ABOUT THE AUTHORS

Josef Vincent Lombardo received the Ph.D. degree at Columbia University and degrees of Litt.D. and LL.D. from the University of Florence, Italy, and Villanova University, respectively. He has had extensive experience in teaching art and engineering drawing at the College of Engineering, New York University, at Columbia University, and at Queens College, where he is now serving as Associate Professor.

Lewis O. Johnson is currently Professor of Engineering Drawing at New York University. He is the co-author of standard texts in descriptive geometry: *Elements of Descriptive Geometry — Part 1, Text;* and *Elements of Descriptive Geometry — Part 2, Problems.* He received the degrees of B.S. (C.E.) and M.S. (C.E.) at the University of Maine.

W. Irwin Short is Departmental Administrative Officer and Professor of Civil Engineering at the University of Pittsburgh and Director of Undergraduate Work in Industry in the Schools of Engineering and Mines at that university. He is a graduate of the Missouri School of Mines and of the University of Pittsburgh, where he received the degree of M.S. (C.E.).

Albert J. Lombardo received the degrees of B.A. and M.A. at New York University. He has served on the staff of Hofstra College, where he taught courses in fine arts and engineering drawing. He is now in the Engineering Department of Otis Elevator Company.

ENGINEERING
DRAWING

ENGINEERING DRAWING

JOSEF VINCENT LOMBARDO
Queens College

LEWIS O. JOHNSON
New York University

W. IRWIN SHORT
University of Pittsburgh

ALBERT J. LOMBARDO, *Editor*

BARNES & NOBLE BOOKS
A DIVISION OF HARPER & ROW, PUBLISHERS
New York, Hagerstown, San Francisco, London

©

COPYRIGHT 1953, 1956

BY HARPER & ROW, PUBLISHERS, INC.

L. C. catalog card number: 56-10847

ISBN: 0-06-460086-6

Manufactured in the United States of America

84   20 19 18 17 16 15 14 13

Foreword

The purpose of this text is to provide a comprehensive, practical guide that will aid the student to master the essentials of engineering drawing. The text is designed to introduce him to each phase of the subject, step by step, and enable him to develop working skill and efficiency.

On deciding to become an engineer, the student accepts definite obligations to a profession characterized by the careful observance of instructions and the accurate performance of assignments. In engineering drawing, one of his first professional courses, he has an opportunity to demonstrate the ability to fulfill these obligations. It is, therefore, assumed that the instructor, who will provide necessary guidance and supervision, including evaluation of the student's progress, will invariably insist upon strict adherence to standard drafting procedures and practices.

ACKNOWLEDGMENTS

The authors acknowledge with deep gratitude and appreciation the cooperation of Keuffel and Esser Company, Braddock Instrument Company, Eugene Dietzgen Company, Otis Elevator Company, the American Society of Mechanical Engineers, and the American Standards Association, including permission to reproduce copyrighted material.

Many thanks are similarly extended to the following engineers, designers, and draftsmen of the Otis Elevator Company for their painstaking work in reading the manuscript and for invaluable suggestions: George Di Nardo, Charles A. Arrata, William Blackwood, Nicholas Di Pinto, Stephen A. Fritsch, Seymour Roberts, Ernest Schoor, Benjamin G. Thorne, Samuel K. Ward, Ernest Wellenkamp, H. Rudolph Yost, and Louis De Sanctis. The authors are also indebted to Professors C. E. Rowe, of the University of Texas, and Clair V. Mann, of the University of Missouri.

Introduction

Engineering drawing is the graphic or visual language of engineers. With drawings the engineer communicates to others the shape, the size, the material, and the other necessary details — hence, the appearance — of any object he wishes to design, build, and operate. The several branches of engineering deal with different objects; still, these objects may all be a part of one major project. Consider, for example, a modern steel mill. The civil engineer has been concerned with the nonmoving parts of the mill, as he has designed and constructed the buildings and roads. The mechanical and electrical engineers have been concerned with the moving parts of the mill, which include the cranes, the elevators, and the rolling equipment. The industrial engineer has made plant layouts that aid production. The chemical engineer has dealt with problems relating to industrial wastes and by-products from the coking of coal; the petroleum engineer, with the problem of liquid and gaseous fuels; the mining engineer, with the solid fuels and ores used in making the steel; and the metallurgical engineer, with the amount and quality of the steel being manufactured.

The student can think of many other projects in which several branches of engineering have combined their efforts to design, construct, and operate. He will have difficulty in bringing to mind any engineering project that has not required the use of drawings.

Regardless of the magnitude or complexity of an engineering drawing, it may be broken down into its principal parts. The principal parts may be grouped as follows (the topics listed are in the same sequence as the chapters in this text):

Control of Appearance (Chapters 1, 2, and 3)

Linework and the use of instruments (Chapter 1)

Geometric constructions (Chapter 2)

viii INTRODUCTION

Lettering (Chapter 3)
Views (Chapters 4, 5, 6, and 7)
  Orthographic projection (Chapter 4)
  Auxiliary views (Chapter 5)
  Sections and conventions (Chapter 6)
  Pictorial views (Chapter 7)
Dimensioning (Chapter 8)
  The use of size and location dimensions so that the magnitude of the object and operations on the object may be defined.
Fasteners (Chapter 9)
  Standard fasteners, such as bolts, nuts, studs, screws, and others used to fasten objects together.
  Conventional representation of fastenings.
  Standard sizes and means of dimensioning fastenings.
Working Drawings (Chapter 10)
  The terminal drawing: the drawing from which work may be done; the drawing that, to be correct, proper, and complete, involves portions or all of the preceding standards and procedures.

In view of the fact that any drawing may thus be broken down into parts, the task of learning to draw may be accomplished by parts. The student should note that the procedures in the first three chapters of this book (dealing with control of appearance) are somewhat mechanical and that this work may be mastered by anyone having normal control of his hands. Visualization of the size and shape of objects, however, is a necessary and important aspect of engineering drawing. It is as vital in this field as it is in all other work of engineers and in all branches of engineering. Mastery of the subject matter of Chapters 4, 5, 6, and 7 is, therefore, an essential preparation for the working procedures outlined in the final chapters of the text.

Contents

ENGINEERING
DRAWING

1

Linework and the Use of Instruments

In the technical and industrial world an engineering drawing employs a visible language consisting of lines, letters, symbols, and numbers to express ideas and convey technical information. A drawing performing these functions in a clear, correct manner, and according to accepted and approved standards, satisfies the requirements of good drafting practice.

Engineering drawing is a highly developed skill involving the use of special instruments. Proficiency in drawing depends upon the proper use of these instruments and upon a knowledge of their limitations. The best way to acquire a "feel" for instruments is by continued, diligent practice. The student can achieve accuracy in technique, as well as in design, if he begins by working slowly, carefully, and neatly. Speed in performance is only a matter of time.

The following statement expresses an indispensable standard which, if it is observed faithfully in the course of an engineer's college and professional career, will redound to his decided advantage.

No work will be accepted which has ink erasures, indented lines, blots, mistakes, or violations of instructions (see Fig. 28); *or incorrect weights of the different lines* (see Figs. 5 and 6 and Mann's Draftsman's Line Gauge in Fig. 7).

The Drawing Table. The ideal drafting table is about 36 to 40 inches high, to permit working in a standing position. The board is placed in the drafting room so that the light comes from the left. There are stools at all drafting tables, and some draftsmen do their best work in a seated position.

1

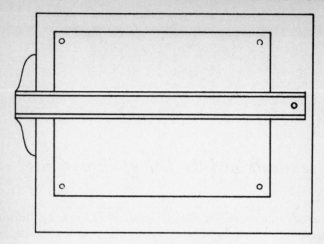

Fig. 1.   The Drawing Board.

Placement of Drawing Paper on the Drawing Board.   Not all companies use the same size of drawing paper.   Convenience in binding, filing, and blueprinting often determines the size of drawing sheets used by a particular manufacturer or engineering firm.   In the absence of a standard size of drawing paper, a sheet larger than the proposed drawing should be used.   This sheet should be "lined up" towards the upper left-hand corner of the drawing board, as shown in Fig. 1.   Fastening the paper to the drawing board in this position will reduce the likelihood of the errors which frequently occur because the blade of the T-square has a tendency to sag when the extreme right end is used.   This precaution is unnecessary, however, if a parallel straightedge or a drafting machine is used.   Then the horizontal edge of the paper is "lined up" with the horizontal edge of the device, and the position of the paper on the board can be anywhere within the working range of the instrument.

Various types of thumbtacks and drafting tapes are available to fasten the drawing sheet to the drawing board.

The Drawing Pencil.   Drafting pencils are available in many grades of hard, medium, and soft leads, and the selection of the proper pencil for each specific function merits consideration.

CHOICE OF PENCIL.   There are several factors which almost dictate the use of a particular grade of pencil under a given con-

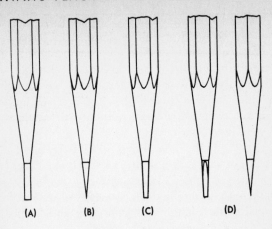

Fig. 2. Pencil Points.

dition. For example, the quality and texture of the drawing paper compel one to use a softer pencil if the paper is hard and "fast." (A "fast" paper is a dry, smooth-surface paper upon which the graphite of the hard pencil will not adhere well.) Rough-textured papers require harder pencils, if accuracy and neatness are to be attained. Another factor influencing the choice of pencil is the effect of atmospheric conditions on drawing paper. A humid day softens the paper considerably. When this condition prevails, a softer pencil is used because the graphite adheres to the surface of the paper more easily — a hard pencil cuts grooves into the paper on such a day. Conversely, a dry day permits the use of harder pencils.

With time and experience, every draftsman develops a preference for a given pencil because it performs best for him under the accustomed pressure he exerts on it in drawing, and also because its legibility, darkness, or lightness suits his aesthetic sense.

Generally, it is recommended that a 5H or 6H pencil be used for layout work and for dimension and extension lines; an H to 3H for drawing the actual object; an H to 2H for lettering, section lines, break lines, and arrowheads; and an F and an HB for freehand technical sketching. Whatever the choice of pencil, however, the draftsman is cautioned to avoid using hard pencils that cut grooves in the paper or soft pencils that tend to blur and smudge.

PENCIL POINTS. The lettered end of the pencil, showing the manufacturer's name and the degree of hardness, should never be sharpened; this practice makes identification of the pencil difficult.

The average drafting room is equipped with specially designed pencil sharpeners which remove the wood from the lead of a pencil without pointing the lead, as shown in Fig. 2A. (If an automatic sharpener is not available, a sharp penknife or a single-edge razor blade can be used to remove the wood.)

A sanding pad or a file is employed to bring the lead to a conical point (Fig. 2B) or to a wedge point (Figs. 2C, D). Fig. 2D shows the face and the profile of a wedge point.

A conical point is generally used, and it is best obtained by rotating the pencil while running the lead back and forth along the *entire length* of the sanding pad, as in Fig. 3.

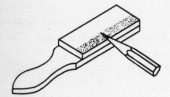

Fig. 3.   Conical Points.   **Fig. 4.**   Pencil and T-square.

A wedge point is used for straight-line work where lines of uniform thickness are desired, and it is obtained by sanding the lead on opposite sides (see Figs. 2C, D).

After the pencil has been sharpened, all the loose graphite should be removed with a clean cloth. The sanding pad should be freed of graphite by tapping it against the inside of a wastepaper basket. Though the pad should be kept close at hand, it should not be left near drawings, and when not in use it should be kept in a paper wrapper or an envelope.

A mechanical pencil, known as an "artist pencil," obviates sharpening because the lead is replaceable and is "fed out" for sanding alone. This pencil eliminates the need for sharpeners and saves a considerable amount of time.

METHOD OF HOLDING THE PENCIL. Fig. 4 shows how a pencil should be held against the working edge of the T-square.

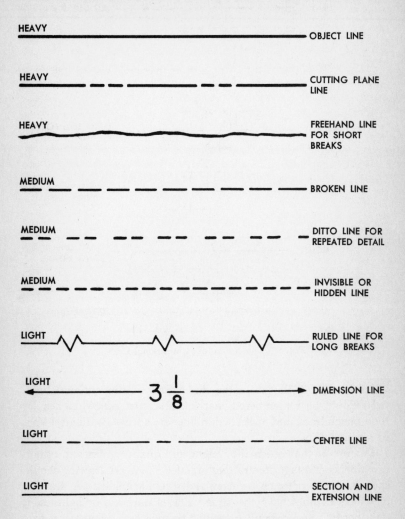

Fig. 5. Conventional Ink Lines (True Weights).

Conventional Lines. The American Standards Association has adopted an alphabet of lines consisting of three weights: heavy, medium, and light lines. Conventional ink lines and their physical characteristics are shown in Fig. 5 and are reproduced in their true

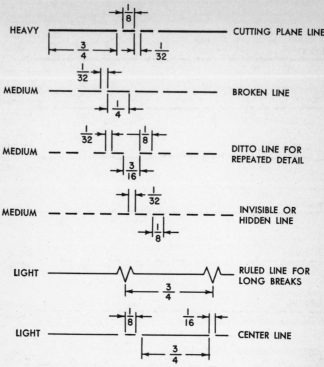

Fig. 6. Dimensions of Conventional Lines.

weights. Fig. 6 illustrates the dimensions of conventional lines. It should be remembered that ink lines are somewhat heavier than pencil lines, and construction lines are always the lightest lines in a pencil drawing.

The use of contrast in the weight and quality of lines to obtain prominence is a favorite drafting practice. A good drawing should show contrasts between primary and secondary lines. A drawing in which all lines have the same value of darkness or lightness is uninteresting and difficult to read. In such a drawing every part is of equal weight and equal prominence; and the significant features, which should be emphasized, are obscured in the monotony of the uniform line.

Horizontal Lines. Let us assume the draftsman is right-handed. In that case, he draws horizontal lines by holding the head of the

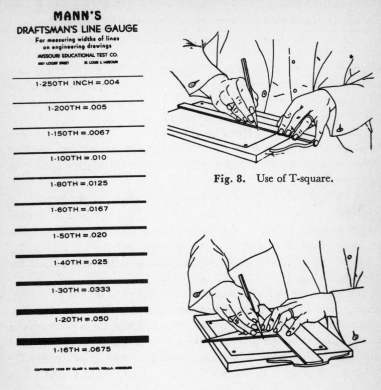

MANN'S
DRAFTSMAN'S LINE GAUGE
For measuring widths of lines
on engineering drawings
MISSOURI EDUCATIONAL TEST CO.

1-250TH INCH = .004

1-200TH = .005

1-150TH = .0067

1-100TH = .010

1-80TH = .0125

1-60TH = .0167

1-50TH = .020

1-40TH = .025

1-30TH = .0333

1-20TH = .050

1-16TH = .0675

Fig. 8. Use of T-square.

Fig. 7. Mann's Line Gauge.   **Fig. 9.** Use of Triangle, T-square.

T-square firmly against the drawing board with the left hand while running the pencil along the working edge with the right hand. The pencil should be held in a vertical plane (Fig. 4) — that is, a plane perpendicular to the paper, but it should be inclined approximately 60° to the right, as in Fig. 8. A line should always be drawn from left to right. If a conical point is used, the pencil should be rotated the full length of the line to insure uniform thickness.

When a parallel edge or a drafting machine is used, the left hand serves only to set the device on the desired point or points, and the same procedure explained in the foregoing paragraph is followed in drawing lines.

A left-handed person must do with his left hand what is here described for the right hand of a right-handed person.

Vertical Lines. The 45° triangle or the 30°–60° triangle is used in combination with the T-square to draw vertical lines.

The T-square is once again held firmly against the drawing board and the triangle is placed along its edge with the right angle of the triangle perpendicular to the T-square, as in Fig. 9. Vertical lines are drawn from bottom to top, or away from the working edge of the T-square, with the pencil held in a vertical plane and tilted approximately 60° to the right, or away from the body.

Use of Triangles to Draw Inclined Lines. The 45° triangle and the 30°–60° triangle have been standardized for drawing inclined lines because of the frequency at which these angles appear in engineering drawing.

A 45° line may be drawn by moving the pencil or pen upward or downward along the hypotenuse of the 45° triangle with either leg of the triangle resting on the T-square, as in Fig. 10. (The leg of a triangle is any side other than the hypotenuse.)

A 30° or 60° line may be obtained in a similar manner, as indicated in Fig. 10.

Triangles may also be used in combination to obtain 15° or 75° lines. Fig. 11 demonstrates the method and direction of linework.

For intermediate angles in the circle or semicircle, a protractor is used. If a 65° slope is desired, the center of the protractor is set at the intersecting point of the horizontal line and its perpendicular divisor. A point is then marked off on the paper at 65° and a line

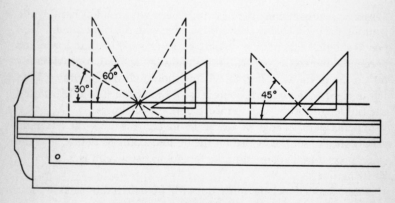

Fig. 10. 45°, 30°, and 60° Lines.

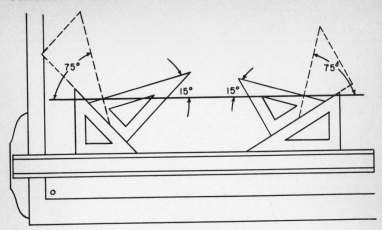

Fig. 11. 15° and 75° Lines.

is drawn between this point and the intersection, as in Fig. 12. (For more accurate construction, see "Tangent Method," p. 50.)

Parallel Lines. Inasmuch as parallel lines are not always vertical or horizontal, it becomes necessary to devise a simple method of drawing parallel lines at any given angle.

The method that is always used to obtain parallel lines consists of "lining up" the hypotenuse of a triangle which has one of its legs

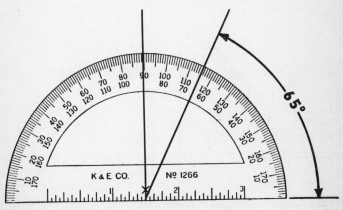

Fig. 12. Use of Protractor for Intermediate Angles.

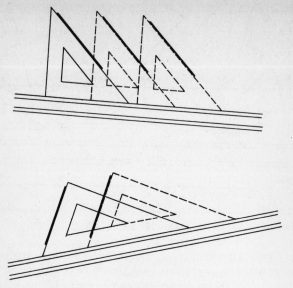

Fig. 13. Parallel Lines with T-square
and Triangle.

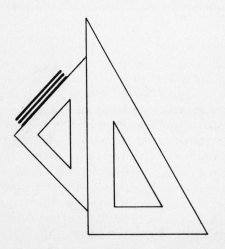

Fig. 14. Parallel Lines with Two Triangles.

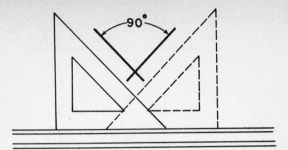

Fig. 15.   Perpendicular Lines with Triangle
and T-square.

Fig. 16.   Dividers.

resting on the T-square, as in Fig. 13, along the line to be drawn. The draftsman then moves the triangle along the working edge of the T-square; by sliding it backward or forward, he can obtain as many parallel lines as he desires. If a required line is very short, two triangles, instead of a triangle and a T-square, may be used to accomplish the same purpose, as shown in Fig. 14.

Perpendicular Lines. Perpendicular lines may be drawn by employing the same method used for drawing parallel lines. The triangle and the T-square are "lined up" in the same way, and the triangle is moved to the intersecting point on the given line. At this point the triangle is turned over, as shown in Fig. 15, and a line is drawn through that point. This is, of course, only one of many ways in which perpendicular lines can be drawn.

The Dividers. The dividers are used for dividing distances into a prescribed number of equal parts, or for transferring dimensions and distances. This instrument (see Fig. 16) is manipulated with one hand, thereby necessitating diligent practice in order to attain speed and accuracy. Proper handling of the dividers is essential to their successful use.

Fig. 17. Division of Lines
into Equal Parts.

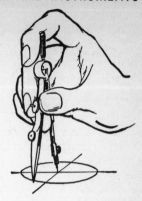

Fig. 18A. Proper Method
of Handling Compasses.

The dividers are held by the thumb
and index finger while the middle and
fourth fingers are used to steady the instrument and to adjust the spreading of
its legs.

When an arc or a line is to be bisected
by trial, the dividers should be set by eye
at the mid-point of the line to be bisected.
The handle of the instrument is held by
thumb and index finger (as in Fig. 16),
and the distances are marked off with
a counterclockwise motion and then a
clockwise motion, or vice versa. If the
dividers fall short, the legs should be readjusted to measure approximately one-

Fig. 18B.
Drawing
Small
Circles.

half of the remaining distance. This trial-and-error procedure is
repeated until the arc or the line is bisected. A draftsman skilled
in the use of dividers can mark off distances accurately and rapidly.

A similar process may be used in dividing arcs or lines into 3, 4, 5,
6, etc. equal parts, as shown in Fig. 17.

Circles. Many compasses are designed for pen-and-ink work
(see Fig. 20A), and are so made that one point is interchangeable
with the other. The needle point should be set so that it projects
about $\frac{1}{64}$ of an inch beyond the pen point, as in Fig. 19.

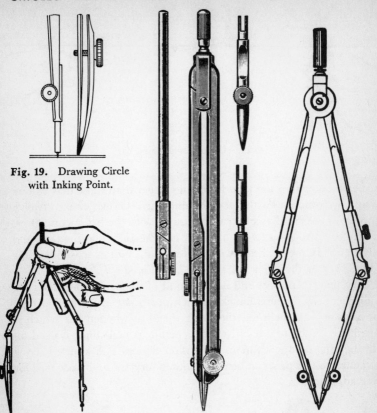

Fig. 19. Drawing Circle with Inking Point.

Fig. 20C. Inking Larger Circles.

Fig. 20A. For Pen-and-Ink Work.

Fig. 20B. Drawing Larger Circles.

Circles with a one-inch to two-inch radius may be drawn with the legs of the compasses straight (Fig. 18B). Larger circles require "breaking the legs" of the compasses at the joints (Figs. 20B, 20C) so that the needle point and the pencil point are perpendicular to the paper. When the inking point is used, care should be taken that the two blades of the inking point are always perpendicular to the paper (Figs. 19, 20C) in order to obtain an even flow of ink and a line of uniform thickness.

When large circles are necessary, a lengthening or extension bar can be attached to the compasses, as shown in Fig. 21.

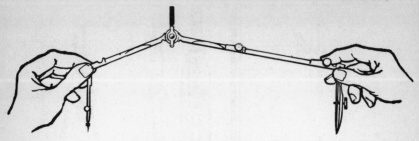

Fig. 21. Use of Lengthening Bar.

Beam compasses are used for circles larger than those that can be made by compasses with a lengthening bar. Circles of from twelve to sixty inches in diameter can be drawn with the beam compasses. There are two basic types of beam compasses. The fundamental difference between these two types is that one has a wooden bar (Fig. 22) and the other has a metal bar (Fig. 23).

The pen (or pencil) and needle point of the beam compasses are called chucks. These chucks, which are designed to fit the type of bar used, are held together by a metal or wooden bar which is available in different lengths. The pen or pencil chuck is fixed on the bar in the approximate dimension desired. A knurled screw attached to this part can be manipulated forward and backward for fine adjustments.

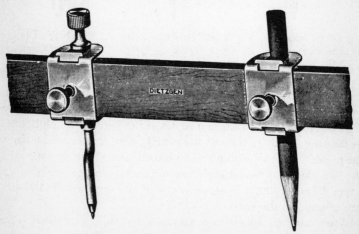

Fig. 22. Beam Compasses with Wooden Bar.

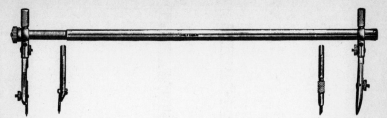

Fig. 23. Beam Compasses with Metal Bar.

The initial step in drawing pencil circles is to mark off the desired radius on the center line of the required circle. The needle point of the compasses must then be set accurately at the intersection of the center lines (see Figs. 18A, 18B). The pencil point is next adjusted to coincide with the marked-off radius. The compasses are held with the thumb and index finger and rotated in a clockwise direction (Figs. 18, 20C). The instrument is tilted to about 60° to the right and the circle is drawn from the bottom and rotated through 360°.

The pencil point should be beveled on one side with a sanding pad (Figs. 18B, 24B). To get a clear, sharp line, this bevel should face

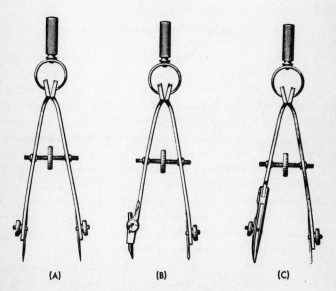

(A)   (B)   (C)

Fig. 24. Bow Divider, Bow Pencil, Bow Pen.

Fig. 25. The Ruling Pen.

outside, or away from the center of the circle.   A hard lead, 4H or 6H, is generally used.

In drawing circles or arcs, the student should avoid holding the instrument by the legs, as this might change the adjustment of the instrument and result in inaccurate circles.   However, when a lengthening bar is attached to a pair of compasses to strike circles that are larger than the normal limit of the instrument, both hands should be used for steadiness and accurate concentricity (Fig. 21).

Figs. 24B and 24C are the common bow pencil and bow pen. Fig. 24A is a bow divider, which is used to divide distances into equal parts.   Bow pencils and bow pens are capable of describing circles of small diameter, because of their short and jointless legs.   Fig. 18A shows how the bow pen should be held and used.

The Ruling Pen.   One of the most frequently used instruments is the ruling pen (Fig. 25), which is used to ink straight lines and irregular curved lines.   It is never used as a freehand instrument.

SELECTION AND CARE OF PEN. A high-speed steel ruling pen is generally the best because this type of steel is suitable for precise machinability and does not wear easily, thus obviating frequent sharpening of the nibs.   The nibs of a ruling pen must be equal in length and elliptical in shape to insure the proper retention and uniform flow of ink.   Nibs that are too sharp or that are blunted are unsatisfactory: sharp nibs do not permit the ink to feed steadily; blunt nibs deliver the ink too rapidly and produce blots at the end of an ink line.

After prolonged use even the highest-quality ruling pen begins to show bright spots or reflections, an indication of wear.   Sharp line-work is not possible with worn-out nibs.   The instrument, however, can be sharpened to its original shape.

Before the ruling pen is put to a honing stone (Arkansas oilstone is considered best), the nibs of the pen must be screwed together until the blades touch.   In sharpening the nibs, the pen should be held in a vertical position (as when drawing with it) and drawn back and forth along the oilstone.   The pen is held at an angle of approximately 30° and oscillated, pendulum fashion, until it reaches a similar position at the other end of the sharpening stone.   By re-peated, complete strokes, the nibs will eventually become equal in length and will assume the proper elliptical shape.   The blades should then be opened slightly and each blade honed separately to a keen edge while the blade is rolled from side to side to maintain its convex surface.

The blades are not properly sharpened until the bright spots or reflections are ground away and disappear.   Blades should not be so sharp as to score or cut the paper.   If the ruling pen has a tendency to do this, it should be honed again.   The inside of the nibs should never be sharpened except to remove the burrs which result from sharpening of the blades.

The leading manufacturers of drafting instruments offer a sharpen-ing service to those who are too inexperienced or too busy to sharpen their own pens, or who prefer the precision work of a machine.

USE OF RULING PEN.   Most engineering and architectural firms make their tracings or drawings in pencil.   This is particularly true of firms which do not need permanent records.   For manufacturers requiring permanent records which can be easily reproduced, draw-ings are made with black waterproof India ink.

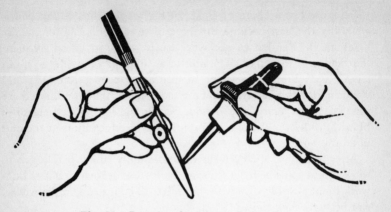

Fig. 26.   Procedure for Inking a Ruling Pen.

Inking a ruling pen is a simple operation if done properly.   Ink is inserted between the partly spread nibs of the ruling pen by the quill which is attached to the stopper of the ink bottle.   The width of the nibs, and, hence, the thickness of the line, are determined by the adjustment screw.   The greater the space between the nibs, the greater the flow of ink.   A small amount of ink should be used at a time.   The ruling pen should be held in the left hand, with the adjustment screw towards the body, while the ink is inserted between the nibs with the right hand.   Fig. 26 demonstrates this technique. Experienced inkers have shown that there is less likelihood of getting ink on the outside surfaces of the nibs when the adjustment screw of the ruling pen faces the body.

Several precautions should be observed in using a ruling pen. (1) A ruling pen should never be filled over a drawing sheet. (2) Ink that has carelessly been allowed to settle on the outside of

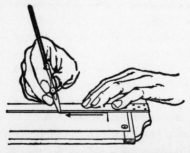

Fig. 27.   Position for Drawing Lines.

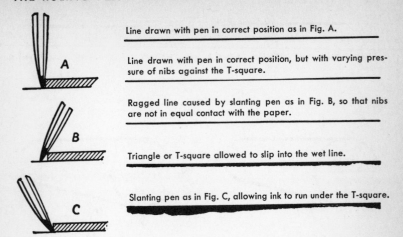

Line drawn with pen in correct position as in Fig. A.

Line drawn with pen in correct position, but with varying pressure of nibs against the T-square.

Ragged line caused by slanting pen as in Fig. B, so that nibs are not in equal contact with the paper.

Triangle or T-square allowed to slip into the wet line.

Slanting pen as in Fig. C, allowing ink to run under the T-square.

Fig. 28. Correct and Incorrect Positions for Linework.

the nibs should be wiped off thoroughly. (3) There should never be more than $\frac{3}{16}$ to $\frac{1}{4}$ of an inch of ink in the pen. Excessive ink is heavy and usually drops out on the paper. (4) When several small lines must be drawn, the pen should contain very little ink, to avoid blots. (5) The ruling pen should be cleaned frequently with a chamois or a soft cloth even when it rules sharp, clear lines. (6) When heavy ink lines are required, they should not be joined or connected while the lines are wet. Square, even corners can be drawn only when one ink line has already dried before a second line is drawn to it.

Fig. 27 illustrates the correct position of the ruling pen when lines are being drawn. The pen must be held with the tips of the thumb, index, and middle fingers, with the adjusting screw facing away from the body. The handle of the pen rests on the long bone of the index finger, as would a pencil in ordinary writing. The thumb and the index finger are in a position to permit manipulation of the adjustment screw, which rests on the side of the middle finger.

Before drawing a line, one should set both nibs of the ruling pen parallel to the guiding edge, as shown in Fig. 28A, by holding the pen in a vertical position slightly inclined in the direction of the stroke (see Fig. 27). The pen is pressed gently against the ruling edge to insure accurate linework. The middle and ring fingers serve as a running support for the hand and guide the pen in main-

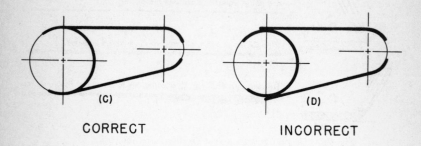

(A)   (B)

THIN LINES ARE PENCIL LINES — HEAVY LINES ARE INK LINES

(C)   (D)

CORRECT   INCORRECT

Fig. 29. Correct and Incorrect Methods of Inking Lines.

taining a constant angle of inclination.   Inking lines requires a free
arm action, except that the end of a line is drawn by a slower movement of the thumb and the index finger alone.   This finger movement prevents overrunning the line and avoids blotting at the ends
of lines.   At the end of each stroke, the pen should be raised off the
paper quickly and the guiding edge should be moved away from the
wet line.

Figs. 28B, C illustrate the undesirable effect of faulty inkwork.
Poor inkwork is a direct outcome of carelessness and disregard of
fundamentals in the use of the ruling pen.

India ink dries rapidly; and, owing to its high carbon content, de-
posits of carbon frequently clog the pen.   The clogging of ink re-
duces the space between the nibs and results in thin, irregular lines
if the pen writes at all.   For this reason the pen should be wiped
often with a soft cloth or a chamois.   Caked ink, whenever it is
present, should never be scraped off with a knife or a sharp instrument.   It is better to wash it away with hot water or a cleaning fluid
intended for such purposes.   When water is used, care should be
taken to dry the ruling pen thoroughly to prevent rust from forming
around the adjustment screw.

If at times the ink does not flow readily, the tip of the ruling pen should be touched to one's finger or to a piece of chamois to induce it to flow. If this fails, the pen should be thoroughly cleaned and the nibs reset to the desired thickness of line before it is used again.

Ink lines are almost always heavier than pencil lines; consequently, the ruling pen should be centered on the pencil line, as in Fig. 29A, and not as in Fig. 29B. The same principle applies also to circular lines drawn by the bow pen or compasses, and to tangents (Fig. 29C). The incorrect method is shown in Fig. 29D.

A draftsman's line gauge, also referred to as the "alphabet of lines," has been established by Professor Clair V. Mann and is reproduced true size in Fig. 7. This line gauge, showing the thickness of lines in fractions of an inch, has been universally adopted by technical draftsmen. (Cf. Figs. 5, 6.)

Irregular Curves. Irregular or French curves are used for drawing all noncircular curves. Great care and skill are required when irregular curves are drawn in ink. Just as the straightedge, T-square, and triangle are used as guiding edges for ruling straight lines, so the irregular or French curve is used as a guide for ruling curved lines.

Drawing an irregular curve requires the plotting of many points. The number of points used depends upon the complexity of the curved line desired. Points should be laid out in pencil at regular intervals along the path of the curved line, as shown in Fig. 30. After the points have been plotted, the required curve can be drawn

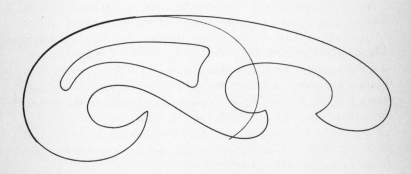

Fig. 30. Plotting of Points for Irregular Curves.

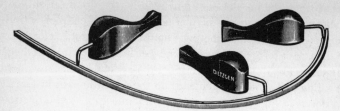

Fig. 31. Splines for Long Curves.

in pencil either freehand or with a French curve. Once a smooth continuous curve is rendered in pencil, inking the line becomes an easier operation. It is advisable not to connect too many points at one time, as the line will generally begin to fall away from the plotted curve. Ragged connections, breaks, sharp points, and lines which do not coincide result from attempting to connect too many points at one setting.

Splines. When long, sweeping curves must be drawn, ship curves or splines (Fig. 31) are used. Owing to the great length of a spline, it is impossible to hold it in place by hand. Lead weights called "ducks" are used to hold the spline on the projected curve.

Method of Erasing. To erase properly is just as important as to observe correct drawing practice. Errors or changes in design are inevitable; consequently, clean erasing is necessary to preserve valuable drawings. The surface of either an ink or a pencil drawing can be rendered useless if an error or changed detail is not erased properly.

An erasing shield and a medium-soft eraser, such as a Ruby pencil eraser, are basic tools. The shield is designed for erasures of straight or curved lines, for lines ruled closely together, and for small circles. The eraser is applied to the desired opening in the shield, and a firm but light stroke is used in one direction only. If the drawing pencil has made grooves in the surface of the paper, a hard flat surface, like a triangle, should be placed under the drawing in the area to be erased. In this way all the graphite from the inner reaches of the groove will be removed. The back of the drawing also should be erased, because grooved paper picks up dirt or graphite from the normal handling of the drawing sheet.

The same procedure is followed with ink drawings, although the process is a much slower one. A gritty ink eraser should never be

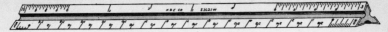

Fig. 32. Architects' Scale.

used in removing ink lines, as the surface of the paper or tracing cloth will be permanently injured.

The hand should never be used to remove erasure crumbs from a sheet of paper. When this careless method is resorted to, the lines are blurred and smudged. A soft cloth or brush is recommended.

Scales. Mechanical drawings are invariably drawn to scale. This means that the mechanism or its parts are drawn either to actual size or to a reduced ratio of the actual size. It would be physically impossible, of course, to draw full size such objects as power plants, skyscrapers, or automobiles; but these can be drawn accurately to the right relative proportion on a reduced scale.

THE ARCHITECTS' SCALE. The architects' scale (Fig. 32) is universally used for computing ratio. This triangular rule contains eleven scales. One is the foot scale, graduated in inches and sixteenths of an inch; the others (appearing two on each edge of the instrument) are as follows:

$$\frac{3}{32}'' \text{ scale and } \frac{3}{16}'' \text{ scale}$$
$$\frac{1}{8}'' \text{ scale and } \frac{1}{4}'' \text{ scale}$$
$$\frac{3}{8}'' \text{ scale and } \frac{3}{4}'' \text{ scale}$$
$$\frac{1}{2}'' \text{ scale and } 1'' \text{ scale}$$
$$1\frac{1}{2}'' \text{ scale and } 3'' \text{ scale}$$

It should always be remembered that each graduation represents one foot. For example, on the $\frac{1}{4}''$ scale, every $\frac{1}{4}''$ that is marked off stands for a foot; and therefore $2''$ on this scale represents eight feet.

Usually the ratio of a drawing is noted in its legend in the following way: $\frac{1}{4}'' = 1'$.

When a change in dimensions is required after a drawing has been completed, some engineering firms do not redraw it to scale. They merely change the affected dimension and underscore that dimension with a heavy dash line to indicate that the dimension is "out of scale."

THE ENGINEERS' SCALE. The engineers' scale is a decimal scale in which the inch is divided into tens or multiples of ten. It is not generally used for machine or technical drawing, although there are

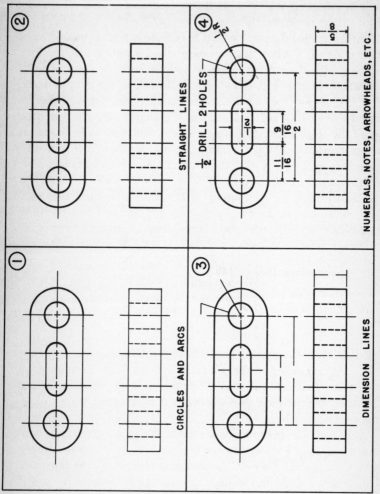

Fig. 33. Correct Order of Inking a Drawing.

a few engineering offices which use the decimal system of measurement.

Order of Inking a Drawing.   In inking a drawing which has already been carefully planned in pencil, the following order, as illustrated in Fig. 33, should prevail:

1. Circles.   These should be inked first; the order should be from smaller circles to larger ones.

2. Arcs.

3. Hidden circles and arcs.   These must be drawn third because the bow pen must be readjusted to obtain a medium line, the conventional symbol for hidden or invisible lines.   (See Appendix, ASA Line and Line Work.)

4. Irregular curves.

5. Horizontal lines.   Horizontal lines that are continued from arcs should be drawn, wherever and whenever possible, from the arc.   A horizontal line should never be drawn *to* an arc if the two lines are to coincide.   The line should be started at the arc and should be drawn horizontally *away* from the arc.

6. Vertical lines.   The same rule that applies to horizontal lines in their relation to arcs also obtains in drawing vertical lines.

7. Inclined lines.   Same rule as in 5 and 6.

8. Center lines. (See p. 149.)

9. Extension and dimension lines.   (See p. 148.)

10. Arrowheads.   (See p. 149.)

11. Section lines.   (See pp. 107–110.)

12. Lettering.

13. Notes, instructions, legend, and title.

2

Geometric Constructions
(Drawing-Board Geometry)

The student of engineering drawing should be familiar with the following geometric constructions, which will appear frequently in his work. Not only does the engineer use these geometric constructions on the drawing board, but also in many design computations he forms the geometric shapes exactly as they are constructed and uses his knowledge of geometric construction in visualizing his procedure in computing. The engineering student will note this almost immediately in his courses in mathematics, surveying, and theoretical and applied mechanics. It is recommended that the student review the principles of plane geometry and their application in any standard textbook.[1]

To Bisect a Straight Line

WITH DIVIDERS. Bisect the given straight line *AB* with a pair of dividers, as in Fig. 34A. Vary the setting of the dividers until line *AB* is equally divided. This method is based on trial and error and is therefore not mathematically accurate.

WITH COMPASSES. Bisect the straight line *CD* with a pair of compasses (Fig. 34B). Using *C* as a center and a radius greater than one-half *CD*, strike one arc above and one arc below *CD*. With the same radius and *D* as a center, repeat the operation. Draw the vertical line *EF* connecting the intersections of the two arcs above and below *CD*. Point *X* bisects *CD*.

[1] A convenient manual for "brush-up" on these principles is *Problems in Plane Geometry, with Solutions*, by Marcus Horblit and Kaj L. Nielsen (College Outline Series). — Ed.

26

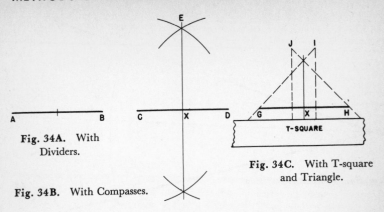

Fig. 34A. With Dividers.

Fig. 34B. With Compasses.

Fig. 34C. With T-square and Triangle.

Fig. 34. Methods of Bisecting a Straight Line.

WITH T-SQUARE AND TRIANGLE. Bisect the line *GH* with a T-square and a 45° triangle (Fig. 34C). Place the 45° triangle on the T-square so that the hypotenuse of the triangle passes through point *G*, and draw line *GI*. Turn the triangle over and repeat the same procedure using point *H*, and draw line *HJ*. Place the vertical edge of the triangle at the intersection of *GI* and *HJ*. The vertical line drawn from this point through *GH* bisects the line.

To Trisect a Straight Line (Fig. 35). Place a 30°–60° triangle on the T-square so that the hypotenuse forms a 30° angle with the line *AB* at point *A*. Draw a line along the hypotenuse. Turn the triangle over and repeat the operation using point *B*. The two lines drawn at 30° through points *A* and *B* intersect each other at point *C*. Place the triangle on the T-square with the hypotenuse

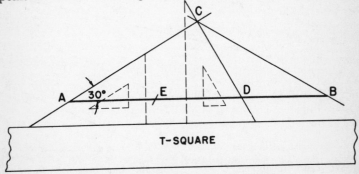

Fig. 35. Method of Trisecting a Straight Line.

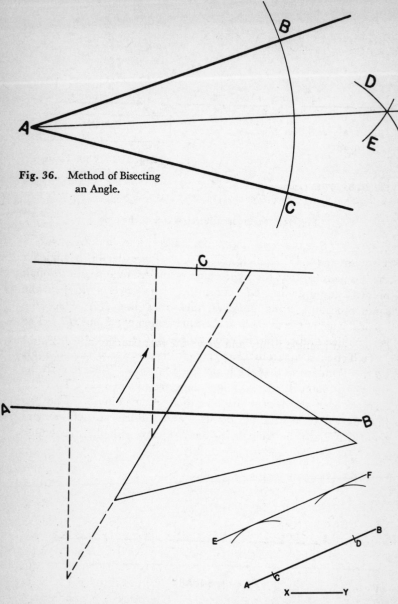

Fig. 36. Method of Bisecting an Angle.

Fig. 37. Line through Point *C* Parallel to Line *AB*.

Fig. 38. Line Tangent to Two Arcs Parallel to Line *AB*.

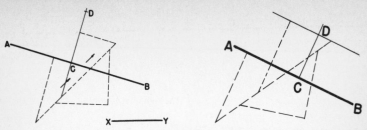

Figs. 39, 40. Alternative Method of Drawing Line Parallel
to a Given Line at a Given Distance.

at point C to make an angle of 60° with AB. The hypotenuse cuts
AB at point D. Turn the triangle over so that its hypotenuse passes
through the same point C, cutting AB at E. $AE = ED = DB$.

To Bisect the Angle ABC (Fig. 36). With A as a center and any
radius, strike the arc BC. With B as a center and any radius, strike
the arc E. Using C as a center with the same radius, strike the arc
D. A line drawn through the intersections of arcs D and E to the
point A bisects the angle ABC.

To Draw a Line through Point C Parallel to Line AB (Fig. 37).
Place the small side of a 30°–60° triangle on the line AB. Place a
second triangle against the hypotenuse of the first triangle. Hold
the second triangle firmly and move the first triangle upward until
its small side passes through point C. The line drawn along this
small side or edge will pass through point C and will be parallel to
AB.

To Draw a Line Parallel to a Given Line at a Given Distance

FIRST METHOD. Given the line AB and the distance XY (Fig.
38). From any two points C and D on AB, strike arcs with a radius
equal to XY. A line drawn tangent to the two arcs will be parallel
to AB.

SECOND METHOD. Given the line AB and the distance XY (Fig.
39). Place the small side of a 30°–60° triangle so that its edge coincides with AB. Place a second triangle against the hypotenuse of
the first triangle. Hold the second triangle securely and move the
first triangle upward as shown in Fig. 39 until its vertical edge
passes through any point C on AB. Mark off the distance XY on line
DC. XY equals DC by construction. A line may be drawn through
point D parallel to AB, as in Fig. 40. The small side or edge of the

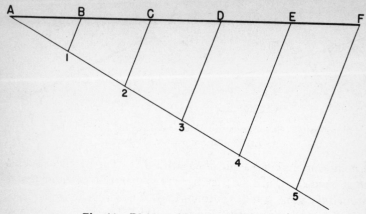

Fig. 41. Division of Line into Equal Parts.

first triangle may be brought up to pass through point *D*, and a line drawn along this edge will be parallel to *AB* at a distance equal to *XY*.

To Divide a Straight Line into Any Number of Equal Parts (Fig. 41). Given the line *AF*, to divide into, say, five parts. From point *A* draw any line *A–5*, marking off five equal divisions of any convenient distance, such as *A–1*, *1–2*, *2–3*, *3–4*, and *4–5*. Draw the line *5–F*. Through points *1*, *2*, *3*, and *4*, draw lines parallel to *5–F* cutting the line *AF*. The distances *AB*, *BC*, *CD*, *DE*, and *EF* are all equal.

To Divide a Straight Line into Proportional Parts (Fig. 42). The procedure used in this construction is the same as previously explained for dividing a line into equal parts (see preceding paragraph and Fig. 41).

Through point *A* draw the line *A–C*. On line *A–C* mark off any distance *A–1*, then mark off distance *1–3*, making it twice the distance *A–1*. Mark off the distance *3–6*, making it three times the distance *A–1*. Draw line *6–B*. Through points *1* and *3*, draw lines parallel to *6–B* which will divide line *AB* into proportions of *1*, *2*, *3*.

To Draw a Line Perpendicular to a Given Line through a Given Point on the Line

BY MEANS OF COMPASSES (Fig. 43). Given the line *AB* and the

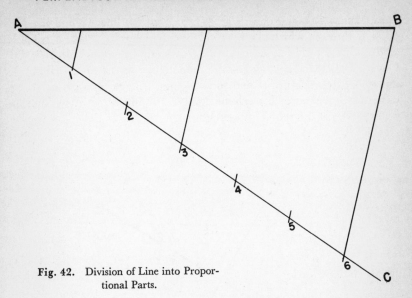

Fig. 42. Division of Line into Proportional Parts.

point *C* through which the perpendicular is to pass. With point *C* as a center and any radius, strike the arcs *D* and *E*. With points *D* and *E* as centers and any radius, strike equal arcs which intersect at *F*. A line drawn between *F* and *C* is the required perpendicular.

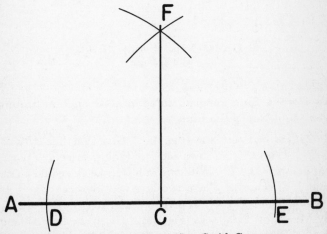

Fig. 43. Perpendicular to *AB* at *C* with Compasses.

By Means of Triangles (Fig. 44). Given the line *AB* and the
point *C* through which the perpendicular is to pass. Place a triangle so that a side adjacent to the 90° angle coincides with *AB*.
Place a second triangle against the hypotenuse of the first. Hold
the second triangle firmly and slide the first triangle upward until
its vertical edge passes through the point *C*. A line drawn along this
vertical edge is the required perpendicular.

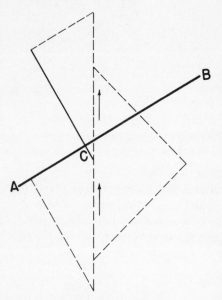

Fig. 44. Perpendicular to *AB* at *C*
with Triangle.

To Draw a Line Perpendicular to a Given Line through a Given Point Not in the Line

By Means of Compasses (Fig. 45). Given the line *AB* and the
point *C*. With *C* as a center and any radius, strike an arc cutting
AB at points *D* and *E*. With any radius strike two equal arcs using
D and *E* as centers. These two arcs will intersect at *F*. A line
connecting points *C* and *F* is perpendicular to *AB*.

By Means of Triangles (Fig. 46). Given the line *AB* and the
point *C*. Place the short side of a 30°–60° triangle on *AB*. Place

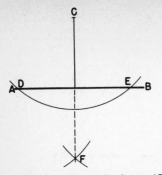

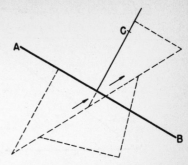

Fig. 45. Perpendicular to *AB*
through *C* with Compasses.

Fig. 46. Perpendicular to *AB*
through *C* with Triangle.

a second triangle against the hypotenuse of the first one.   Hold the
second triangle firmly and slide the first triangle upward until its
long or vertical edge passes through point *C*.   A line drawn along
this vertical edge will be perpendicular to *AB*.

To Construct a Triangle with Three Given Sides. Given
AB, *BC*, and *CA* (Fig. 47).   On any line mark off *A′B′* equal to *AB*.
With *B′* as a center and a radius equal to *BC*, strike an arc.   With

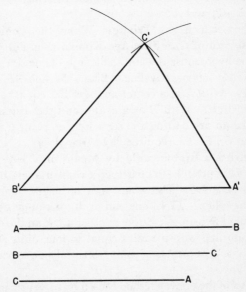

Fig. 47. Triangle with Three Given Sides.

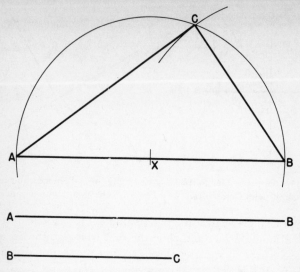

Fig. 48. Right Triangle with Hypotenuse and One Side Known.

A' as a center and a radius equal to CA, strike an arc intersecting the first arc at C'. The required triangle is formed by connecting the points B', C', and A'.

To Construct a Right Triangle When the Lengths of the Hypotenuse and of One Side Are Known (Fig. 48). Given the length of the hypotenuse AB and the length of one side BC. Mark off the distance AB on any line. Bisect the line AB, calling the midpoint X. With X as a center and a radius equal to AX or BX, draw a semicircle. With B as a center and the distance BC as a radius, strike an arc cutting the semicircle at point C. Draw the lines BC and CA for the required right triangle.

To Construct a Right Angle by Means of a 3–4–5 Triangle (Fig. 49). It is possible to construct a right triangle by using the proportions of 3–4–5. Using any unit of length, mark off three units on a base line. From one end of this base line, strike an arc with a radius of five units. Strike another arc from the other end of the same base line with a radius equal to four units. The intersection of these arcs locates a point which falls on a perpendicular to the base line.

A variation of the above method is used by surveyors in laying out a right angle by means of a 100-foot tape (Fig. 50). Let it be re-

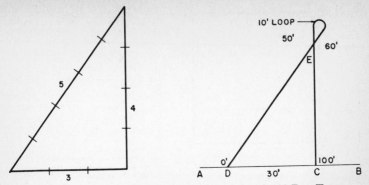

Figs. 49, 50. Right Angle with Triangle and with 100-Foot Tape.

quired to construct a right angle at *C* with the line *AB* as its base. From point *C* measure 30 feet along *AB* to point *D*. One man now holds the 0 end of the 100-foot tape at point *D* and another man holds the 100-foot end of the tape at point *C*. A third man, holding the 50-foot and 60-foot marks of the tape together at point *E* to form a 10-foot loop as shown in the drawing, changes his position until equal tension is applied to both sides of the tape. The point *E* locates a point on a line perpendicular to *AB* through point *C*.

To Construct an Equilateral Triangle

By Means of Compasses (Fig. 51). *AB* is the length of each side. With *A* as a center and *AB* as a radius, strike an arc. With *B* as a center and the same radius, strike an arc which intersects the first arc at *C*. Connect the points *A*, *B*, and *C* for the required equilateral triangle.

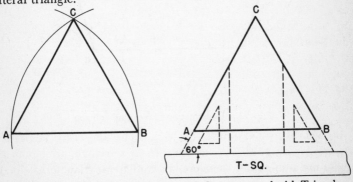

Figs. 51, 52. Equilateral Triangle with Compasses and with Triangle.

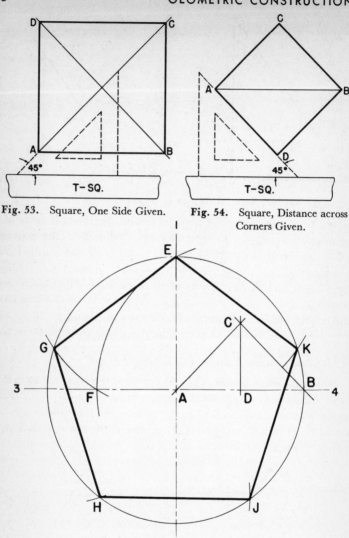

Fig. 53. Square, One Side Given.

Fig. 54. Square, Distance across Corners Given.

Fig. 55. Construction of Regular Polygon.

By Means of Triangles (Fig. 52).   The sum of the angles of a triangle equals 180°.   When the sides of a triangle are equal, the angles are also equal; therefore, an equilateral triangle has angles of 60°.

Fig. 56.   Construction of Five-Point Star.

AB is the length of each side.   Place a 30°–60° triangle on a T-square and construct a 60° angle at both *A* and *B*.   Produce the sides of these angles until they intersect at *C*, forming an equilateral triangle.

To Construct a Square with the Length of One Side Given.
AB is the given length of a side (Fig. 53).   At *A* and *B* erect perpendiculars using the T-square and triangle as shown in the illustration.   Through points *A* and *B*, draw 45° diagonal lines intersecting the two perpendiculars at points *C* and *D*.   Connect *C* and *D* for the required square.

To Construct a Square with the Distance across Corners Given.
AB is the given distance across corners (Fig. 54).   Through points *A* and *B* draw lines at 45°.   Turn the triangle over and draw lines at 45° in the other direction through the same points.   These lines will intersect at points *C* and *D*, completing the required square.

To Inscribe a Regular Pentagon (Fig. 55).   Construct center lines *1–2* and *3–4* so that they intersect each other at right angles. Draw a circle whose center is *A* and whose radius is *AB*.   Bisect radius *AB*, locating point *D*.   With *D* as a center, strike an arc through the intersection of the circle and center line *1–2* at *E*. Continue this arc through center line *3–4* at *F*.   With *E* as a center and *EF* as a radius, strike the arc *FG*.   The distance *EG* is the length of each side of the pentagon.   All the corners of the pentagon may be located by marking off the distance *EG* around the circle with a pair of compasses, establishing points *H*, *J*, and *K*.

A five-point star can be constructed by extending the sides of the pentagon until they intersect as demonstrated in Fig. 56.

To Construct a Regular Hexagon with the Distance across Corners Given (Fig. 57). Given the distance *AB*. Construct a circle with the distance *AB* as its diameter. Construct the hexagon by using a T-square and the 30° angle of a 30°–60° triangle as shown in the diagram. The inscribed hexagon in the circle is the required construction.

To Construct a Regular Hexagon with the Distance across Flats Given (Fig. 58). Given the distance *CD*. Construct a circle with the distance *CD* as its diameter. Construct the hexagon by using a T-square and the 60° angle of a 30°–60° triangle as shown in the illustration. Draw lines tangent to the circle as shown in the diagram. The hexagon circumscribed about the circle is the required construction.

To Construct a Regular Octagon with the Distance across Flats Given

THE SQUARE METHOD (Fig. 59). *AB* is the given distance across flats. Construct a square *ABCD* and draw the diagonals *AC* and *BD*. Construct another square *EFGH* with side equal to *AB* so that its diagonals, *EG* and *FH*, are horizontal and vertical. An octagon is formed by connecting the points where the sides of the two squares intersect.

THE INSCRIBED CIRCLE METHOD (Fig. 60). *AB* is the given distance across flats. Draw a circle with *AB* as its diameter. To construct the octagon, use a T-square and a 45° triangle and draw lines tangent to the circle as shown.

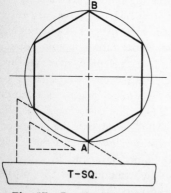

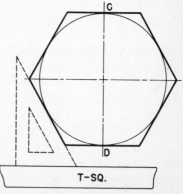

Fig. 57. Regular Hexagon with Distance across Corners Given.

Fig. 58. Regular Hexagon with Distance across Flats Given.

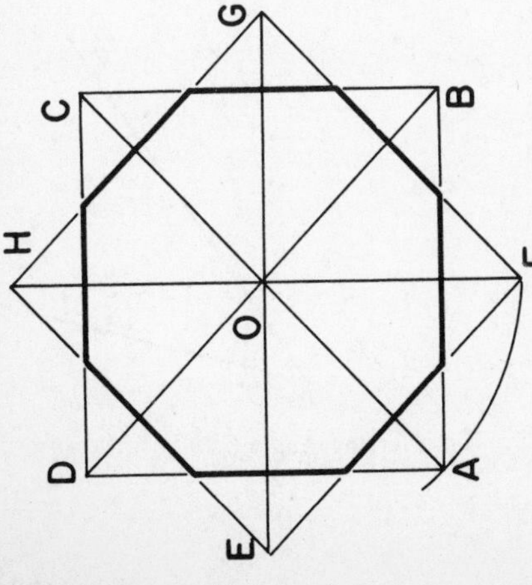

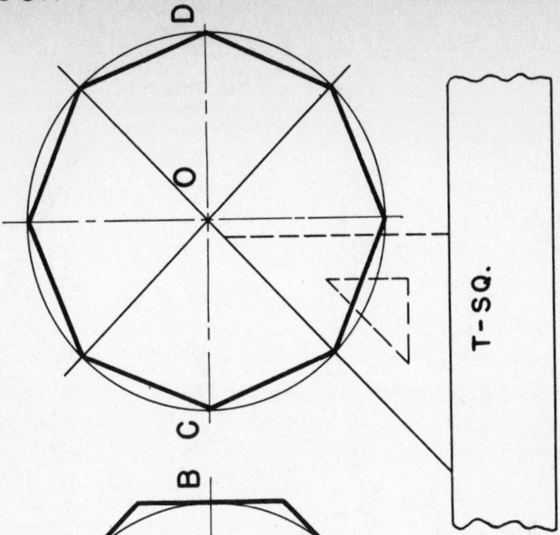

Fig. 61. Distance across Corners Given.

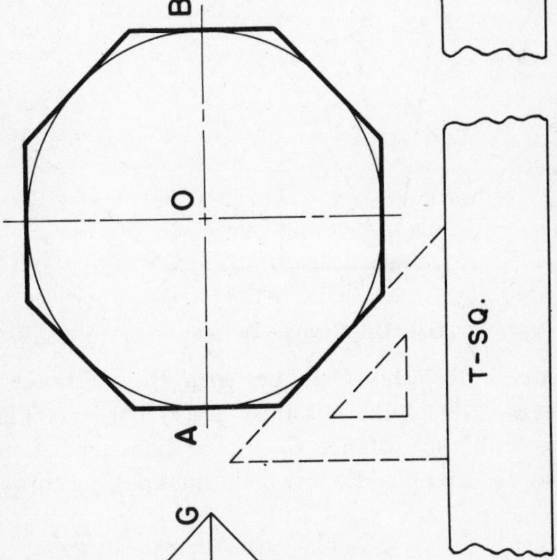

Fig. 60. Inscribed Circle Method.

Fig. 59. Square Method.

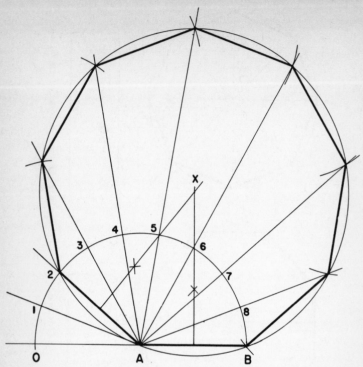

Fig. 62. Regular Polygon.

To Construct a Regular Octagon with the Distance across Corners Given. *CD* is the distance across corners (Fig. 61). Draw a circle with the distance *CD* as its diameter. Using the T-square and a 45° triangle, draw two 45° lines passing through the

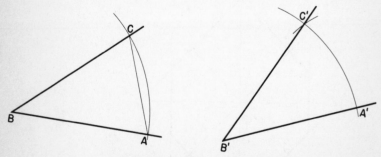

Fig. 63. Transferring Angle *CBA*.

center of the circle as shown. The corners of the octagon are located at the points where the 45° lines, plus the horizontal and vertical center lines, cut the circumference of the circle. The octagon is constructed by connecting these points.

To Construct a Regular Polygon with Any Number of Sides (Fig. 62). *AB* is the length of the sides. With *A* as a center and *AB* as a radius, draw the semicircle *OAB*. Divide this semicircle into as many equal parts as the desired number of sides of the polygon. In Fig. 62, the semicircle has been divided into nine equal parts, *0–1, 1–2, 2–3, 3–4, 4–5, 5–6, 6–7, 7–8, 8–B*. Draw line *A2*. Find the perpendicular bisectors of lines *A2* and *AB* which intersect at point *X*. With *X* as a center, and the distance *XB* as a radius, draw a circle. From point *A* draw lines passing through points *3, 4, 5, 6, 7*, and *8*, located on the semicircle previously subdivided, and extend these lines to intersect the circumference of the circle. These intersections locate the corners of the required polygon.

To Transfer an Angle. Transfer the angle *CBA* (Fig. 63A) so that its base will be *B'A'* instead of *BA*. With point *B* as a center and with any radius, strike an arc cutting the two sides of the angle at *A* and *C*. With point *B'* as a center and with a radius equal to *AB*, strike an arc cutting the line *B'A'* at *A'*. Measure the length of the chord subtended by the arc *AC* with a pair of compasses. With *A'* as the center and a radius equal to the chord *AC*, strike an arc cutting arc *A'C'* at *C'*. Draw the line *B'C'* to complete the transference of the angle as shown in Fig. 63B.

To Transfer a Plane Figure about a New Base. Given the plane figure (Fig. 64) *ABCDEFGHJKA*. Let it be required to transfer this figure so that its base *AB* will become *A'B'*.

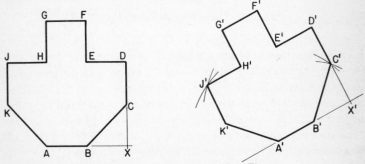

Figs. 64, 65. Transferring a Plane Figure.

OFFSET METHOD. Measure the distance BX and lay this same distance off on the new base $B'X'$. Erect a perpendicular at X'. Lay off $X'C'$ equal to XC. The other corners of this plane figure can be located by repeating this operation (Fig. 65).

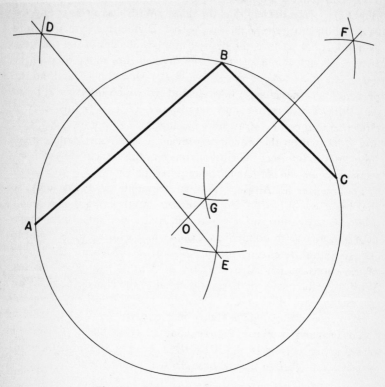

Fig. 66. Circle through Points A, B, C.

TRIANGULATION METHOD. Using B' as a center and the distance BC (Fig. 64) as a radius, strike an arc. With A' as a center and AC as a radius, strike an arc. These two arcs intersect at C', locating a point on the transferred figure corresponding to the point C. Similarly, J' could be located by striking an arc with AJ as a radius and A' as a center, then striking another arc with BJ as a radius and B' as a center. The intersection of these two arcs will locate the point J' in Fig. 65.

To Construct a Circle Given Three Points Not in the Same Straight Line (Fig. 66). *A*, *B*, and *C* are the three given points. Draw lines *AB* and *BC* connecting the three points. Construct the perpendicular bisector of *AB* which is *DE*, and the perpendicular bisector of *BC* which is *FG*. These bisectors intersect at point *O*. With *O* as a center and *OA* as a radius, draw a circle as illustrated. This circle will pass through the points *A*, *B*, and *C*.

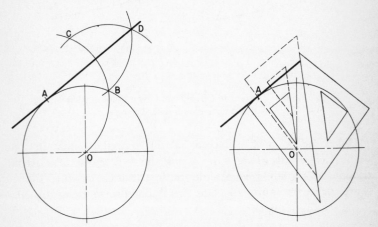

Figs. 67, 68. Tangent to Circle through Given Point on Circumference.

To Draw a Line Tangent to a Circle through a Given Point on the Circumference

BY MEANS OF COMPASSES (Fig. 67). Given the point *A* on the circumference of the circle. With *A* as a center and a radius equal to the radius (*OA*) of the circle, strike an arc *CBO*. With *B* as a center and the same radius (*OA*), strike the arc *CD*. Using point *C* as a center and the same radius (*OA*), strike the arc *BD*. A straight line drawn through points *A* and *D* will be tangent to the circle at the given point *A*.

BY MEANS OF TRIANGLES (Fig. 68). This method is preferred and recommended. A line tangent to a circle at any point is perpendicular to the radius of the circle at that point. In accordance with this principle of plane geometry, a line tangent to a circle through a given point can be simply constructed by the use of two triangles.

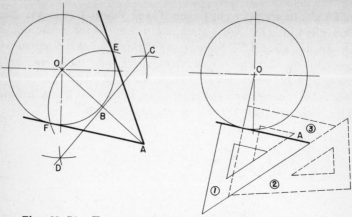

Figs. 69, 70.   Tangent to Circle from Given Point outside Circle,
with Compasses and with Triangle.

Given the point *A*. Place a 30°–60° triangle so that its long
vertical edge falls along *OA*. Using the hypotenuse of a second
triangle as a guiding edge, slide the first triangle down so that its
short edge passes through point *A*. A line drawn along this edge
is the required tangent.

To Construct a Tangent to a Circle from a Given Point outside the Circle

By Means of Compasses (Fig. 69).   From the given point *A* draw
a line connecting that point with the center of the circle *O*. Construct the perpendicular bisector *CD*, bisecting the line *OA* at point

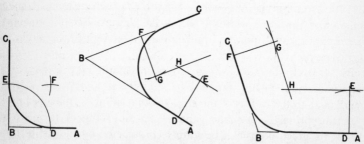

Figs. 71, 72, 73.   Circular Arcs Tangent to Two Lines.

B. With point *B* as a center and *OB* as a radius, strike the arc *EOF*. Draw lines joining points *A*, *E* and *A*, *F*. These two lines pass through the given point *A* and are tangent to the circle.

By Means of Triangles (Fig. 70). This method is preferred and recommended. Triangle (1) is placed so that one of its edges is tangent to the circle and passes through the given point *A*. Draw a line along this edge. Using the guiding edge of another triangle (2) as shown, slide the first triangle (1) upward so that its vertical edge passes through the center of the circle, thereby locating the point of tangency accurately. It is apparent from the diagram that only one of two possible conditions is shown.

To Draw a Circular Arc of Given Radius (R) Tangent to Two Lines

When the Two Lines Are at Right Angles (Fig. 71). With *B* as a center and radius *R*, strike an arc cutting the line *CB* at *E* and the line *BA* at *D*. Using the same radius with points *D* and *E* as centers, strike the arcs intersecting at *F*. With point *F* as a center and the same radius, draw the required arc *DE*.

When the Two Lines Form Any Angle (Figs. 72, 73). At any point *D* erect a perpendicular to line *BA*. Mark off radius *R* on the perpendicular to locate point *E*. Repeat same procedure, using any point *F* to locate point *G*. Draw a line through point *E* parallel to line *BA*, and another line through point *G* parallel to line *BC*. These two lines intersect at point *H*, the center of the required arc.

To Draw a Circular Arc with a Given Radius (R) Tangent to a Given Circular Arc and a Given Straight Line. Given the circular arc of radius R_1 and the straight line *AB*. At any point *C* erect a perpendicular to line *AB*, as in Fig. 74. Mark off the radius *R* on this perpendicular to locate point *D*. Draw a line through point *D* parallel to line *AB*. It is apparent that any circular arc of radius *R* that is to be tangent to the circular arc of radius R_1 must have its center a distance of radius *R* away from the arc of radius R_1. Therefore, draw an arc with a radius of $R_1 + R$ intersecting the line through *D* at point *E*. Point *E* locates the center of the arc which is tangent to the given line and to the given circular arc. In Fig. 75, the same procedure is used except that the radii must be subtracted instead of added.

To Draw a Circle of Given Radius (R) Tangent to Two Circles or Circular Arcs. Given two circles whose centers are A and B with radii of R_1 and R_2 respectively. With A as a center and a radius of $R_1 + R$, strike an arc. With B as a center and a radius of $R_2 + R$, strike an arc. These two arcs intersect at point C, which is the center of the required circle (Fig. 76). In Fig. 77, the same procedure is followed except that in this case the radii have to be subtracted in one instance.

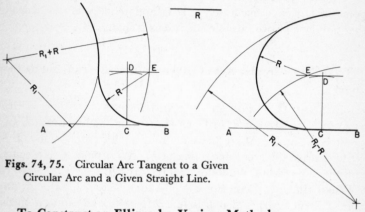

Figs. 74, 75. Circular Arc Tangent to a Given Circular Arc and a Given Straight Line.

To Construct an Ellipse by Various Methods

Foci Method — True Ellipse (Fig. 78). Let it be required to construct an ellipse by the foci method with a major axis of AB and a minor axis of CD. With point D as a center and a radius equal to OB, strike an arc cutting the major axis at points E and F, the foci of the ellipse. Divide the distance from O to E into a number of units, such as $1, 2, 3, 4, 5$. Take the distance from A to 2 and with E as a center strike an arc. Take the distance from B to 2 and with F as a center strike an arc. The intersections of these arcs determine points on the curve which make possible the plotting of the ellipse. This operation is repeated, using the points $1, 3, 4,$ and 5, until a series of points are obtained so that a smooth curve can be drawn by connecting the points with an irregular curve.

String Method (Fig. 78). This method is not accurate enough for the draftsman but is explained here because it is a common method of laying out ellipses for flower gardens and the like where accuracy is not necessary.

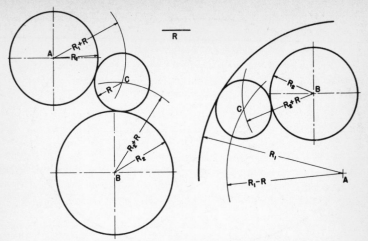

Figs. 76, 77. Circle Tangent to Two Circles or Circular Arcs.

The foci, E and F, are located in the same manner as described. Pins are driven in at these foci points. A piece of string the length of the major axis AB is fastened at one end to pin E and at the other end to pin F. Taking a pencil or any other marking device, the string is pulled taut and the pencil is moved along the string, keeping it tight at all times, until the complete ellipse is drawn. The inaccuracy of this method is due to the stretching of the string and the winding of the string around the pins as the ellipse is being described.

CONCENTRIC-CIRCLE METHOD — TRUE ELLIPSE (Fig. 79). Let it be required to construct an ellipse with a major axis AB and a minor axis $C'D'$ by the concentric-circle method. With point O

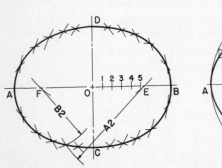

Fig. 78. Ellipse, String Method.

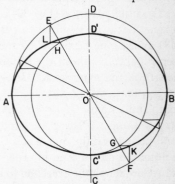

Fig. 79. Concentric-Circle Method.

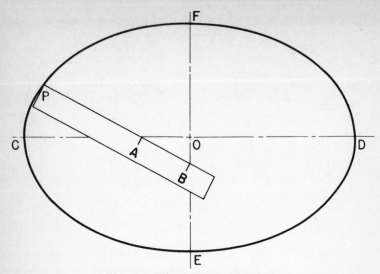

Fig. 80.   Ellipse, Trammel Method.

as a center, which is the intersection of the major and minor axes, draw two circles, one with a radius of *OB* and the other with a radius of *OD'*.   Draw any diametral line *EF*.   At points where the diametral line cuts the circumference of the outer circle, draw vertical lines *FK* and *EL*.   At points where the same diametral line cuts the inner circle, draw horizontal lines *GK* and *HL*.   The intersections of these lines locate points on the ellipse.   Sufficient points plotted this way may be connected with an irregular curve to form a smooth ellipse.

TRAMMEL METHOD (Fig. 80).   This method is preferred by draftsmen.   Let it be required to construct an ellipse with a major axis *CD* and a minor axis *EF* by the trammel method.   On a piece of scrap paper, mark off the distance *PB*, making it equal to half the length of the major axis, *OD* or *OC*.   On the same piece of scrap paper, mark off the distance *PA*, making it equal to half the length of the minor axis, *OF* or *OE*.   A piece of paper so marked is known as a trammel.   Place point *B* on the trammel on the minor axis *EF*, and point *A* on the major axis *CD* as shown.   Mark point *P*.   The trammel is now moved in order to plot a series of points with point *P*.   Care should be exercised to keep points *B* and *A* on the trammel on the minor and major axes while the various positions of *P* are located, thus generating a true ellipse. A smooth curve may be obtained with an irregular curve by connecting the points located by point P on the trammel.

FOUR-CENTER METHOD (Fig. 81). An approximate ellipse may be constructed by the four-center method. This ellipse is composed entirely of circular arcs and is drawn by a pair of compasses, eliminating the use of the irregular curve. Let the length of the major axis be AB and that of the minor axis be CD. Draw line CB joining the ends of the major and minor axes. With point O as a center and OB as a radius, strike an arc cutting the minor axis at point E. With C as a center and CE as a radius, strike an arc cutting the line CB at point F. Find the perpendicular bisector GH of the line FB, which cuts the major axis at J and the minor axis at K. Points K' and J' are found in the same way. Using J as a center and a radius JB, strike the arc MBL. Repeat this process, using J' as the center

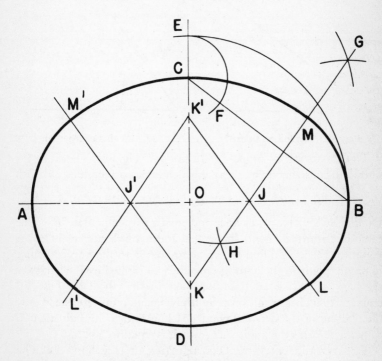

Fig. 81. Ellipse, Four-Center Method.

and a radius $J'A$. With K as a center and a radius KC, strike the arc $M'CM$. Repeat this procedure, using K' as a center and a radius $K'D$ to draw arc $L'DL$.

This ellipse is used generally, as it is close enough to a true ellipse for most purposes and is the easiest of the approximate ellipses to construct.

To Construct Angles by the Tangent Method. In making drawings, it is sometimes necessary to construct angles other than those possible by the use of the 45° and 30°–60° triangles. These angles are generally constructed by means of a protractor, but this method is not accurate.

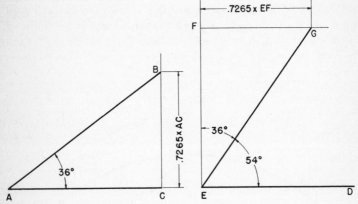

Fig. 82. Angle Less than 45°.   **Fig. 83.** Angle Greater than 45°.

To Construct an Angle Less than 45° (Fig. 82). Let it be required to construct an angle at A which makes an angle of 36° with the line AC. From trigonometry it is known that $\tan A = \dfrac{BC}{AC}$. On line AC lay off any distance and erect a perpendicular CB. The table of natural tangents shows that the natural tangent of 36° is equal to .7265. To find the value to lay off on the perpendicular to obtain point B, the natural tangent is multiplied by the length of the base AC. It is advisable to make the length of the base AC equal to 10 inches as this saves multiplying and requires instead only the shifting of the decimal point. A line drawn through point B to point A forms the angle BAC, which is equal to 36°.

To Construct an Angle Greater than 45° (Fig. 83). Let it be required to construct an angle at E which makes an angle of 54°

with the line *ED*. The tangent method of constructing angles is inaccurate for angles greater than 45°.   In order to use this method for large angles, a perpendicular *EF* is erected as in Fig. 83, and the complementary angle of the 54° angle is constructed with this perpendicular.   The complement of the 54° angle is 36°.   At any point *F* erect a perpendicular *FG* to line *EF*.   It is best to make the length of *EF* equal to 10 inches for the same reason given in the preceding paragraph.   On the perpendicular *FG* lay off the value obtained by multiplying the natural tangent of 36° with the length of the base *EF*.   A line drawn from point *G* to point *E* forms the angle *FEG* of 36° or the complementary angle *GED* of 54°.

3

Lettering

In the control of the appearance of a drawing, excellent lettering may offset to some extent faulty linework and geometric construction, but never in the control of appearance can excellent linework and geometric construction offset, or counterbalance, poor lettering. Lettering makes or breaks the appearance of anything on which it is placed, be it drawing, report, homework problem, textbook assignment, or placard.

Freehand lettering differs from writing in that the work of lettering is done with finger motion, each entire stroke being made by the movement of the fingers; at the end of the stroke the pen or pencil is lifted from the paper. Writing is done with a sweeping motion with the pen or pencil trailing across the paper, which produces an uneven width of stroke.

Poor penmanship is no excuse for poor lettering. In fact, there are but two reasons for poor lettering: one is the lack of normal control over the hands; the other is laziness. Every draftsman must acquire the skill to letter clearly. He can do so by means of continued practice.

Before attempting to letter, the student should first learn the form and characteristics of every individual letter of the alphabet. This he can do by drawing the letters again and again until he is satisfied that he is able to reproduce the alphabet legibly and with ease.

The Single-Stroke Gothic Alphabet. The single-stroke Gothic alphabet (Figs. 84, 85) is the simplest style known and is used almost universally for technical drawings. Vertical (Figs. 84, 85) and inclined (Figs. 86, 87) letters may be used, as both types are recommended by the American Standards Association. Lettering is

ABCDEFGHIJKLMN

OPQRSTUVWXYZ&

Fig. 84. Vertical Letters, Gothic.

ABCDEFGHI

JKLMNOPQR

STUVWXYZ&

Fig. 85. Vertical Letters, Gothic.

ABCDEFGHIJKLMN

OPQRSTUVWXYZ&

Fig. 86. Inclined Letters, Gothic.

ABCDEFGHI

JKLMNOPQR

STUVWXYZ&

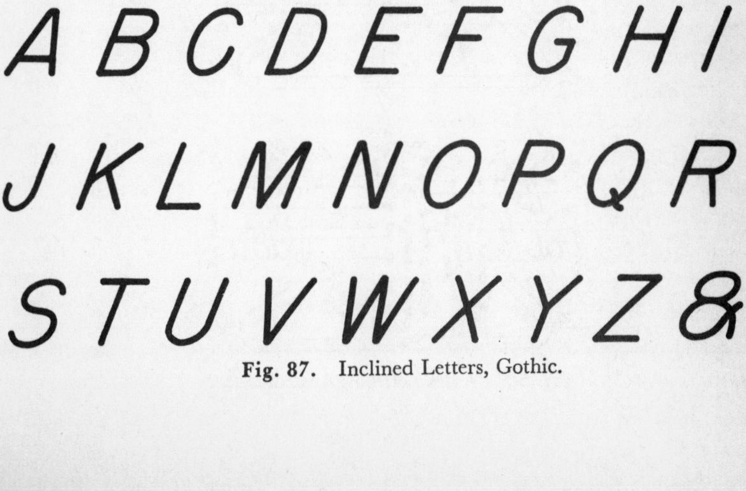

Fig. 87. Inclined Letters, Gothic.

Fig. 88.   Vertical Guide Lines.

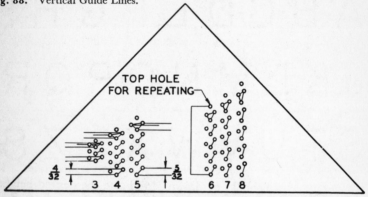

Fig. 89.   Braddock-Rowe Lettering Triangle.

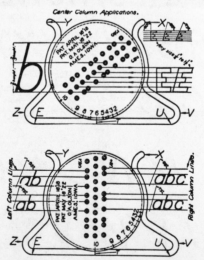

Fig. 90.   Ames Lettering Instrument.

usually done freehand, although many industrial companies require a mechanically drawn alphabet. During World War II, the United States government required all technical drawings to be lettered with the LeRoy Lettering Set, a product of Keuffel & Esser Co. Most of the lettering in this chapter has been executed with this instrument. However, the single-stroke Gothic alphabet can be mastered easily, and every engineering student should learn how to letter freehand.

Preparation of Pencil for Lettering. An F, H, or 2H pencil may be used for lettering in pencil, depending upon the personal choice of the draftsman. It is essential that a well-sharpened conical point be maintained on the pencil to obtain uniformity and clarity of line. Care must be taken not to use a needle-point pencil, as such an edge will cut into the surface of the paper. When the pencil has been sharpened to a fine point, the draftsman should then draw several lines on scrap paper, rotating the pencil in his hand, to dull the point slightly and to keep a symmetrical point on the pencil.

Method of Inking. Before inking, all letters and words should be carefully planned and penciled. The draftsman should never ink letters without first having executed them completely in pencil.

Guide Lines. A good letterer always uses guide lines. Two horizontal lines should be drawn to indicate the desired height of the letters. Vertical guide lines are then drawn at random across the length of the horizontal lines, as shown in Fig. 88. These lines are drawn with a triangle and a T-square and should be drawn in lightly. They are not intended to help the student space his letters or words, but are used solely to aid in drawing straight, vertical letters.

The *Braddock-Rowe Lettering Triangle* (Fig. 89) is a very useful instrument in drawing and spacing guide lines for lettering. It is particularly time-saving in spacing horizontal lines for upper- and lower-case letters.

The *Ames Lettering Instrument* (Fig. 90) is also useful and practical as a device in drawing guide lines. The authors, however, prefer the Braddock-Rowe Lettering Triangle because of its many uses as a triangle. Every student is urged to obtain one.

With both these lettering instruments, a sharp-pointed pencil is placed in the countersunk holes and the instrument is then drawn back and forth along the blade of the T-square with the pencil.

GUIDE LINES FOR INCLINED LETTERS (Figs. 91, 92). The angle of inclination is determined by a 2-and-5 triangle as shown, and is approximately $67\frac{1}{2}°$. A protractor can also be used to obtain this angle. A special triangle is manufactured with a hypotenuse of $67\frac{1}{2}°$. Besides this special triangle, the Braddock-Rowe Lettering Triangle and the Ames Lettering Instrument can also be used to obtain the recommended angle for inclined letters.

Fig. 93 shows guide lines for large and small capital letters. The small capitals should be drawn about two-thirds the height of the large letters.

Several lines of lettering should be spaced so that they can be read easily. It is recommended that the space between lines of lettering be about two-thirds the height of the letters, as shown in Fig. 94. The guiding principle should be legibility, regardless of any set rule.

The order and direction of lines in drawing capital letters and numerals are shown in Figs. 95 and 96. The student should familiarize himself with this procedure before he begins to letter.

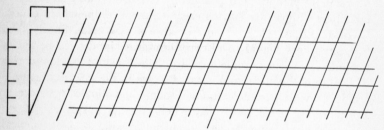

Fig. 91. Guide Lines for Inclined Letters.

Fig. 92. Guide Lines for Inclined Letters.

Fig. 93. Guide Lines for Capital Letters.

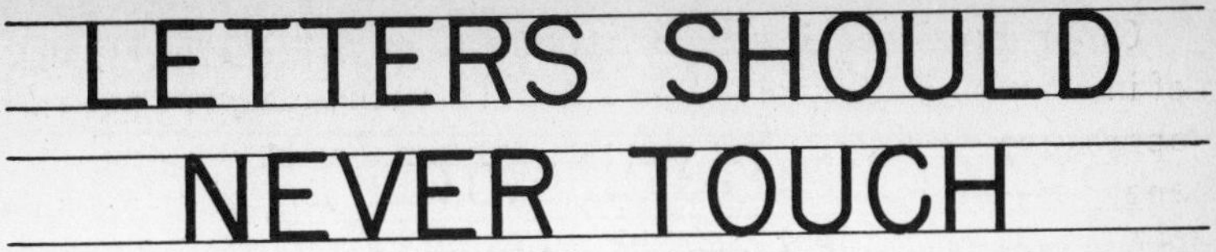

LETTERS SHOULD
NEVER TOUCH

Fig. 94.   Spacing between Lines.

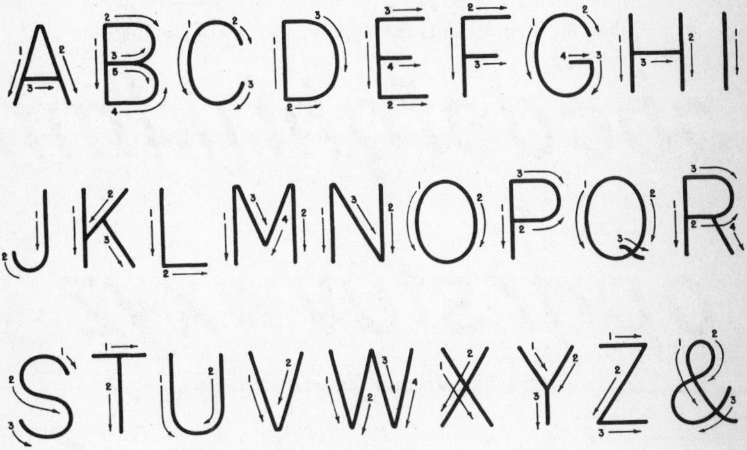

ABCDEFGHI
JKLMNOPQR
STUVWXYZ&

Fig. 95.   Order and Direction of Lines.

1234567890

Fig. 96.   Order and Direction of Lines.

abcdefghijklmn

opqrstuvwxyz

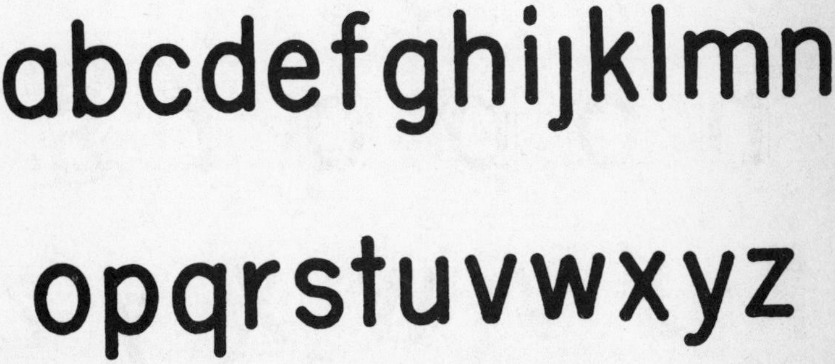

Fig. 97.   Lower-Case Letters.

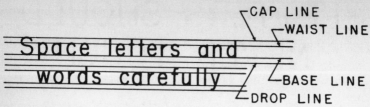

CAP LINE
WAIST LINE
Space letters and
words carefully
BASE LINE
DROP LINE

Fig. 98. Guide Lines for Upper- and Lower-Case Letters.

abcdefghijklmn
opqrstuvwxyz

Fig. 99. Inclined Lower-Case Letters.

a b c d e f
g h i j k l m
n o p q r s
t u v w x y z

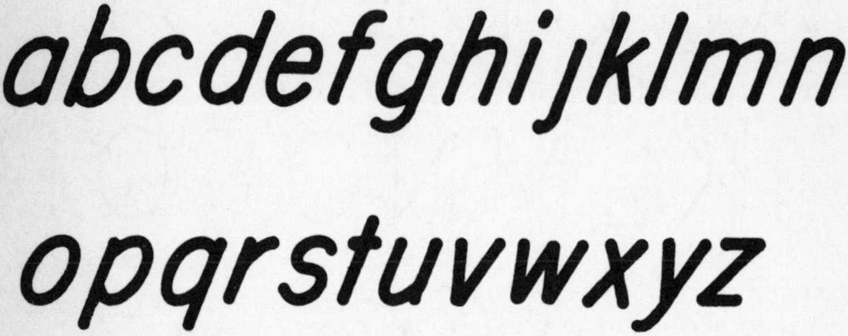

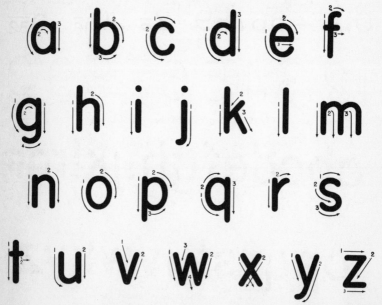

Fig. 100. Order and Direction of Lines.

GUIDE LINES FOR LOWER- AND UPPER-CASE LETTERS. The lower-
and upper-case alphabet is shown in Figs. 97, 98. Inclined lower-
case letters are shown in Fig. 99. In lower- and upper-case letters,
the lower-case letters are drawn about two-thirds the height of the
capital letters, as shown in Fig. 98. Letters *b*, *d*, *f*, *h*, *k*, *l*, and *t* are
drawn full length. Letters *g*, *j*, *p*, *q*, and *y* extend below the base
line one-third the height of the letters, as shown in the diagram.
Spaces between lines of lower- and upper-case letters are also
one-third the height of the full letters, as illustrated. Here again,
the principle to observe in spacing lines is legibility.

Vertical or inclined guide lines for lower- and upper-case letters
follow the same practice already explained in this chapter for capital
letters.

The order and direction of lines in drawing lower-case letters are
shown in Fig. 100.

GUIDE LINES FOR NUMERALS AND FRACTIONS. Whole numbers
and fractions drawn vertically are shown in Figs. 101, 102. Inclined
whole numbers and fractions are shown in Figs. 103, 104.

$$0123456789 \quad 2\tfrac{1}{2} \quad 10\tfrac{7}{16} \quad 5\tfrac{17}{32}$$

Fig. 101. Whole Numbers and Fractions, Vertical.

$$0123456789$$

$$3\tfrac{1}{4} \quad 5\tfrac{7}{8} \quad 1\tfrac{3}{4} \quad 8\tfrac{2}{3} \quad \tfrac{9}{16}$$

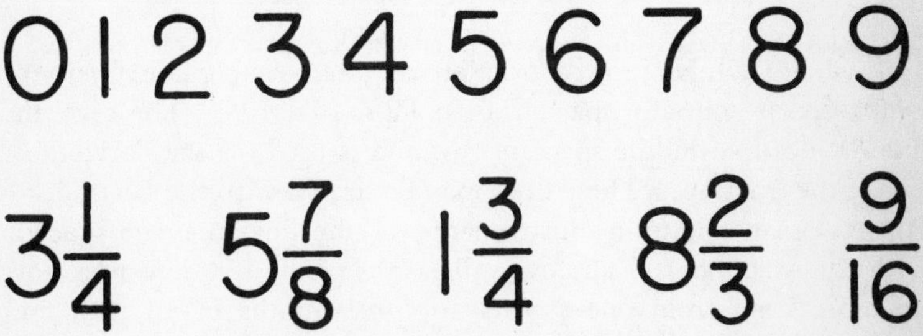

Fig. 102. Whole Numbers and Fractions, Vertical.

$$0123456789 \quad 2\tfrac{1}{2} \quad 10\tfrac{7}{16} \quad 5\tfrac{17}{32}$$

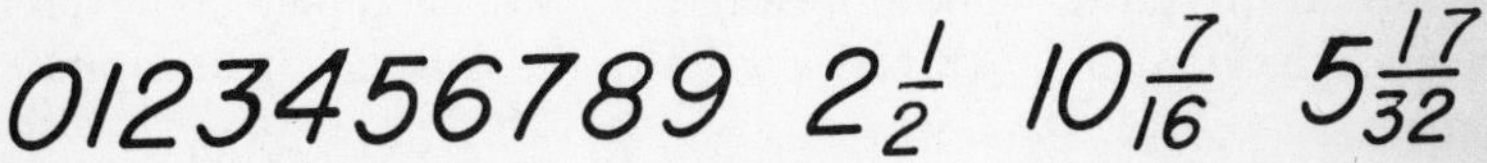

Fig. 103. Whole Numbers and Fractions, Inclined.

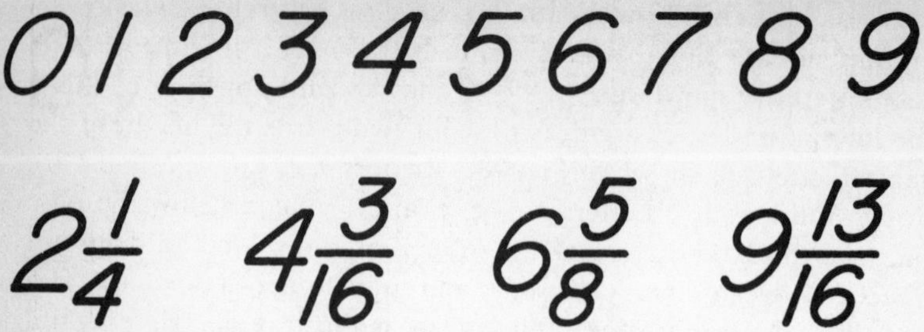

0 1 2 3 4 5 6 7 8 9

$2\frac{1}{4}$ $4\frac{3}{16}$ $6\frac{5}{8}$ $9\frac{13}{16}$

Fig. 104. Whole Numbers and Fractions, Inclined.

Fig. 105. Guide Lines for Whole Numbers and Fractions.

Fig. 106. Guide Lines for Whole Numbers and Fractions.

A whole number and a fraction require seven guide lines, of which six are equally spaced, as in Figs. 105, 106. The seventh line divides the middle space in two and is used for the horizontal bar of the fraction. These lines may be drawn with the Braddock-Rowe or Ames lettering instruments, or the lines may be spaced with a bow divider. The over-all height of the fraction need not be more than from one-quarter to three-eighths of an inch for ordinary dimensions. The whole number is almost always three-fifths the height of the fraction, as shown in Fig. 106.

The Ampersand. The ampersand (&) is the accepted abbreviation for the word *and*. It is always drawn the same height as capital letters.

Method of Spacing. The secret of easily read words is good spacing. Spacing is the most difficult aspect of lettering, and it can

POOR SPACING

Fig. 107. Equal Spacing of Letters.

GOOD SPACING

Fig. 108. Correct Spacing of Letters.

SPACING

Fig. 109. Equal Areas between Letters.

be learned only by constant application and practice, especially because it is done by eye. Certain rules or practices, however, must be observed to insure good spacing. Letters, for example, must never touch. Nor must they be spaced so closely together as to create the illusion that they touch each other. Spaces between words should be adequate enough to permit easy reading.

The letters in a word cannot be spaced uniformly. When letters are spaced equally, as in Fig. 107, they do not hold together as words and, consequently, reading becomes difficult and confusing. Words should be spaced as in Fig. 108, where the letters are so arranged as to leave about the same amount of area between them. Spacing, then, should not be based on a constant mathematical value, as in Fig. 107, but should vary according to the shape and form of the letters in order to achieve a balance of approximately the same area between them. Fig. 109 shows that the areas between letters are approximately equal.

To maintain approximately equal areas between letters, the following rules should be carefully noted. Greater space should be allowed between vertical letters when they occur side by side, such as *M* and *I*, *I* and *H*, *I* and *N*, or other similar combinations. Less space should occur between circular letters, such as between *O*'s (*book*, *moon*, *soon*, etc.), or between *O* and *C*, *O* and *G*, *D* and *O*,

O and *T*, and so forth. Still less space should be allowed between *L* and *E*, *L* and *L*, *A* and *C*, *T* and *T*, *A* and *T*, *V* and *A*, etc. Some letters in combination actually overlap, such as *L* and *T*, *A* and *Y*, *L* and *Y*. The student should make a list of the more common combinations of letters which need special attention for proper spacing.

4

Orthographic Projection

This chapter deals with the theory and methods of orthographic projection. The student will be required to apply the knowledge he has acquired in the study of the preceding chapters. He should not attempt to dimension a drawing while he is studying the material in this chapter.

Views of an object are drawn so that those using the drawing may know the shape, the size, and the material from which the object is to be made. Before an object can be built, its shape must be indicated on paper so that the builder may have a guide. The reader should realize that as a student he learns to draw by drawing views of objects already made, but that as an engineer he will first make the drawings (design the objects) so that the objects can be made in accordance with his drawings.

Single and Multiple Views. In most cases the important view is the contour (front) view, which in drawing terminology is the view that best shows the shape or contour of the object. The front of a building or monument usually tells most about its shape; but the side of an automobile tells most about its shape, and in a drawing of an automobile the contour (front) view would be a view looking directly at the side of the automobile.

It would be extremely difficult to construct a building, monument, or automobile from a single view; so additional views are necessary. In the case of the automobile, views of all the component parts would first have to be drawn. These comprise the details, and the drawings are detail drawings. Detail drawings are also working drawings. The detail drawing shows every detail in regard to shape, size, and material necessary to make the object. In other words, it is a working drawing in that work may be done by using

63

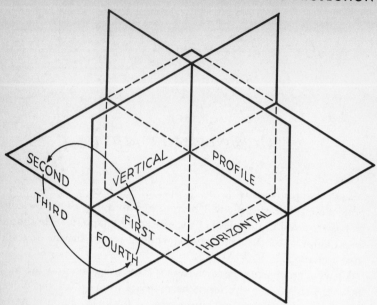

Fig. 110.   Three Planes of Projection.

the drawing and its instructions as a guide for the construction of the object.

The number of views necessary to describe an object depends entirely on its complexity. A gasket for a cylinder head may be described by a single view. A bolt or nut may be described by two views, a front view and a side (end) view, or by a single picture view. A very complex object may require a number of views, such as front, side, top, bottom, auxiliary, and section views. These views are made by projection; consequently, we have the term *orthographic projection*. Enough views must be drawn to describe the object completely. If one view and a note will describe the object sufficiently well, no more views need be drawn.

Theory of Projection. There are three principal planes of projection — horizontal, vertical, and profile — as illustrated in Fig. 110. These planes intersect each other at right angles, forming the first, second, third, and fourth angles or quadrants. Theoretically, an object can be projected in any one of the four angles. An object projected in any angle or quadrant so that its sides are parallel to the principal planes will show the object in its true size and shape.

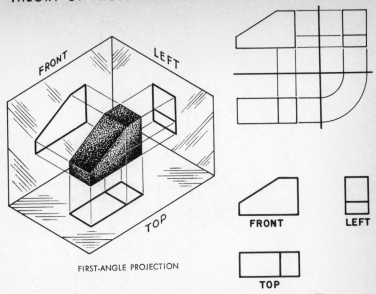

FIRST-ANGLE PROJECTION

Fig. 111. Projection from Position in Front of Vertical Plane.

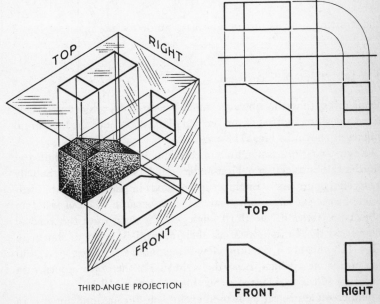

THIRD-ANGLE PROJECTION

Fig. 112. Projection from Position above Horizontal Plane.

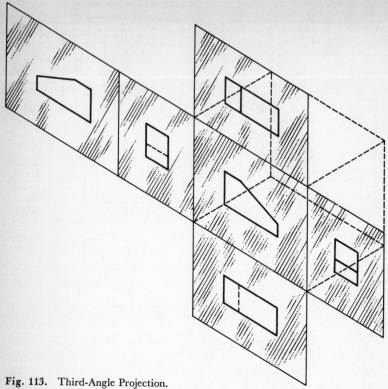

Fig. 113. Third-Angle Projection.

Remember that the observer should view every object projected from a position in front of the vertical plane and above the horizontal plane, as shown in Figs. 111 and 112.

Engineering draftsmen are concerned chiefly with first-angle and third-angle projection. First-angle projection is used primarily in foreign countries. Engineering methods in America make third-angle projection more practical. This is because when views of an object projected in the third angle are revolved onto the vertical plane, all the views appear in their natural position as shown in Figs. 113 and 114. The top view is seen above the front view, and the profile view which shows the right side of the object appears on the right of the front view. (See Figs. 111 and 112.)

Third-angle projection is used exclusively throughout this text in conformity with standard practice in the United States as determined

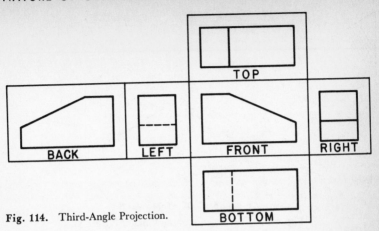

Fig. 114.   Third-Angle Projection.

by the American Standards Association, the American Society of Mechanical Engineers, and the American Society for Engineering Education.

Nature of Orthographic Projection.   The problem continually confronting the engineering draftsman is to represent a three-dimensional object on a sheet of paper which has only two dimensions.   Such drawings must give the mechanic or shopman a complete description of the object to enable him to construct it with facility and without error.   There are several methods of representing a three-dimensional object on a sheet of paper — namely, by photographs, by picture drawings, and by orthographic projections.

Photographs are not always practicable because the object must be made before it can be photographed.   Moreover, the interior of the object cannot be seen and the back view can be shown only by another photograph.   Photographs also have a tendency to distort the object somewhat, so that true relationships between the different views of the object cannot be fully expressed.

Picture drawings also are limited in their usefulness because, as in photographs, interior details are not shown.   During World War II, however, many factories made use of pictorial drawings of simple objects to enable the untrained person with limited skill to perform minor operations on these objects.   (A summary of different types of pictorial drawings is provided in Chapter 7.)

Regardless of the type of representation used to show an object, all methods of representation make use of lines of sight, or projectors.

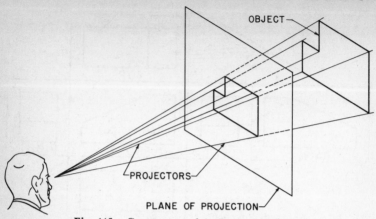

Fig. 115. Convergence of the Lines of Projection.

If the projectors converge to a point or are inclined to a plane placed between the observer and the object (Fig. 115), the resulting projection of the object on this plane will be distorted. This type of representation is known as *perspective projection* and is used principally by architects to show how a proposed building will appear when completed. Fig. 115 shows how projectors converge. This kind of projection is more nearly what the eye actually sees than is any other type of graphic representation. The plane which is inserted between the observer and the object is known as the *plane of projection*.

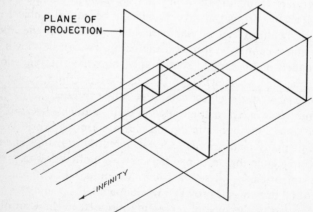

Fig. 116. Projectors Perpendicular to Plane.

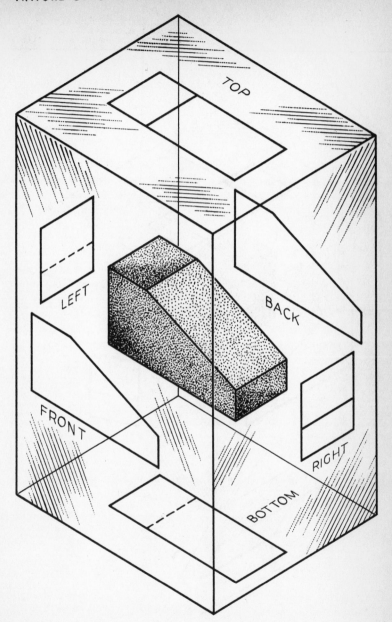

Fig. 117. The "Glass-Box" Method.

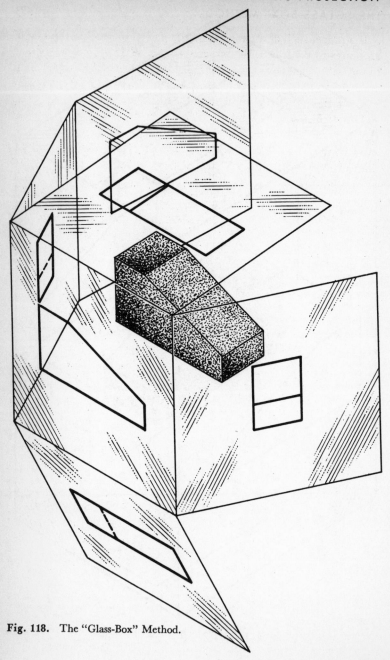

Fig. 118. The "Glass-Box" Method.

If a plane, such as a pane of glass, is placed parallel to the side of an object to be drawn, the projectors may be drawn perpendicular to the pane of glass, as shown in Fig. 116. The resulting projection on the glass will be an *orthographic projection* of that side of the object and will show that side in its true size and shape.

The "Glass-Box" Method. The student can easily visualize the method of orthographic projection by making a careful study of Fig. 117. Perpendicular projectors are drawn from all sides of the object onto the various faces of the "glass box." Six

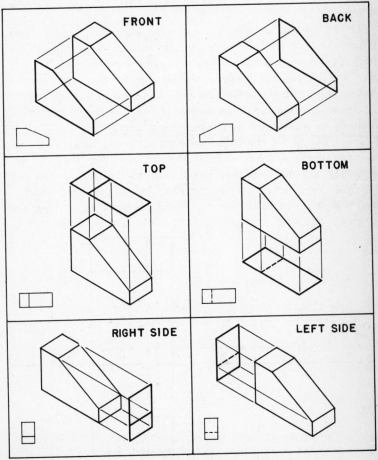

Fig. 119. Views Obtained by Looking at Object Perpendicularly.

orthographic projections are obtained by connecting these points properly.

Fig. 118 shows how the various sides of the "box" are connected or hinged together and how they are rotated until they take the position shown in Fig. 113. Fig. 114 shows how these six views appear on a sheet of paper when they coincide with the front plane.

Practical Method. Fig. 119 shows that the *front view* or *front elevation* is obtained by looking at the front face of the object perpendicularly. All other views are likewise obtained by looking at the various faces of the object perpendicularly as shown in the same diagram.

The "glass-box" method is a cumbersome one. It is possible to obtain the same results by arranging the various views of the object so that the *top view* and *bottom view* are in line vertically with the *front view* and by placing the *left* and *right* sides of the object in line horizontally with the same *front view*, as shown in Figs. 114, 120. In the *left-side view* and the *bottom view* of Figs. 114 and 120, invisible features are represented by a broken or hidden line.

Inspection of Fig. 120 will show that the *front view* and the *back view* are alike; that the *top view* (also known as the *plan view*) and the *bottom view* are alike; and that the *right-side view* (or *right-end view*) and the *left-side view* (or *left-end view*) are alike, in that they both describe and designate the same shape. Therefore, since these views are alike, the *back*, the *bottom*, and the *left-side views* are omitted in Fig.

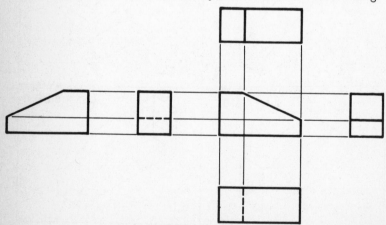

Fig. 120. Arrangement of Identical Views.

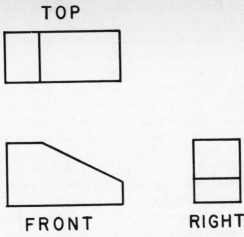

Fig. 121.   Three Essential Views.

121.   The remaining three views — *top*, *front*, and *right* — describe the shape of the object adequately enough for it to be constructed. It would follow then that in this case three views are sufficient to give a complete description of the shape of the object.

Rules for Projection.   Before the student attempts to construct an orthographic projection, he should have a thorough understanding of the following rules.   Most of these rules are illustrated in Fig. 122.

1. The front view and the top view are in the same vertical line.

2. The front view and the end views are in the same horizontal line.

3. The width of the top view is equal to that of the end views.

4. The length of the top view is equal to that of the front view.

5. The height of the end views is equal to that of the front view.

6. A surface that is parallel to a plane of projection will show true size and shape when projected onto that plane.

7. A line that is parallel to a plane of projection will show true length when projected onto that plane.

8. A line that is inclined to a plane of projection will appear shorter than its true length when projected onto that plane.

9. A line that is perpendicular to a plane of projection will appear as a point when projected onto that plane.

10. A surface that is perpendicular to a plane of projection will show as a line when projected onto that plane.

11. A surface that is inclined to a plane of projection will appear foreshortened when projected onto that plane.

Selection of Views. As has already been illustrated, it is not always necessary to show every view of an object to give an adequate description of that object (cf. Fig. 121). In drawing an orthographic projection of an object, then, it is necessary to select and represent only those views that will describe the object completely.

A study of the object should be made to determine its front view. This is the first step in constructing an orthographic projection. Generally, the front view is the one which shows the greatest contour or irregular shape. If any doubt exists as to which view fulfills this condition, the view selected as the front view should be the one having the greatest length.

Lét it be required to select the front view of the object illustrated in Fig. 123A. It should be evident upon inspection that the front view should be taken in the direction indicated by the arrow since it fulfills both of the requirements (as to shape and length) stated in the preceding paragraph.

Using this front view as a basis, the other five views of the object would appear as shown in Fig. 123B. Since not all these views are necessary for a complete understanding of the object, three of them

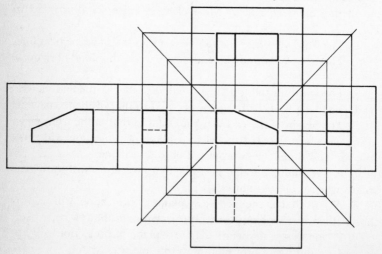

Fig. 122. Figure Illustrating Rules for Projection.

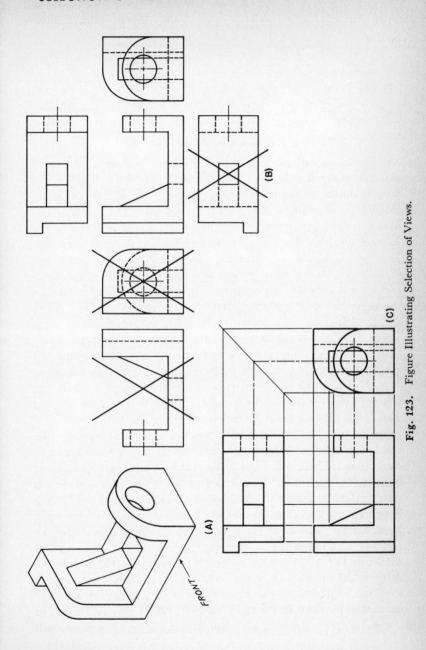

(B)

(A)

(C)

Fig. 123. Figure Illustrating Selection of Views.

FRONT

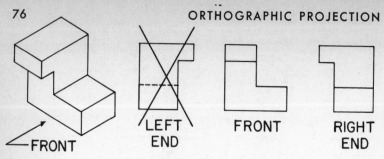

Fig. 124.   Selection of Right-End View.

have been crossed out.   The back view is eliminated because it
shows nothing that is not shown in the front view.   The bottom
view is similar to the top view except that more of the details are
invisible, and consequently it may be omitted.   The left-end view
and the right-end view, except for certain invisible features, are
likewise similar.   The general practice is to show the end view which
has fewer hidden lines; therefore, the left-end view is crossed out.
If, however, there is no difference between two end views, the right-
end view is generally represented.   It should be remembered that
the right-end view is always placed to the right of the front view,
and the left-end view is placed to the left of the front view.

Fig. 123C shows the three-view drawing of the object under discussion.   Construction lines have been retained to show the beginner how certain points are projected from one view to the other.

In Fig. 124, the right-end view is selected in preference to the
left-end view because of the invisible feature found in the left-end
view.   All parts in the right-end view are visible.

Points.   If a point is located in any two views, its position in the
third view can be determined when the previously stated rules of
projection are followed.   Using Fig. 125A as an illustration, it can
be seen that the front surface of the front view will appear in the top
view as the line nearest the front view.   Similarly, this same surface
appears in the end view as a line which is also nearest the front view.
By making use of this fact, it is possible to transfer the lengths of the
surfaces from either the top view to the end view or vice versa, as
shown in Fig. 126A.   This is done by means of a 45° line drawn
through the intersection of the lines which are the continuation of
the lines representing the same surfaces in the two views.   For
example, any point in the top view (Fig. 126A) may be located in
the end view by drawing a horizontal line through the point until

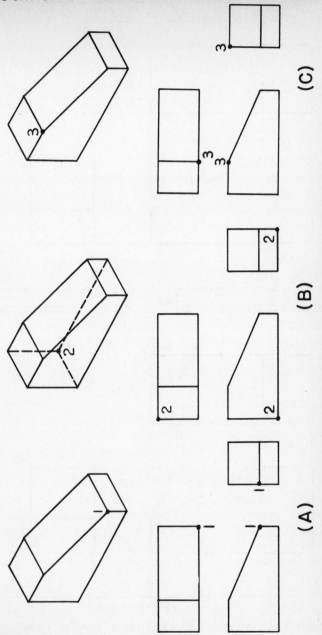

Fig. 125. Determination of Views by Location of Points.

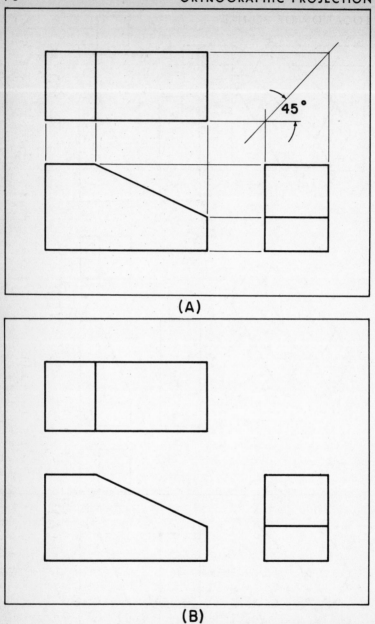

(A)

(B)

Fig. 126. Location of End View by Projection from Top Views.

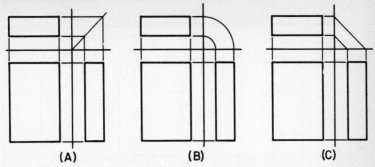

Fig. 127.   Three Methods of Projection.

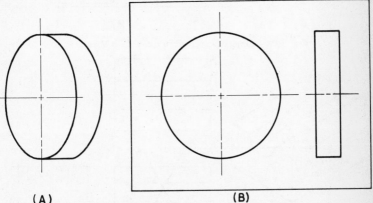

(A)   (B)

Fig. 128.   Object Described in Only Two Views.

it meets the 45° line, and thence vertically downward until it meets another horizontal line drawn through the same point in the front view. The intersection of these two lines determines the third projection of the point. This is also illustrated in Fig. 123C. In the finished drawing, construction lines are removed as in Fig. 126B.

In addition to the method of projection just explained, where the end view is located by projecting from the top view as in Fig. 126A, there are several other methods that are sometimes used. These methods are shown in Figs. 127B and 127C. The authors, however, feel that the procedure outlined in Fig. 126A, and again shown in Figs. 123C and 127A, is superior to these other methods.

The discussion of orthographic projection to this point has dealt with three views of an object. In many cases an object can be completely described in only two views. Consider, for example,

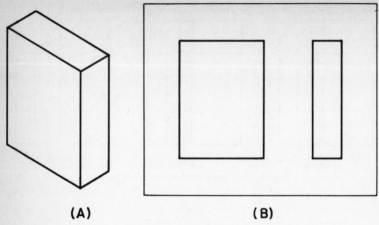

(A)   **(B)**

Fig. 129. Object Described in Only Two Views.

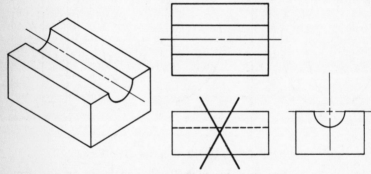

Fig. 130. Object Described in Only Two Views.

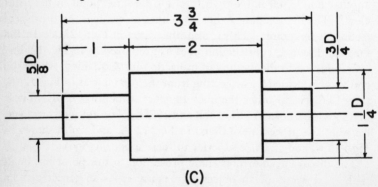

(C)

Fig. 131. Cylindrical Object Described in One View.

the circular object shown in Fig. 128A. Fig. 128B shows a two-view drawing of this object. If a top view had been drawn, it would have been identical with the end view. Consequently, the top view was omitted as unnecessary. The same reasoning holds true for the objects shown in Figs. 129 and 130.

It is frequently possible to describe a cylindrical object in one view, as in Fig. 131, providing a center line (see p. 149) is used and the diametric dimensions are indicated by *D*, the standard abbreviation for "diameter."

Procedure for a Three-View Drawing. The following steps are recommended in planning a three-view drawing.

1. Prepare drawing paper with a border and some form of title box or title strip.

2. Select the views that best describe the object.

3. Make a rough sketch of the selected views on scrap paper.

4. Measure the horizontal and vertical distances from border to border.

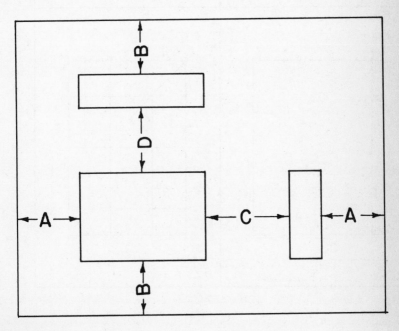

Fig. 132. Spacing a Three-View Drawing.

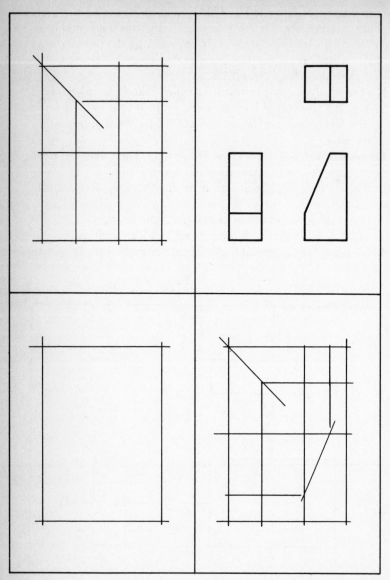

Fig. 133. Weight of Lines in a Three-View Drawing.

5. Add the length of the front view to that of the end view. Subtract this measure from the horizontal distance between the vertical borderlines of the drawing sheet. The remainder is the length that is available for spacing. Fig. 132 shows the spacing of a three-view drawing. Spaces *A* are equal, and *C* is larger than *A*, but should not be more than one-half larger than *A*. The reason for this larger space between the front and end views is that the additional space is required for dimensioning. In Chapter 8 on Dimensioning, it is shown that wherever possible dimensions should be placed between views.

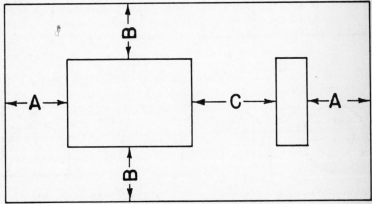

Fig. 134. Spacing in a Two-View Drawing.

6. Add the height of the front view and the depth of the top view and subtract the total length from the vertical distance between the horizontal borderlines. Divide the remaining distance as indicated in the preceding paragraph so that spaces *B* are equal, and *D* is not more than one-half larger than *B* (cf. Fig. 132). Note that there is no relationship between the sizes of spaces *A* and *B*.

7. In planning an orthographic projection, draw all views in lightly with a 6H pencil. Be sure to work on the three views alternately without attempting to complete one view before starting on the others.

8. After the three views are completely drawn, darken the lines to the proper weight as indicated in Fig. 123. It is recommended that a 2H pencil be used for visible outlines, a 4H pencil for invisible lines, and a 6H pencil for center lines.

9. Erase all construction lines.

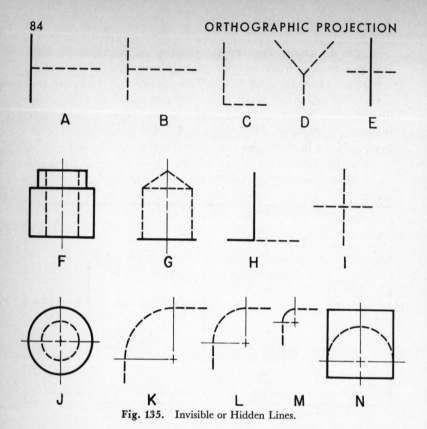

Fig. 135. Invisible or Hidden Lines.

Procedure for a Two-View Drawing. The same procedure is followed in laying out a two-view drawing as in the case of a three-view drawing, except for the spacing of the views. Fig. 134 shows the proper spacing of a two-view drawing on a sheet of paper. The distance C is not more than one-half larger than A.

Invisible or Hidden Lines. Invisible or hidden lines are medium in weight or lighter than visible lines and are represented by $\frac{1}{8}''$ dashes separated by $\frac{1}{32}''$ spaces. Invisible lines are used to indicate the edge or contour of an object which cannot be seen, as shown in Figs. 123B and 125B. Invisible lines should be carefully drawn and their junctures with other lines should be accurately represented. The following rules should be observed in drawing invisible lines.

1. Invisible lines terminating at or starting from other lines begin with a dash as shown in Figs. 135A and B.

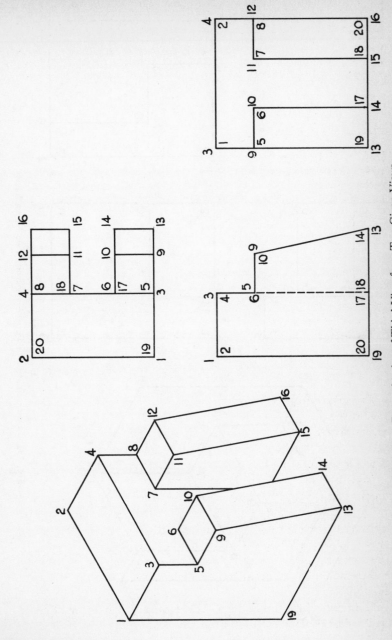

Fig. 136. Determination of Third View from Two Given Views.

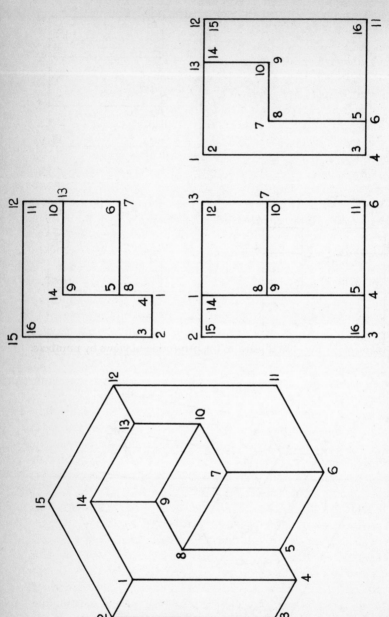

Fig. 137. Determination of Third View from Two Given Views.

2. When invisible lines intersect each other a sharp corner is formed as in Figs. 135C, D, and G.

3. An invisible line that crosses a visible line is drawn so that a space occurs on either side of the visible line as in Figs. 135E and F.

4. An invisible line which is a continuation of a visible line should start with a space as shown in Fig. 135H. The first dash should not be connected with the visible line.

5. When two invisible lines in different planes appear to cross, the invisible line closer to the observer is drawn through the farther one as shown in Fig. 135I.

6. Invisible circular arcs start with dashes at the points of tangency as shown in Figs. 135K, L, and N.

7. Very small invisible arcs are not broken as shown in Fig. 135M.

Procedure for Construction of a Third View from Two Given Views. The student will not infrequently be given two orthographic views of an object and will be required to construct a third view. In the discussion of orthographic projection, under the paragraph on points, it was shown how certain points were assigned numbers (cf. Fig. 125) and how other views were determined by these points. If this method of numbering points in the two given views is applied, the third view or projection can be easily located and drawn. Fig. 136 illustrates the projection of views by numbers. Extreme care should be taken in numbering the same points in each view. After numbering all corners in both given views and determining their location in the third view, all that remains to be done is to connect these points correctly.

This method of projection has its disadvantages, since (a) it is a slow process, (b) visibility of lines must be determined by inspection, and (c) curved and sloping surfaces are difficult to determine. Figs. 136 and 137 have been included to help the student acquire some practice in this method of determining the third view.

The following practice is recommended in numbering points. When points are visible, numbers are placed outside the corners. When points are not visible, numbers are placed inside the corners.

Fillets and Rounds. Sharp corners on castings are avoided because the cooling of the metal causes the crystals to line up perpendicular to the surface, thereby creating a weak spot at the corners. The filling in of interior angles is known as *filleting*, and the rounding off of exterior edges is known as *rounding*. (See Fig. 138.) These

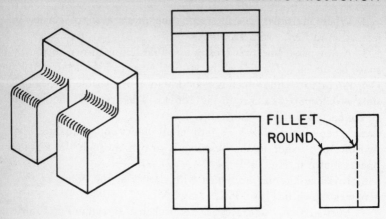

Fig. 138. Fillets and Rounds.

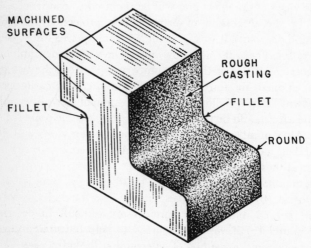

Fig. 139. Fillets and Rounds — Machined Surfaces.

fillets and rounds are found on all castings unless they are machined off when the surface is finished. (See Fig. 139.)

On drawings, fillets and rounds are represented only on those views in which they appear as circular arcs. In all other views a line should be drawn representing the points where the surfaces would intersect if the fillet or round were omitted.

5

Auxiliary Views

We have shown that when the surface of an object is projected onto a plane parallel to it the projected surface will appear in true size and shape. Frequently, however, the draftsman encounters an object with an inclined surface which will not appear in true size and shape in any of the six ordinary planes of projection (Fig. 114). When an inclined or slanting surface occurs, it becomes necessary to construct an additional view to describe that surface adequately.

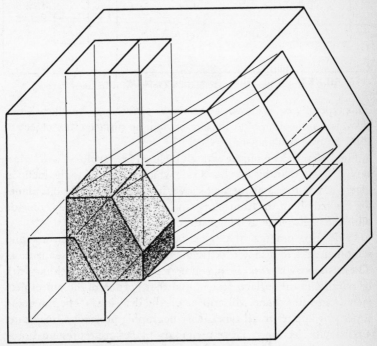

Fig. 140. Object with Inclined Face in "Glass Box."

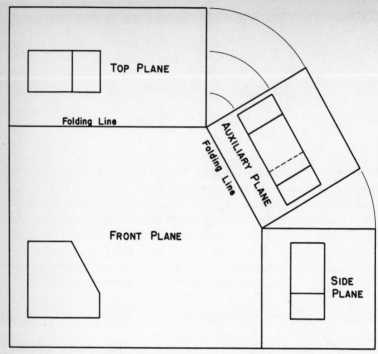

Fig. 141. "Glass-Box" Method for Object with Inclined Face.

This type of view is known as an *auxiliary view*. An auxiliary view, then, is a projection of a slanting or oblique surface of an object to show its true size and shape.

Fig. 140 shows an object with an inclined face enclosed in a "glass box." Note that this box has a side which is parallel to the inclined face. Using the same method shown in Fig. 118, the various planes are hinged about the front plane and are rotated until they coincide with the front plane as demonstrated in Fig. 141.

In drafting practice, the "glass-box" method is cumbersome and seldom used, and it should be used only for purposes of visualization. The customary method is to assume a plane, either coinciding with or parallel to the surface drawn, and that portion of the object projected onto this plane will appear on the drawing. The foregoing statement applies to all types of orthographic projection, including auxiliary projection. These imaginary planes are represented only in cases where an auxiliary view is being constructed. This pro-

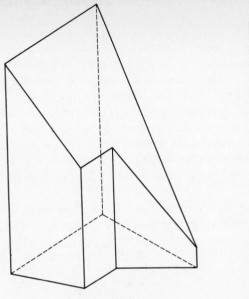

Fig. 142. Object Requiring
Auxiliary View for
Complete Description.

*Direction of sight to
obtain true size of
sloping surface*

Fig. 143. Two Views of
Object in Fig. 142.

cedure can be illustrated by making a drawing of the object shown in
Fig. 142, in which an auxiliary view is necessary for a complete
description of the object. Fig. 143 shows two views of this same object, and it is evident that the inclined face does not appear in true
size or shape. In order for this slanting surface to appear in true
size and shape, it is necessary to look at it in a direction perpendicular
to the inclined face, as shown by the arrow in the drawing.

Imagine a plane as being placed so that it is parallel to the inclined face, at any convenient distance from the face, as shown in
Fig. 144. If this plane is rotated about some line in the plane until
it coincides with the plane of the front elevation, the resulting view
shows the true size and shape of the inclined face. This line about
which the plane is rotated is called a *reference line* and is shown in
Fig. 145.

Reference lines can be placed anywhere on this imaginary plane, but if the object is such that the auxiliary view will be symmetrical, the reference line should then be placed so that it is on the line of symmetry. This line is known as the *symmetrical reference line* (Fig. 148, *R'L'*). When the object is not symmetrical, as in Fig. 143, the reference line can be taken at any convenient place, as shown in Fig. 145. This line is known as the *nonsymmetrical reference line*.

Construction of an Auxiliary Drawing. The first step in making an auxiliary drawing is to draw a reference line so that it is parallel to the line which shows the inclined surface. If a plane is imagined as being parallel to the inclined face, any line on that plane will also be parallel to the inclined face. This is illustrated in Fig. 145.

Draw light projection lines at right angles from all points on the inclined face, and lay off (along these lines from the reference line)

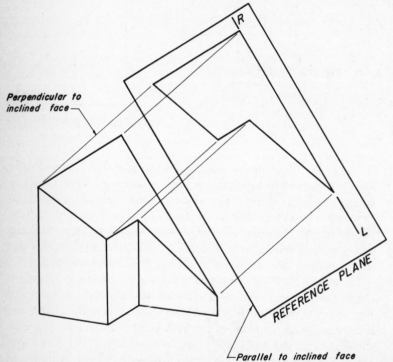

Fig. 144.   Plane Parallel to Inclined Face.

the perpendicular distances from the near edge of the surface as shown in the plan view. The true distances of the lines are present in this view. This procedure is illustrated in Fig. 147, which shows the true size and shape of the inclined face. In this diagram, the distance *1'–2'* is laid off perpendicular to the reference line in the auxiliary view and is equal to line *1–2*, measured perpendicular to the reference line in the plan view.

It must be remembered that inclined surfaces require an auxiliary view to show their true size and shape. Auxiliary views showing only inclined surfaces may be used advantageously as a means of (1) eliminating difficult projections, (2) showing true relationships for dimensioning, and (3) simplifying drawings to avoid confusion.

The auxiliary plane is always imagined to be hinged to the plane to which it is perpendicular and is revolved into the plane of the paper as shown in Fig. 141.

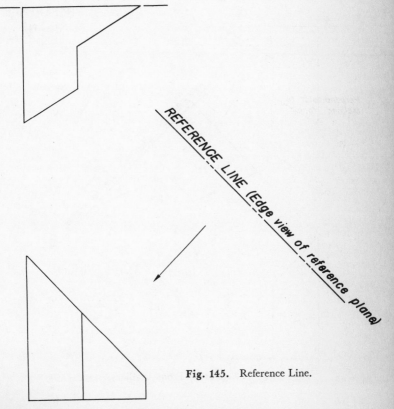

Fig. 145. Reference Line.

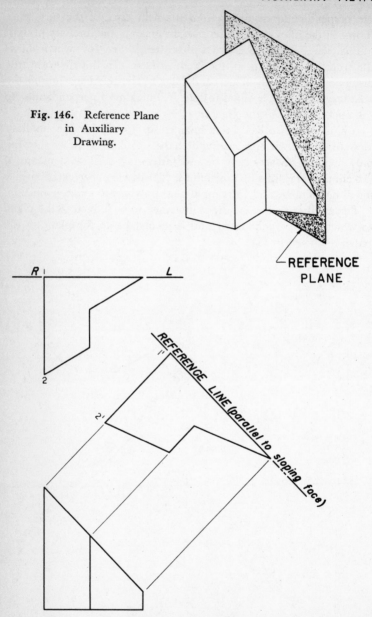

Fig. 146. Reference Plane
in Auxiliary
Drawing.

REFERENCE
PLANE

R   *L*

2

REFERENCE LINE (parallel to sloping face)

2'

Fig. 147. Front Auxiliary.

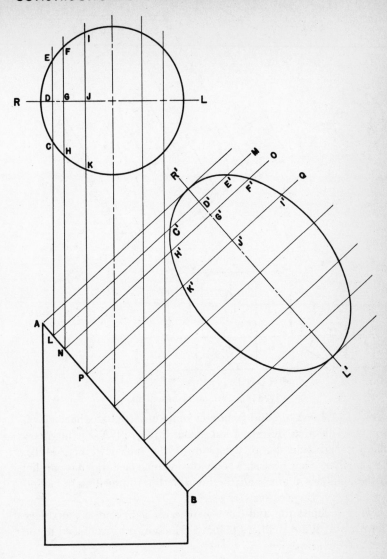

Fig. 148. Use of Symmetrical Reference Line.

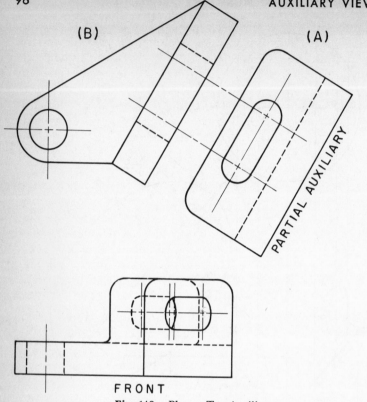

(B)   (A)

PARTIAL AUXILIARY

FRONT

Fig. 149. Plan or Top Auxiliary.

Fig. 149 shows top and front views and a partial auxiliary elevation. In the auxiliary elevation shown in Fig. 149A, the auxiliary
plane is perpendicular to the plane of the top view (Fig. 149B).
The auxiliary view need show only the inclined face which is parallel
to the auxiliary plane, and the invisible lines immediately behind
it which may be necessary for clarity.

Fig. 150 shows top and front views with right and left auxiliary
views in which the auxiliary planes are imagined to be hinged to the
plane of the front view.

A front auxiliary drawing is Fig. 151, with its front and side views.
This auxiliary plane is hinged to the plane of the side view.

Fig. 148 shows the auxiliary view of an inclined surface containing
curves and indicates the method of construction. Draw $R'L'$ any
convenient distance from and parallel to the inclined face AB.

Draw several lines, perpendicular to the center line or diameter RL, through the circle of the plan view, extending these lines downward to the inclined face.   From these points in the inclined face, draw lines parallel to AR' and BL'.   Points C and E are equidistant from the center line; consequently, CD is equal to DE.   This is also true of points F and H, I, K, etc.   On line LM, mark off $C'D'$ equal to CD, and $D'E'$ equal to DE, so that points C' and E' are equidistant from $R'L'$.   Repeat this operation several times to obtain sufficient points to plot the ellipse of the auxiliary view.   Connect these points with an irregular curve to obtain the required auxiliary view.

Classification of Auxiliary Views.   An auxiliary view obtained by projecting from a principal view that shows the inclined surface as a line (Figs. 147 and 148) is called a *single* or *primary auxiliary view*. Single or primary auxiliary views can be subdivided into *plan* or *top auxiliary views*, *front auxiliary views*, and *end* or *side auxiliary views*, depending upon the view from which the auxiliary view is projected.   The auxiliary view in Fig. 147, then, is known as a front auxiliary view since it is projected from the front elevation.   Fig. 149 shows a plan or top auxiliary view.   Fig. 150 shows a right front auxiliary view and a left front auxiliary view.

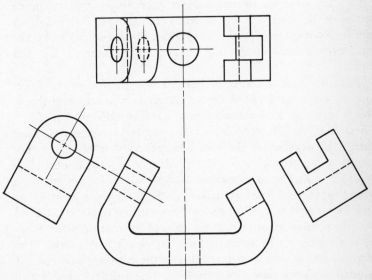

Fig. 150.   Right Front and Left Front Auxiliary Views.

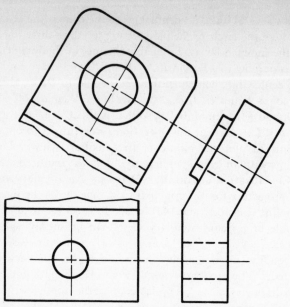

Fig. 151.   Front Partial Auxiliary.

Auxiliary views are further classified according to the amount or portion of the object actually shown.   For example, Fig. 147 shows only the sloping face — this is known as a *partial auxiliary* and is the type most commonly used.   Fig. 151 is another example of a partial auxiliary.

Occasionally, it is desired to indicate how the rest of the object appears when the inclined face is shown in true size and shape. This is known as a *complete auxiliary* and is illustrated in Fig. 152.

Sectional Auxiliary Views.   The occasion sometimes arises when it is necessary to show an auxiliary view in section.   (For discussion of sections, see p. 105.)   This type of view, illustrated in Fig. 153, is known as a *sectional auxiliary view*.   In this figure, a cutting plane *A–A* has been passed through the front elevation to show the desired cut.   (For discussion of cutting plane, see p. 106.) Arrowheads should be used at the ends of the cutting plane to indicate the direction in which the auxiliary view is to be taken.   The reference line is then drawn parallel to the cutting plane and the required auxiliary view is constructed.   This auxiliary view is then sectioned to indicate that the auxiliary view is also a sectional view.

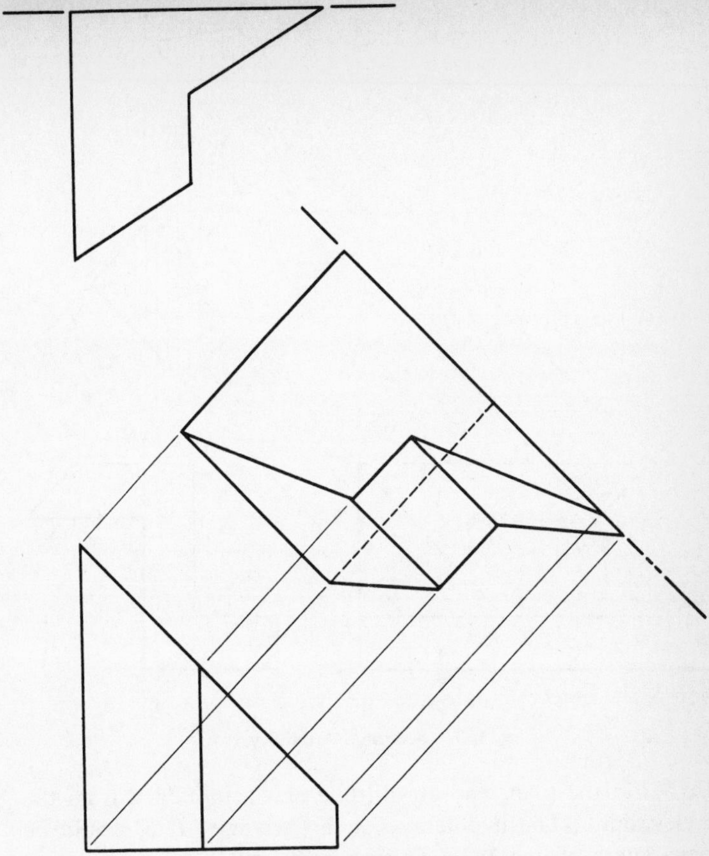

Fig. 152.   Complete Auxiliary.

This type of auxiliary may be either a complete or a partial view, depending on which is required.

True Length of a Line.   There are several methods of finding a true length of a line.   A draftsman should be familiar with all these methods because they have special applications to various problems.

In Fig. 154A, let it be required to find the true length of the line 1–2.   If an auxiliary view were constructed that showed the inclined face in true size and shape, the line 1–2, as well as line 1–3, would appear in true length.

Another method of finding the true length of the line 1–2 (Fig. 154B) would be to construct a right triangle, with the base equal to the

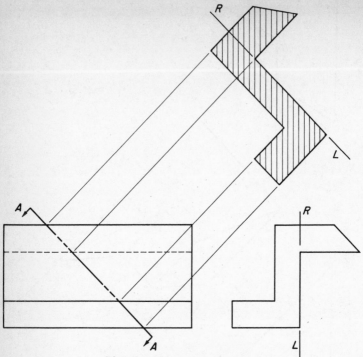

Fig. 153. Sectional Auxiliary.

length *1–2* in the plan, and an altitude of *x* as obtained from the front elevation. The hypotenuse of this triangle, *1'–2*, would be the true length of line *1–2*. This procedure is known as the *true-length diagram method*.

In Fig. 155, let it be required to find the true length of any line on the surface of a right circular cone that passes through the apex of the cone. It is evident from the drawing that all of these lines, such as *0–1* or *0–2*, are equal in length. The true length of any of these lines is shown in the front elevation by line *0'–1'*. It can be seen from Fig. 155 that when a line, such as *0'–1'*, appears in true length, the other projection of this line *0–1* appears as a horizontal line. Therefore, the following rule can be stated: if a line appears horizontal in one view of a right circular cone, the other view shows the true length of the line.

The application of the foregoing rule to a particular problem is

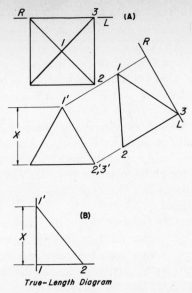

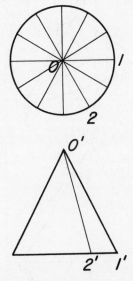

Fig. 154. True-Length Diagram Method.

Fig. 155. True Length of Line — Right Circular Cone.

illustrated in Fig. 156.   Let it be required to find the true length of
the line *1–2*.   It will be seen by inspection that line *1–2* does not
appear horizontal in either view.   With a radius of *1–2* and *1* as a
center, strike an arc with a pair of compasses.   Draw a horizontal
line through point *1* until it intersects the arc of radius *1–2* at point
X.   By projecting point *X* to *X'* in the front elevation, the line
1'–X' gives the true length of line *1–2*.

Double or Secondary Auxiliary Views.   Occasionally the
draftsman requires an auxiliary view of an inclined face which does
not appear as a line in any of the principal views.   The view necessary to show the oblique face in true size and shape is called a
double or *secondary auxiliary view* since two separate steps are required
in its construction.

In Fig. 157, let it be required to find the true size and shape of the
oblique face *1–2–3*.   Since this face does not appear as a line in any
of the given views, a view must be drawn to satisfy this condition.
In order to construct an auxiliary view so that surface *1–2–3* will
appear as a line, every line that shows true length in the surface of
the given view must be made to project in a point.   For example,
the line *1'–3'* appears in true length in the front elevation, and if a
new view were constructed so that this line appeared as a point, the

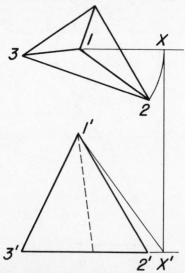

Fig. 156.   Problem of Ending True Length of Line *1–2*.

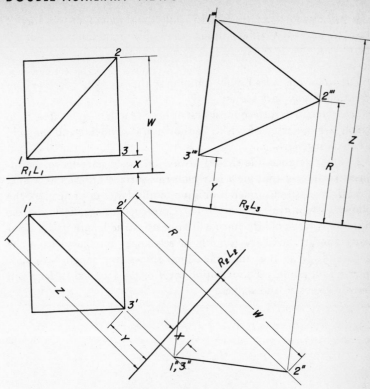

Fig. 157. Double Auxiliary.

surface $1'–2'–3'$ would appear as a line.   If a reference plane were
taken perpendicular to $1'–3'$ and rotated about the reference line
(R_2L_2) lying in the plane, the surface $1–2–3$ would appear as a line.
By laying off the perpendicular distances (the distances of points
1, 2, and 3 from the reference line R_1L_1) along the proper projectors
from R_2L_2, points $1''$, $2''$, and $3''$ are located.   These points, when
connected, give the edge or line view of the oblique plane $1–2–3$.   To
find the true size and shape of this face, another reference line R_3L_3
is drawn at any convenient location and parallel to $1''$, $2''$, and $3''$.
From points $1''$, $2''$, and $3''$ project perpendicular lines to R_3L_3.
Lay off from R_3L_3, along the proper projectors, the perpendicular
distances that point $1'$, $2'$, and $3'$ are from R_2L_2, locating points
$1'''$, $2'''$, and $3'''$.   When these points are properly connected, the
true size and shape of the oblique face are obtained.

It will be noted that in Fig. 157 only the sloping face was carried through the two auxiliary projections. The remaining portions of the object may be obtained in a manner similar to the method just described.

The following rules briefly summarize the procedure for the construction of auxiliary views:

1. An inclined surface must first appear as a line in the view from which it is projected, if it is to be shown in its true size and shape in an auxiliary view.

2. The reference line should always be taken parallel to the inclined surface in that view in which this surface appears as a line.

3. If the desired surface is oblique to all planes of projection, the following steps are necessary. (a) Construct an auxiliary view so that a line in the oblique face will appear in true length. (b) Construct another auxiliary (double or secondary auxiliary) from the first auxiliary so that the line which shows true length will now appear as a point. The resulting view of the inclined surface will show in true size and shape.

6

Sections and Conventions

Often it is difficult to show clearly the true shape or construction of interiors by means of exterior views. This source of confusion is generally eliminated by the drawing of partial views or full-section views of the object. In these drawings, one must visualize a portion or section as having been removed or cut away; consequently, interior details and construction become clearly visible. Invisible lines become visible in all section views (see Figs. 160–164).

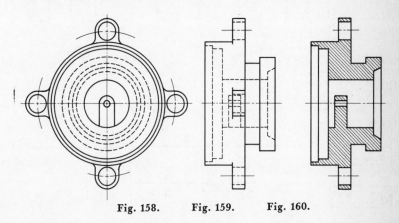

Fig. 158.　　　Fig. 159.　　　Fig. 160.

Figs. 158–160 show a comparison between an ordinary end elevation and a section view (Fig. 160), which simplifies the object and makes it more easily understood. Other types of section views are shown in Figs. 161–164.

Section views must be shown in a way that is consistent with *conventions*. In engineering drawing a convention is any drawing procedure based upon approved practice and accepted generally in industry. One of the principal functions of the American Standards Association has been to induce American industry to standardize drawing procedures and drafting room practices.

Cutting Plane. A cutting-plane line is used in the drawing of an object to show where the section has been removed. The cutting plane is indicated only in the view showing the plane as a line. The cutting-plane line shown in Fig. 165 is illustrated in full scale or dimension. It is represented as a heavy line and is composed of a $\frac{3}{4}''$ line, a $\frac{1}{32}''$ space, a $\frac{1}{16}''$ line, a $\frac{1}{32}''$ space, a $\frac{1}{16}''$ line, and a $\frac{1}{32}''$ space, then repeating a $\frac{3}{4}''$ line, etc. Arrowheads on the cutting-plane line are used to indicate the direction in which the remaining portion of the object is to be viewed (Figs. 161–163). The part of

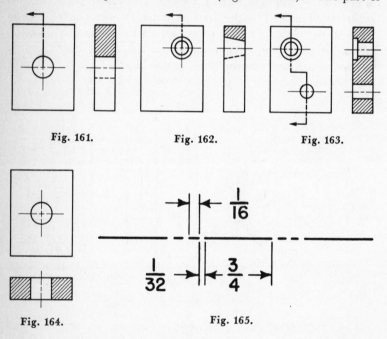

Fig. 161.   Fig. 162.   Fig. 163.

Fig. 164.   Fig. 165.

the object in front of the cutting-plane line is visualized as having been removed. Whenever it is obvious that the cutting plane passes through the center line (Figs. 158, 164), the cutting-plane line symbol may be omitted.

Construction of Section Views. The following procedure is observed in the drawing of section views.

1. The object should be first studied and visualized pictorially (Fig. 166).

2. The type of section showing the clearest description of the object should be determined, and the cutting-plane line should then be indicated.

3. The portion of the object in front of the cutting-plane line should be imagined as having been removed (Fig. 167) and the student should then make an orthographic projection of the remaining portion for the desired section view.

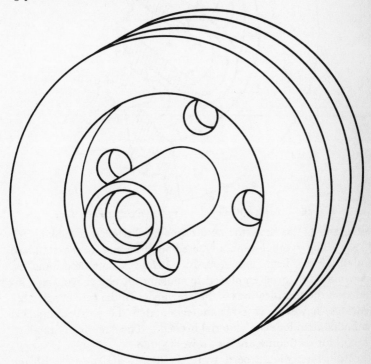

Fig. 166. Pictorial View.

Section Lining or Crosshatching. Lines drawn across the section view at 45° are known as section lines or crosshatching, and are inserted (1) to indicate precisely the cut surface of the cutting

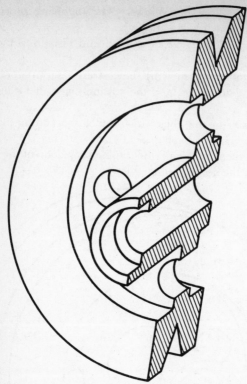

Fig. 167. Portion Removed in Front of Cutting-Plane Line.

plane, and (2) to show the kind of material needed in making the object. The symbol generally used in drawings is the standard symbol for cast iron (Figs. 160, 163, 164). A note describing the exact material to be employed in making an object is always included in the specifications of the drawing. In the case of assembly drawings, however, it is recommended that the correct standard symbol be used for each material needed. The American Standard symbols for sectioning are shown in Fig. 168.

Section lines should be drawn very lightly and at 45° with the horizontal. These lines should be spaced by eye at from $\frac{1}{16}''$ to $\frac{1}{8}''$ apart, depending on the size of the area to be sectioned. Usually they are drawn $\frac{1}{16}''$ apart. Great care should be taken in spacing section lines uniformly, as the slightest variation will be readily noticed.

AMERICAN STANDARDS

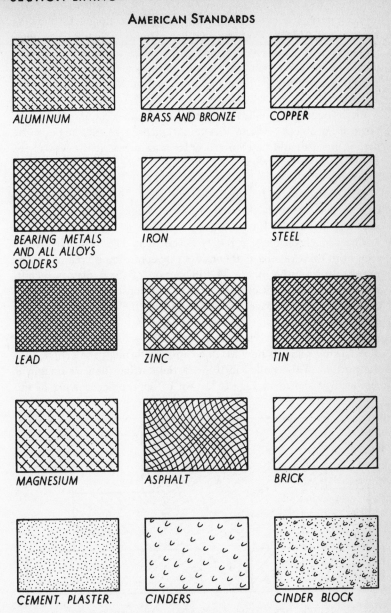

ALUMINUM   BRASS AND BRONZE   COPPER

BEARING METALS   IRON   STEEL
AND ALL ALLOYS
SOLDERS

LEAD   ZINC   TIN

MAGNESIUM   ASPHALT   BRICK

CEMENT. PLASTER.   CINDERS   CINDER BLOCK

Fig. 168. Symbols for Sectioning.

Very narrow areas or thin pieces may be sectioned by showing them in solid black. When several thin pieces adjoin one another, white lines should separate them. Fig. 169 shows how adjacent pieces of the same material should be sectioned. In cases of this type it is permissible to draw section lines at 30° and 60° with the horizontal.

Occasionally, it will be found that section lines run parallel to the edge of an object. When this condition prevails, the angle of the section lines should be changed. In cases where it is necessary to show several section views of an object, the section lines should be changed.

Full Section. A full section is the view obtained by passing a cutting plane entirely through an object (Figs. 160, 164, 171) or a machine (Figs. 187, 188).

The end elevation of a pulley is shown in Fig. 170. It can be seen from this drawing that considerable confusion is created by the number of invisible lines. A full section of the pulley is recommended to clarify its interior details and construction. The procedure outlined on page 106 is followed for the construction of this sectional view.

The pulley is first visualized pictorially as shown in Fig. 166. The cutting plane is now assumed to pass through the center, and the portion of the pulley in front of the cutting plane is imagined removed as shown in Fig. 167. An orthographic drawing of the

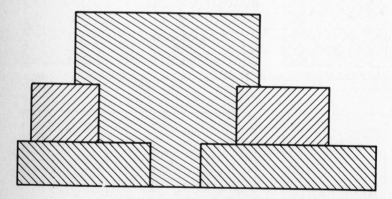

Fig. 169. Method of Sectioning Adjacent Pieces
of the Same Material.

remaining portion is then constructed as in Fig. 171, and section lines are drawn where the material has been cut by the cutting plane as indicated in the drawing.

It should be noticed that in this drawing the cutting-plane line has been omitted, as it obviously passes through the center line.

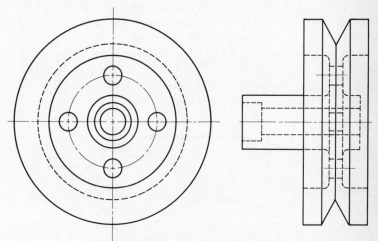

Fig. 170.   End Elevation of Pulley.

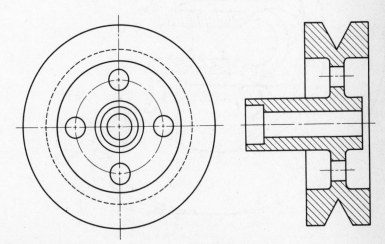

Fig. 171.   Full-Section View.

Half Section. A half section is a view in which only one-quarter has been removed from the object (Figs. 161, 172).

In half sections, the cutting-plane line ends on the center line of the object as in Fig. 161. This center line divides the sectioned from the unsectioned part of the object as shown in Figs. 161, 173.

Fig. 173 shows the orthographic drawing of the remaining portion of the pulley after one-quarter has been removed. It should be noted that the invisible lines in the unsectioned part are permissible only when they are necessary for dimensioning.

The junctions of sectioned and unsectioned portions of an object are separated by a center line. Theoretically, a solid line should be shown; but since the portion of the object is only imagined to be removed, a center line is generally used.

Fig. 172. Half-Section View.

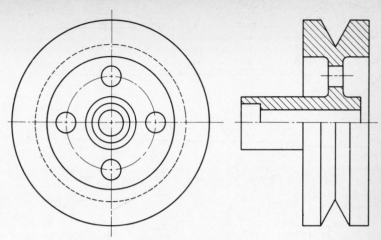

Fig. 173. Half-Section View.

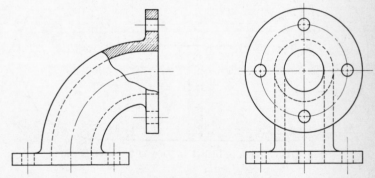

Fig. 174. Partial Section.

Partial or Broken Section. A partial or broken section is used to show a particular interior detail, where a larger section view is not required. This kind of section is made as if a piece were broken from the object, leaving an irregular line for the junction of the sectioned and unsectioned parts. An example of a partial section of a flanged elbow is shown in Fig. 174.

Revolved Section. A revolved section is used to show the true shape of an object, such as a handle, spoke, etc. Fig. 175 shows two views of a wrench. Without the revolved section, the exact shape of the handle would be unknown. This revolved section is obtained

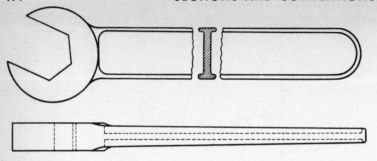

Fig. 175. Wrench, Including View of Revolved Section.

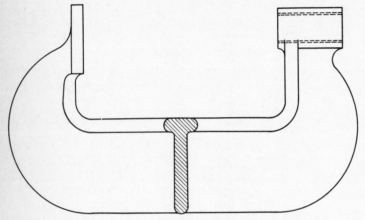

Fig. 176. C-clamp, Including View of Revolved Section.

by passing the cutting plane perpendicular to the axis of the piece to be sectioned. The portion of the object cut by the cutting plane is revolved until it coincides with the plane of the paper. Since this revolved section is superimposed on one of the original views, any line of the object interfering with the revolved section may be broken, as in the case of the wrench (Fig. 175), or omitted, as shown in the drawing of the C-clamp (Fig. 176).

A drawing of a handwheel is shown in Fig. 177, together with a revolved section to indicate the true shape of the spoke. This information is given neither in the front elevation nor in the full-section view. Consequently, a revolved section is absolutely necessary to obtain a description of the spoke.

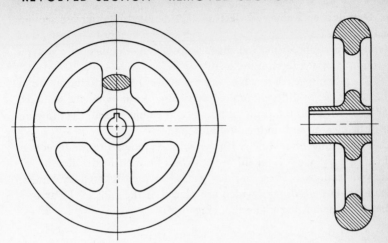

Fig. 177. Handwheel and Revolved Section.

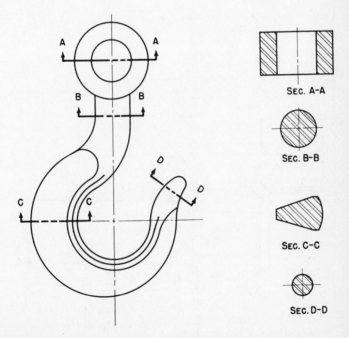

Fig. 178. Drawing of Detailed or Removed Section.

Detailed or Removed Section. A detailed or removed section serves the same purpose as a revolved section except that, instead of being superimposed on the drawing itself, the detailed or removed section is shown separately, as in Fig. 178.

The advantages of this type of section are that (1) dimensions can be added, (2) a different scale may be used in drawing the sections, and (3) with this information noted on the object itself, the drawing will be clearer and understood at a glance.

The cutting-plane line, with arrowheads indicating the direction in which the view is taken, must always be used in detailed or removed sections. These various sections are designated by letters, such as *A–A*, *B–B*, etc., which are placed at the ends of the arrowheads of the cutting-plane line (Fig. 178).

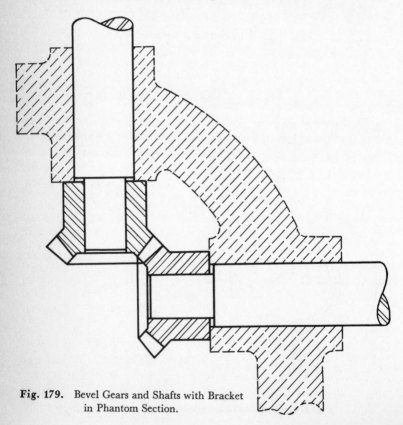

Fig. 179. Bevel Gears and Shafts with Bracket in Phantom Section.

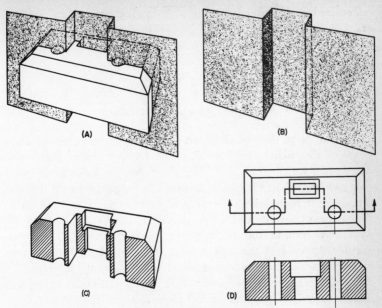

Fig. 180. Offset Section.

Phantom Section. A phantom section is made by not removing the part of the object in front of the cutting plane. This is done to show the interior construction of a part without disturbing its relationship with the exterior front part which remains intact. In phantom sections, the section lines and the outline of the object are broken to indicate that they are invisible. This type of phantom sectioning is frequently used.

A common use of the phantom section is to show the relationship between a removed part and the part represented. Fig. 179 shows the drawing of a set of bevel gears and their shafts. The portion shown in phantom section is the bracket supporting the gears and shafts. This type of representation is often used to show the relationship between a new piece of mechanism and an old part of the same mechanism. The old part or existing piece is the one shown in phantom section.

Offset Section. In the different types of section views already discussed, the cutting plane has almost always passed continuously through the object as a straight line. Many objects are designed in such a way, however, that certain features which require section-

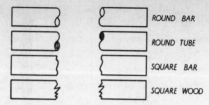

ROUND BAR

ROUND TUBE

SQUARE BAR

SQUARE WOOD

Fig. 181. Conventional Breaks.

ing do not lie in the same straight line. By changing the direction of the cutting plane, it is possible to show all the desired features in one section view.

It can be seen in Fig. 180A that the cutting plane passes through the object to include all the inaccessible features. Fig. 180B shows the cutting plane removed. Fig. 180C shows how the object appears with the portion in front of the cutting plane removed. The ortho-graphic drawing of the object, with the portion of the object in front of the cutting plane removed for sectioning, is shown in Fig. 180D. It should be noticed that there are no lines in the sec-tion view to show that the cutting plane changes directions.

Conventional Breaks. Fig. 181 shows a series of conventional breaks approved by the American Standards Association.

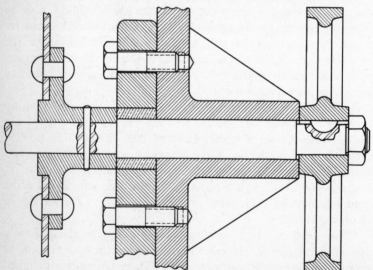

Fig. 182. Conventional Violations of Sectioning.

Conventional Violations of Sectioning. In certain cases, section lines are omitted despite the indication of the cutting plane. These omissions are known as conventional violations of sectioning. The reason for this practice is to facilitate the reading of drawings. The general rule to remember in such cases is as follows: objects that are not sectioned when their longitudinal axis is parallel to the cutting plane include webs, ribs, spokes, shafts, bolts, rivets, nuts, keys, cotter pins, screws, etc. Fig. 182 shows a drawing containing a number of violations of sectioning. In this drawing, the rivets, taper pin, tap bolts, shaft, Woodruff keyway, and nut display conventional violations of sectioning.

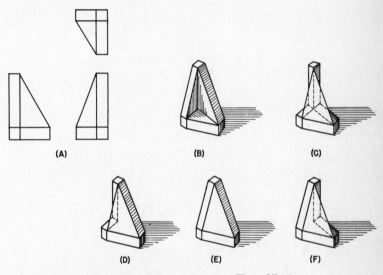

Fig. 183. Solutions Based on Three Views.

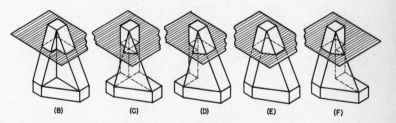

Fig. 184. Use of Cutting Planes.

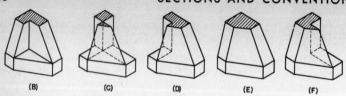

(B)   (C)   (D)   (E)   (F)

Fig. 185. Tops Removed.

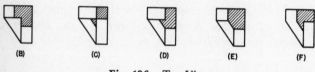

(B)   (C)   (D)   (E)   (F)

Fig. 186. Top Views.

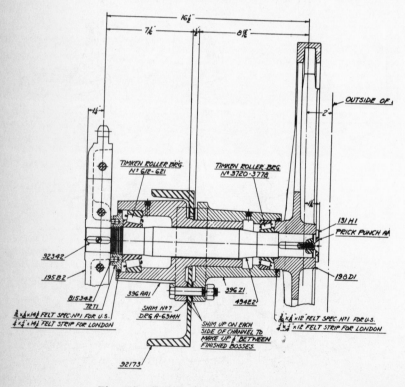

Fig. 187. Full-Section View of a Machine.

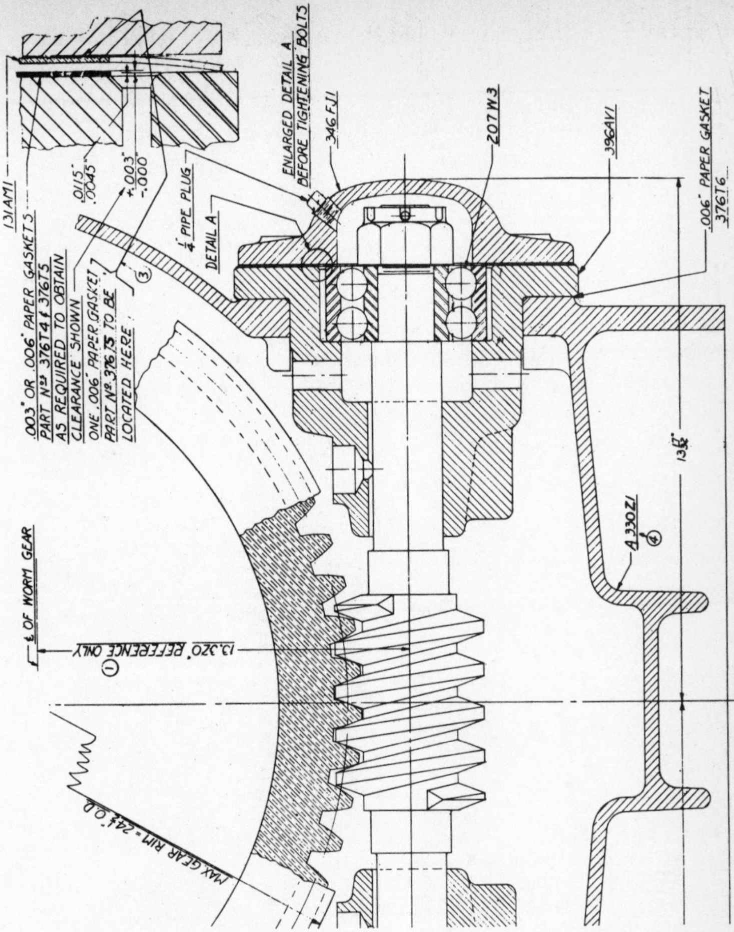

Fig. 188. Full-Section View of a Machine.

Special Sections. In certain types of drawings, sectional views are absolutely necessary as a guide in making the correct object from the drawings.

Fig. 183A shows three views of an object. A study of these three views will show that a number of possible solutions exist, any one of which would be correct. Figs. 183B, C, D, E, and F are picture drawings of five possible solutions. If cutting planes were used parallel to the base in the five possible solutions, as shown in Figs. 184B, C, D, E, and F, and the tops were removed, as in Figs. 185B,

C, D, E, and F, the top views would then appear as in Figs. 186B, C, D, E, and F. If this sectional plan view were to take the place of the plan in the original three-view drawing (Fig. 183A), the person making the object would then be restricted to only one solution.

7

Pictorial Views

Two-dimensional, multiview orthographic projections can be read and interpreted only by those having special training. Pictorial drawings, on the other hand, enable even a layman to obtain a visual, three-dimensional concept of the objects represented. During World War II such drawings were used extensively to illustrate various steps in the manufacturing processes of machine parts, as thousands of workers recruited by defense industries lacked the technical training to understand orthographic projection. Similar drawings have also been commonly used in advertising. It should be remembered, however, that pictorial drawings give only an over-all description of the external surfaces of an object and a three-dimensional concept of its form, shape, and mass.

The two principal types of pictorial drawings are (1) axonometric projection and (2) oblique projection.

AXONOMETRIC PROJECTION

In axonometric projection, the object is so placed as to show three faces or surfaces in one view. This is accomplished by placing the object so that its faces are inclined to the plane of projection. In the section on Orthographic Projection (Chapter 4), Fig. 117 shows an object enclosed in a "glass box." Assume that this object, instead of having its faces parallel to the co-ordinate planes as shown, is rotated and tilted in such a way that all faces are inclined. If perpendiculars are projected to one of the planes — e.g., the vertical plane — the resulting view will be an axonometric projection of the object.

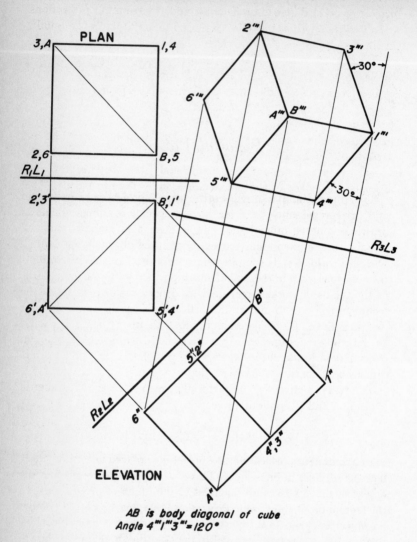

Fig. 189. Isometric Projection — First Method.

There are three sorts of axonometric projections: (1) isometric projections, (2) dimetric projections, and (3) trimetric projections.

In *isometric projection* the object is placed so that its faces are equally inclined to the plane of projection. This is the most common type of axonometric projection and is the one which will be discussed in this chapter. In *dimetric projection* the object is placed so that two of the faces are equally inclined to the plane of projection. In *trimetric projection* the object is placed so that all faces are unequally inclined to the plane of projection. The latter two types of axonometric projections are rarely used by the beginner.[1]

Isometric Projection. In isometric projection, as previously stated, the faces are equally inclined to the plane of projection. As a result, the edges of the object are equally foreshortened. The name *isometric* is derived from this equal foreshortening of the edges. The word *isometric* comes from the Greek (*iso*, equal, and *metron*, measure) and means "equal measurement."

There are several methods to show how an isometric projection is obtained. Two of these methods or "proofs" are given in Figs. 189, 190. In both proofs illustrated, a cube is used because its *body diagonal* will appear as a point when the faces of the cube are equally inclined.

Fig. 189 shows two views of a cube which has a body diagonal $A-B$. If a new view is constructed so that the diagonal $A-B$ appears as a point, the resulting view will be an isometric projection of the cube. The procedure used in the construction of this view is similar to that for the construction of a double auxiliary view (see Fig. 157).

FIRST METHOD. The object is to obtain a view of the cube in which its diagonal $A-B$ appears as a point. Since this line does not appear in true length in either of the given views, it becomes necessary to construct a new view which fulfills this condition. R_2L_2 is drawn at any convenient distance parallel to one of the projections of line $A-B$. By projecting perpendiculars from points $1'$, $2'$, $3'$, $4'$, A', and B' to R_2L_2 and laying off the distances that 1, 2, 3, etc. are from R_1L_1 along the proper projectors, points $1''$, $2''$, $3''$, etc. are located. The diagonal $A-B$ is now shown in true length and is represented by $A''B''$. R_3L_3 is drawn at any convenient distance

[1] For information concerning dimetric and trimetric projections, see Hoelscher, R. P., Springer, C. H., and Pohle, R. F., *Industrial Production Illustration*, McGraw-Hill, 1946.

perpendicular to $A''B''$ and the distances from R_2L_2 to $1'$, $2'$, $3'$, etc. are marked off on the proper projectors from R_3L_3. The points $1'''$, $2'''$, $3'''$, etc. are thus located. When these points are connected, the resulting figure is an isometric projection of the given cube in which the body diagonal $A–B$ appears as a point. If this view is rotated clockwise until the projector $1''–1'''$ is horizontal, it will be found that the edges $4'''–1'''$ and $1'''–2'''$ make angles of 30° with this line, and that $B'''–1'''$ is vertical. This is the usual position for the axes in isometric projections.

SECOND METHOD. Fig. 190 shows another method of approach to the theory of isometric projection. Fig. 190A is a conventional orthographic projection. In Fig. 190B the plan has been rotated so that the vertical faces make equal angles with the plane of projection. The cube must now be tipped until the top face makes the same angle with the plane of projection as the vertical faces. In Fig. 190C the end elevation is the same as the end elevation in Fig. 190B, except that it is inclined. The object is tipped until the body diagonal is a horizontal line. The angle between AB and the vertical, and between BC and the horizontal, is found to be 35°16'.

It is evident on inspection that no matter how much the end elevation is rotated, the width of the plan and the front elevation will be the same in Fig. 190C as in Fig. 190B. A new plan and front elevation can be drawn by projecting the end elevation in Fig. 190C and the front elevation in Fig. 190B. This new front elevation is the required isometric projection. The edges of the cube in this isometric projection either make an angle of 30° with the horizontal or are vertical. It should also be noted that the edges of the cube are foreshortened in the isometric projection and that these edges are all foreshortened equally.

In constructing an isometric projection it is not necessary to go through the entire procedure as outlined in Figs. 189 and 190, provided that a special isometric scale is used to determine the foreshortening of the lines. The method of constructing an isometric scale is shown in Fig. 191.

Isometric Drawing. If a regular scale had been used, instead of the isometric scale, for the drawings mentioned in the foregoing paragraphs, the resulting figure would be an *isometric drawing*. The only difference between an isometric projection and an isometric drawing is in the scale used.

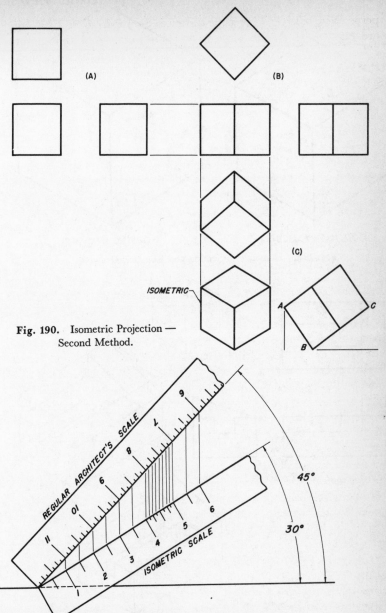

Fig. 190. Isometric Projection —
Second Method.

Fig. 191. Method of Constructing Isometric Scale.

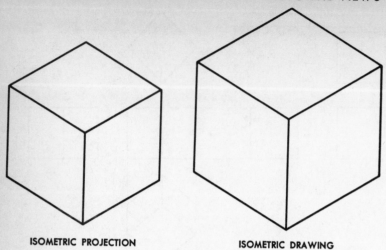

ISOMETRIC PROJECTION   ISOMETRIC DRAWING

Fig. 192. Isometric Projection and Isometric Drawing.

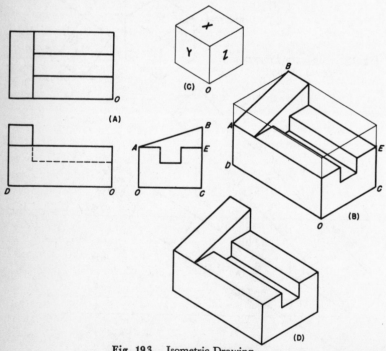

Fig. 193. Isometric Drawing.

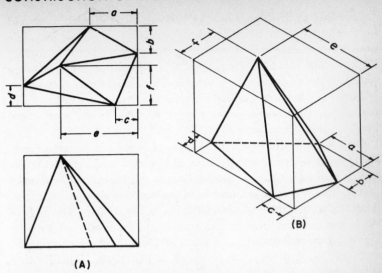

Fig. 194. Isometric Drawing of Object with Nonisometric Lines.

Fig. 192 illustrates this difference between an isometric projection and an isometric drawing. The figures are identical except for size, the isometric drawing being approximately 22 per cent larger. It is much easier, therefore, to construct an isometric drawing as no special scale is necessary — and the picture value is the same as that of the isometric projection.

Construction of an Isometric Drawing. Let it be required to construct an isometric drawing of the object shown in Fig. 193A. Select any point O as a starting point and construct a box which has the over-all dimensions of the object. This box should be so constructed that one edge is vertical and that the other two edges make angles of 30° with the horizontal, as indicated in Fig. 193B. Fig. 193C is drawn to show that the front elevation will be in plane Y, the plan view in plane X, and the end elevation in plane Z. By combining the actual views mentioned, Fig. 193B is obtained. Fig. 193D shows the finished drawing after the box construction has been removed.

Any line on the object parallel to the edges of the box construction, such as OC, OD, and CE, is known as an *isometric line* and can be drawn in true length. Any line, such as AB, is known as a *nonisometric line* and does not appear in true length.

Invisible or Hidden Lines in Isometric Drawings. It should be noted that all invisible lines have been omitted in the isometric drawing in Fig. 193D. Invisible lines have a tendency to confuse the untrained person; consequently, they are omitted in almost every type of picture drawing. The only exception to this rule occurs when it is impossible to obtain a clear understanding of an object without invisible lines, as in Figs. 194A, B. In all such cases, invisible lines are indicated.

Objects with Nonisometric Lines. Let it be required to construct an isometric drawing of the object shown in Fig. 194A. It can be seen on inspection that all lines in this object will be nonisometric lines. A box is constructed around the view as indicated. This box is then drawn in isometric, as in Fig. 194B. The ends of these nonisometric lines are located in the isometric drawing by laying off the dimensions, shown in Fig. 194A, on the isometric axes and connecting these points as shown in Fig. 194B. The drawing is completed with the removal of the box construction.

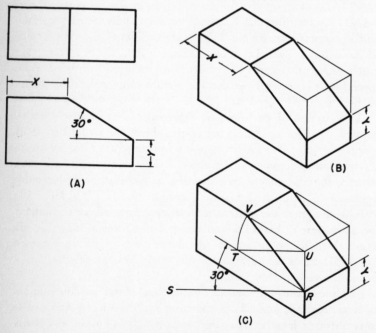

Fig. 195. Inclined Lines in Isometric.

Isometric Angles. The occasion sometimes arises when an object drawn in isometric is dimensioned in such a way (as in Fig. 195A) that an inclined line may be located by means of several different methods.

Fig. 195B shows how the isometric drawing would be constructed if the two distances X and Y were given. These distances locate the extremities of the line.

Fig. 195C shows the method of construction when the line is dimensioned by use of one of the distances, such as Y, and the angular measurement. In Fig. 195C, let it be required to construct a line through point R, making an angle of 30° with the base of the object. Draw a horizontal line RS. Lay off the required angle of 30° with SR as its base, giving the angle TRS. Through point U, which is vertically above R and at the same elevation at which the inclined line is to terminate, draw another horizontal line cutting the line RT at T. With U as a center and UT as a radius, strike an arc cutting the top edge of the isometric box at V, which is at the other extremity of the inclined line. Locate the required line by drawing a line joining R and V. Locate the other edge of the sloping surface which is parallel to the line RV by projecting both points R and V isometrically until they cut the opposite sides of their respective isometric faces. Complete the inclined face by drawing a line through these points.

Isometric Circles. It should be evident from an inspection of Figs. 196 and 197B that any circle in isometric will appear as an ellipse. These isometric circles or ellipses can be drawn by means of either an approximate method or an exact method.

APPROXIMATE METHOD. The easier and more commonly used method of constructing an isometric circle is the approximate method, which requires the use of a pair of compasses. It should be remembered, however, that this is only an "approximate" method and that the only points which are exactly the same as in a true ellipse are those where the arcs are tangent to the isometric square enclosing the circle, such as at point X in Figs. 196K, L, M.

Figs. 196K, L, and M show the three isometric faces of a cube. Let it be required to construct by the approximate method an isometric circle completely enclosed in each of these faces. Draw the longest diagonals AB. With a T-square and the 60° angle of the 30°–60° triangle, draw a line through corner D which makes an

angle of 60° with the horizontal
and cuts the diagonal *AB* at *E* and
the edge of the isometric square
at point *X*. Repeat this construction by drawing a 60° line through
point *C*, to locate point *F*. With
point *D* as a center and a radius
DX, strike an arc which will pass
through the point of tangency of
lines *AC* and *BC*. With point *C*
as a center and the same radius
DX, strike another arc which will
pass through the point of tangency
of lines *AD* and *DB*. Using *E* as
a center and a radius *EX*, strike
an arc tangent to the two arcs previously drawn. Complete
the ellipse by repeating the
same procedure with *F* as
the center.

EXACT METHOD. Let it
be required to make an isometric drawing of Fig. 197A
by using the exact method
of constructing isometric circles.

A series of points is located on
the given orthographic view of the
circle. Horizontal and vertical
lines are drawn through these points
to the edges of the object. These
horizontal and vertical distances

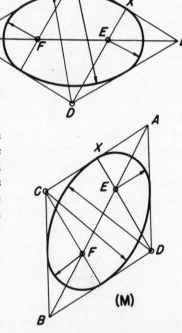

Fig. 196. Isometric Circles —
Approximate Method.

are laid off on the proper isometric axes, the intersections of which locate a point on the curve of the ellipse to be constructed. An illustration of this method is shown in Figs. 197A and B. After sufficient points have been located in this manner, they are joined together in a smooth curve by means of an irregular curve. It will be noticed that there is another circle of the same radius, indicating the depth of the hole, Z distance in back of the front face. The isometric drawing of this second circle is obtained by drawing 30° lines through a number of points on the first or front ellipse, and measuring the distance Z along these lines. These points are also connected by means of an irregular curve to complete the visible portions of the second ellipse or isometric circle.

Isometric Circles on Nonisometric Planes

CASE I. The plane containing the circle is perpendicular to one of the isometric planes. The construction of an isometric drawing of this type can best be explained by studying Fig. 198. Fig. 198A shows two orthographic projections. By means of the box method of construction, as explained for Fig. 195, the object is drawn without the ellipse on the inclined face. In Fig. 198B, an isometric square is drawn on the face *B–H–G–F* to enclose the isometric circle. A

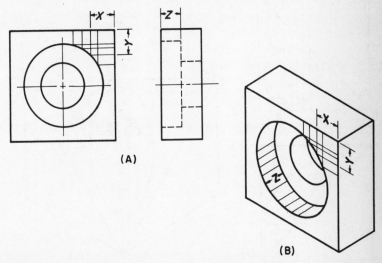

(A)

(B)

Fig. 197.   Isometric Circle — Exact Method.

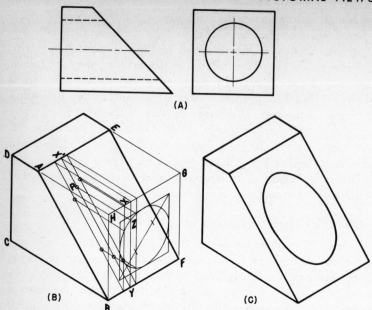

Fig. 198.   Isometric Circle on Nonisometric Plane — Case I.

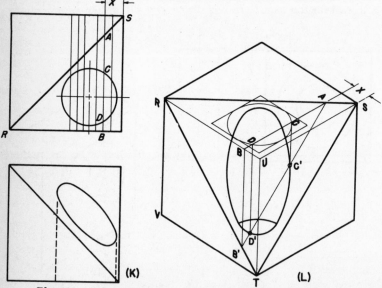

Fig. 199.   Isometric Circle on Nonisometric Plane — Case II.

series of planes is then passed parallel to the face D–A–B–C. One of these planes might, for example, cut a line XX' on the face A–E–G–H and the line XY on the face B–H–G–F. This same plane would also cut the sloping surface A–E–F–B along the line $X'Y$ and the isometric circle constructed on face B–H–G–F at a point Z. From point Z an isometric line is drawn parallel to AH, cutting the line $X'Y$ at P. Point P is a point on the required ellipse. By constructing a number of similar planes, sufficient points may be obtained to draw the ellipse by means of an irregular curve. Fig. 198C shows how the completed object appears after the construction lines are removed.

CASE II. Fig. 199K shows two orthographic views of an object with a circle on its oblique face, from which it is desired to construct an isometric drawing. By means of the box method of construction the object is drawn with the ellipse on the inclined face temporarily omitted. An isometric square is drawn on the top face to enclose the isometric circle, as shown in Fig. 199L. A series of parallel planes is passed in the orthographic view as shown in Fig. 199K. One of these planes cuts the diagonal of the top face at A, the isometric circle at C and D, and the edge of the top face at B. This same plane cuts the face R–U–T–V along the line BB', and the oblique face R–S–T along the line AB' which is parallel to ST. By means of projections vertically downward from C and D until the line AB' is cut, points C' and D' are located; these are points on the required ellipse. By passing a number of similar planes, one may obtain sufficient points to complete the drawing of the ellipse with an irregular curve.

Irregular Curves in Isometric. Let it be required to construct an isometric drawing of the object shown in Fig. 200A. In an object of this type it is necessary to plot the irregular curve by the method used in Fig. 197. Even if the radii of all the curves were known, it would be impossible to draw the curves by the approximate method, as these curves are not tangent to any straight planes at the quarter points.

Fig. 200B shows how the method of box construction is applied to a figure of the type shown in Fig. 200A, and also the construction of the holes and the cylinder. Notice that, in the construction of the cylinder, the top face was drawn first and that perpendiculars were dropped from the centers of the arcs for a distance which cor-

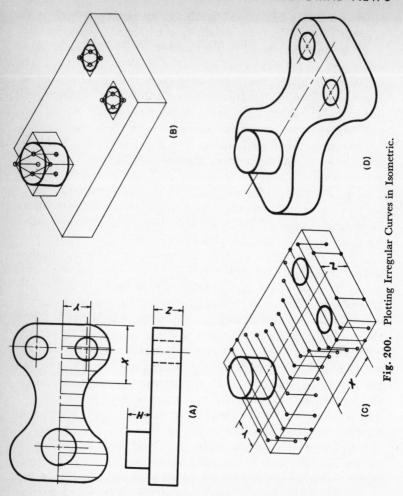

Fig. 200. Plotting Irregular Curves in Isometric.

responds to *H*, the height of the cylinder, which was obtained from the front elevation. By using these centers and the same ellipsoidal co-ordinates used for the top ellipse, one may draw the visible portions of the bottom ellipse.

The plan of Fig. 200A is divided so that the co-ordinates of various points on the irregularly curved edge may be obtained. It should be noted that it is necessary to locate the co-ordinates of only one side when the object is symmetrical.

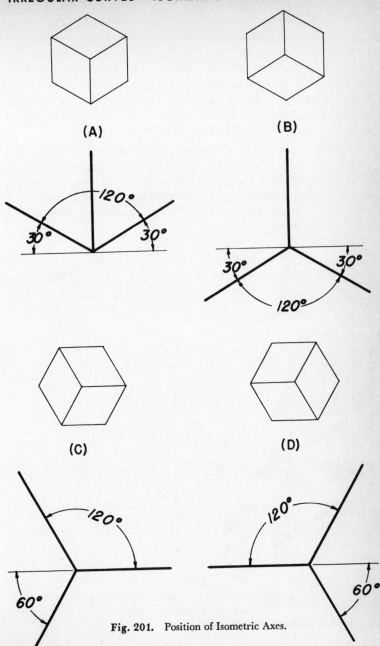

Fig. 201. Position of Isometric Axes.

Fig. 200C shows how these co-ordinates, obtained from the ortho-graphic view, are transferred to the isometric drawing. After these points have been located on the top face, the bottom face may be obtained by dropping vertical lines from these points and laying off the distance Z, which represents the depth or thickness of the object. If these points are joined with an irregular curve and the construction lines are removed, the completed isometric drawing will be made to appear as shown in Fig. 200D.

Position of Isometric Axes. In the foregoing discussion and diagrams of isometric drawings the most commonly used position of the axes has been the same as shown in Fig. 201A. Occasionally it is necessary or desirable to show an object as seen from the bottom looking up. In such cases the position of the isometric axes will be

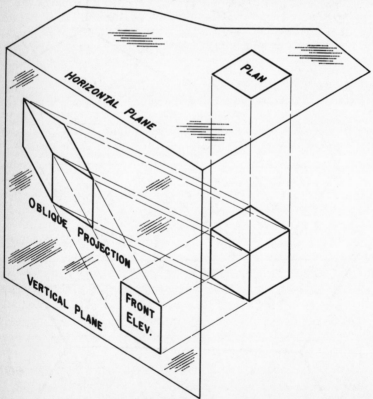

Fig. 202.   Example of Oblique Projection.

the same as in Fig. 201B. Similarly, occasions may arise when it will be advantageous to represent isometric axes as shown in either Figs. 201C or 201D.

OBLIQUE PROJECTION

In oblique projection, the object is projected onto the plane of projection by oblique projectors rather than by the perpendicular projectors that are used in orthographic and isometric drawings.

Fig. 202 shows a cube in space enclosed in a partial section of the "glass box." The analysis of orthographic projection showed that the plan and the front elevation of an object are obtained by projecting perpendiculars from the object to the projecting planes. If these projectors are drawn parallel to each other at an angle other than 90°, the resulting projection will be an *oblique projection*. Since these projectors are parallel, any face of the object that is parallel to the plane of projection (picture plane) in an oblique projection will appear in its true size and shape, just as it does in orthographic projection.

Position of Axes. From the discussion in the preceding paragraph it has been established that two of the axes make an angle of 90° with each other. The third and receding axis may be at any angle, depending on the angle that the projectors make with the picture plane. The angle that these projectors make with the picture plane also determines the amount of foreshortening of the receding axis. Therefore, it is evident that there are any number of possible conditions in which an object can be represented in oblique projection. The most common position of the receding axis is at 45° with the horizontal. The 45° angle has been used throughout this text.

Types of Oblique Projection. A *cavalier drawing* and a *cabinet drawing* are two types of oblique projection. When the length on the receding axis is shown in true length, the resulting picture drawing is known as a *cavalier drawing*. When the length on the receding axis is taken as one-half the true length, the resulting picture drawing is known as a *cabinet drawing*.

Fig. 203A is a two-view orthographic drawing of an object from which a cavalier drawing and a cabinet drawing have been made. Fig. 203B shows how the object appears as a cavalier drawing, and

Fig. 203C shows how the same object appears as a cabinet drawing. It is clear that the cabinet drawing appears better proportioned than the cavalier drawing. Although a cabinet drawing may be more difficult to draw than a cavalier drawing, owing to the foreshortening of the receding axis, it is the one generally preferred.

The receding axis in a cabinet drawing may slope upward at 45° and either to the left or right as shown in Fig. 204, or it may slope downward either to the left or right depending upon which faces must be shown.

Construction of a Cabinet Drawing. Let it be required to construct a cabinet drawing of the pulley shown in Fig. 205, with its upper right quarter removed for sectioning. It should be noted that this pulley is built up of cylinders which have their ends in five different but parallel planes, the centers of which have been marked on the section view, Fig. 205B, by points C, D, E, F, and G.

Starting at point C, Fig. 206A, horizontal and vertical center lines are drawn, including a center line at 45° with the horizontal. Center D, located $\frac{3}{4}''$ in back of center C, is marked off on the receding axis as one-half that distance $(\frac{3}{4}'')$ or $\frac{3}{8}''$. Centers E, F, and G are located in a similar manner by laying off one-half the distances shown in the sectional view, Fig. 205B.

Circles are then drawn with points C, D, E, F, and G as centers, Fig. 206B. There are two circles, with diameters of $\frac{9}{16}''$ and $1''$ respectively and a common center at point C, shown in the front plane of Fig. 205A. Using point C as a center in Fig. 206B, circles with these diameters $(\frac{9}{16}''$ and $1'')$ are drawn.

Point D in Fig. 205B is the center of two circles with diameters of $1''$ and $1\frac{1}{2}''$. Using point D as a center in Fig. 206B, two circles are drawn with these diameters $(1''$ and $1\frac{1}{2}'')$. The same procedure is repeated and circles are drawn in Fig. 206B, using centers E, F, and G, with their respective diameters obtained from Fig. 205B.

It should be remembered that this pulley is built of cylinders the ends of which are shown by the circles just drawn. By drawing 45° lines tangent to the circles representing the ends of the cylinders, the draftsman forms the cabinet drawing of each individual cylinder. Any portion of a circle representing the back face of a cylinder which might fall below the point of tangency of these 45° lines would be invisible and, consequently, it would not be shown. Invisible

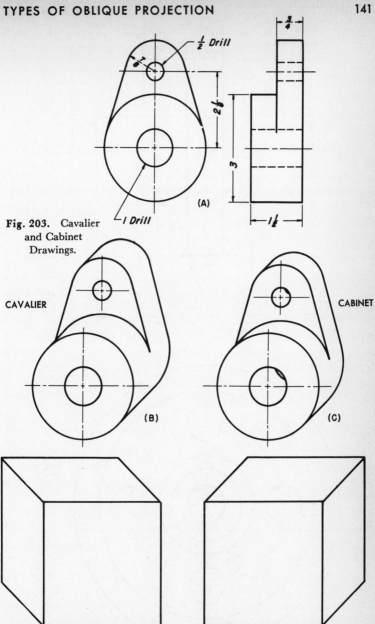

½ Drill

1 Drill

Fig. 203. Cavalier and Cabinet Drawings.

CAVALIER

CABINET

(A)

(B)

(C)

Fig. 204. Position of Axis in Cabinet Drawing.

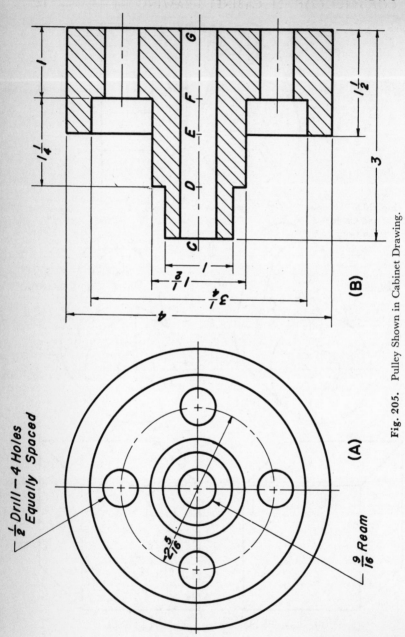

Fig. 205. Pulley Shown in Cabinet Drawing.

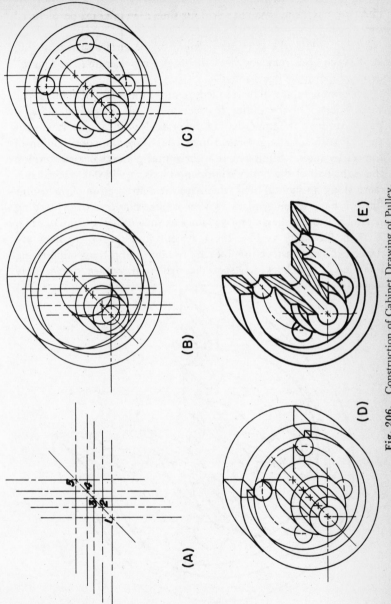

Fig. 206. Construction of Cabinet Drawing of Pulley.

lines, as has been said, are seldom shown in picture or pictorial drawings.

In Fig. 206C, the invisible portions of the circles drawn in Fig. 206B have been removed, and the circles representing the four $\frac{1}{2}''$ drilled holes have been added.

This problem, it will be recalled, requires the removal of the upper right quarter of the pulley for sectioning. If a vertical plane is passed through the upper half of the pulley's vertical axis, it will cut vertical surfaces along vertical lines which are the continuation of the center lines. Similarly, if a horizontal plane is passed through the right half of the pulley's horizontal axis, it will cut vertical surfaces along horizontal lines which are the continuation of the center lines of that particular plane. Both of these planes cut the receding portions of the pulley along 45° lines as shown in Fig. 206D. Fig. 206E is the same as Fig. 206D, except that the object lines are darkened, the construction lines are removed, and the section lining is added. The back parts of the drilled holes are drawn only when they are visible.

Fig. 207.   Sectioning in Cabinet Drawing.

SECTIONING PICTORIAL DRAWINGS

Procedure for Sectioning Pictorial Drawings. In sectioning pictorial drawings it is advisable to incline the section lines so that they are not parallel to any of the object's edges. These section lines should be drawn so that if they were continued or extended they would meet in pairs on the center line.

In the cabinet drawing shown in Fig. 207, the section lining is inclined 30° and 60° so that if the two cut surfaces were made to coincide the section lining would come together in pairs on the center line.

In isometric drawings the section lining is best drawn at a 60° angle for all cut surfaces. If a quarter of an object is removed, the section lines should still be drawn at 60°, but they should be made to slope in different directions. With this one exception, the practice prevailing for cabinet drawings is the same as for isometrics. (For the proper method of dimensioning pictorial drawings, both isometric and cabinet, see Chapter 8.)

ADVANTAGES AND DISADVANTAGES OF ISOMETRIC AND CABINET DRAWINGS

Cabinet Drawing vs. Isometric Drawing. When circles appear in a series of parallel planes, it is much easier to construct a cabinet drawing than an isometric drawing. When circles are not in parallel planes and, consequently, must be plotted on the receding axis, cabinet drawing is an unsatisfactory type of representation because the work involved in plotting curves and circles is too time-consuming.

Pictorial Drawing vs. Orthographic Projection. Pictorial drawings are more easily visualized and understood by the untrained person than is the usual orthographic projection, with its conventional two or three views. For objects requiring the representation of much detail, however, it is very difficult to draw in either isometric or cabinet and still show all the detail necessary. Moreover, certain objects appear too badly distorted when drawn in either of these two methods of pictorial representation. Pictorial drawings are also difficult to dimension.

Regardless of the advantages or disadvantages, isometric and cabinet drawings serve a very useful purpose in the description of objects.

8

Dimensioning

If the student has mastered the subject-matter on the control of appearance (Chapters 1, 2, and 3) and on views (Chapters 4, 5, 6, and 7) he should be able to construct a professional-appearing drawing of an object using the views necessary to describe its shape completely. The next step is to learn to dimension the drawing so that the object may be made to the correct size and the parts of the object bearing distance relationships to each other may be located one in respect to the other.

The study of dimensioning involves working on *size* and *location* dimensions. A good drawing improperly dimensioned is worthless insofar as the dimensioning of the object is concerned. Therefore, although professional appearance and correctness will be required in all work, the information in this chapter on dimensioning must be emphasized and applied throughout the succeeding chapters of the text.

Not only must an object be drawn properly according to the designer's specifications before it can be manufactured, but also the drawing must contain all pertinent information regarding size, how the object is to be made, whether it is to be cast, forged, or machined. This information must be provided as a guide to the skilled mechanic to help him construct the object accurately.

A good draftsman should be familiar with machine-shop practices, forging, foundry work, patternmaking, and so forth. Unless he understands these processes thoroughly, the engineer or draftsman cannot outline or recommend the most efficient and economical way of manufacturing an object. The mechanic looks to the draftsman for guidance and for accurate information. Consequently,

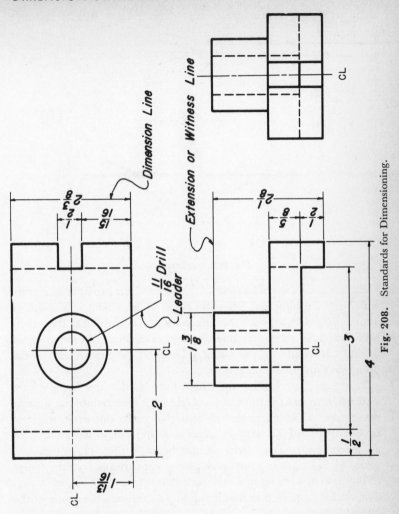

Fig. 208. Standards for Dimensioning.

drawings should contain all necessary dimensions, notes, and other data concerning the object to facilitate the mechanic's task.

A properly dimensioned drawing shows extension lines, dimension lines terminated by arrowheads, easily read numerals indicating size, finish marks, and notes.

Dimension Standards.   Fig. 208 shows the accepted standards for dimensioning.   (See also Figs. 5 and 6.)

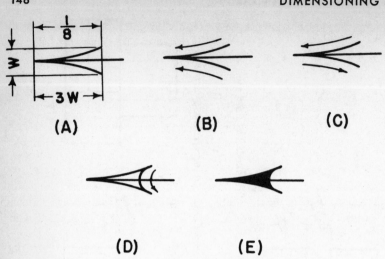

Fig. 209. Arrowheads.

EXTENSION OR WITNESS LINES. Extension lines are light solid lines which are brought out from the edges of an object. A space of about $\frac{1}{16}''$ is left between the object and the beginning of the extension line. An extension line should never touch the edge of an object. It should extend about $\frac{1}{8}''$ beyond the arrowheads of the dimension line to which it refers.

LEADERS. Leaders are light solid lines leading from a note or a dimension to some feature of an object to which the note or dimension refers. The leader should be drawn preferably at an angle of between 45° and 60° with the horizontal and should terminate with an arrowhead. The leader should begin with a horizontal line about $\frac{1}{8}''$ in length and should be placed approximately at the center of the note or dimension. A leader that refers to a hole, as in Fig. 208, should be placed so that it would pass through the center of the hole if it were continued.

Leaders should usually be drawn as straight lines with a ruling edge, but should never be horizontal or vertical lines. A leader can also be drawn as a curved line when space is limited, as indicated in Fig. 208.

DIMENSION LINES. Dimension lines are light solid lines which indicate the distance between two points or parts of an object. They are almost always drawn between two extension lines. Dimension lines are broken near the center to provide for a numeral or a fraction to indicate the length of the measurement. In structural drawing, however, the dimension line is not broken and the numeral is placed above the dimension line. The dimension line should be spaced between $\frac{3}{8}''$ to $\frac{1}{2}''$ away from the object, and approximately $\frac{3}{8}''$ away from other dimension lines when more than one are used.

In dimensioning an object, a rule to remember is never to have dimension lines cross each other.

ARROWHEADS. Arrowheads are placed at the ends of dimension lines to enable one to locate the termination of the dimension lines at a glance. Arrowheads are drawn as shown in Fig. 209. In general, arrowheads should be approximately $\frac{1}{8}''$ long, or three times as long as they are wide, as drawn in Fig. 209A. Figs. 209B and 209C show two alternative orders of strokes in forming arrowheads. Experience has proved, however, that the arrowhead shown in Fig. 209B can be drawn with greater ease. The arrowhead shown in Fig. 209D is seldom used in engineering drawing and should be avoided. The arrowhead in Fig. 209E is the one most commonly used and is recommended by the American Standards Association.

An important rule to remember is that all arrowheads must be the same size on the same drawing.

CENTER LINES. Center lines are light lines composed of alternating $\frac{3}{4}''$ lines and $\frac{1}{8}''$ lines separated by $\frac{1}{16}''$ spaces. Center lines are used to designate the axis of symmetry of an object. They can be used as extension lines to locate holes, in which case they are extended as center lines and not as extension lines. This is illustrated in the plan view of Fig. 208.

In those views of an object where a hole or a circular part is shown circular, the center line should be drawn so that the two perpendicular center lines intersect each other at the $\frac{1}{8}''$ lines, as shown in the plan view of Fig. 208.

FINISH MARKS. Finish marks are symbols to indicate special surface finishing. These symbols tell the mechanic whether a part is to be machined or smoothed in a specified manner. A machine part that is cast or forged normally has a rough surface. Portions of these objects require machining to permit proper mating to other parts.

Patternmakers always build out their patterns in excess of the indicated dimensions for those surfaces which are later to be finished or machined. This maintains the necessary thickness of metal after it has been machined down to the finished dimensions.

There are several types of finish marks in use today. The American Standards Association recommends the use of a 60° "V," as shown in Fig. 210. This "V," made freehand and approximately $\frac{1}{8}''$ high, is drawn so that it touches with its point the surface that is to be finished. The "V" is used only in views where the surface that is to be finished appears as a line (see Fig. 210). The "V" alone

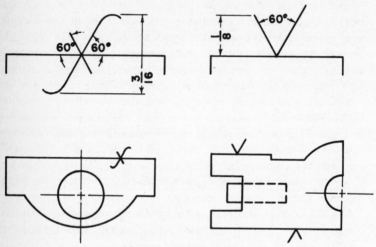

Fig. 210. Finish Marks.

does not specify the type of surface finish desired; consequently, a system of numbers has been established to indicate the required type of finish. This system of numbers is based on the root mean square height of the irregularities in micro-inches. For example, if the number "5" appeared in the throat of the "V," it would signify that the surface must be finished so that the irregularities should not vary in height by more than five-millionths of an inch.[1]

The old type of finish mark, an "f" symbol, is still being used by some manufacturers. This symbol should be made freehand and placed on the drawing as shown in Fig. 210.

[1] A more detailed explanation of this number system of indicating and checking finished surfaces can be found in *Control of Surface Quality*, by James A. Broadston, and is obtainable from The Surface Checking Gage Company, Hollywood, California.

Theory of Dimensioning.   All machine parts are composed of or built up from elementary geometric solids, such as prisms, pyramids, cylinders, cones, spheres, etc.   It follows, then, that the dimensioning of any machine part can be broken down into the dimensioning of the elementary shapes (size dimensioning) and the location of these elementary shapes in relation to one another (location dimensioning).

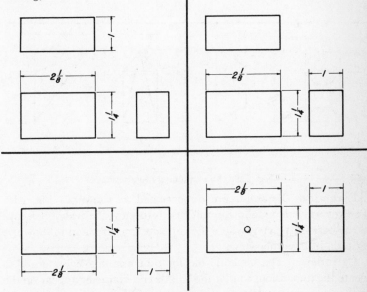

Fig. 211.   Dimensioning of Prism.

Basic Rules for Placing Dimensions

1. Dimensions should be placed between views.

2. If it is not possible to dimension an object clearly between views, the next best position is outside the views.

3. If the first two rules cannot be conveniently followed, then the dimensions must be placed on the views themselves.

4. Dimensioning to invisible lines should be avoided wherever possible.

Prisms.   Fig. 211 shows the approved methods of dimensioning a prism.   The general rule to remember is to show the length and height in the front view or front elevation, and the depth in one of the other views.

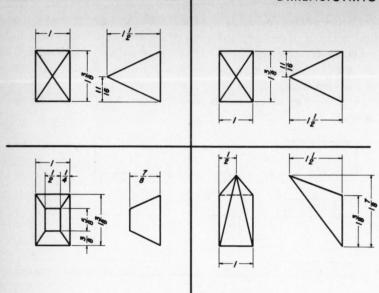

Fig. 212.   Dimensioning of Pyramids.

Pyramids.   Pyramids are dimensioned as shown in Fig. 212. The general rule to follow in this case is to show the two dimensions of the base in the view where they appear true size, and to show the altitude in the other view.

Cylinders.   The general rule for dimensioning cylinders is to locate the dimensions so that the length and diameter appear on the same view.   Where a hole or a negative cylinder exists, it is best to dimension by a note when the method of producing the hole is known (cf. Fig. 213B).

The approved methods of dimensioning cylinders are shown in Fig. 213.   The method used in Fig. 213B is preferred to the one shown in Fig. 213C.   The method illustrated in Fig. 213C is generally used when the numeral is followed by a D (diameter) and the circular or plan view is omitted.

A good rule to remember in dimensioning cylinders is the following: the only dimension that should appear on a plan view, showing cylinders as circles, is the diameter of the circular center line of bolt circles in the flange of the object, as illustrated in Fig. 214 (circular dimensioning).   This figure also shows how a piece should be dimensioned when it is built up entirely of cylinders.

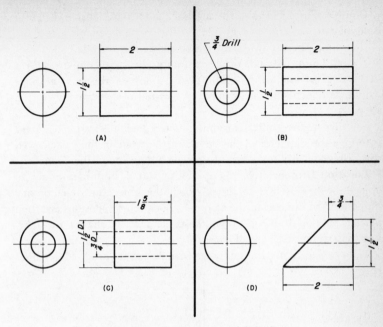

Fig. 213. Dimensioning of Cylinder.

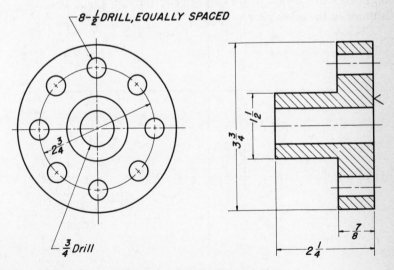

Fig. 214. Circular Dimensioning.

Cones. Fig. 215 shows the methods used to dimension different types of cones. The general rule for dimensioning a cone is to show all the dimensions on the view which shows the altitude.

Two different methods of dimensioning the same cone are shown in Figs. 215B and 215C. The choice between the two methods would be dependent solely upon its method of construction in the shop.

Another method of dimensioning a cone which is frequently used is to give the diameter of the base and the angle of the vertex. In this instance it is not necessary to show a diagram of the cone.

Location Dimensions. As previously stated, in dimensioning an object the first step is to break down the object into elementary shapes and to dimension the shapes. Location dimensions are then placed on the drawing to tie these elementary shapes together. Location dimensions are of several types.

1. Locating center lines of holes with respect to other center lines (Fig. 216A).

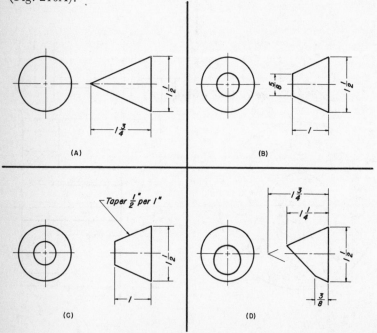

Fig. 215. Dimensioning of Cones.

2. Locàting surfaces from center lines of holes (Fig. 216B).

3. Locating cènter lines from finished surfaces (Fig. 216C).

4. Locating finished surfaces with respect to other finished surfaces (Fig. 216D).

Fig. 217 shows a completely dimensioned drawing. Instead of numbers, L has been used to indicate location dimensions and S to indicate size dimensions. It will be noted that many of the rules previously set forth are illustrated in this drawing.

Over-All Dimensions. Over-all dimensions should be shown for all .drawings. An over-all dimension, which is neither a size dimension nor a location dimension, must show the summation of all intermediate dimensions. The only exception to this rule is that the over-all dimension is never given to pieces having circular ends (Fig. 217).

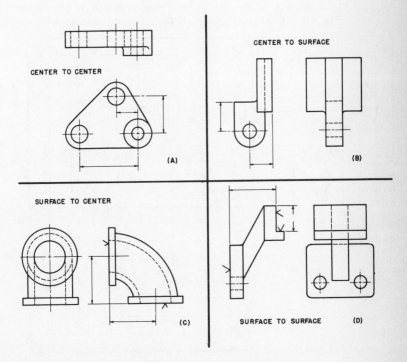

Fig. 216. Location Dimensions.

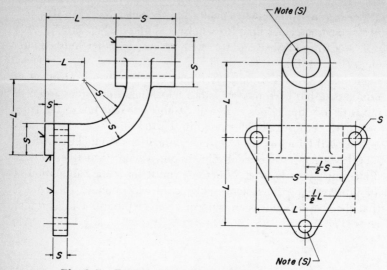

Fig. 217. Example of Completely Dimensioned Drawing.

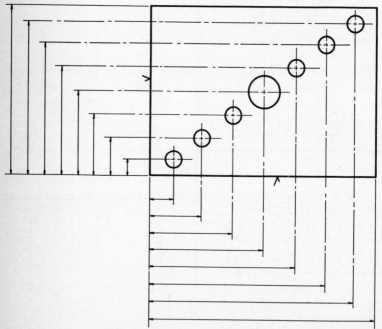

Fig. 218. Base-Line Dimensioning.

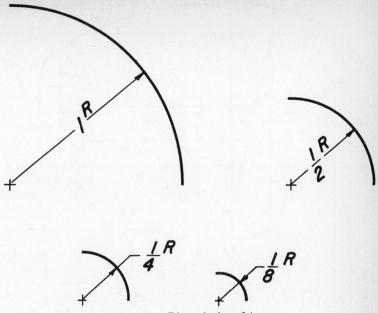

Fig. 219. Dimensioning of Arcs.

Base-Line Dimensions. In certain types of precise work, dimensions are sometimes referred to as "center line" or "base line." The purpose of base-line dimensioning is to prevent cumulative errors, for each dimension is independent of all others. Fig. 218 shows an example of base-line dimensioning. The dimensions used in this kind of work are always expressed in decimals, since fractional dimensions are not sufficiently accurate.

General and Recommended Practice in Dimensioning

METHOD OF DIMENSIONING ARCS. Fig. 219 shows the approved method of dimensioning arcs. The numeral giving the length of the radius should always be followed by R, which is the standard symbol for "radius." The dimension line should have only one arrowhead, which should touch the arc. The center of the arc should be clearly marked.

METHOD OF DIMENSIONING IRREGULAR CURVED LINES. The method of dimensioning curved lines recommended by the American

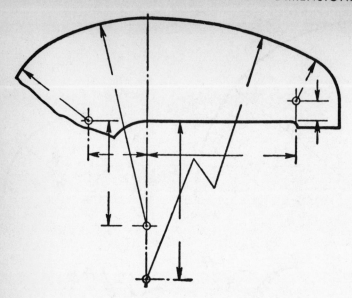

Fig. 220.   Dimensioning of Curved Lines with Radii.

Standards Association is shown in Figs. 220 and 221 (see Appendix, p. 379).   Figs. 222 and 223 show other methods of dimensioning curved lines which are widely used in industry.

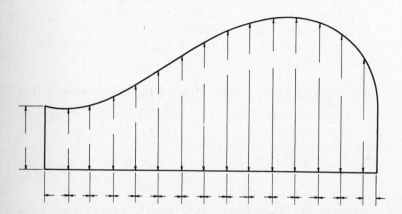

Fig. 221.   Dimensioning of Curved Lines with Offsets.

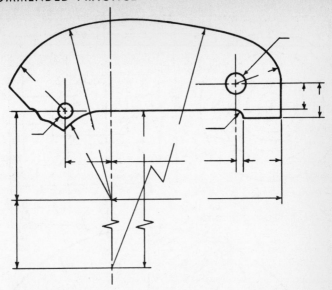

Fig. 222. Common Method of Dimensioning Curved Lines.

USE OF CONTINUOUS AND STAGGERED DIMENSIONS. In many cases where there are a series of parallel dimensions, it is desirable to have the breaks in the dimension lines staggered to give sufficient space for the numerals and for clarity in reading. Fig. 224 illustrates this rule.

METHOD OF DIMENSIONING IN UNDESIRABLE AREAS. In dimensioning inclined lines, avoid the shaded areas indicated in Fig. 225.

METHODS OF DIMENSIONING IN LIMITED SPACES. Dimensions

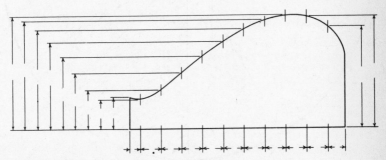

Fig. 223. Common Method of Dimensioning Curved Lines.

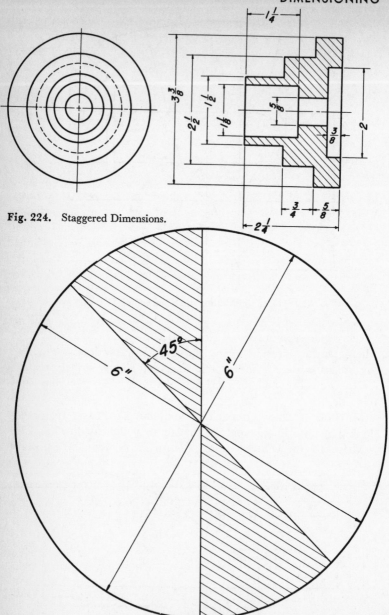

Fig. 224.   Staggered Dimensions.

Fig. 225.   Dimensioning in Undesirable Areas.

should never be crowded into small spaces.   Fig. 226 shows several suggested methods of dimensioning where the space is limited.

METHODS OF DIMENSIONING ANGLES.   Fig. 227 shows several recommended methods of dimensioning angles.

Notes.   In making drawings of machine parts, it is found that dimensions alone are insufficient to describe an object completely. In such instances, it is necessary to supplement the dimensions by additional notes.

Acquaintance with machine-shop methods and practices is of invaluable aid in helping the draftsman to place the proper notes on a drawing.   An example of the value of knowing machine-shop practice is illustrated by Fig. 228, a diagram showing several holes. If the draftsman dimensions these holes by giving only their diameters, the mechanic making the object will not know which of the various methods of production to use — as, for example, drilling, reaming, coring, and boring.   The draftsman, in cases of this type, should state specifically by a note or notes the method to be used in the making of these holes.

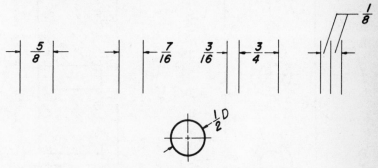

Fig. 226.   Dimensioning in Limited Space.

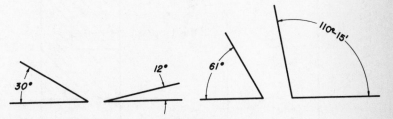

Fig. 227.   Methods of Dimensioning Angles.

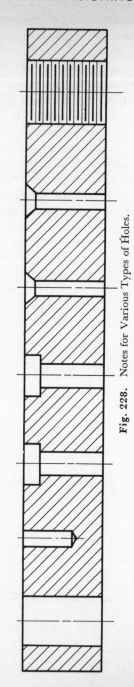

Fig. 228. Notes for Various Types of Holes.

$\frac{13}{32}$ Drill–C.B. for $\frac{3}{8}$–Fil. Hd. Mach. Scr.

$\frac{1}{4}$ Drill–C's'k. for $\frac{1}{4}$ Fl.Hd.Mach.Scr.

$\frac{7}{8}$ Tap–1–8NC–2

–10(.1935)Drill–$\frac{3}{4}$ Dp.

$\frac{1}{4}$ Drill–80° C's'k. to $\frac{1}{2}$ D.

$\frac{3}{8}$ Drill–$\frac{5}{8}$ C.B. X $\frac{1}{4}$ Dp.

$\frac{3}{4}$ Drill

Notes should always be expressed in a definite form. Fig. 228 shows the accepted form of notes for various types of holes.[1] The size of the hole is stated first, then the operation to be used in making it. Where several operations are performed on the same hole, the steps are listed in the order in which they should be made. Fig. 228 also shows methods of indicating counterbored and countersunk holes for screws. Either method of notation is correct.

In the case of drilled holes, in numbered or lettered sizes, the number or letter of the drill should be followed by its decimal equivalent in parentheses. (See Fig. 228.)

Additional Rules for Dimensioning. In addition to the foregoing rules for dimensioning, the following general rules should be observed.

1. Dimensions should read from the bottom and right-hand side of the sheet of paper unless the unilateral system of dimensioning is used. The unilateral system of dimensioning has all dimensions placed so that they read from the bottom of the sheet.

2. Dimensions should be placed on the view which shows the part being dimensioned in its greatest contour.

3. Dimensions should never be repeated unless they are absolutely necessary to avoid confusion.

4. A line of the drawing or the edge of an object should never be used as a dimension line.

5. Holes should be located in the view where they appear as circles, and the dimension should be referred to the center line of the hole and never to the side of the hole.

6. A circle is dimensioned by its diameter and never by its radius. Where there is any possibility of doubt that a diameter is being used, the dimension should be followed by a *D*.

7. Notes should always be lettered horizontally.

8. Drawings of machine parts are expressed in inches up to 72 inches.

9. Inch marks may be omitted in a drawing if all dimensions are in inches.

10. Shorter dimensions should be placed inside longer ones to avoid having extension lines cross dimension lines.

---

[1] The ASA standard abbreviations for dimensioning and notes are listed in Z 32.13 1950, *Abbreviations for Use in Drawings*.

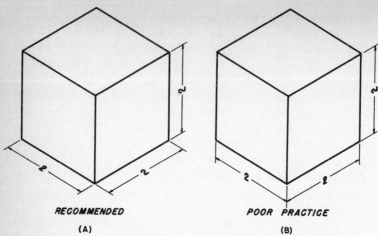

Fig. 229. Recommended and Poor Practices in Dimensioning.

11. If a dimension is placed on a sectioned view, the cross-sectioning should be omitted from the portion of the object where the numerical value of the dimension appears. In other words, the numeral should be surrounded by white space so that it can be easily read. (See Fig. 225.)

12. Unnecessary dimensions should be avoided.

13. The workman should never be required to scale a drawing, or add and subtract to arrive at a required dimension.

14. If dimensions are changed without changing the drawing accordingly, each new dimension should be underscored with a dark line indicating it is "out-of-scale."

Rules for Dimensioning Pictorial Drawings. Pictorial drawings used for construction purposes must be dimensioned. The following rules should be borne in mind in dimensioning isometric and cabinet drawings.

ISOMETRIC DRAWINGS

1. All dimension and extension lines, dimensions, and arrowheads should be contained in the same isometric plane as the part of the object being dimensioned.

2. All dimensions should read toward the bottom front corner, as shown in Fig. 229A.

3. In dimensioning the base of an object, avoid if possible the position of the extension lines as shown in Fig. 229B. Extension

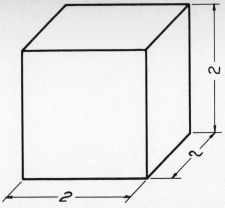

Fig. 230. Dimensioning of Cabinet Drawing.

lines placed in the position indicated give the impression that the object is supported on these extension lines as legs.

4. Dimension numerals should be placed so that they can be enclosed in a box the sides of which are parallel to the extension and dimension lines as illustrated in Fig. 229A.

5. Notes should be placed horizontally.

6. Dimensions may be placed on the object when necessary.

CABINET DRAWINGS

1. Fig. 230 shows the recommended positions of dimensions for a cabinet drawing.

2. The receding axis is dimensioned as though it were full size, but the dimensions or numerals themselves should be compressed as shown in Fig. 230.

3. Dimensioning rules 3, 4, 5, and 6 under isometric drawings also apply to the dimensioning of cabinet drawings.

9

Fasteners

This chapter on fasteners concludes the study of the separate parts of the working drawing preparatory to the study of the next chapter on the working drawing as a whole. A thorough knowledge of fasteners is essential to the preparation of working drawings.

Function and Types of Fasteners. The function of a fastener is to hold machine parts together. There are two types of fasteners in general use: (1) *removable fasteners*, such as bolts, screws, keys, and pins, and (2) *permanent fasteners*, such as rivets. Both types of fasteners are so widely used that every draftsman should study them carefully and familiarize himself with the standard method of representing them.

SCREW THREADS

Standardization of Screw Threads. The first known reference to the screw is found in the writings of Archimedes (287–212 B.C.), but the screw was not used to any great extent until the Middle Ages. Screw threads were not interchangeable; the nut for one bolt would not fit another bolt of the same size. This condition existed until about 1860 when William Sellers devised a thread which was widely adopted and became known as the "Sellers thread" or the "United States thread." This thread was standardized and used satisfactorily until the mass production of automobiles and industrial machinery required a still more exacting thread.

In 1918, the Bureau of Standards, in co-operation with leading manufacturers and engineering societies, helped to create the

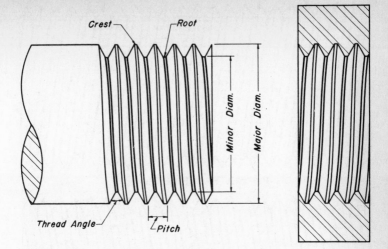

Fig. 231. Terminology of Threads.

National Screw Thread Commission authorized by an Act of Congress. The thread developed by this Commission has the same profile as the Sellers thread, but the range of sizes and number of threads per inch are much greater than those designed and developed by Sellers. This thread is known as the "American Standard thread" and is the type referred to throughout this text unless otherwise specified.

Terminology. In order to acquire a working knowledge of threads, the student should become acquainted with Fig. 231 and with the following definitions.

External Thread: A thread on the outside of a member.

Internal Thread: A thread on the inside of a member.

Major Diameter: The largest diameter of a screw thread. This term is applicable to both internal and external threads.

Minor Diameter: The smallest diameter of a screw thread. This term is also applicable to both internal and external threads.

Pitch (*P*): The distance from any point on a screw thread to the corresponding point on the next screw thread measured parallel to the axis of the screw.

$$\text{Pitch (in inches)} = \frac{1}{\text{number of threads per inch}}$$

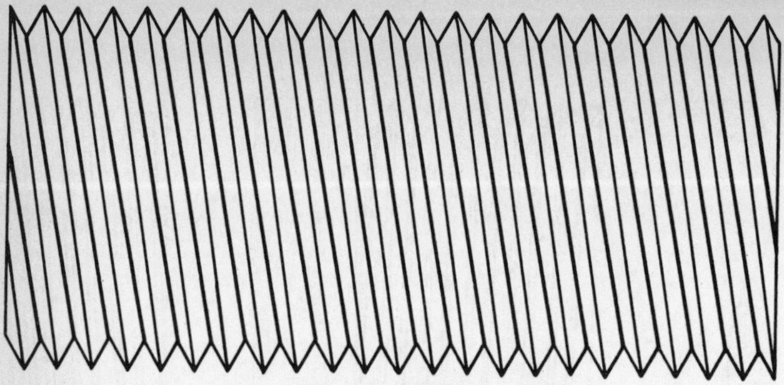

Fig. 232. Right-Hand Thread.

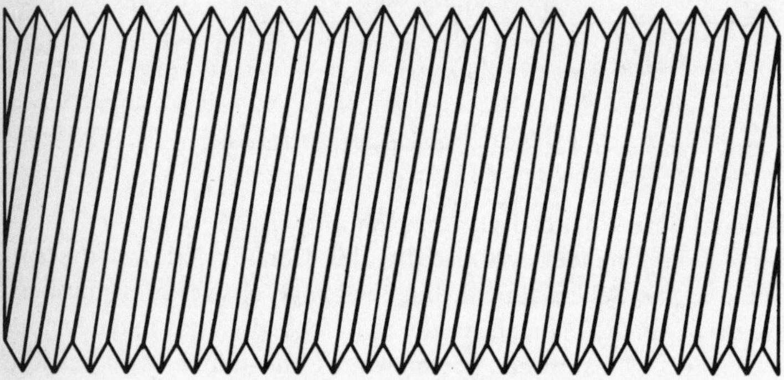

Fig. 233. Left-Hand Thread.

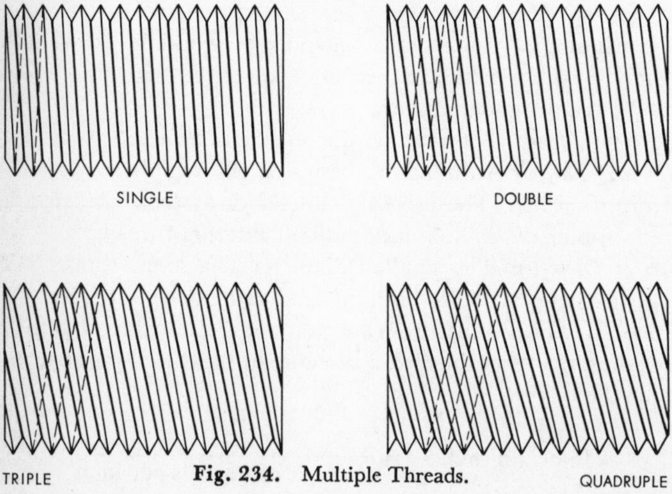

SINGLE

DOUBLE

TRIPLE

Fig. 234. Multiple Threads.

QUADRUPLE

Lead: The distance a screw thread advances axially in one turn. In the case of a single-thread screw, the lead and the pitch are the same. On a double-thread screw, the lead is twice the pitch, etc.

Crest: The top surface joining the two sides of the thread.

Root: The bottom surface joining the sides of two adjacent threads.

Depth of Thread: The distance betweeen the crest and root of a thread, measured normal to the axis.

Thread Angle: The angle included between the sides of the thread, measured in an axial plane.

Right-Hand and Left-Hand Threads. A *right-hand* thread is one that tightens when turned in a clockwise direction. This is the type of thread most commonly used (Fig. 232). A thread which must be turned in a counterclockwise direction to be tightened or to advance into a threaded hole is a *left-hand* thread (Fig. 233). The two diagrams of these threads show that a right-hand thread always slopes from upper left to lower right, whereas the left-hand thread slopes from lower left to upper right.

Multiple Threads. The layman thinks of a thread as a continuous groove cut around a piece of rod. This is true only in the case of a single thread, in which the pitch is equal to the lead. Certain requirements sometimes make it necessary to have two, three, four, etc. continuous threads cut side by side around the rod. These threads have leads of respectively two, three, four, etc. times the pitch. The chief reason for having multiple threads is to permit the screw to enter a nut or threaded hole faster without using a coarser thread. Moreover, whereas the single thread has only one point of entrance into a nut, a double thread has two points of entrance which are spaced 180° apart; a triple thread has three points of entrance spaced 120° apart, and so forth.

A good example of a multiple thread is the cap on a fountain pen. When the cap is unscrewed from the pen and turned in a counterclockwise direction, a number of clicks will be heard with only one revolution of the cap. These clicks indicate the number of points at which the thread could be engaged if the cap were rotated in the opposite direction. If four clicks are heard, for example, the fountain pen has a quadruple thread.

The drawings in Fig. 234 show how the slope of the threads varies as the multiplicity of the threads increases. It should be noted that in a thread with an odd number of multiples the crest is always directly opposite a root.   In a thread with even multiples, the crest is always opposite another crest.

Use of Screw Threads.   Screw threads are used for three general purposes: (1) they are most commonly used on fasteners, such as bolts and nuts, cap and machine screws, and so forth; (2) they are used in certain types of setscrews designed for adjustment purposes, such as the gasoline and air-intake adjustment on the carburetor of an automobile; (3) they are also used for transmission of power, as are the threads found on a lifting jack.

Types of Screw Threads.   The drawings in Fig. 235 show the profiles of some of the more common types of threads, and their dimensions.

AMERICAN STANDARD THREAD (Fig. 235A).   This thread is the standard thread in the United States.   It was formerly known as the "United States Standard" (USS) of the "Sellers profile."   The letter N, signifying "National," is used to designate this thread.

The American Standard includes five series of screw threads which differ from one another in pitch, or the number of threads per inch, for a given diameter.   The series is comprised of (1) coarse thread (NC); (2) fine thread (NF); (3) 8-pitch thread; (4) 12-pitch thread; and (5) 16-pitch thread.

In addition to the five series of threads mentioned, there is another series of threads having the same profile as the American Standard. This thread is very fine and is called the Society of Automotive Engineers (SAE) thread, sometimes erroneously classified as the National Extra Fine (NEF) thread.

SHARP-V THREAD (Fig. 235B).   The sharp-V thread is similar to the American Standard thread except that the crests have not been cut off or the roots filled in.   This thread is commonly used in boiler work or wherever it is necessary to have leak-proof joints.

ACME THREAD (Fig. 235C).   This thread is utilized for the transmission of power.   Fig. 235C shows a profile of the thread and the necessary dimensions for laying it out.   It is accepted practice to use a 30° angle in the drawing of the acme thread to represent the true thread angle of 29°.   The point of failure in the square thread can be readily seen by comparing its profile with that of the acme thread.   The comparison also shows how this defect has been eliminated in the acme thread by leaving more material at the critical point, thereby making the acme thread much stronger.

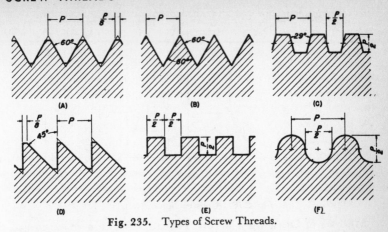

Fig. 235. Types of Screw Threads.

BUTTRESS THREAD (Fig. 235D). This is a special thread which permits the transmission of power in one direction only. It is used in the recoil mechanism of heavy guns and in the inertia starters of aircraft engines.

SQUARE THREAD (Fig. 235E). This thread is used for power transmission; it is found chiefly in jacks, vises, etc. It is an easy thread to cut in the lathe, and this accounts for its wide adoption. Its principal defect is that it shears at the root diameter. This shortcoming brought about a modification of the square thread which resulted in the development of the acme thread (Fig. 235C).

KNUCKLE THREAD (Fig. 235F). This thread is the only one that can be both rolled and cast; though very crude, it has many uses. It is used, for example, on the bases of light bulbs and in the screw tops on glass jars.

OTHER THREADS. There are many types of screw threads not illustrated in this chapter because they are not commonly used in the United States. One of these threads is the *Whitworth* or *British Standard*. This thread is similar to the American Standard thread, except that it has a thread angle of 55° and that the crests and roots are rounded off instead of being flat.

Another such thread is the *International Standard* thread, which has the same profile as the American Standard thread. The only difference is that it is measured in the metric system. It is standard throughout Europe, except in England, and is used in the United States on spark plugs.

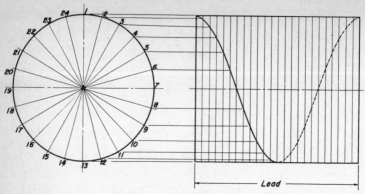

Fig. 236. Construction of Helix.

Method of Drawing a Screw Thread. Before a screw thread can be drawn, certain information must be known, such as form of thread, major diameter, number of threads per inch, whether there is to be a single or multiple thread, and whether the thread is to be right- or left-handed.

One method of making a screw thread is to move a cutting tool longitudinally along a shaft while the shaft is rotated. The thread thus cut takes the form of a *helix*, whose construction is shown in Fig. 236. It can be seen from Fig. 237 that one helix is formed for the major diameter of the thread, and another helix of different size for the minor diameter. It is obvious from this diagram that it would be very laborious to construct drawings of threads in this manner. Consequently, this type of representation is rarely used.

CONVENTIONAL REPRESENTATION OF THREADS. It has already been shown how laborious it would be to construct the helices for a true projection of a thread. In the conventional method of representing a thread, the helices are drawn as straight lines. Fig. 237 shows a screw thread as it actually appears, and Fig. 238 shows the same thread with the helices drawn as straight lines. By comparing these two diagrams, it can be seen that the difference between the two methods is so slight that construction of helices is not worth a great expenditure of time and energy.

AMERICAN STANDARD OR SHARP-V THREAD. The American Standard thread and the sharp-V thread are both drawn in the same way. This is made possible by the elimination of the flat portions on the crests and roots of American Standard threads.

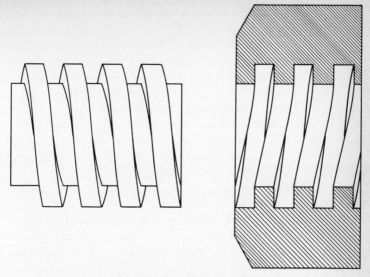

Fig. 237. True Projection of Thread.

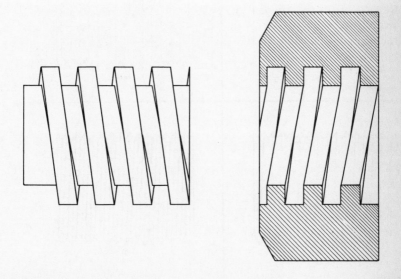

Fig. 238. Conventional Representation of Thread.

These flat portions are really so small that they can be omitted in a drawing without being noticed.

Let it be required to draw an American Standard or sharp-V thread. The pitch distance is first laid out along the entire length of the thread, and lines are drawn through these points at angles of 60° as shown in Fig. 239A. Since this is to be a single thread, a crest must appear directly opposite a root as indicated in Fig. 239B. The next step is to connect the crests as illustrated in Fig. 239C. The final step is to draw lines connecting the roots as shown in Fig. 239D. If the drawing is to be inked, the lines joining the roots should be heavier than those connecting the crests.

SQUARE THREAD. Let it be required to draw a double, right-hand square thread. Draw lines a distance equal to $P/2$ in from the crest lines of the thread. Starting at any convenient point, lay

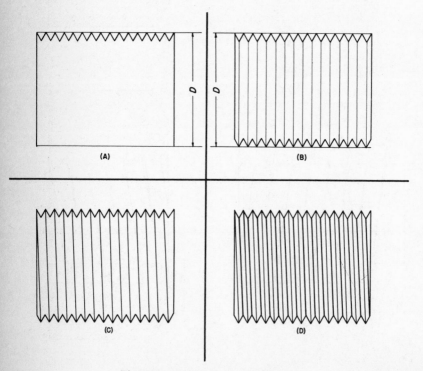

Fig. 239. American Standard Thread.

off the distance *P/2* along the length of the thread as shown in Fig. 240A. Since this is to be a double thread, a crest is to be shown opposite a crest. Fig. 240B shows how this profile appears with the construction lines removed. Fig. 240C shows the lines connecting the crests. The invisible lines were drawn in principally to show how certain visible lines were obtained. Fig. 240D shows the completed thread.

ACME THREAD. Let it be required to draw a single, right-hand acme thread. Draw lines a distance of *P/2* in from the crest lines. Also draw lines a distance of *P/4* in from the crest lines. The length of the threaded portion is then divided by lines set a distance of *P/2* apart, as shown in Fig. 241A. The next step is to draw lines, making angles of 75° with the horizontal, through the intersection of the lines that are a distance of *P/4* in from the crest and the lines perpendicular to the axis of the screw, as shown in Fig. 241B. It should be noted that the 75° lines slope in the same direction at

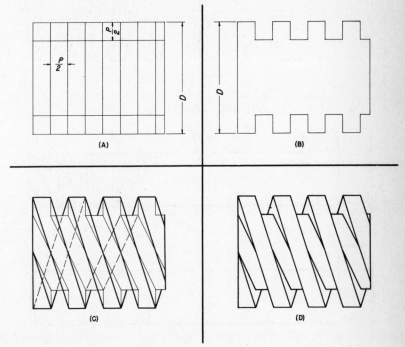

Fig. 240. Square Thread.

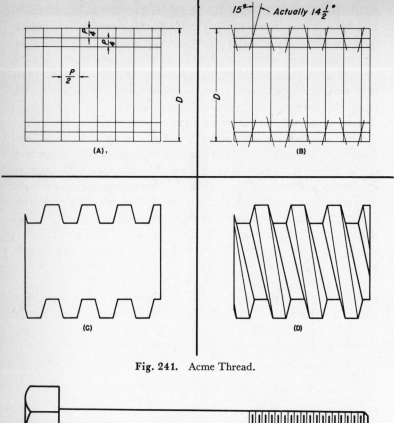

Fig. 241. Acme Thread.

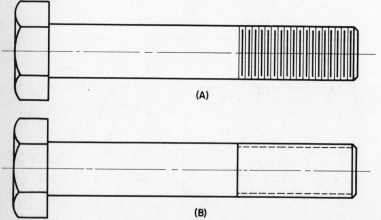

Fig. 242. External Thread Symbols.

both ends of the vertical lines for a single thread. In the case of a double thread, the lines slope in opposite directions. The actual $14\frac{1}{2}°$ thread angle, shown in Fig. 241B, represents a single face of an acme thread. The $14\frac{1}{2}°$ angle adjacent to it makes a complete angle of 29° between the two thread faces (cf. Fig. 235C). Fig. 241C shows the profile of the threads with construction lines removed. Fig. 241D shows the completed thread in which the lines joining the crests and roots have been added.

Thread Symbols. The thread representations which have been shown and discussed in this chapter are to be used only when they appear 1″ or more than 1″ in diameter on a drawing. When they are shown less than 1″ in diameter, it is recommended that the symbols shown in Figs. 242A and 242B be used.

EXTERNAL THREAD SYMBOLS. Fig. 242A is known as the *American Standards Association regular thread symbol*, and it is recommended that this symbol be used on assembly drawings. The light lines representing the crests of the thread are not spaced according to scale. It is recommended that these lines be spaced not closer than $\frac{3}{32}″$. The lines representing the roots of the thread are drawn heavier. These lines are spaced midway between the crest lines, and should

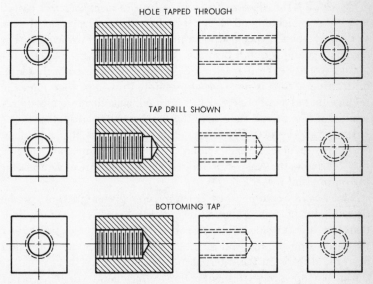

Fig. 243. Regular Symbols for Internal Threads.

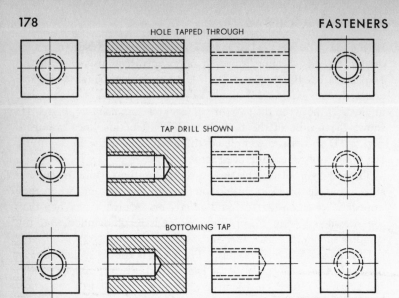

Fig. 244. Simplified Symbols for Internal Threads.

terminate a minimum of $\frac{1}{16}''$ from the lines representing the major diameter of the thread.

Fig. 242B is the *American Standards Association simplified thread symbol*, and its use is recommended for detail drawings. The reason the use of these symbols is specified for a particular type of drawing is that anyone reading a detail drawing (cf. Chapter 10, p. 260), for example, would be familiar with the various symbols used in that kind of drawing. This is not true of assembly drawings; therefore, the regular thread symbol (Fig. 242A) is used, since it more closely resembles a true thread than does the simplified thread symbol.

INTERNAL THREAD SYMBOLS. Fig. 243 shows the American Standard regular thread symbols for use on internal threads. Fig. 244 shows the American Standard simplified thread symbols for use on internal threads.

Threads in Section. Fig. 231 is a true representation of a screw thread. In this figure, the nut or internal thread is in section, and, therefore, the far side of the thread is visible. This explains why the threads on the internal member slope in the opposite direction from the threads on the external member.

Fig. 245 shows the treatment of threads in general when they occur on a section drawing.

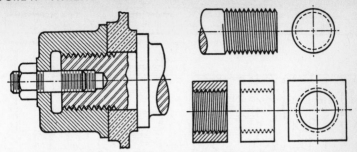

Fig. 245. Treatment of Threads on a Section Drawing.

Classification of Screw-Thread Fits.[1] The American Standards Association, in standardizing screw threads, established a classification of fit between the two mating parts to promote ease of assembly. The four commonly used classes of fit are as follows.

CLASS 1.   The Class 1 fit is recommended only for screw-thread work where clearance between mating parts is essential for rapid assembly and where shake or play is not objectionable.

CLASS 2.   The Class 2 fit represents a high-quality commercial screw-thread product and is recommended for the great bulk of interchangeable screw-thread work.

CLASS 3.   The Class 3 fit represents an exceptionally high-grade commercially threaded product and is recommended only in cases where the high cost of precision tools and the continual checking of tools and products are warranted.   This fit is used where shake or play is not desired.

CLASS 4.   The Class 4 fit is intended to meet very unusual requirements, even more exacting than those for which Class 3 is recommended.   It is a selective fit, used if initial assembly by hand is required.   It is not, as yet, adaptable to quantity production.

Other classifications of fits are discussed in greater detail on pp. 191–192 of this section.   Thread dimensions and tap drill sizes are found in Appendix Table 1.

Screw-Thread Notes.   The type of thread is indicated by special notes.

EXTERNAL THREADS.   External screw threads are designated on a

[1] Cf. ASA Bl.1 — 1935, *Screw Threads for Bolts, Nuts, Machine Screws, and Threaded Parts.*

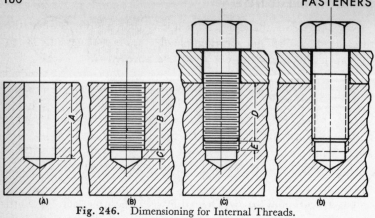

Fig. 246. Dimensioning for Internal Threads.

drawing, bill of material, etc. by listing the following items in order
in a note.

1. Diameter of screw
2. Number of threads per inch
3. Type of thread (NC, NF, N, SAE, Square, etc.)
4. Class of fit
5. Right- or left-hand (RH, LH)
6. Multiple (single, double, triple, etc.)

A thread is assumed to be single and right-hand when it is not
otherwise specified in a note.

Examples:

$\frac{1}{2}$–13 NC–2   1–10 N–2

$\frac{3}{4}$–16 NF–3   1$\frac{1}{4}$–12 N12–3

#10–24 NC–2   1$\frac{1}{2}$–6 NC–2, LH Double

1–5 Square   1–4 Acme, LH

INTERNAL THREADS. Internal threads, such as threaded holes,
are designated by a note which lists the items in the following order.

1. Diameter of tap drill
2. Depth of tap drill
3. Diameter of thread
4. Thread specification
5. Class of fit
6. Depth of thread

Example: $\frac{7}{8}$ Drill — 2 Deep, 1–8 NC–2 × 1$\frac{3}{4}$ Deep.

Fig. 246 shows the depth dimensions that are used when the threaded hole does not pass completely through a piece, or when the depth dimensions are not given in a note.

Fig. 246A shows the way in which the hole formed by the tap drill appears. The dimension A is usually taken as $1\frac{1}{2}D$, where D is the major diameter of the thread. For soft metals, such as brass, aluminum, etc., this distance is increased to $2D$; and for steel the distance is reduced to $1D$.

Fig. 246B shows the same hole after the tap has been screwed into the hole made by the tap drill. Note that the thread does not extend to the bottom of the drilled hole. The reason for this is that the chips formed by the tap drill fall to the bottom of the hole and cause the tap drill to jam. Leaving clearance at the bottom eliminates this condition. The dimensions shown in Fig. 246B are taken so that $A = B + C$, and C is taken as $\frac{1}{4}D$.

Fig. 246C shows the tapped hole with a fastener in place. Note that the end of the fastener does not extend to the bottom of the threaded hole. The reason for this can be seen by inspecting the tap in Fig. 247, and observing how the first few threads cut by the tap are imperfect owing to the tapering of the tap at the bottom.

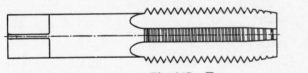

Fig. 247. Tap.

The dimensions shown in Fig. 246C are taken so that $B = D + E$, and E is taken as $\frac{1}{4}D$. The American Standard regular thread symbol is used in Fig. 246, whereas Fig. 246D is the same type of fastener except that the American Standard simplified symbol is used instead.

BOLTS AND NUTS

The American Standards Association classifies squarehead bolts and nuts in two groups: unfinished and semifinished.[1] Hexagonal-head bolts and nuts are classified in three groups: unfinished, semi-finished, and finished.

[1] Cf. ASA B18.2 — 1941, *Wrench-Head Bolts and Nuts and Wench Openings.*

Classification. The following definitions, extracted from the above-mentioned pamphlet, apply to both square and hexagonal bolts and nuts.   (Also see Appendix Table 2.)

UNFINISHED.   Unfinished boltheads and nuts are not machined or treated on any surface except in the threads.

SEMIFINISHED.   Semifinished boltheads and nuts are provided with a smooth bearing surface for the proper seating of the parts they bolt together.   Boltheads have either a washer-face or a plain, but smooth, bearing surface on the underneath side of the head. Nuts have either a washer-faced surface or a circular bearing surface which is produced by chamfering the corners on the underside of the nut.

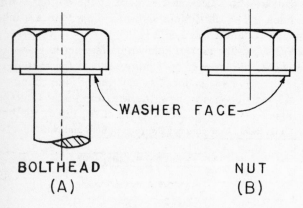

BOLTHEAD   NUT
   (A)   (B)

Fig. 248.   Washer Face.

FINISHED.   Finished boltheads and nuts are the same as semi-finished except that the surfaces, other than the bearing surface, have been so treated as to provide a special appearance.   The finish desired on all nonbearing surfaces of finished boltheads and nuts should be specified by the purchaser.

Washer Face.   The washer face is a circular boss turned or otherwise produced on the bearing surface of a bolthead or nut to relieve the corners (see Fig. 248).   A circular bearing surface can also be produced by chamfering the corners of the nut.

Height of Head.   The height of head is the over-all distance from the top to the bearing surface and includes the thickness of the washer face where provided.   (See Appendix Table 3.)

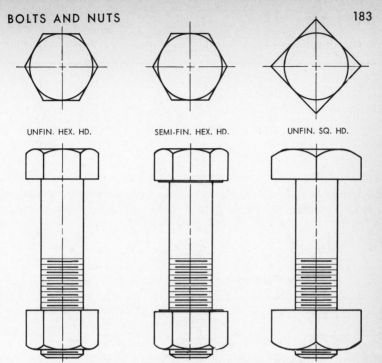

UNFIN. HEX. HD.   SEMI-FIN. HEX. HD.   UNFIN. SQ. HD.

Fig. 249. Conventional Drawings of Bolts and Nuts.

Thickness of Nut. The thickness of nut is the over-all distance from the top to the bearing surface and includes the thickness of the washer face where provided. (See Appendix Table 3.)

American Standard Bolthead and Nut. Fig. 249 shows the conventional way of drawing several of these bolts and nuts. It is common practice, however, never to make a detail drawing of bolts and nuts when they are standard.

Let it be required to draw a bolthead or nut of any given size. By consulting Table 3 in the Appendix, the distance across flats of the head or nut can be found. This distance is approximately $1\frac{1}{2}$ times the diameter of the bolt. The steps shown in Fig. 250 illustrate the procedure to be followed in the construction of a hexagon with a 30°–60° triangle when the distance across corners is given. The drawings in Fig. 251 show the various steps in the construction of the front view of a bolthead or nut. It should be pointed out that no matter from what direction a bolthead or nut is viewed, it should always be drawn as though it were seen across corners.

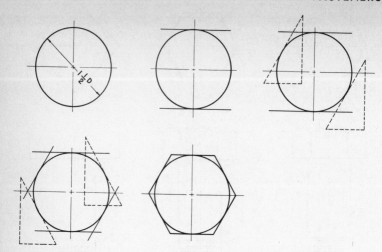

Fig. 250. Construction of Hexagon with 30°–60° Triangle.

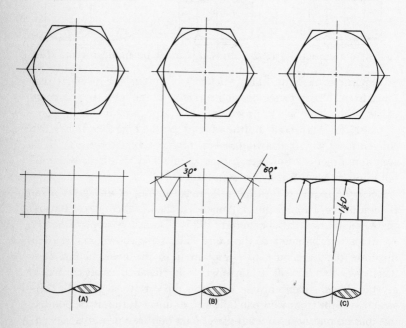

Fig. 251. Front View of Bolthead and Nut.

Bolt Specifications. In describing or specifying bolts in correspondence, bills of materials, etc., the items should be put in note form in the following order.

1. Diameter of bolt.

2. Length of bolt (measured from underside of head to end). See Appendix Table 3.

3. Material, if other than steel.

4. Finish of bolt (unfinished, semifinished, etc.)

5. Series (omit if bolt is regular series).

6. Style of head (square or hexagonal) and state BOLT.

7. Style of nut if different from head of bolt.

8. Thread specification (type and fit).

Example: $\frac{3}{8}$x3 brass, Fin. heavy, Hex. Hd. bolt and nut $\frac{3}{8}$-8NC-2.

Studs. A stud bolt is not a bolt in the true sense. It is a piece of rod with right-hand threads on both ends to hold two or more pieces together.[1] One end is screwed into a threaded hole. The other end has a nut affixed to it which, when tightened, holds two pieces firmly together, as shown in Fig. 252A.

The American Standards Association has not yet standardized studs; consequently, detail drawings must be made for all studs.

The method of dimensioning studs is shown in Fig. 252B.

When a stud is shown in place, as in Fig. 252A, or is specified in correspondence, it is necessary to list the items in the following order.

1. Diameter.

2. Length and state STUD.

3. Material, if other than steel.

4. Thread specification (nut end).

5. Length of thread (nut end).

6. Type of nut.

7. Thread specification (stud end).

8. Length of thread (stud end).

Example: $1 \times 3\frac{7}{8}$ Stud; 1–14NF–2, $1\frac{1}{2}$ long, Unfin. Hex. Hd. Nut; 1–8NC–2 $\times 1\frac{3}{4}$ long.

When the thread on both ends of the stud are the same, this note can be listed as follows: $1 \times 3\frac{7}{8}$ Stud; 1–14NF–2, $1\frac{1}{2}$ long both ends; with Unfin. Hex. Hd. Nut.

Cap Screws. Cap screws are fastening devices used to fasten two pieces of material together by passing through a clearance hole in one member, and screwing into a threaded or tapped hole in the

[1] In rare cases, one end may have a right-hand thread and the other end a left-hand thread.

$1 \times 3\frac{7}{8}$ Stud; 1-14NF-2, $1\frac{1}{2}$ long, Unfin. Hex. Hd. Nut; 1-8NC-2 x $1\frac{3}{4}$ long

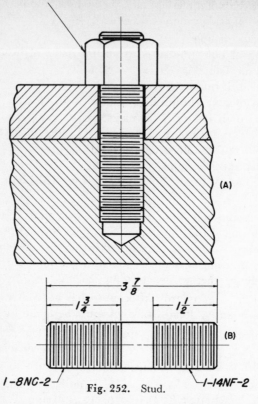

Fig. 252. Stud.

other member. Cap screws come in six different styles of heads.
Fig. 253 shows five of these types. The type not shown is the fluted
socket head, which is similar to the hexagonal socket-head cap screw.
The dimensions of all six types of cap screw heads will be found in
Appendix Tables 4, 5, and 6.

Cap screws are specified by note and the items should be listed as
shown in the sample notes on Fig. 253.

Machine Screws. Machine screws are very much like cap
screws. The only difference between them is that machine screws
are smaller in diameter and have only four types of head, shown in
Fig. 254. The American Standards Association's dimensions for
these screws can be found in Appendix Table 7.

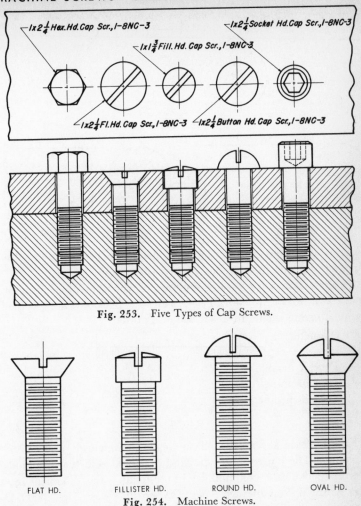

Fig. 253. Five Types of Cap Screws.

FLAT HD. FILLISTER HD. ROUND HD. OVAL HD.

Fig. 254. Machine Screws.

Setscrews. Setscrews are used to prevent relative motion between two pieces. An example illustrating this point is the use of a setscrew to fasten a pulley onto a piece of shafting, so that when the shaft rotates the pulley will rotate with it.

When setscrews were first used they had square heads, and were considered dangerous when affixed to rotating pieces as they had a tendency to become easily entangled with clothing. The safety

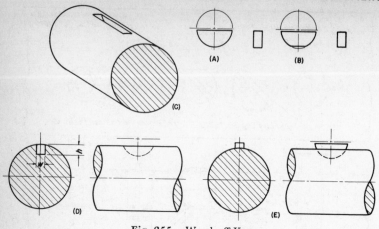

Fig. 255. Woodruff Keys.

setscrew was then designed with a slot or socket for tightening purposes, thus limiting the use of the square head.

Setscrews come in a variety of points, of which the more common ones are shown in Appendix Tables 8 and 9. Setscrews are specified by note, listing the items in the following order.

1. Diameter
2. Length
3. Type of head
4. Type of point
5. Thread specification

KEYS

Keys are used as a means of fastening pulleys, wheels, cranks, etc. to shafts. There are many types and sizes of keys for various kinds of work. The most common key in use today is the Woodruff key. Figs. 255A, B show the two types of Woodruff keys. Figs. 255C, D show the key seat cut in the shaft. Fig. 255E shows how the key would appear after being placed in the key seat cut in the shaft. Dimensions for the various sizes of Woodruff keys and their key seats can be found in Appendix Table 10. Similar data for other keys commonly used in present-day practice may be found as follows in the Appendix: Pratt and Whitney keys (Table 11), square and flat plain parallel stock keys (Table 12), plain taper stock keys (Table 13), and gib-head taper stock keys (Table 14).

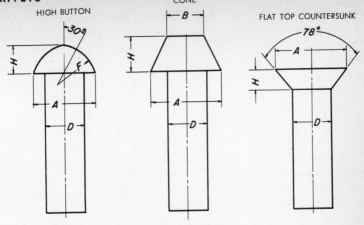

Fig. 256. Rivetheads.

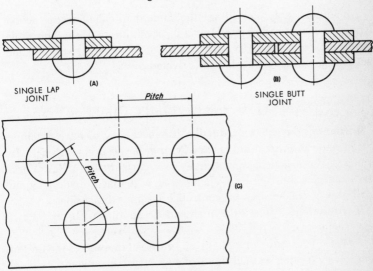

Fig. 257. Methods of Using Rivets.

RIVETS

Rivets are widely used in structural work, particularly for bridges, and for boilers. Riveting is slowly being replaced, however, by welding, which is cheaper because it saves time and labor.

The heads of rivets come in a variety of styles depending on the type of work to be done.   Fig. 256 shows the more common types of rivetheads. Fig. 257 demonstrates several methods of joining pieces of material together with rivets.   Fig. 257A, for instance, shows a single-riveted *lap joint*, so called because it has only a single row of rivets.   Other types of lap joints are double-riveted, triple-riveted, etc., depending upon the number of rows of rivets.

When a riveted joint has more than a single row of rivets, as shown in Fig. 257C, the distance between the centers of the rivets must not be less than the minimum pitch distance, which is usually three times the diameter of the rivet; the rivets must also be staggered in such instances.

Fig. 257B shows a single-riveted *butt joint* with splice or cover plates.   Other types of butt joints are double-riveted, triple-riveted, etc., depending on the number of rows of rivets on each side of the joint.

Appendix Table 15 will aid the student to calculate the actual length of a rivet before and after it is driven into place.   This table shows the desired grip, or true length, of the driven rivet, and the actual size of the rivet before it is riveted over.

FIT OF MATING PARTS (LIMIT DIMENSIONS)[1]

In present-day mass production it is necessary to have machine parts made in large numbers and with great accuracy in size.   In much of the practical work being done, parts made in New York, for example, must be interchangeable with parts made, say, in California.   These sizes are controlled by limit dimensions.

Terminology.   The student should be familiar with the following special terms.

Nominal Size: A designation given to the subdivision of the unit of length having no specified limits of accuracy but indicating a close approximation to a standard size.

Basic Size: The exact theoretical size from which all limiting variations are made.[2]

Allowance: An intentional difference in the dimensions of mating parts; or the minimal clearance space which is intended between

[1] Cf. ASA B4.1 — 1947, *Limits and Fits for Engineering and Manufacturing.*
[2] *Ibid.*

mating parts. It represents the condition of the tightest permissible fit, or the largest internal member mated with the smallest external member. Its purpose is to provide for different classes of fit. Example: a shaft dimensioned 0.749 in. and a hole dimensioned 0.750 in. represent an allowance of 0.001 in. The same hole with a shaft dimensioned 0.751 in. represents an allowance of 0.001 in. also; but, as the shaft is larger than the hole, this allowance becomes a negative quantity.

Tolerance: The amount of variation permitted in the size of a part. Note that in the example under *Allowance*, the ideal condition and the tightest fit permissible have been given; but in manufacturing large numbers of pieces these sizes could not be produced exactly; consequently, variations must be made that will not prevent their proper functioning but will enable them to be produced. These variations must therefore tend toward greater looseness. Therefore, if a manufacturing tolerance of 0.001 in. were required on each member, they would be dimensioned as follows.

$$\text{Shaft } \frac{0.499''}{0.498''} \qquad \text{Hole } \frac{0.500''}{0.501''}$$

Limits: The following classification of fits is recommended.[1]

Loose Fit (Class 1) — Large Allowance. This fit provides for considerable freedom and embraces certain fits where accuracy is not essential. Examples: machined fits of agricultural and mining machinery; controlling apparatus for marine work; textile, rubber, candy, and bread machinery; general machinery of a similar grade; some ordnance material.

Free Fit (Class 2) — Liberal Allowance. For running fits with speeds of 600 r.p.m. or over, and journal pressures of 600 lbs. per sq. in. or over. Examples: dynamos, engines, many machine-tool parts, and some automotive parts.

Medium Fit (Class 3) — Medium Allowance. For running fits under 600 r.p.m. and with journal pressures less than 600 lbs. per sq. in.; also for sliding fits; and for the more accurate machine-tool and automotive parts.

Snug Fit (Class 4) — Zero Allowance. This is the closest fit which can be assembled by hand and necessitates work of con-

[1] *Ibid.*

siderable precision. It should be used where no perceptible shake is permissible and where moving parts are not intended to move freely under a load.

Wringing Fit (Class 5) — Zero to Negative Allowance. This is also known as a "tunking fit" and is practically metal-to-metal. Assembly is usually selective and not interchangeable.

Tight Fit (Class 6) — Slight Negative Allowance. Light pressure is required to assemble these fits and the parts are more or less permanently assembled, such as the fixed ends of studs for gears, pulleys, rocker arms, etc. These fits are used for drive fits in thin sections or extremely long fits in other sections and also for shrink fits on very light sections. Used in automotive, ordnance, and general machine manufacturing.

Medium Force Fit (Class 7) — Negative Allowance. Considerable pressure is required to assemble these fits and the parts are considered permanently assembled. These fits are used in fastening locomotive wheels, car wheels, armatures of dynamos and motors, and crank disks to their axles or shafts. They are also used for shrink fits on medium sections or long fits. These fits are the tightest which are recommended for cast-iron holes or external members as they stress cast iron to its elastic limit.

Heavy Force and Shrink Fit (Class 8) — Considerable Negative Allowance. These fits are used for steel holes where the metal can be highly stressed without exceeding its elastic limit. These fits cause excessive stress for cast-iron holes. Shrink fits are used where heavy force fits are impractical, as on locomotive wheel tires, heavy crank disks of large engines, etc.

Allowable tolerances in various classifications of fits are found in Appendix Tables 16–23.

Computation of Limit Dimensions[1]

BASIC HOLE SYSTEM. The most·common method of calculating limit dimensions is the basic hole system. By looking at the various tables of fits in the Appendix, it can be seen that one dimension of the hole is always the basic size. These tables were designed for use with the basic hole system.

Example: suppose the limit dimensions are to be determined

[1] *Ibid.*

of a $2''$ shaft with a Class 2 fit in a $2''$ hole. The nominal size of the hole is $2''$. Referring to the tables, the limits on the hole are $\dfrac{2.0000 + 0.0000}{2.0000 + 0.0016} = \dfrac{2.0000}{2.0016}$. The limits on the shaft are

$$\frac{2.0000 - 0.0022}{2.0000 - 0.0038} = \frac{1.9978}{1.9962}.$$

It will be noted from this example that the smallest dimension is above the line and the largest one is below the line. Likewise the dimensions of the shaft are expressed with the large dimension above the line and the small one below the line. The reason for expressing these dimensions in this manner is that the machinist in making these parts tries to make the piece the size of the dimension above the line. In the case of the shaft, if the machinist should remove a slight extra amount he still would be within the limits of the dimension below the line. The same reasoning applies to the hole.

BASIC SHAFT SYSTEM. In certain special cases it is sometimes necessary to have a number of pulleys, bearings, couplings, etc. having the same nominal size affixed to a piece of shafting. In a case of this type the basic shaft system is used.

The tables of fits can be converted to the basic shaft system by adding or subtracting the allowance to or from the basic shaft size, and then proceeding as for the basic hole system.

Example: suppose the limit dimensions are to be determined for a $2''$ shaft with a Class 5 fit in a $2''$ hole. Converting the basic shaft system to the basic hole system, we have the following results.

Basic shaft $\pm$ allowance $=$ basic hole

$2.0000 - 0.0005 = 1.9995$

The limits on the hole are $\dfrac{1.9995 + 0.0000}{1.9995 + 0.0008} = \dfrac{1.9995}{2.0003}$

The limits on the shaft are $\dfrac{1.9995 + 0.0005}{1.9995 + 0.0000} = \dfrac{2.0000}{1.9995}$

10

Working Drawings

The working drawing is the terminal drawing, which requires consolidation of all information already presented in this text, together with additional data to be developed in this chapter. Such drawings must be correct, proper, and complete.

The working drawing is the key to the construction of all mechanical, structural, architectural, and electrical contrivances. It is the graphic representation of an object with all the information necessary for its manufacture. The object represented should be so fully described that no additional data will be required to construct or erect it. Such a drawing consists of a pictorial representation of the shape of the object, shows its size and its material specifications, and provides a descriptive title conforming to the generally accepted conventions of the industry or trade.

Frequently, structural and architectural drawings require so many detailed explanatory notes on methods of workmanship and so many specifications of materials that confusion would result if all these data were placed on the working drawing. This information is, instead, set forth in a separate document in a form established by each firm but generally known in all trades as a specification sheet.

Working drawings may be classified under the broad headings of *detail drawings* and *assembly drawings*.

DETAIL DRAWINGS

Any device, system, or structure is initially conceived and drawn as an assembly, but it is later broken down into its individual parts and detailed for manufacture. The individual part, or detail, is customarily drawn in several orthographic views so that a complete description of its shape, size, and material specification is furnished to the workman who must make the piece.   In the interest of simplicity it is desirable to limit the number of views used; the liberal use of sectioning should be encouraged to obtain greater clarity.

Much time is saved when a part which is uniform in cross-section is detailed in one view only.   This is generally the case in machine-shop practice, where the objects are primarily cylindrical.   To facilitate reading of the drawing, the side view showing the circular shape of the object need not be used if the center line of the object and the diameter (abbreviated D) are given (Fig. 258).   These data

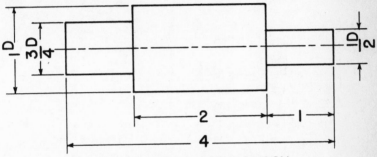

Fig. 258.   Detail Drawing of Cylindrical Object.

are essential, since the outline of a cylindrical object is shown merely as one or more rectangular shapes adjacent to each other and since the only clue to its cylindrical form is indicated by a center line and diametral dimensions (see Fig. 258).

The long line and short line, known as the *center line*, is commonly used to denote the axis of symmetry of a symmetrical object and is drawn through the center of all views of holes and circular objects. The use of diametral dimensions completes the description of the cylindrical object drawn in one view.

Individual Parts.   Wherever the manufacturing process is geared for mass production, the individual part is generally detailed on a single drawing sheet.   However, an individual part does not necessarily consist of one piece.   It may be made up of separate pieces that are permanently assembled by riveting, soldering, welding, or other means of assembly.   This procedure is used with less complex geometric structures, such as the cam in Fig. 259.

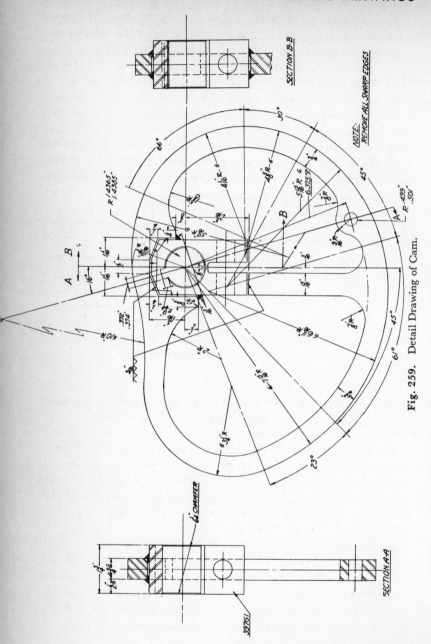

Fig. 259. Detail Drawing of Cam.

Subassemblies are usually necessary where the welded, brazed, or soldered pieces are assembled with offset parts or have other characteristics that compel the detailer to show the separate parts in their exact relationship to each other.

Requirements

SHAPE DESCRIPTION. Except in rare cases, orthographic projection is used almost exclusively for working drawings. Usually only three views are required to represent the form of an object adequately. Wherever parts are symmetrical, or nearly symmetrical, as with bushings, shafts, and coil springs, one view may adequately convey all the essential data regarding the size and shape of the part. A sufficient number of views, however, should always be employed to give a full description of the object, even if this procedure entails five or six views.

SIZE DESCRIPTION. It has long been established in the manufacturing process that all dimensional descriptions of detailed parts should be complete so that nothing will be left to the judgment of the workman. In order to obviate the necessity of the shopman's making calculations to obtain desired dimensions, all dimensions should be accurate, clear, and distinct. Dimensions should be neatly and systematically placed. They should be kept outside the outline of the part and preferably placed in a horizontal position.

Certain dimensions, such as installation dimensions, which have little bearing on the manufacturing of the part must be kept separate from production dimensions (see Fig. 303).

Choice of Views. The arrangement of views of an object is generally subject to the contour of the object and its intricacy. Although it is desirable to detail the individual part in the same position as it appears in the layout or assembly, this is sometimes confusing to the shopman and can cause unnecessary trouble. Some authorities say that detailing in this manner facilitates the reading and checking of the drawing, and clarifies the relationship of the parts, thereby making it easier for the assembler to erect the mechanism. It must be remembered, however, that the purpose of a detail drawing is to provide the mechanic with all the information he needs to make the part, and only those views which will aid his understanding of the drawing need be shown. The views shown and the position which they occupy on the drawing sheet should,

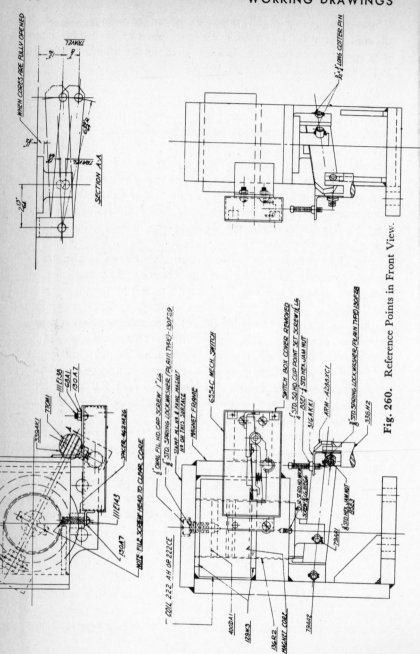

Fig. 260.   Reference Points in Front View.

in the judgment of the draftsman, contain all the data needed to manufacture the actual part.

In selecting the front or main view, several things should be borne in mind. The front view should be chosen to give, at a glance, the general profile or contour of the object. All other views are taken or developed from the front view. The front view of the detailed part, however, is not necessarily the front view when the object is assembled in the mechanism. It would be impractical to detail a piece at an odd angle simply because it is placed at that angle in the assembly. It is more desirable to consider the part according to its logical base surface or according to the position it will occupy in the processes of manufacture and inspection. In this way, if the part is not detailed in the same view as in the assembly drawing, reference points and additional dimensions may be provided to facilitate assembly of the piece, as in Figs. 260 and 261.

In locating parts that are to be machined, the part should always be drawn in the same position as it will appear when the specific operation is performed in the machine. For example, screw machine parts should be shown with the chucked end, or head, at the left, as in Fig. 262, because all machine operations are from the right to the left.

When the choice of end view or side view is made, the view which presents the least number of hidden or invisible lines and which conveys the best idea of the contour of the piece should be employed. The need for either view may be obviated if a note can better serve its purpose, or if a section view can be better used than an outside one, or if an auxiliary view may more adequately convey information to the shopman or mechanic.

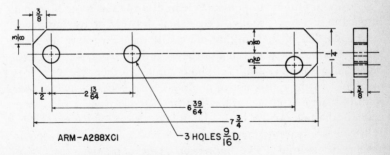

Fig. 261. Additional Dimensions in Front View.

Styles of Drafting.   There are many styles of drafting technique which are peculiar to the profession or trade in which they are developed.   Whatever the technique used, there is always opportunity for some artistic representation.

In the field of architecture, there is a positive need for artistic refinement, because the fine linework required and the pictorial characteristics of the subject matter are features which interest and attract the prospective buyer.

The ironclad rules set down in patent drawings by the United States Patent Office establish a very exact technique so that deviations from accepted practice are likely to disqualify a drawing.   The size of the drawing sheet, the restriction to the use of India ink, the character and color of linework, the size and type of lettering, etc. make all such drawings rigidly uniform in character.

There is almost an absence of formalized drafting style in tool design.   Positive linework and clarity seem to be the keynotes. Many things are left to the imagination because that type of drawing is done in close proximity to the shop, where the skill and judgment of the workman are usually just as good as those of the designer or draftsman.   Besides, many tools, jigs, and fixtures are not produced in great quantity, and a rough drawing is adequate for the needs of the work.

The ideal in good drafting style should embody the best points of the above-mentioned techniques.   The choice of views, their pleasing disposition on the drawing page, the contrasts of good linework, and the concise, logical arrangement of dimensions and notes are compositional principles which measure up to *style* in drawing.

The accomplishment of good style in drawing has some practical implications, too.   Usually, the original drawing or tracing never leaves the files of the drafting office.   If the drawing is used for sales promotion or advertising purposes, it must be reproduced as a blueprint, photostat, vandyke, photo-offset, or other type of reproduction.   In the reproductive process, even the best drawings lose some of their sharpness.   If the drawing is reduced in size and then printed, the fine quality of line often loses its distinctive character. It becomes apparent, therefore, that a neat, clear-cut drawing is absolutely essential.   The impression made upon the prospective purchaser should not be lessened by a poor drawing.

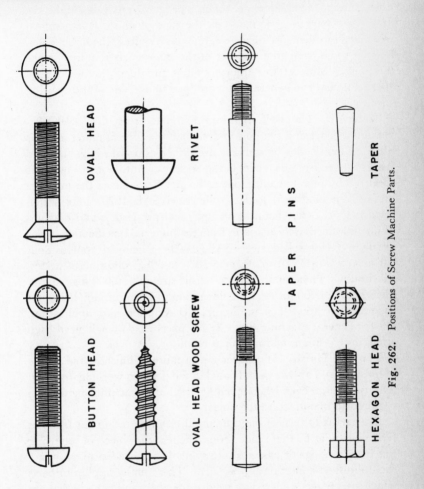

Fig. 262. Positions of Screw Machine Parts.

OVAL HEAD

RIVET

BUTTON HEAD

OVAL HEAD WOOD SCREW

TAPER PINS

HEXAGON HEAD

TAPER

Specifications. Facts about the size and shape of an object are not sufficient information to enable the shopman to produce that object in the machine shop. The workman must also know the material a part is to be made of, the type of finish, whether heat treatment or other specialized treatment is required, the size of holes, and, in some cases, the number of the same parts required in the assembly. Most of this information is provided in the form of specific notes or in general notes grouped to one side of the drawing sheet.

Material. The well-organized manufacturing firm uses conventional codes and symbols to designate the type of material to be used. These codes or symbols are either established by the firm itself or taken from the codes of the Society of Automotive Engineers (SAE). By merely calling out or listing the name of the material and its code number (e.g., Hot rolled steel, SAE, 1020), information regarding its type, chemical and physical properties, and machinability is immediately available from the material specification. For example, "Hot rolled steel, SAE, 1020. Chemical composition: carbon 15% to 25%; manganese 30% to 50%; phosphorus .045% maximum. Physical properties: tensile strength 60,000 lbs./sq. in.; yield point 28,000 lbs./sq. in.; elongation in 2" minimum 25%, and reduction of area 45% minimum. Description and application: (1) for general machine use; (2) for parts that do not need high strength; (3) forges and machines readily."

Types of Finish. Whenever a part must be finished, the degree of finish should always be indicated in the detailed working drawing. This is essential even when it is obvious that a machine operation is required to manufacture the object.

If a part is to receive only the usual cleaning treatment (such as removing material that is not a component of the object, or removing fins from forgings or castings), no symbols are needed to designate the unfinished condition of the part. This usually applies to parts which are brazed, soldered, or welded together, and to parts that are pressed, drawn, rolled, forged, or cast.

When a standard material, such as wire, cold rolled steel, sheet steel, brass rod, etc. is of adequate accuracy for the function it is to perform, there is no need for finished dimensions. A nominal dimension is sufficient with an optional designation of "commercial size" added to help clarify the specification of the item.

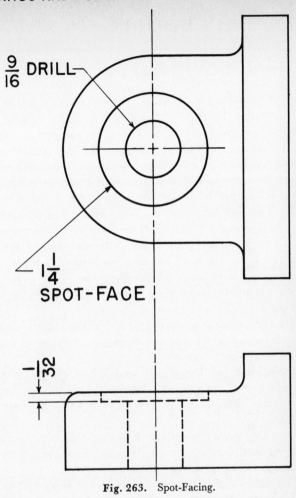

Fig. 263. Spot-Facing.

The degree of machined surface finishes will be shown on drawings according to the symbols used in the chapter on Dimensioning.

Castings and Forgings. If one of the standard finishes is used for forgings or castings, the allowances for machining are not indicated on the drawing. If it is desirable for some reason to use a special finish or allowance, this should be indicated on the drawing, wherever needed, by the use of phantom lines.

Wherever there is a surface on a casting or forging that calls for machining, the patternmaker or smith builds out the pattern or die to allow enough stock for finishing.

For a more detailed description of patternmaking for castings, see pp. 238–247.

Method of Spot-Facing.   Spot-facing is an economical, efficient type of finishing.   Instead of finishing an entire surface, this machining device provides a finished seat on castings or forgings for the bearing surface of flanged bushings, boltheads, washers, etc. After a hole has been drilled, reamed, or bored, a rotating milling cutter is applied to the rough surface of the piece, producing a smooth "spot" perpendicular to the center line of the hole (see Fig. 263).   The spot-face must be large enough in diameter to permit the flanged bushing, bolthead, etc. to fit without interference. The depth of the spot-face is usually left to the discretion of the shopman, who can see at first hand just how much spotting is needed to smooth the irregular surface.   If, however, the metal to be spot-faced is thin, a depth limit can be set by providing a dimension, such as $\frac{1}{64}''$ or $\frac{1}{32}''$.

In spot-facing a small boss, the diameter of the spot-face should be specified at least $\frac{1}{16}''$ larger than the diameter of the boss so that no unnecessary fins or burrs are left.

Use of Necking (or Grooving) and Chamfering.   Necking (or grooving) and chamfering are two machining procedures that promote greater facility in the assembly of shafts to bearings, housings, etc.

There are three types of shoulders to a shaft that may be turned on a lathe — namely, the square shoulder, the filleted shoulder, and the angular shoulder.   (See Fig. 264.)

The square shoulder is the plainest type but is limited in use because it cannot withstand excessive strain at the corner. It has some advantages, however, in that it affords a flat surface for perfect mating of parts and can also be used as an end bearing.

The filleted shoulder is more commonly used for the additional strength it provides at the corner.   A good mating surface can be obtained with this type of shoulder by chamfering the housing as shown in Fig. 265.   Chamfering is also used at the end of most shafts and semifinished or finished bolts to facilitate assembly and for better appearance (Figs. 266A, 266B).

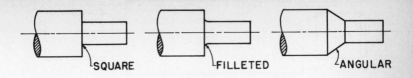

Fig. 264. Types of Shoulders.

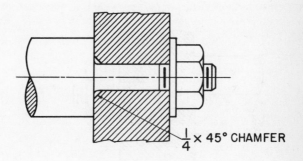

$\frac{1}{4}$ × 45° CHAMFER

Fig. 265. Filleted Shoulder.

CHAMFER & NECK TO
    THREAD DEPTH

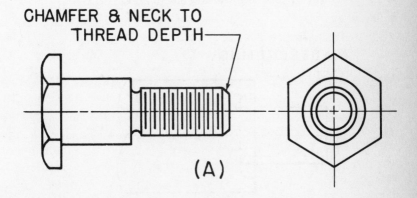

(A)

Fig. 266A. Example of Chamfering and Necking.

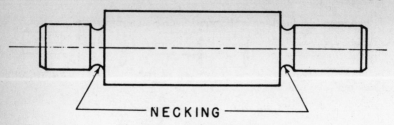

— NECKING —

Fig. 266B.   Example of Necking.

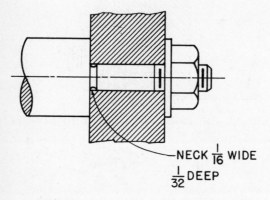

— NECK $\frac{1}{16}$ WIDE

$\frac{1}{32}$ DEEP

Fig. 267.   Shoulder Requiring Strength at Corner.

UNDERCUTTING

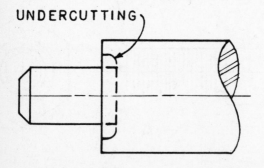

Fig. 268.   Alternative Type of Undercutting.

The angular shoulder is the most economical of all the shoulders to produce in quantity, but it is not so strong at the corner as the filleted corner shoulder (see Fig. 264).

Necking or grooving is the machining process of undercutting or recessing a cylindrical piece. The "neck" or groove is cut to provide a perfect mating of parts at the shoulder corner. This obviates the chamfering of the housing, which is necessary with a filleted-cornered shoulder; but it cannot be used where strength at the corner is essential (Fig. 267). This type of finish has other functions, too. The grooves are cut at the end of threads or provide space for a threading tool at the shoulder. Thus a full thread can be made almost to the very edge of the shoulder (Fig. 266A). After a cylinder has been turned, a groove is cut at the shoulder when a grinding operation is required. This provides clearance for the grinding tool, thereby preventing the grinding wheel from striking the side of the shoulder.

Another type of undercutting is illustrated in Fig. 268. As in the necking or grooving operations, described above, this alternative type of undercutting eliminates the need for chamfering the smaller diameter of the shaft and facilitates more accurate fit of the shaft to its housing.

Drilled Holes. If the diameter of the finished size of a drilled hole is satisfactory for the function that it must perform, the size of the hole may be indicated in a note as "$\frac{1}{2}''$ Drill," or if the size of the hole is standard for a drill number (cf. Appendix Table 1) it may be indicated as "#10 (.190″) Drill." If a letter-sized drill is used, it will be noted as "$\frac{\text{X (.3970″)}}{\text{Drill}}$." Whenever the same-sized drills are equally spaced on a circular piece the size of the drill, the quantity of the same drill and their spacing can be written as "$\frac{13}{16}$ Drill, 5 Holes Equally Spaced," as in Fig. 269. If the holes are unequally spaced they are located by indicating angular dimensions.

Reamed and Bored Holes. Accurate holes that require a smooth surface and are held to close tolerances are either reamed or bored. In reaming, the hole is drilled undersize and then a reamer is applied to size the hole to the given tolerance so that the hole becomes smooth, straight, and round. (For standard and oversize reamers, see Appendix Table 24.) This process is indicated on the

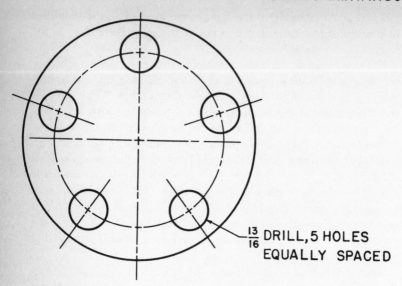

$\frac{13}{16}$ DRILL, 5 HOLES
EQUALLY SPACED

Fig. 269.   Drilled Holes.

drawing by the symbols "$\sqrt{}$Ream $\frac{.249''}{.251''}$" or finish ground by the symbol "$\sqrt{}$Ground $\frac{.749''}{.751''}$."   Boring is somewhat similar to reaming except that the hole is enlarged and made concentric by the use of a boring tool.   The basic difference between reaming and boring is that reaming is limited by the available sizes of the reamer whereas boring can be done to any odd sizes.

Countersinks and Counterbores.   A countersunk hole is a cone-shaped recess cut at one end of a hole to accommodate a countersink flathead screw or bolt.   A counterboring is the enlarging of one end of a hole to a given size and depth to receive the head of a screw or bolt.   This type of bore has parallel sides and a square shoulder.   The size of the hole and countersink or counterbore varies with the type and size of screw or bolt to be used.   Therefore either of these machining operations is indicated in a note as in Figs. 270 and 271.   The actual diameter and depth of the countersink or counterbore is a standard measurement and is determined by the diameter of the bolt or screw used.

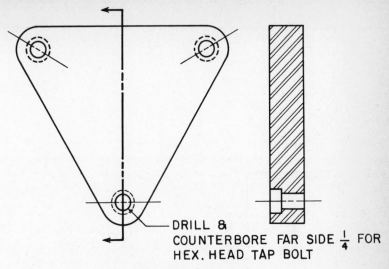

DRILL &
COUNTERBORE FAR SIDE $\frac{1}{4}$ FOR
HEX. HEAD TAP BOLT

Fig. 270.   Counterbore.

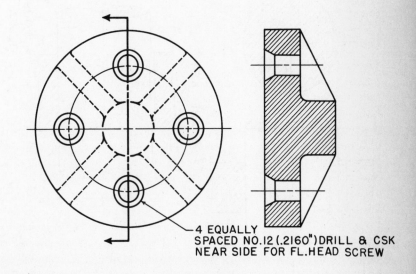

4 EQUALLY
SPACED NO.12(.2160")DRILL & CSK
NEAR SIDE FOR FL.HEAD SCREW

Fig. 271.   Countersink.

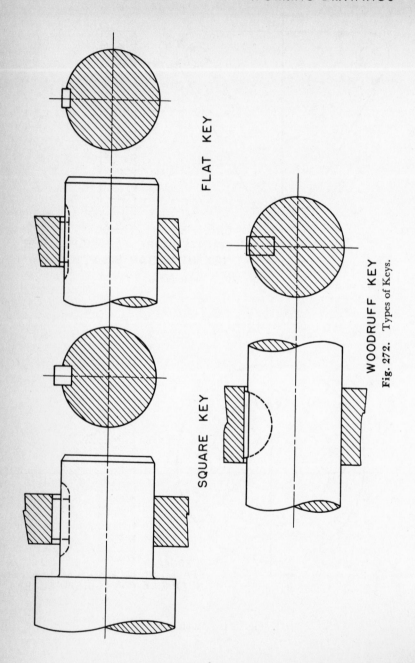

FLAT KEY

SQUARE KEY

WOODRUFF KEY

Fig. 272. Types of Keys.

The main function of countersinks and counterbores is to provide clearance for moving parts or parts that are so close together that the height of an ordinary screw or bolthead would interfere with the assembly of the pieces. They are also used to improve the appearance of the assembled product.

See Appendix Table 25 for sizes of the clearance holes for countersinking flathead screws in thin metal stock.

Keys and Keyways. A keyway is a groove milled into a shaft and the hub of its mating part to receive the key which locks both into place. The function of the key is to prevent motion between the shaft and the gear, pulley, or lever to which it is locked.

There are many types of keys, but the most widely used ones are flat, square, and Woodruff keys, as shown in Fig. 272. (Cf. Appendix Tables 10–14.)

The flat key is used in cases where a deep groove would greatly weaken the hub of the mating piece or shaft.

The square key, as well as the flat key, is used for light-duty work. In specifying these two keys, there are certain rules of proportion which should be observed. The depth of the keyway, measured at the side of the keyway and not at the center line, should equal one-half the height of the key ($\pm .005''$). The depth in the hub, measured also at the side of the groove, should be one-half the height of the key plus $\frac{1}{64}''$ ($\pm .005''$). The length of the key should equal one and one-half times the diameter of the shaft but may be made to suit the length of the hub, torque, etc.

The Woodruff key is specified according to established standards. The key number indicates the nominal key dimensions set up by the American Standards Association. The last two digits give the nominal diameter in eighths of an inch, and the preceding digits give the nominal width in thirty-seconds of an inch. Thus 404 means a key $\frac{4}{32}'' \times \frac{4}{8}''$ (or $\frac{1}{8}'' \times \frac{1}{2}''$). Number 1010 indicates a $\frac{10}{32}'' \times \frac{10}{8}''$ (or $\frac{5}{16}'' \times 1\frac{1}{4}''$) key.

A good method of proportioning a Woodruff key to a specific shaft is to lay it out so that its radius is one-half the radius of the shaft and its width is equal to one-fourth the diameter of the shaft. The radius of the key should be taken at a center one-half the width of the key above the shaft.

Pins. A pin is a small shaft whose chief use is in systems of levers of mechanical linkage. It may be either free-moving or

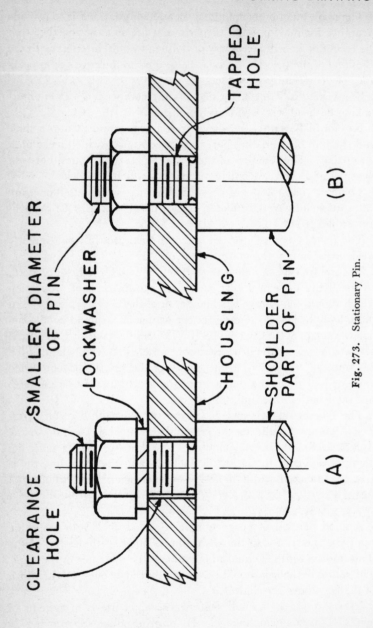

Fig. 273. Stationary Pin.

fixed (stationary) in a housing. (See Appendix Tables 26 and 27 for these two types of pins.)

The pin is designed to provide a grip or surface, upon which a lever, arm, or link can move, and the necessary holes at either end for the insertion of cotter pins. (Appendix Table 28 suggests appropriate pins for any desired purpose. This table also gives the location and size of drilled holes for the particular size and length of cotter pin required. Appendix Table 26 provides the appropriate clearance hole in the lever, arm, or link for the pin selected or used.)

The two most common methods of stationary-pin design are (1) riveting over one end, and (2) welding one end to its housing. Both methods require the design of a shoulder pin. (Appendix Table 26 lists the recommended size of clearance holes for the smaller diameter of the shoulder pins. Once the size of the clearance hole has been determined, Appendix Table 27 provides the following data: (1) the correct size of the smaller pin diameter, (2) the method of machining, riveting, or welding of the smaller pin diameter to its housing, and (3) the minimum diameter of the shoulder of the pin.)

Another accepted method of producing a stationary pin involves threading the smaller diameter of the pin and bolting it to the housing. (See Figs. 273A and 273B.) The disadvantage of this method is that the threaded part of the pin, plus the lockwasher and nut, form a projection which may present clearance difficulties where levers must move in close proximity. There is also the risk, when this method is used, that the nut may work itself loose — this could not happen with the riveted or welded methods.

The hole in the housing may be a clearance (in which case the nut and the lockwasher hold the pin in place [see Fig. 273A]), or the hole may be tapped into the housing, thereby providing a more secure or positive bearing for the pin and employing the nut as a locknut (see Fig. 273B). It should be noted that this method also requires a shoulder pin.

Gauges. The word "gauge" has numerous meanings. For engineers and draftsmen, a gauge is an exact measurement of a distance from one point, or center line, to another point, or center line. There are certain recommended gauges, for instance, for the location of holes in structural shapes. (Appendix Table 29 lists the prescribed gauges for structural angles, channels, and beams. Appendix

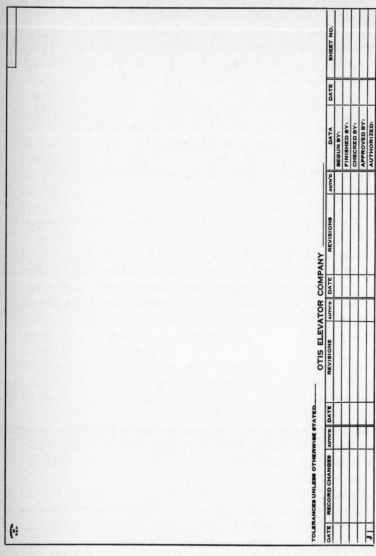

Fig. 274. Title Block.

Table 30 furnishes the minimum gauges in angles for bolts and nuts. For situations where it is necessary to work to closer gauges than those recommended in Table 29, Table 30 outlines the absolute minimum gauges permissible in structural angles.)

Title. The drawing, with its notes and dimensions, must bear a title block with the name of the piece, the manufacturer, the scale, the date, the draftsman's name, the tracer's name, the name telling by whom approved, the drawing number, and the change record. The title block varies with the firm, trade, or system set up by the manufacturer. Most large firms have established their own standard title block, printed on standard-sized sheets of tracing cloth or paper. The draftsman fills in all the required information. (An example of the Otis Elevator Company's title block is reproduced in Fig. 274.)

NAME OF PIECE. The name of a part is generally chosen according to its appearance or function. However, each trade uses names and terminology peculiar to itself. At times, neither of these factors is considered in naming a piece. For instance, a name may be given to a part or machine simply because that name has advertising appeal.

MANUFACTURER. The manufacturer's name always appears on the drawing sheet whether it is a printed form or a title block drawn by the draftsman. The address of the firm or plant is usually included.

SCALE. The size of the piece to be drawn generally determines the scale in which it will be drawn. Ideally, it is desirable to represent detail drawings in full scale. But when the part is large, it may not fit on a standard sheet of paper if it is detailed to scale; in this case, the scale may be reduced to a simple ratio of one-half or one-quarter size. Conversely, if the part is small and a full-scale drawing of it is not sufficiently clear, or if it is impossible to indicate all the details, it is desirable to draw it double or triple scale to facilitate reading.

Wherever it is necessary to draw a piece not in actual size, a full-scale drawing of one external view should be added to one side of the drawing sheet. In this way, a person trained to read and interpret a drawing does not have to visualize the part in its actual size.

Whenever minor dimensional changes must be made to a drawing without changing the picture, it is permissible to use out-of-scale dimensions. All out-of-scale dimensions should be underscored (for example, $\underline{2''}$ or $\underline{\frac{3}{4}''}$) because the picture is then no longer true to scale. Besides, the underscored dimensions serve as a clue to the tracer, who might otherwise redraw the piece as he originally found it, thereby perpetuating the out-of-scale condition.

DATE. The "begun date" is the date on which the draftsman starts to draw the piece. It should be the first notation the draftsman puts down after tacking his drawing sheet to the board. If a tracing is remade because a drawing has been lost, destroyed, or ruined, the original "begun date" is used again as a matter of record. The official date of the drawing may be the "begun date" or the "finished date" depending on the ruling established by the individual firm. The effective date of the drawing however, reverts to the date of revision whenever it occurs. Some firms establish the official date of the drawing on the date of authorization, revision, or record change.

DRAWN BY AND TRACED BY. The initials of the draftsman or tracer are placed next to the legend "Drawn by" or "Traced by," respectively. In all cases the initials should be separate letters. The use of monograms is most undesirable. Some firms permit the draftsman to use his full name.

CHECKED BY AND APPROVED BY. The rules to be followed in these two instances are substantially the same as for "Drawn by" and "Traced by."

PART NUMBER AND DRAWING NUMBER. The key to the records of a manufacturing firm centers around the part number and drawing number. Most firms have an elaborate system of numbering parts and drawings in order to manufacture, record, and order all items that are used.

The part number serves as an identification of the part in the files of the drafting room, the specifier, the shop, and the man who assembles the mechanism from individual parts. In many cases, the part number is the same as the drawing number except for a suffix number. Whatever the system used, the part number and drawing number are the basic elements of the entire system.

CHANGE RECORD. In the course of drawing, specifying, and manufacturing, there are occasions when a drawing must be changed to comply with a request from the factory, the specifier, or the

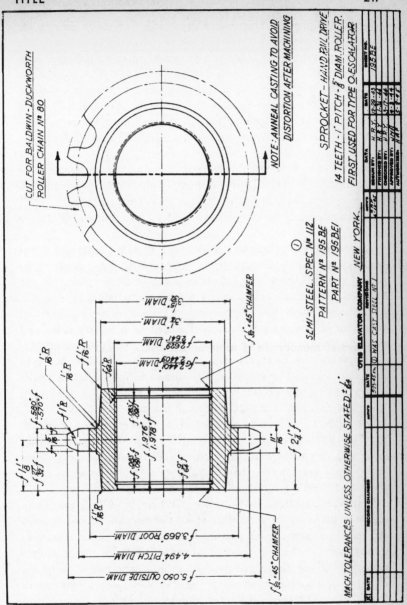

Fig. 275. Revision Shown in Title Block.

designing engineer. This does not include a checker's request for changes, because the drawing has not yet been put into production and any number of changes can be made without the need for a record change.

The date of the revision is very important because it definitely establishes the effective date of the drawing. Once the drawing has been released for production, all changes must be recorded so that up-to-date blueprints may be distributed to all departments concerned.

The revision is usually numbered, the number appearing in a circle next to the revised part on the drawing. A brief explanation of the revision is made in the revision space, as shown in Fig. 275. This becomes a readily accessible record of the origin and character of the revision.

Approved Violations of Projection. In many instances it has been found that the true projection of a drawn object is very confusing and awkward and results in visual misconceptions of the detailed part. As a result, many objects are detailed in violation of the established rules of true projection. The use of approved violations of projection minimizes the need for auxiliary views and saves time for drawing and allotted space on the drawing sheet.

HOLES IN CIRCULAR OR FLANGED OBJECTS. Drilled holes in flanges or circular objects should be shown in true relations to the center line of the holes and the other edge of the flange, even though the section is not taken through the axes of the holes.

View B in Fig. 276, a true section of the flanged cover, is misleading and difficult to visualize correctly. View A in the same diagram provides a clearer picture of the disposition of the holes. View A shows the holes in their true radial distance from the center of the piece and slightly rotated into the plane of the section.

SYMMETRICAL VIEWS OR SECTIONS. When the oblique part of an object is projected in section or view, the angular portion is foreshortened, creating an undesirable representation of the object, as shown in Fig. 277A. It is better to violate the rules of true projection by revolving the oblique portion so that it is parallel to the plane of projection and then showing the end view accordingly, as in Fig. 277B. This presents a truer representation than the view that is theoretically correct.

RIBS IN SECTION. When a section is taken longitudinally through

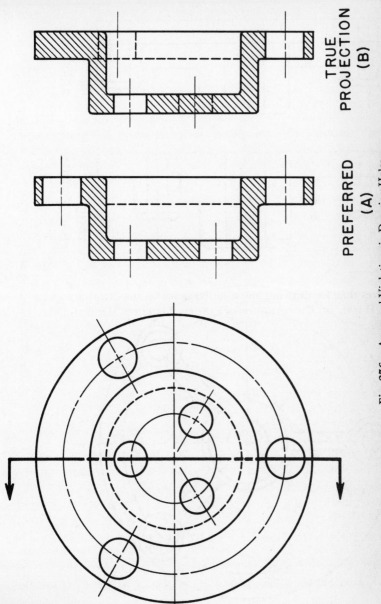

Fig. 276. Approved Violations in Drawing Holes.

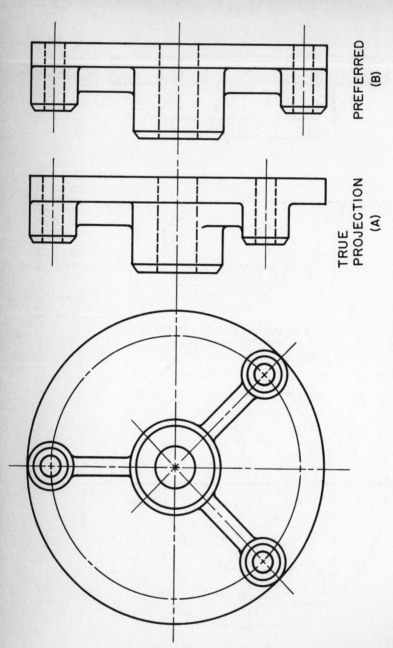

PREFERRED
(B)

TRUE
PROJECTION
(A)

Fig. 277. Projection of Oblique Part.

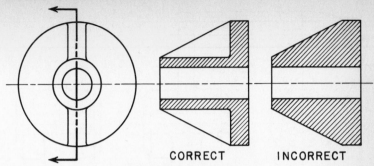

Fig. 278. Rib in Section.

a rib, the rib is not cross-sectioned or cross-hatched, because it is then misleading and hard to understand. It is projected as though the cutting plane were immediately in front of the rib, as shown in Fig. 278. This presents a truer picture of what the object really represents. In addition to webs and ribs, screws, bolts, nuts, taper pins, cotter pins, and washers are never sectioned.

ALIGNMENT OR ROTATED METHOD. An object which has one part offset at an angle is generally aligned in end view with foreshortening. The angular portion is revolved in end view or section much as the rib of a pulley is rotated to give a clearer picture of the object shown. (This method is shown in Fig. 279.)

BOLTHEADS. In working drawings, when a hexagon bolt is shown across corners in one view it is shown again across corners in the other view, instead of across flats, so that the space requirement for the larger dimension of the bolthead is shown (see Fig. 280). If the hexagon-head bolt were drawn across flats, it would appear like a square-head bolt; and, therefore, it would be difficult to identify the bolt as a hexagon-head bolt. A view shown across corners is always preferred, as illustrated in Fig. 280.

DEVELOPED SHAPES. When a bent piece is detailed, it is customary to show it in a developed view and in a developed length, as illustrated in Fig. 281. The purpose of this unconventional treatment is twofold: (1) to ascertain the actual length of the piece, and (2) to locate the holes in the same relationship as they would be when punched or drilled before the metal is bent. The established principle that the shopman should not be required to make calculations to obtain data regarding the making of the piece is another reason for providing the shopman with the developed length.

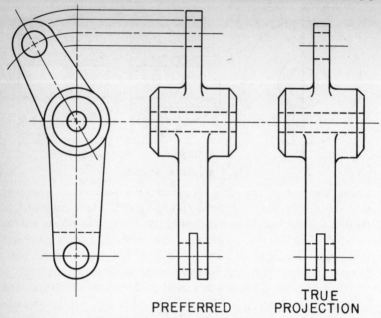

PREFERRED

TRUE
PROJECTION

Fig. 279. Alignment or Rotated Method.

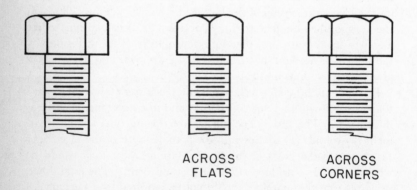

ACROSS
FLATS

ACROSS
CORNERS

Fig. 280. Views of Bolthead.

(Many designs require the actual development and intersection of surfaces. These are treated as a separate section of working drawings.)

UNTRUE PROJECTION. Frequently, the simple device of moving a line slightly out of true projection has its justification if by this practice an important phase of the drawing becomes clearer. When, in a side-view projection, two details of a part coincide so that they appear as one line, as shown in Fig. 282A, a clear picture of the part is not obtained. If lines *C* are moved slightly out of true projection, as in Fig. 282B, a far clearer picture is presented.

INTERSECTIONS. Many machine parts are designed with two or more intersecting curved portions. When these parts are detailed, it is expedient to conventionalize the points of intersection rather than plot the curves as they actually exist. (This method is shown in Figs. 283 to 290.) It is another desirable departure from the theory of true projection.

The intersection of holes, cylindrical forms, and curved and bent objects is conventionalized for reasons of clarity and facility of drawing and reading. The examples shown in Figs. 283 to 290 are

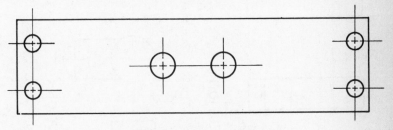

DEVELOPED LENGTH

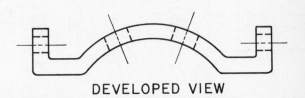

DEVELOPED VIEW

Fig. 281.   Detail of Bent Piece.

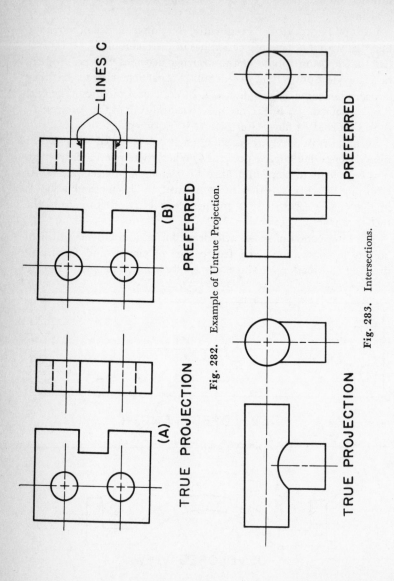

Fig. 282. Example of Untrue Projection.

Fig. 283. Intersections.

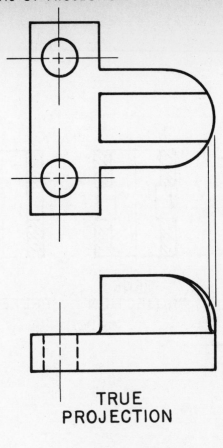

TRUE
PROJECTION

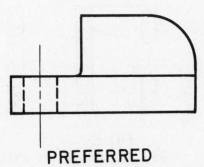

PREFERRED

Fig. 284. Intersections.

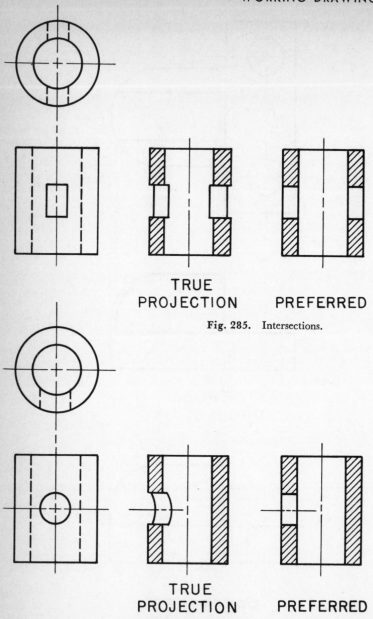

TRUE
PROJECTION   PREFERRED

Fig. 285.   Intersections.

TRUE
PROJECTION   PREFERRED

Fig. 286.   Intersections.

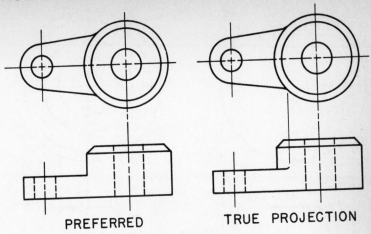

Fig. 287. Intersections.

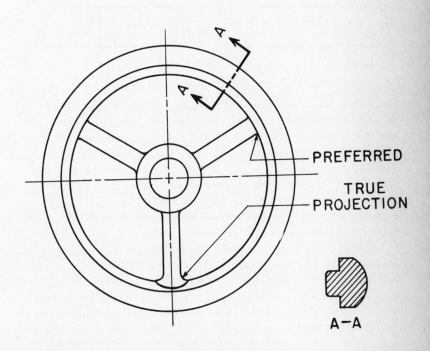

Fig. 288. Intersections.

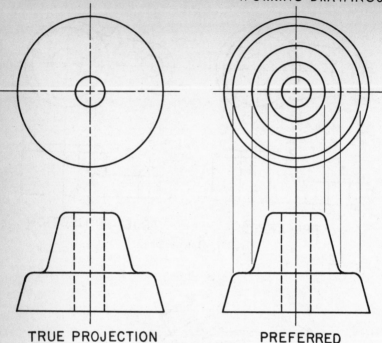

TRUE PROJECTION   PREFERRED

Fig. 289. Intersections.

generally accepted in engineering offices. (Where it is necessary to manufacture an object to rigid specifications, the intersections of surfaces must be accurately developed. In such cases, these intersections are represented as separate views in the working drawings.)

Fillets and Rounds. A *fillet* is a radial surface connecting two surfaces that are usually at right angles to each other. The fillet is used to avoid sharp internal angles in cast pieces that may have a tendency to crack or fracture. Greater strength is obtained by adding a fillet to such a critical point.

The radius of the fillet depends on the amount of strength needed, the amount of clearance desired, and the type and thickness of the metal. Generally, the size of fillets should be equal in radius to the thickness of the wall to which the fillet is applied. Fillets should be, wherever possible, uniform in size throughout the casting. When there is no special reason for giving the dimension of the fillet's radius, the fillet is indicated in the drawing and the dimension is left to the judgment of the patternmaker.

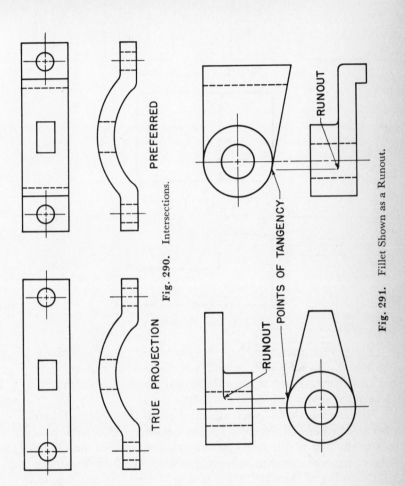

PREFERRED

Fig. 290.   Intersections.

TRUE PROJECTION

RUNOUT

POINTS OF TANGENCY

RUNOUT

Fig. 291.   Fillet Shown as a Runout.

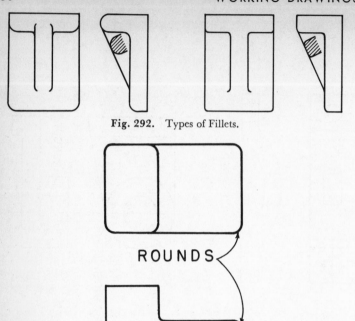

Fig. 292. Types of Fillets.

Fig. 293. Rounds.

The fillet is shown only in the views where its actual shape is indicated. In some views the fillet is shown as a "runout," a conventional way of indicating a theoretical line at the point of intersection, as shown in Figs. 291 and 292.

Exterior rounded corners are called *rounds* (Fig. 293). External corners are normally rounded for easy handling and for appearance. As in the case of fillets, the patternmaker dimensions the radius of the corner when the corner is not dimensioned on the drawing.

Grouping of Details. Some industrial firms group two or more details on one drawing sheet instead of detailing each part on a separate piece of paper. This method is economical if only a limited number of the parts are intended for production. In mass production, however, this method is decidedly inadequate both from the point of view of the drafting room and from that of the filing and record department.

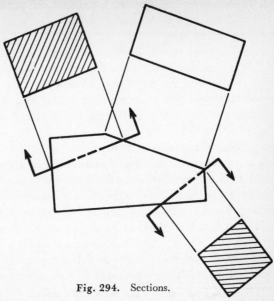

Fig. 294.   Sections.

In many instances, particularly where the device is small or where it consists of few parts, both the assembly and the detail are shown on one drawing sheet.   Wherever the device is large, the maximum number of details are placed on several sheets, and the assembly is drawn on a separate sheet.   The pitfalls of this method are over-crowding and poor arrangement of views in an effort to economize on space.

Grouped drawings are usually drawn in smaller scales for the obvious reason that more drawings can fit on one sheet.   When parts are detailed in reduced scale, it is desirable to maintain the same scale throughout.

Careful thought by the draftsman is necessary when detailing parts.   He must consider proper spacing and wisely chosen views, and he must plan the drawing as a logical and pleasing unit.   It is very often helpful to "rough-in" the parts and their views, allowing for sufficient space between views to permit proper dimensioning and the addition of notes, if necessary.

It is also desirable to allow enough space to show sections in their logical position at right angles to the cutting plane, as shown in Fig. 294.   This practice has the advantage of establishing the precision of the section by direct projection and makes it easier to understand the engineering significance of the part.

Tabulated Drawings. Most large industrial establishments, whose manufacturing process frequently involves thousands of parts, find that many similar parts whose features are alike can be easily tabulated. Variations in dimensions, wherever they occur, are designated by letters and recorded next to the part number; thus one drawing serves as many, each with an individual set of dimensions. (See Fig. 295.)

This method of detailing is economical, particularly with firms carrying a line of items that are similar but that are produced in graduated sizes. Such firms usually stock their bins with these standard items for immediate use or delivery.

Standard Parts. Numerous commercial commodities are produced by firms that specialize in such products. For example, nuts and bolts, screws, washers, bushings, bearings, springs, spring rings, lubricator fittings, oil seals, shims and gaskets, cotter pins, taper pins, dowels, and rivets are purchased by companies whose manu-

SINGLE ROW - RADIAL - DEEP GROOVE - BALL BEARINGS
PURCHASED

BEARING - BALL
SINGLE ROW
RADIAL
BOOK I

WITHOUT SHIELDS, SPECIFY - MRC 30, 200-S, 300-S, 400-S SERIES OR EQUAL
WITH SINGLE SHIELD, SPECIFY - MRC 30-F, 200-SF, 300-SF, 400-SF SERIES OR EQUAL
WITH DOUBLE SHIELD, SPECIFY - MRC 30-FF, 200-SFF, 300-SFF, 400-SFF SERIES OR EQUAL

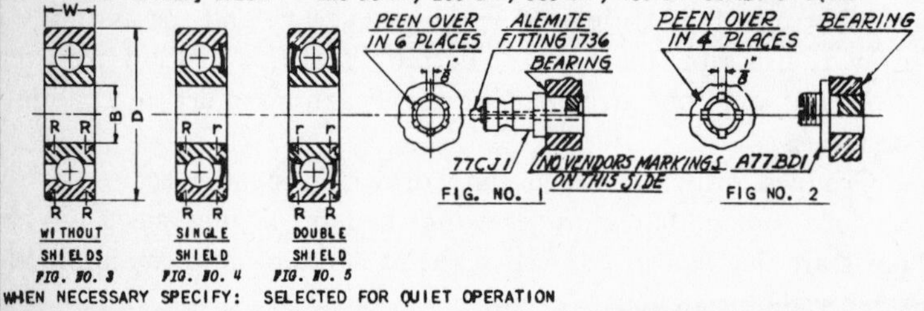

WHEN NECESSARY SPECIFY: SELECTED FOR QUIET OPERATION

PART NO.	MFRG. NO. OR EQUAL †	B	D	W	R *	r *	FIG. NO.	REMARKS
207Z1	MRC 404-S SPL.RAD.R	.7870 .7874	2.8346 2.8340	.748 .743	†† .04		3	** Selected For Quiet Operation
207Z2							1	207Z1 With Pin And Alemite Fitting
207Z3	MRC 202-SFF	.5903 .5906	1.3780 1.3775	.4331 .4281	.025	.012	5	
207Z4							2	207Z3 With Pin
207Z5	MRCf 203-S	.6690 .6693	1.5748 1.5743	.4724 .4674	.04		3	
207Z6	MRC 36	.2359 .2362	.7480 .7476	.2362 .2312	.02	.02	3	

Fig. 295. Tabulated Drawing.

facturing facilities do not encompass commercial parts of this nature. However, these items are generally drawn and included in the commodity lists of the purchaser because the engineering departments of the purchasing firms need the basic information regarding the parts.   The picture of each part, with its dimensions and material specifications, is information that is needed by the designing engineer.   When a commercial part is detailed, the catalog number, name, or trade-mark of the manufacturer is usually included with the basic data.   (Fig. 295 shows all the desired information.)   There are, however, certain large firms which do not permit any information on a drawing which would in any way identify the manufacturer.   The nature of such a working drawing lends itself readily to the tabular type.

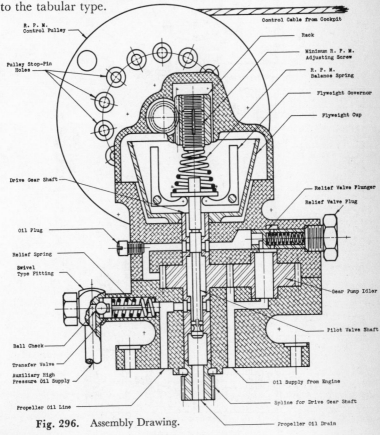

Fig. 296.   Assembly Drawing.

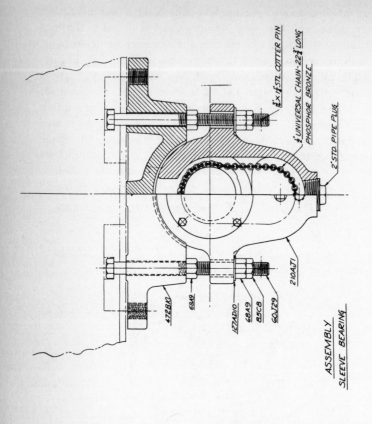

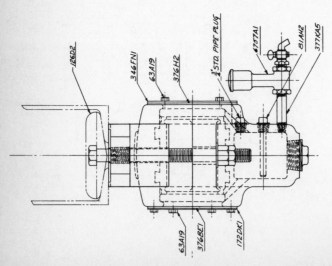

Fig. 297. Assembly Drawing.

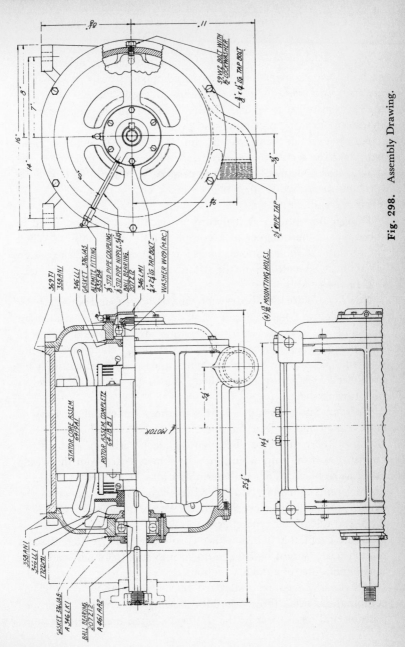

Fig. 298. Assembly Drawing.

ASSEMBLY DRAWINGS

A drawing illustrating an assembled mechanism or structure, showing the exact relationship of its component parts, is known as an *assembly drawing*. (The assemblies in Figs. 296, 297, and 298 should be studied carefully, for they contain much valuable information on drafting procedure and practice.)

An assembly drawing may be shown in one, two, or three views with as many sections as needed, depending on the intricacy of the machine or structure. Wherever possible, it is desirable to draw a mechanism with one main view plus a cross-section view, as in Figs. 297 and 298.

Design Assembly. A structure or machine is first conceived in the mind of the designer as a complete unit or assembly. When the function of the assembled parts has been established, the design assembly is turned over to the draftsman to be drawn into details and final assembly.

New layouts are usually drawn by the designer to full size wherever practicable, and are generally not dimensioned. The draftsman marks off his distances with dividers and applies these distances to his drawing when full scale is used in detailing. If the scale is not the same as the layout, the draftsman measures distances with his architect's scale and converts them to a larger or smaller scale on his drawing sheet.

Unit or Subassembly. It is sometimes impossible to draw a complicated mechanism on one sheet of paper without creating confusion and disorder. Frequently, mechanisms of this nature consist of several units which may be shown apart from the whole as subassemblies. These subassemblies may be treated as separate, distinct units and may be referred to by notes or numbers on the general assembly whenever a general assembly is used. (Fig. 299 is an example of this type of assembly.)

In the event that the machine is so closely interrelated that its mating parts cannot be broken down into subassemblies, one must make liberal use of auxiliary sections.

Individual parts are designated by names, numbers, letters, or combinations of all three. Besides showing each part in its proper position and identifying it, the draftsmen often must provide more

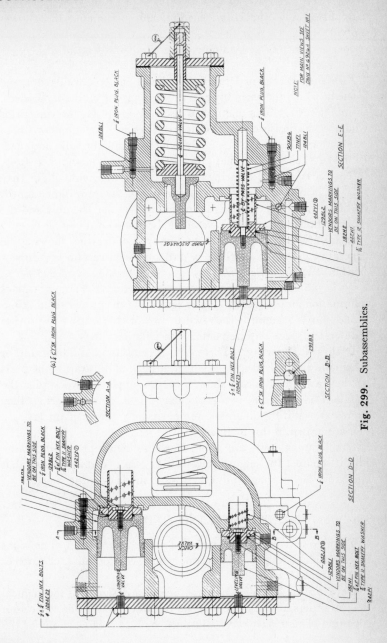

Fig. 299. Subassemblies.

careful assembly instructions (see Fig. 300). The notes designating individual parts assist the assembler in assembling the parts in proper sequence or in obtaining the desired adjustment for the various parts.

Assembly Working Drawings. An assembly working drawing is one in which the assembly and its parts appear on the same sheet, as in Fig. 301. This method is used by many engineering firms whose work consists either of simple devices or of machines or whose production is limited to one model which eventually is discontinued. In the latter case, individual production drawings are not necessary.

The parts of each drawing may be detailed individually or they may be drawn only in the assembly where they are dimensioned. At times the simpler parts are dimensioned on the assembly and the more complicated parts are detailed elsewhere on the same sheet.

Installation Drawing. An outline type of drawing showing the general contour of a machine or structure with certain key dimensions is called an *installation drawing*. (See Figs. 302 and 303.)

An installation drawing serves several functions. First, it displays information for the erection of the device and the proper relationship of its units. Second, it is drawn in two or three views to provide data on the space requirements for installation.

Diagram Drawing. There are several types of diagram or schematic assembly drawings which, instead of illustrating the parts as they actually appear, show them in simple linework plus the standard symbols of the particular phase of engineering they represent. Wiring diagrams, piping layouts, power-plant layouts, etc. are drawn in this manner.

Small piping units are often drawn as they appear, but large layouts compel the engineering firm to resort to diagrams so that the entire layout may be indicated on a single drawing sheet.

PATTERNMAKING AND CASTINGS

The frequent use of cast pieces of varied shapes and dimensions in mechanical design warrants our special consideration of patternmaking for castings.

Decision on Use of Casting. Before a designer of mechanical devices orders a part to be cast, he must determine whether or not a casting of that part can be justified by reason of economy or the

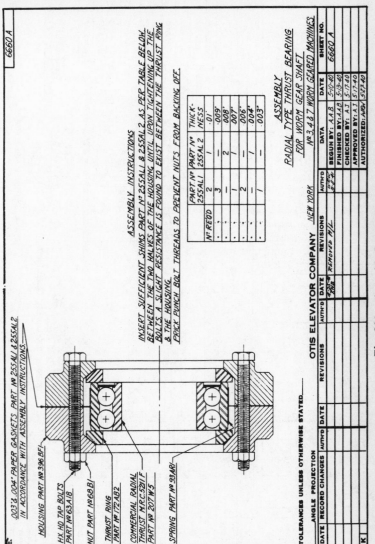

Fig. 300. Assembly Instructions.

1. Units are to be furnished with keys for keying the couplings on high speed and on both ends of the slow speed shafts.
2. Units must be good for delivering a torque of 1300 inch pounds on the slow speed shaft when the high speed shaft is operating at 1800 RPM.
3. The slow speed gear is to be of high grade phosphor bronze.
4. The high speed gear is to be made of Phenol canvas or Phenol liner.
5. The worms are to be of S.A.E. Specification #1020 steel, case hardened and polished.
6. The starting efficiency must not be less than 15% for operation from the high speed shaft.
7. The running efficiency, when operating at 1800 RPM on the high speed shaft, must not be less than 50%.
8. All joints and connections must be substantially protected against oil leakage when the unit is in its normal operating position and the oil level is at its required height.
9. Inasmuch as this unit is to be used on top of an elevator car, quietness of operation under full load and no load is essential. This company reserves the right to reject the units which, in our judgment, are not sufficiently quiet.
10. The high speed and intermediate speed shafts are to be provided with thrust bearings, each consisting of a Tobin bronze washer keyed to the shaft and a hardened and ground steel washer free to rotate between the cast iron housing and the cast iron end cap. The thrust washers are to be equipped with suitable oil grooves for lubrication. The slow speed shaft is to be equipped with hardened and ground steel thrust washers between the hub of the bronze gear and the cast end cap.
11. Radial bearings shall be of the sleeve type and must be so designed as to amply receive and distribute lubricating oil from inside the housing.
12. End play in worm shaft shall not exceed .005". End play in intermediate and slow speed shafts shall not exceed .003".
13. The weight of the unit less the oil shall not exceed 50%.

ASSEMBLY PART N°	GEAR RATIO
604941	225 to 1
604942	170 to 1
604943	127 to 1
604944	100 to 1
604945	96 to 1
604946	300 to 1
604947	112 to 1
604948	80 to 1

ASSEMBLY
WORM GEAR REDUCTION UNIT

FULL SIZE SECTION THROUGH SLOW SPEED SHAFT

CONSTRUCTION OF HUB OF SLOW SPEED GEAR

2 SPECIAL INGO WOODRUFF KEYS, ⅛ THICK ⅝ LONG

OIL GROOVE, ¼ DEEP ⅜ WIDE

UNHARDENED & GROUND STEEL WASHERS

⅜ KEY 3½ LONG

LUBRICATING INSTRUCTION PLATE

LUBRICATING INSTRUCTION PLATE

IS SUPPLIED AND MOUNTED BY VENDOR

HIGH SPEED SHAFT

NO BEARINGS TO BE SAME AS SHOWN FOR SLOW SPEED SHAFT

NEW METHOD OF OIL DRAINBACK

PURCHASED CHINFIELD SMITH CO OR EQUAL

SLOW SPEED SHAFT

½″ HEX HD CAP SCREW

HEX HD CAP SCREW

DRILL FOR TAPER PIN IN REAM WHEN ASSEMBLING

HEX HD CAP SCREW

HEX HD CAP SCREW

HEX HD CAP SCREW

MELLON HD GASKET

PIPE PLUG

PIPE PLUG

No 30 (.1287) DRILL C'DRILL FOR RIVET ONE AT ASSEMBLY

Fig. 301. Assembly Working Drawing.

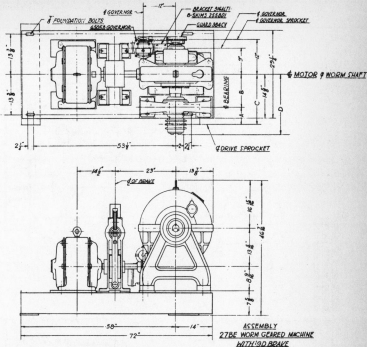

Fig. 302. Installation Drawing.

requirements of good design. Cost studies must be made in order to ascertain whether or not the part may be produced more economically by use of other methods, such as machining the part from a solid piece of metal or perhaps riveting or welding small parts together. If the alternative methods were more costly, the designer would be justified in ordering a casting. Again, in some cases, the intricacy of the part makes casting more suitable than the other methods.

The Drawing. In the drawing of a casting, it is most important that the part be designed so that the cast piece can easily be withdrawn from its mold. Frequently, a split pattern is necessary for the production of a complicated piece, though this requirement does not present any great difficulty either to the patternmaker or to the foundryman.

Care must be taken not to design too heavy a wall in any part of the casting. A thick wall does not cool evenly with other parts of

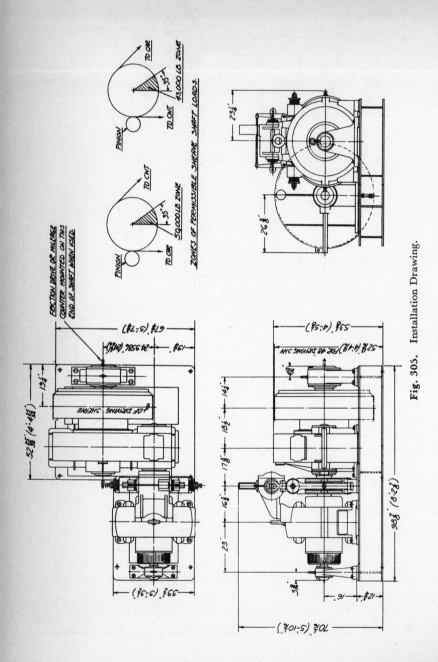

Fig. 303. Installation Drawing.

the casting, and metal brittleness may occur at that point, resulting in eventual failure of the part under normal stresses. The necessarily slow process of cooling is accompanied by a shrinkage of metal which causes defects in any part that is of more than normal thickness.

The Pattern. The patternmaker lays the draftsman's sketch out in full scale directly on the wood from which the pattern is to be shaped. For this work he uses a special patternmaker's scale which has dimensions slightly larger than those of a standard scale. This scale automatically allows for the shrinkage of the metal during the cooling process.

Since shrinkage in metal varies with the type of metal, a careful patternmaker employs scales for the particular type of metal used. The variations in dimensions from the standard are as follows: casting iron, $\frac{3}{32}$ to $\frac{1}{8}$ inch per foot; common brass, $\frac{3}{16}$ inch per foot; yellow brass, $\frac{7}{32}$ inch per foot; bronze, $\frac{3}{32}$ inch per foot; aluminum, $\frac{7}{32}$ to $\frac{1}{4}$ inch per foot; and steel casting, $\frac{3}{16}$ inch per foot.

Wherever the draftsman's sketch calls for finished surfaces, the patternmaker allows an additional thickness of metal approximating $\frac{1}{8}$ of an inch. In the machining process, the additional $\frac{1}{8}$ inch of metal is cut away and the desired thickness of metal is still maintained.

If the casting is designed with surfaces or projections at right angles to each other, a certain amount of taper is allowed by the patternmaker to facilitate withdrawing the casting from the mold. This taper is known as "draft" for patterns. Usually the slope or draft is designed to taper away from the top "face," or the surface deepest set in the mold. The draft in most cases is approximately $\frac{1}{8}$ of an inch per foot.

Patterns not requiring draft are those with no parts at right angles to each other.

Simultaneously with the submission of the draftsman's sketch to the patternmaker, and sometimes even before that stage, a blue print is sent to the materials and methods department for study. Tool and jig designers are requested to study the piece for their recommendations regarding the best way to make the piece. These designers may require the patternmaker to add an additional projection on the casting to serve as a prop for leveling the piece for the machining and drilling processes, as in the clamp lever in

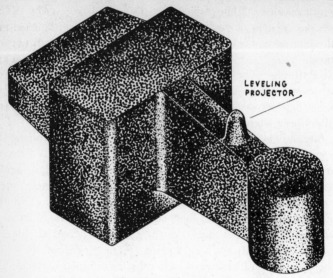

Fig. 304.   Clamp Lever.

Fig. 304. The projections are later cut, milled, or burned off, when their function is no longer required. This procedure is highly successful in mass production.

A pattern cannot be made from a piece of green wood. Since the wood must be well-seasoned and free of warps, the inner layers of logs, the "heartwoods," are best for patternmaking. The outer layers, or "sapwoods," which have a tendency to warp, are not recommended. White pine, maple, birch, mahogany, fir, and cherry are commonly used. The most desirable wood is white pine, which is easy to shape or fashion into odd pieces and also takes glue and varnish best.

The fillets and rounds in patterns are made with pieces of leather, available in large rolls, which are precisely shaped to the various radii. These leather pieces obviate the delicate fashioning of wood to small dimensions. A further advantage is that they take glue easily.

Finally, the wood pattern is finished with several coats of varnish which prevent warping of the wood and protect the surfaces of the pattern from the damp sand used in the construction of the mold.

The Casting.   After the piece has been cast, the casting is washed and any excessive scaliness is removed in special acid baths.   The piece is now ready for marking.   Surfaces to be left unfinished are usually painted black; surfaces to be machined are painted red.

The piece then goes to the machine shop.   A layout man, specially trained for this work, lays out dimensions on the piece itself.   His functions in the shop are comparable to those of a layout draftsman in the engineering department.   He uses a steel-pointed scriber to scratch out dimensions and hole centers.

The layout man's dimensioning is done on a "surface plate," a large cast-iron table top which is precisely square and level.   Normally, one surface is finished first, as, for example, the top surface in the case of the clamp lever in Fig. 305.   All dimensions are then measured-off from this finished surface or reference line.

Finishing one surface also provides a good flat space on which the piece may be clamped and centered for further measurement and machining or drilling.   The portion to be finished can be treated with an end mill, planed with a shaper, or even cut with a

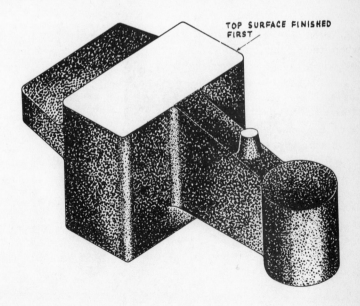

TOP SURFACE FINISHED
FIRST

Fig. 305.   Clamp Lever.

rotary cutter. Usually the piece is put through a rough cutter, then through a fine cutter.

When all finished surfaces have been completed (see Fig. 306), the next step is to measure-off hole centers. In all hole operations the piece is generally fixed in place and the devices used in drilling, milling, etc., are moved to meet the requirements called for in the blue print.

Fig. 307 shows a clearance hole drilled into the hub of the clamp lever. Fig. 308 shows two counterbored holes cut through the main body of the piece. These holes may be drilled first and then counterbored, or they may be drilled and counterbored in one operation with a combination drill and counterbore. The leveling projector is then removed. The completed clamp lever, with the final drilling and tapping of the two holes in the flange, is shown in Fig. 309. Fig. 310 shows how this piece is dimensioned.

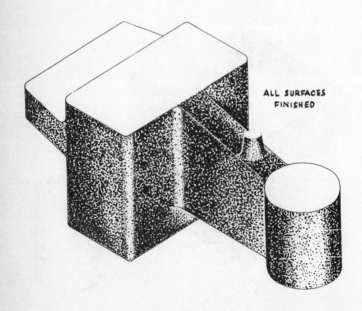

ALL SURFACES
FINISHED

Fig. 306. Completion of Finished Surfaces.

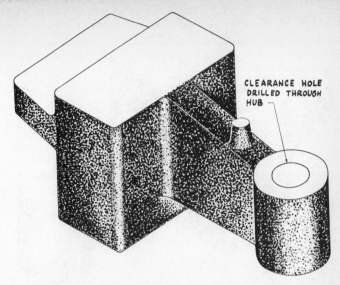

Fig. 307. Clearance Hole Drilled into Hub of Clamp Lever.

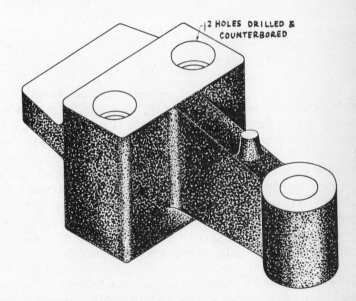

Fig. 308. Counterbored Holes.

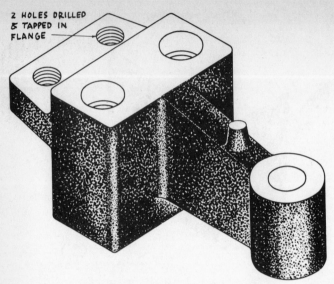

2 HOLES DRILLED
& TAPPED IN
FLANGE

Fig. 309.   Completed Clamp Lever.

WELDING

There are three methods of welding: (1) autogenous or gas welding, (2) electric resistance welding, and (3) electric arc welding. Autogenous or gas welding unites pieces of metal by melting the ends of these pieces with a high-temperature gas flame.   The pieces fuse when the metal attains the proper fluidity.   Electric resistance welding permits a large volume of electric current at diminished pressure or voltage to pass through the abutted pieces of metal. This creates intense heat at the point of contact, melting the metal and causing it to fuse upon the exertion of some pressure on the joint. In electric arc welding, an electric arc of intense heat is created by connecting one wire of the electric circuit to the piece to be welded and the other wire to a welding electrode.   The great heat produced at the joint fuses the pieces together into a solid weld.   The electrode serves as the negative pole and the metal piece serves as the positive pole.

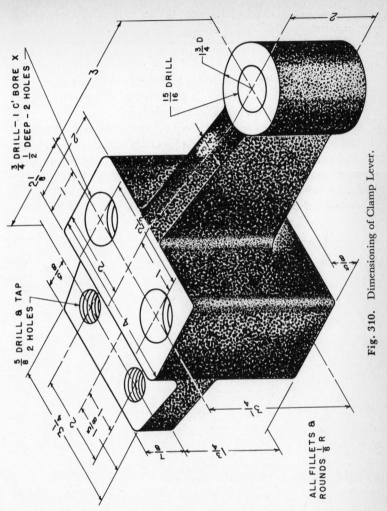

Fig. 310. Dimensioning of Clamp Lever.

One or two per cent of the length of the final piece (which consists of two or more parts) is allowed for expansion or contraction after welding. Because of this variation in dimensions, all machining processes, such as finishing and drilling, are done after the piece has been welded. Greater accuracy is attained by means of this procedure.

Care should be taken to avoid recommending heavy welds or long continuous welds.   These types of welds generally cause "locked-in" stress to appear in the piece which must then be reheated to relieve the stress.   If the piece is not reheated, it is apt to fail at a critical time.

Intermittent welds on jobs that require much welding are effective without causing lock-in stresses.   Smaller welds, strategically placed, will accomplish similar results without stress hazards.

The classification of welds is based either on the type of ends of the parts to be welded or on the method of treatment of these ends. (Useful data on welding standards and symbols may be found in the reference booklet on welding, *Graphical Symbols for Welding* [ASA Z32.2.1 — 1949], published by The American Society of Mechanical Engineers.)

11

The Development and Intersection of Surfaces

A surface is generated by the movement of a line through space. (Movement of a straight-line segment along itself is not considered movement of the line, as a straight line is said to be infinite in length.) If the line moves in accordance with a specific law, the result will be a definite surface. In such cases, the moving line is termed the *generatrix*, and any fixed position of the line is called an *element of the surface*.

CLASSIFICATION OF SURFACES

Ruled Surface. A ruled surface is any surface that is generated by a straight line. Ruled surfaces fall into three categories: (1) *singly-ruled*, on which only one straight-line element may be passed through a point on the surface; (2) *doubly-ruled*, on which two straight-line elements may be passed through a point on the surface; and (3) *plane*, on which an infinite number of straight-line elements may be passed through a point on the surface.

Developable Surface. A developable surface is one which may be rolled or unfolded upon a plane. Contiguous straight-line elements must either intersect or be parallel (the latter type are assumed to intersect at infinity). These surfaces are also known as *singly-curved*.

Warped Surface. A warped surface is a ruled surface which does not meet the requirements for developability. Contiguous elements are neither intersecting nor parallel. One can obtain approximate development of warped surfaces by breaking them down to small approximations of developable surfaces.

Doubly-Curved Surface. A doubly-curved surface is a surface which is generated by a curved line and on which a straight line cannot be drawn. Consequently this surface does not satisfy the requirements for developability. Here again, a development of the surface may be approximated by the same method as the one used for warped surfaces.

Surface of Revolution. A surface of revolution is a surface generated by the rotation of a line in a plane about an axis in the same plane. These may be singly- or doubly-curved. (Note that the hyperboloid of one nappe is also a doubly-ruled warped surface.)

Recapitulation. The classification of surfaces may be summarized as follows.

$$
\text{Ruled} \begin{cases}
\text{Plane} \\
\text{(Developable)} & \begin{cases} \text{Prism} \\ \text{Pyramid} \end{cases} \\[2ex]
\text{Singly-Curved} \\
\text{(Developable)} & \begin{cases} \text{Cylinder} \\ \text{Cone} \\ \text{Convolute} \end{cases} \\[2ex]
\text{Warped} \\
\text{(Non-developable)} & \begin{cases} \text{Hyperbolic Paraboloid} \\ \text{Hyperboloid of One Nappe} \\ \text{Cylindroid} \\ \text{Conoid} \end{cases}
\end{cases}
$$

$$
\text{Non-ruled} \begin{cases}
\text{Doubly-Curved} \\
\text{(Non-developable)} & \begin{cases} \text{Sphere} \\ \text{Ellipsoid} \\ \text{Paraboloid} \\ \text{Torus} \end{cases}
\end{cases}
$$

DEVELOPMENT

Development is the process of laying out a geometric surface upon a plane in such a way that it may be folded to show the developed surface. This process is used extensively in all forms of sheet metal work, particularly in the making of ducts, skylights, cornices, and drains. In order for a geometric surface to be developable, all of its component surfaces must be developable, that is, it must be possible to roll the surface on a plane so that all contiguous elements intersect. (Note that in the case of pyramids, prisms, and polyhedra, each of the faces will coincide simultaneously with the plane used for the development, while each of the edges will act as an axis of rotation until the next face is brought into coincidence with the plane.)

In laying out a development, the draftsman should remember two important points. (1) He should study the surface (or surfaces) for symmetry, and (2) he should aim to utilize the shortest seam in construction of the surface. Symmetry is a first consideration, for it may enable the draftsman to limit his work to the development of only one-half of the surface. The shorter of the two lines of symmetry should always be taken as the cutting edge, as this will require a minimum of work in putting the pattern together. There is another value in symmetry; for example, if one selects a frustum of a right circular cone, which is to be developed by triangulation, it is necessary to develop from a line of symmetry to either side in order to avoid distortion that would result if the error were allowed to accumulate all in one direction.

Development of a Right Prism. Fig. 311 shows a right prism,

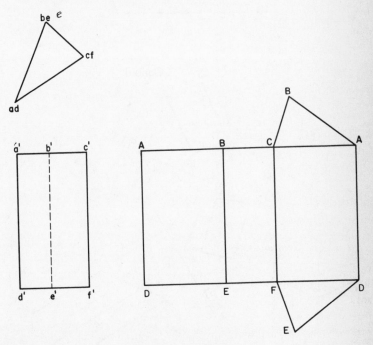

Fig. 311. Right Prism.

with the development at the right. In order to develop the various component plane faces of the prism, one must obtain the true shape of each face. Since a right prism is made of rectangular lateral faces, all that is required for the development of each face is the true length of two adjacent sides. The top and bottom triangular bases

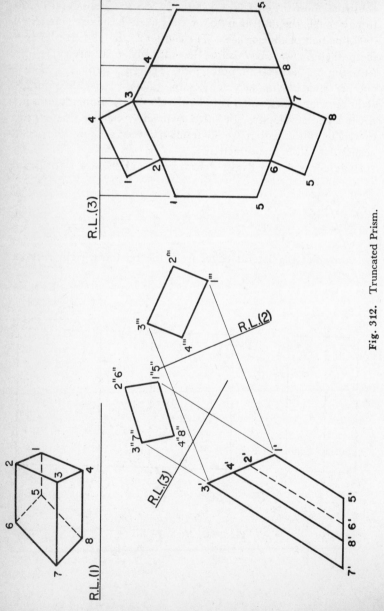

Fig. 312. Truncated Prism.

can be simply constructed if the true length of its three sides is determined.

From the position of the prism, it will be seen that the lateral edges are parallel to the plane of projection in elevation, while the top and bottom faces are parallel to the plane of projection in plan. This means that the lateral edges are seen in true length in elevation, and the edges of the bases are seen in true length in plan. Since all lateral edges are equal in length, the cutting edge can be placed on any edge. It has been placed on edge *AD*. The adjacent rectangular faces have been developed in their consecutive order. The top and bottom faces have been developed on edges *CA* and *FD*, respectively, although these could also have been developed on either of the other two edges. When the development is folded along the edges, and the corresponding points are brought into coincidence, the right prism represented in projection will be produced.

Development of a Truncated Prism. Fig. 312 represents a truncated prism, inasmuch as the planes of the bases are not at right angles to the lateral edges, as may be seen from the elevation. A simple way of developing is to obtain a right section and treat it the same as the right prism, measuring the points 1 through 8 on the corresponding lateral edges from the reference right section, which has been taken at plane (*3*) in elevation.

It is important to note that *R.L.* (*3*) represents the edgewise view of a plane at right angle to the lateral edges. Therefore, the projection on plane (*3*) shows the true shape of the right section which is used in laying off the true distance between the lateral edges in development.

The plan shows that the lateral edges are parallel to the plane of projection in elevation and therefore provide the true length of these edges.

It should be noted that the lower base, being parallel to plane (*1*), will show in true shape in plan. Also, the upper base, being parallel to plane (*2*), will show in true shape in projection on plane (*2*).

The actual development is straightforward and easily becomes apparent if one follows the reference points successively. Note that edge *1–2* makes the shortest seam.

Development of an Oblique Prism. The oblique prism shown in Fig. 313 is treated in exactly the same way as the truncated prism, the only difference being that both bases are parallel to each other, therefore congruent. The development to the right has been carried out by use of the right section $WXYZ$ obtained by means of reference plane (3). It is important to note that before the right section could be established, it was necessary to obtain a view on plane (2) to which the lateral edges are parallel. In this view the true lengths of the lateral edges on either side of the reference plane are also seen. If the points in the development are followed in consecutive order, the entire process will be clarified.

Development of a Right Circular Cylinder. Theoretically, a right circular cylinder may be considered to be a right prism having an infinite number of lateral faces. The circular bases can be divided into any number of small arcs, and can be assumed to be approximated by their chords. The right cylinder, when rolled out on a plane, will form a rectangle whose sides will be equal to the altitude and to the circumference (πD). It is, therefore, customary to carry out the development of the right circular cylinder

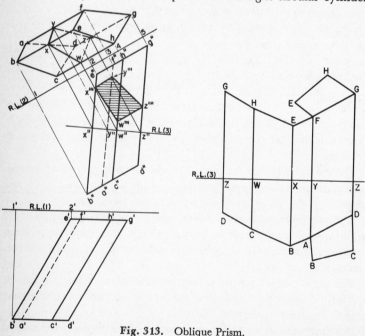

Fig. 313. Oblique Prism.

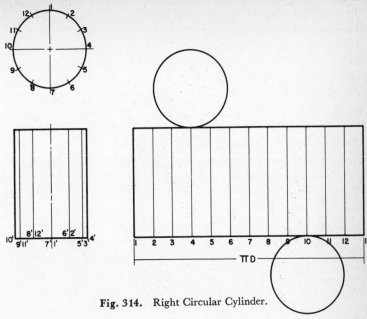

Fig. 314. Right Circular Cylinder.

as shown in Fig. 314. The lengths 12, 23, 34, etc. are actually the rectified arcs indicated in projection, their length being $\frac{\pi D}{12}$ in this case.

The two bases are the true circles which are seen in plan and which may be placed at any convenient place on the development. This development when rolled into shape will give the exact cylinder represented in the projection.

Development of a Truncated Right Circular Cylinder. Now that the development of the right circular cylinder has been considered, it should be a simple matter to obtain the development of the truncated right circular cylinder shown in Fig 315.

One should obtain the development of the right circular cylinder, as before, and number each of the elements. Since the true length of each of the numbered elements is seen in elevation, one need only transfer the true length of each of the elements to its corresponding numbered element. It should be noted that there is symmetry about elements *4* and *10*. Of course, the cutting edge has been selected along element *4* because it is the shorter one.

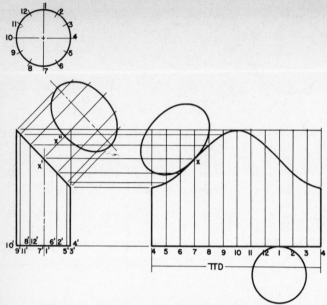

Fig. 315. Truncated Right Circular Cylinder.

The lower base is a circle as before, and it is seen in true size in plan. The upper base is an ellipse. The minor diameter is equal to the diameter of the circle; the major diameter is represented in plan by *10–4* which, being parallel to the plane of projection in elevation, is seen in true length. The supplementary projection to the upper right shows the ellipse in true shape. (When the minor and major diameters are known, the ellipse can be easily constructed by the trammel method.) Unlike the circular base, the elliptical base must be located accurately by matching any point such as X on the element *7*.

Development of an Oblique Circular Cylinder. Fig. 316 shows an oblique circular cylinder. Observation of the position of the elements discloses that they are not parallel to either plane in plan or elevation. Therefore, the first requirement is to obtain the supplementary projection on plane (*2*) showing the true length of the elements.

The right section can be taken through any point in supplementary projection, such as plane (*3*). The projection on plane (*3*) shows

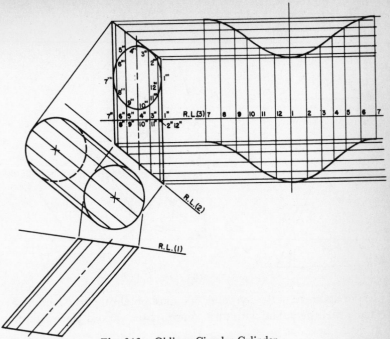

Fig. 316. Oblique Circular Cylinder.

the true shape of the right section which is an ellipse. This projection also shows the edgewise view of the cylinder. Since it would be difficult to divide the ellipse into equal segments, the circular base is divided instead, in this case into 12 equal parts, and the divisions are obtained on the ellipse without regard to uniformity.

It is apparent that symmetry occurs about elements *1* and *7*. One may take advantage of this symmetry in order to simplify the development. The distances between the elements in the development are taken equal to the chords from the right section. A small but permissible error is introduced by this method. In circles with a diameter of 2″ or less, twelve divisions involve a tolerable error; for larger circles, it is customary to increase accuracy by taking twenty-four divisions. Inasmuch as the bases are circles, they may be placed at any point in the development.

Development of a Right Pyramid. The right pyramid shown in Fig. 317 is made up of four lateral faces and a base. In obtaining

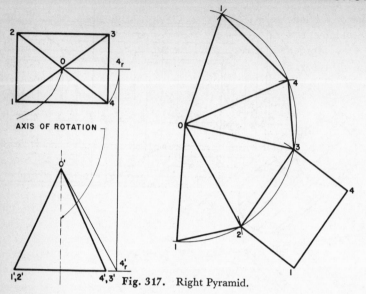

AXIS OF ROTATION

Fig. 317. Right Pyramid.

the development of this pyramid, one must obtain the true length of each of the edges, and with these construct the various plane figures in their respective order.

Examination of the projections shows that only the base is parallel to a plane of projection, for it is parallel to the plane of projection for the plan. Therefore, the entire base is seen in true size in plan.

The four edges, *01*, *02*, *03*, and *04* are all of equal length due to their symmetry. This means that if the true length of any of them is found, then the true length of all of them will be known. It is possible to introduce a supplementary plane parallel to the line, either in plan or elevation, and thereon obtain the true length of the lateral edge. The true length could also be obtained by rotation parallel to one of the existing planes of projection, and this has been done in plan, parallel to the plane of projection in elevation. The axis of rotation has been taken through *0*, perpendicular to the plane of projection in plan. Point *0*, being on the axis of rotation, remains fixed, while point *4* has been rotated to point *4_r*. The true length of *04* is now seen in elevation.

In the development, the edge *01* has been made the cutting edge, and the four lateral faces of the pyramid have been laid out in proper sequence. The base has been placed adjacent to edge *23*, one of the long sides, thus saving space on the sheet used for the development.

Development of an Oblique Pyramid. The oblique pyramid shown in Fig. 318 is developed in precisely the same manner as the right pyramid, with the exception that the lateral edges are no longer of the same length, and the true length of each edge must be found separately. The rotation of each of the edges is readily ascertained from the drawing.

At this point one should consider a simple procedure, which will aid in finding the true lengths, and which can be carried out on a relatively small corner of the drawing, as indicated in the upper right-hand corner of the figure. As may be seen, on the view where the axis of rotation projects as a point, the rotating point moves on the arc of a circle (path of rotation), while, on the view to which the axis of rotation is parallel, the point travels in a plane at right angles to the axis (plane of rotation). These two facts indicate a right triangle relationship; the length of the two legs is known, and the hypotenuse represents the true length of the line. The base of the pyramid is again parallel to the plane of projection in plan;

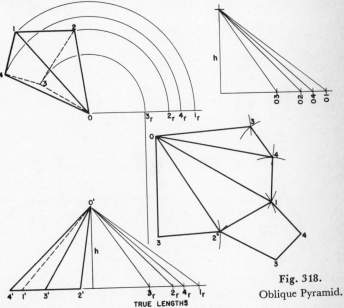

Fig. 318.
Oblique Pyramid.

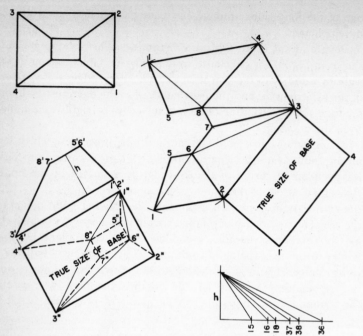

Fig. 319. Frustum of Pyramid.

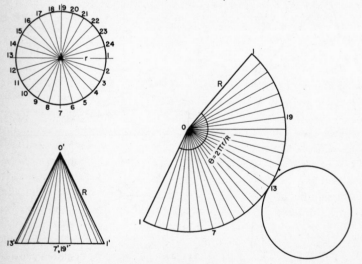

Fig. 320. Right Circular Cone.

therefore, the true size is shown in plan. The development has been carried out by reconstructing each of the lateral faces by means of the three known sides. The base is adjacent to the edge *12*.

Development of a Frustum of a Pyramid. The frustum of the pyramid shown in Fig. 319 is developed by the method already described, that is, by finding the true length of all the edges making up the faces of the frustum, and then reconstructing the faces in their proper sequence.

It will be noted that edges *12*, *34*, *56*, and *78* are parallel in plan, that edges *14*, *23*, *58*, and *67* are parallel in elevation and that the true lengths are available. Nevertheless, the supplementary view was obtained to simplify the finding of the true lengths of the other necessary edges. These true lengths are indicated at the lower right-hand corner of the drawing. In addition to finding the true length of the lateral edges, it was also required to find the true length of one diagonal of each of the lateral faces; in this instance these are irregular quadrilaterals, and the development had to be obtained by the process of triangulation.

For purposes of practice or review, this problem may be solved by extending the lateral edges of the frustum to the apex of the pyramid; the development will be obtained by considering as a large and a small pyramid, then discarding, that portion of the development which would correspond to the small pyramid above the upper base of the frustum. It is suggested that a truncated pyramid be selected for development, that is, a portion of a pyramid in which the two bases are not parallel to each other.

Development of a Right Circular Cone. As in the cases of the prism and the cylinder, the cone may be regarded as a pyramid with an infinite number of lateral faces. In development of the cone, however, fewer faces must of necessity be considered. Again, the base is divided into a number of arcs, and, in the development, the chord is assumed to approximate the arc. In this procedure a small amount of error is introduced, which, for practical purposes, is not significant. If greater accuracy is desired, the divisions can be made smaller. The right circular cone, in Fig. 320, can be developed exactly by considering the geometrical and mathematical relationships involved. If the slant height of the cone is R, it will be seen that, in the development of the cone, the rolling process will describe a sector of a circle of the radius R. If the radius

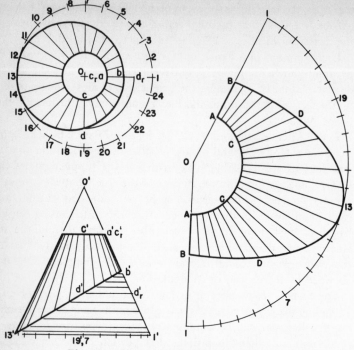

Fig. 321. Truncated Right Circular Cone.

of the base is r, the length of the arc of the sector will be $2\pi r$. The angle, θ, of the sector, in radians, will then be $2\pi r/R$. The circle of the base has been divided into 24 equal parts. If the sector is also divided into the same number of equal parts, the elements in projection will correspond exactly to the elements in development. The base, being a circle, may be placed at any point in the development of the conical surface corresponding to points on the circle of the base.

Development of a Truncated Right Circular Cone. Fig. 321 represents a truncated cone, which will be recognized as a portion of the right circular cone shown in Fig. 320. Therefore, it should be apparent that the development will be simplified by obtaining the development of the entire cone as before, and then eliminating the portion cut from each of the elements.

In projection, only elements *01* and *0–13* are parallel in elevation, and their true length is immediately available. To obtain the true

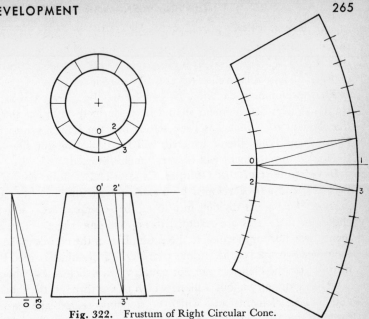

Fig. 322. Frustum of Right Circular Cone.

length of the other elements, it is necessary to rotate them into parallelism in elevation about an axis perpendicular to the plane of projection in plan, such as is seen for element *CD*. After the correct length has been laid off on each of the elements in the development, a smooth curve is passed through the points with the aid of a French curve. Since the portion of the cone above the upper base of the truncated cone represents a smaller cone, the upper arc will also be a sector of a circle.

Development of a Frustum of a Right Circular Cone. Whenever the apex of a right circular cone from which a frustum has been obtained is available, the method just described should be used because it is the simplest method. However, if the apex is not available, or if the slant height of the cone is too long, the method of triangulation, as shown in Fig. 322, will have to be used. The frustum is divided by elements evenly spaced. The chords *02* and *13* are assumed to approximate their subtended arcs. Thus, the conical surface is now assumed to be divided into a number of equal trapezoids. The required dimensions, in reconstructing these trapezoids in development, are its four sides and the diagonal. To the left of the elevation are shown the true lengths of long sides and diagonals, found by means already explained. The true length of the long sides is also available at the contours of the cone in elevation, since they are parallel in elevation. The true lengths of the chords are available in plan, as they are parallel in plan.

The development can now be carried out but, first, a word of caution. The development should be performed on either side of the element *01*, which has been selected as the line of symmetry. If this is not done, the entire error will be thrown on one side and the folded development will be very much distorted.

Development of the Oblique Cone. The oblique cone (see Fig. 323) must be developed by means of triangulation. For this purpose the base is divided into a number of equal arcs, and the chords of these arcs are assumed to approximate them. The elements drawn from the apex to the extremities of the chords make up the other two sides of the various triangles. It should be noted that in this case the elements are not equal. Nevertheless, the oblique cone has symmetry about a plane which passes through the shortest and longest elements and which corresponds to a plane passing through the apex and the center of the base, and perpendicular to the plane of the base. This plane of symmetry is utilized, and the divisions are made symmetrical on either side of the plane. The

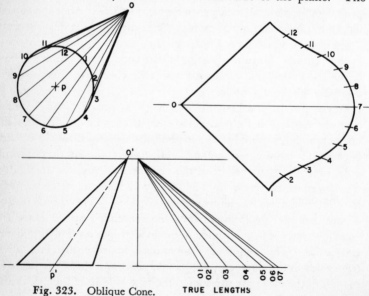

Fig. 323. Oblique Cone.　TRUE LENGTHS

plane of symmetry may be seen in edgewise view in plan, made up by elements *01* and *07*, and the symmetrical elements may easily be recognized on either side of this plane.

To the right of the elevation are shown the true lengths of elements *01* to *07*, found as before by rotation about an axis through *0* perpendicular to the plane of projection in plan. The true lengths of the elements *08* to *0–11* are available from their symmetrical counterparts.

The development is carried out about the element of symmetry *07*, thereby giving the shortest cutting line *01*.

Transition Pieces. Transition pieces are connecting pieces between ducts or openings, which direct the flow of gases. These connections are made of sheet metal, or of some other material which cannot be stretched, and must, therefore, be folded or bent along straight-line elements. In short, the surfaces making up the transition pieces must be developable surfaces.

The main requirement is that the end openings of the transition pieces match, as closely as possible, the openings which they are connecting. However, there are other factors which will enter into a properly designed transition piece.

As indicated, the surfaces employed are to be developable, symmetry is to be taken advantage of whenever available, and the shortest edge is to be made the cutting edge. Furthermore, the change in cross-section should be made as gradual as possible, and no re-entrant angles should be permitted, as they would restrict the free flow of gases and cause turbulence, thereby increasing the resistance of the system. This objective is generally accomplished satisfactorily by breaking up the transition piece into as many surfaces which will be tangent, each to each, as may be required. Where this procedure is not possible, the closest approximation is employed.

A simple transition piece and its development are shown in Fig. 324. This piece connects a circular opening to a rectangular opening, both lying in planes that incline toward each other. The first step in the design of a smooth transition piece is to pass planes through all the straight sides, making these planes tangent to the circular opening. A fundamental rule in regard to a line tangent to a plane curve states that the tangent line must lie in the plane of the curve. Further, it is known that two intersecting lines deter-

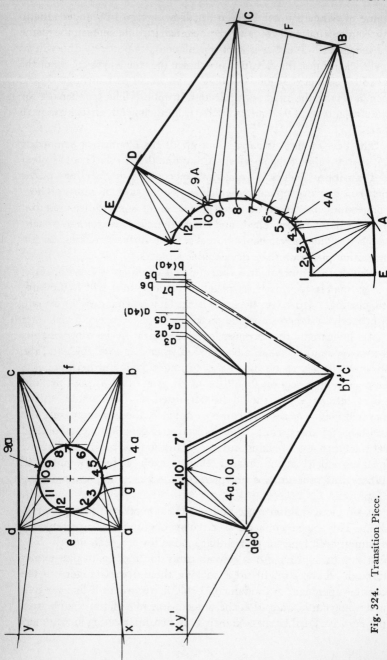

Fig. 324. Transition Piece.

mine a plane. In other words, a line must be drawn tangent to the circle from the point where the straight line pierces the plane of the circle. The tangent lines will come from infinity and will be parallel to lines *AD* and *BC*, which are parallel to the plane of the circle. In this way, we obtain the points of tangency *1* and *7*, and the two tangent planes *AD1* and *BC7* become plane portions of the transition piece. Line *AB* pierces the plane of the circle at point *X*, and line *CD* at point *Y*. From these two points, the two lines tangent to the circle at points (*4A*) and (*9A*) are constructed. Here again, the two tangent planes *AB*(*4A*) and *CD*(*9A*) become plane portions of the transition piece.

The circular opening is now divided into four parts by the four tangent planes. Each of the four arcs along with each of the four points *A*, *B*, *C*, and *D* determines four portions of oblique cones (developable surfaces) and is tangent to the four planes already mentioned. These conical portions are *A1234*(*4A*), *B*(*4A*)*567*, *C789*(*9A*), and *D*(*9A*)–*10*–*11*–*12*–*1*.

The development of the transition piece will be accomplished by the method of triangulation, involving the determination of the true lengths of all the sides making up the triangles. The circle has been divided into twelve parts, and the chords have been assumed to approximate the length of their arcs. Plane *E17F* will be seen to be a plane of symmetry, with line *E1* the shortest element; therefore, it is made the cutting edge. *E1* is perpendicular to line *AD*, and this fact is apparent in the development. The development is laid out on either side of line *F7*.

Fig. 325 shows very much the same type of transition as Fig. 324, with the exception that the angle between the planes of the two openings is 90°. Points *1* and *7*, the points of tangency giving the planes *AB7* and *CD1*, are obtained as before. The tangent lines *X*(*5A*) and *Y*(*9A*) coincide in projection in elevation with the entire tangent plane passing through the edges *AD* and *BC*. The development will be seen to have been made on either side of the line of symmetry *F7*, and the cutting edge along *E1*.

Fig. 326 is a transition piece connecting a circular opening and an elliptical opening, with their planes inclined to each other. The surface employed to connect these openings is a convolute, which is a developable surface. This surface is generated by the tangent plane to the two openings as it rolls in contact with these openings.

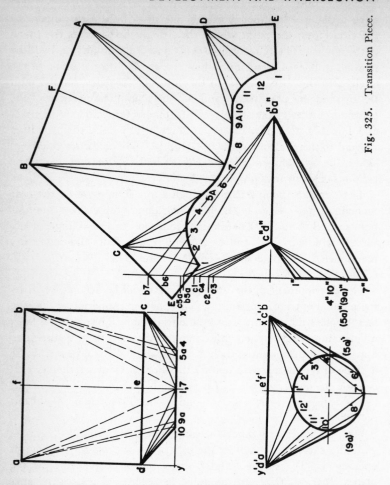

Fig. 325. Transition Piece.

As already stated, the tangent to a plane curve lies in the plane of the curve. Therefore, if a tangent line be drawn at a point on one of the openings, and, from the point where this tangent pierces the plane of the second opening, a tangent be drawn to the second opening, then the plane determined by these two tangent lines represents the tangent plane passing through the two points on the curves. The line joining these two points of tangency determines one of the straight-line elements of the convolute. Similar points of tangency and elements are found at regular intervals; the surface

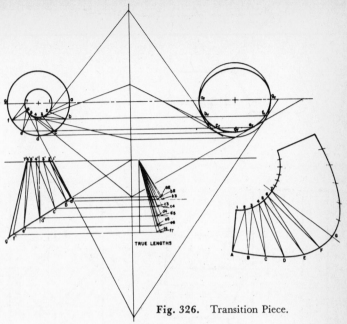

TRUE LENGTHS

Fig. 326. Transition Piece.

is then developed by the method of triangulation. In actual solution of the problem, the plane of the ellipse was rotated into the plane of the circle about the line of intersection of the two planes, thus permitting the ellipse to be seen in true shape in plan. The tangent lines could have been drawn first on either of the two openings. Instead, they were drawn to the ellipse because it is simpler to draw a tangent at a point on the ellipse than to draw a tangent to the ellipse from a point outside the ellipse. The ellipse was rotated about its major diameter *AG* until it projected as a circle. This circle was then divided into twelve equal arcs, but, because symmetry exists about the major diameter, only one of the symmetrical halves was divided. At the points of division the tangents to the circle were drawn; then the circle and the tangents were counter-rotated to the original position of the ellipse. The tangents were extended to the ellipse, intersecting the plane of the circle along the line of intersection of the two planes. From these latter points it was a simple matter to draw the tangents to the circle. The various points of tangency were numbered *1* to *7*. The elements of the convolute had been obtained.

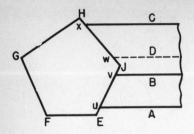

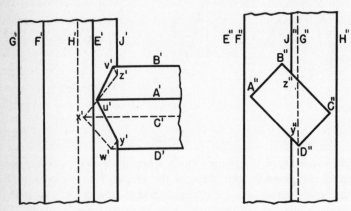

Fig. 327. Intersection of Two Prisms.

In the development of the convolute, the successive elements partition the surface into small segments, and, together with the chords subtended by the arcs of both curves, form warped quadrilaterals, such as *A12B*. These warped quadrilaterals are divided into two triangles, as shown by line *A2*. It should be appreciated that *A2* on the convolute is not actually a straight line, and that a certain amount of error is introduced by assuming it as such, but if the points taken are close enough, this discrepancy is small. The lengths of the chords of the circle are taken from the plan, and the lengths of the chords of the ellipse are taken from the ellipse rotated in plan. The true lengths of the elements and of the diagonals are found as before. The development is carried out simultaneously on either side of the line of symmetry *A1*.

INTERSECTIONS

The draftsman is very frequently confronted with the problem of finding the intersections between surfaces. The line of intersection between two surfaces may be defined as the line common to both surfaces, but this definition is not very useful. A better definition, which would point the way to a uniform, simplified treatment of all problems in intersections, may be presented as follows: a line of intersection is the locus of all points which are the intersections of two lines, one on each of the surfaces. Since lines must lie on the same surface in order to intersect, the correct procedure is clarified.

In other words, the intersections between surfaces are lines, and lines are a succession of points. In order to obtain a point, one must obtain the intersection between two lines. These two lines must be taken one on each of the two surfaces, but in order for these two lines to intersect, they must be on the same surface. Therefore, one uses a third surface, drawing simple lines that cut the two given surfaces. This third plane (like any other plane used for the purpose of providing additional points on the line of intersection) is termed an auxiliary cutting surface. Although the auxiliary cutting surfaces may include any surface that cuts simple lines from the given surfaces, they are usually planes, spheres, cylinders, or cones. The plane surface, the only cutting surface considered in this chapter, is probably the ruled surface most commonly employed.

All the loci (all points in succession) on the line of intersection are joined by a smooth curve with the aid of a French curve. In the case of intersections of planes, the intersections are straight lines, and these may be drawn with the aid of a straight edge when two points, or a point and a direction, have been determined.

If one of the surfaces projects in edgewise view, one can find points on the line of intersection after ascertaining where that surface is pierced by a line in the other surface. In employing this procedure, we must remember that the essential factor is the intersection of two lines, one on each of the surfaces.

Intersection of Two Prisms Intersecting at Right Angles. The two prisms shown in Fig. 327 intersect at right angles. One has lateral edges perpendicular in plan; the other has lateral edges perpendicular in side elevation. The prisms have been made indefinite in length, in order to permit the use of simplified notation. Each of the lateral edges is designated by capital letters, with appropriate notation.

In plan, the lateral faces EJ and HJ project in edgewise view. Therefore, it is possible to note the points which each of the lateral edges A, B, C, and D of the other prism pierce. These pierce points, called U, X, V, and W, will be identified as points common to three planes. For instance, point V is common to lateral faces AB, BC, and EJ.

In side elevation, the lateral faces of the second prism appear in edgewise view, and one can readily locate the points (Y and Z) at which lateral edge J pierces the lateral faces AD and BC.

One can now draw the lines of intersections between the various planes; the sum total of these comprises the line of intersection between the two prisms. Proper visibility of the line of intersection is established by means of the usual rules applicable to visibility.

Intersection of Two Prisms Not Intersecting at Right Angles. The intersection of two prisms not intersecting at right angles is shown in Fig. 329. But one must first deal with a problem indicated by Fig. 328. This problem is one of finding the point P at which the line AB pierces the plane $CDEF$. To solve this problem, one can pass any plane through the given line (there are an infinite number of such planes), obtaining the line of intersection between this plane and the given plane, and then finding the intersection of the given line with the line of intersection of the two planes. It is apparent that the given line can pierce the given plane only along the line of intersection.

In the solution of this problem, the simplest plane to pass through the given line is one of the projecting planes, either in plan or elevation. The plane actually used is the projecting plane in plan, and the two edges CD and EF of the given plane pierce this projecting plane at points X and Y. By projection of the points X and Y to their corresponding projections in elevation, the co-ordinate projection of the line of intersection is obtained and the point of intersection with line AB is found. This point (P) is projected back to the plan.

Again considering the intersection of the two prisms, note that points V, W, and X have been found in the same way as before. From plan, it is seen that edge C pierces faces EF and EG. In finding

these pierce points, one employs a plan view projecting plane through
C, and parallel to the edges E, F, and G.   This projecting plane cuts
elements *1* and *2* from the second prism, and the elevation projection
of these elements shows the required piercing points of the lateral
edge C.

The line of intersection can now be drawn with due regard for
proper visibility.

Intersection of Two Pyramids.   The intersection of two pyramids is shown in Fig. 330.   In the solution of this problem, it will
be noted that plan projecting planes of the three edges OA, OB,
and OC have been employed.   The intersections of these projecting
planes have been taken with lateral face EFG.   The pierce points

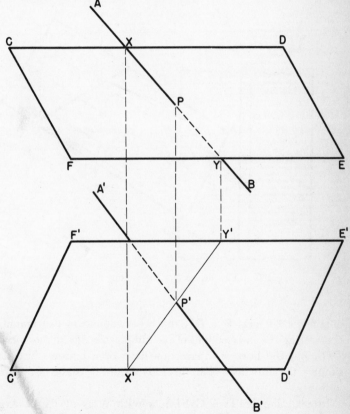

Fig. 328.   Two Prisms Intersecting at Right Angles.

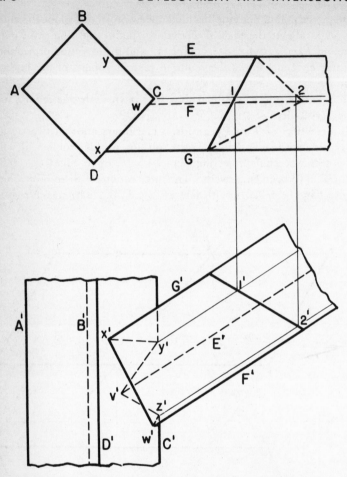

Fig. 329. Two Prisms Not Intersecting at Right Angles.

obtained on lateral face *DFG* have been found in like manner by considering the intersections of the same projecting planes with face *DFG*, but the lines of intersection have been omitted in order to simplify the drawing. Careful study should be made of the correct visibility.

Intersection of Two Cylinders with Axes at Right Angles. When one is dealing with the intersection of two right circular

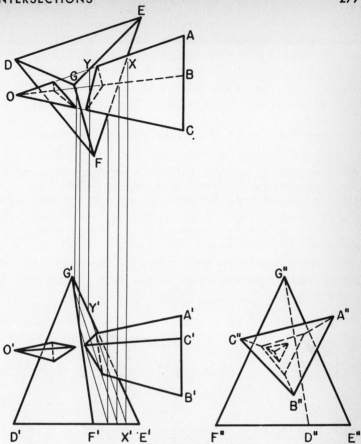

Fig. 330. Intersection of Two Pyramids.

cylinders with axes at right angles, such as those shown in Fig. 331, auxiliary cutting planes parallel to both axes, cutting elements from the two cylinders, can be used, as in this case, or the cutting planes may be parallel to one axis and perpendicular to the other, cutting elements from one cylinder and circles from the other.   When one of the cylinders projects in edgewise view, however, one view of the line or lines of intersection is already available, and, to obtain other views of them, it is necessary only to transfer the points to their corresponding elements.

In order to simplify the solution, one selects in advance the elements through which to pass the cutting planes, evenly spaced around the circumference of the smaller cylinder. The elements cut from the larger cylinder are readily obtained because they project as points in plan. It will be seen that each cutting plane will give either two or four points. The four points found by the cutting plane through elements *2* and *12* have been marked Y_1, Y_2, X_1, and X_2.

It is important to note that certain points are considered critical because of either their position in space or their significance in a particular projection, and they must be found in order that the proper detail of the line of intersection may be shown.

In the problem being considered, all the points on the contour elements must be found. It is easy to handle the contour points for the smaller cylinder by passing cutting planes through these elements. In finding the contour points for the larger cylinder, in elevation, one must project the two contour elements to the side elevation, where these elements are seen to pierce the surface of the smaller cylinder.

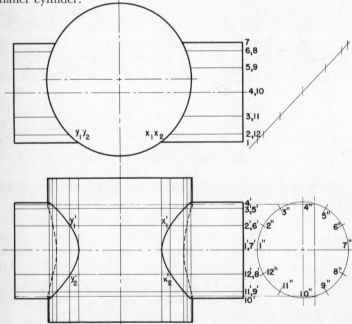

Fig. 331. Two Cylinders with Axes at Right Angles.

Intersection of Two Cylinders with Inclined Axes. The intersection of the two cylinders shown in Fig. 332 may be treated as in the preceding problem, inasmuch as it is still possible to pass cutting planes parallel to both axes. In this instance, no attempt was made to select in advance the elements through which the cutting planes will be passed. It is essential, however, to pass cutting planes through the elements projecting as contour elements.

Points X and Y found by the use of the cutting plane passed through elements *1* and *2* clearly indicate the correct procedure.

Intersection of Two Right Circular Cones with Parallel Axes. When the two axes of the right circular cones are parallel to each other, and perpendicular in plan, as in Fig. 333, the simplest type of cutting surfaces are planes perpendicular to the axes, cutting circles from each of the two cones. The intersections of these circles will give points on the line of intersection.

The critical points to consider are the highest point, found by taking a cutting plane through the two axes, and the contour points, located by finding, as accurately as possible, the points in plan where the projection of the contours cut the line of intersection.

Intersection of a Right Circular Cone and a Right Circular Cylinder. Fig. 334 shows the intersection of a right circular cone and a right circular cylinder, but the method here recommended is also applicable to the intersection of any other cone and cylinder. One may pass cutting planes through the apex of the cone and parallel to the axis of the cylinder, thereby cutting elements from both surfaces; or, alternatively, one may regard the edgewise view of the cylinder as representing one projection of the line of intersection, and then transfer the points to the other projections by projecting them on elements containing these points. Points *1*, *2*, *3*, and *4* show how this is done. Owing to the symmetrical position of the cylinder in relation to the cone, the number of critical points to be found is quite limited. These are points *3* and *4* and the contour points.

Intersection of Two Oblique Cylinders. The intersection of two oblique cylinders, such as those in Fig. 335, can be readily obtained by the use of cutting planes which are parallel to both axes. One can establish the direction of these cutting planes by passing two intersecting lines through any point, such as *A*, each parallel to one of the axes. As these planes cut the bases, they must cut elements

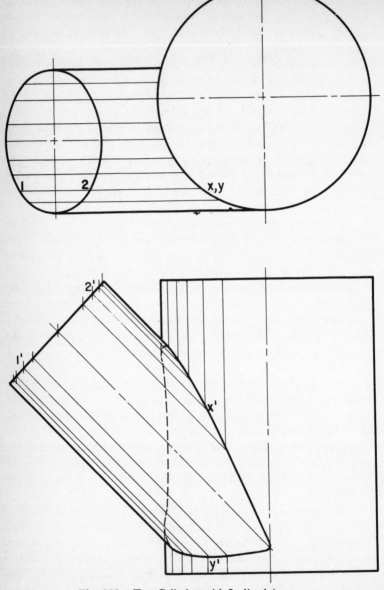

Fig. 332. Two Cylinders with Inclined Axes.

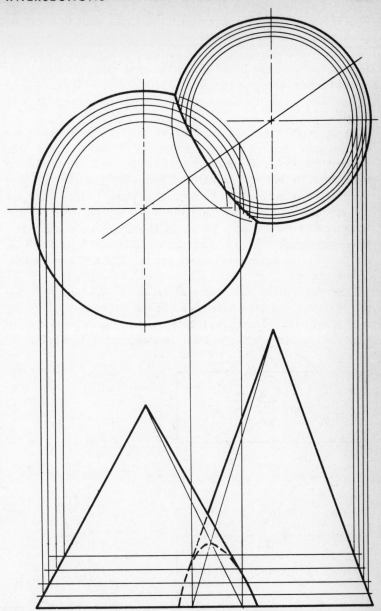

Fig. 333. Two Right Circular Cones with Parallel Axes.

from the cylinders. If these elements intersect, their intersections provide points on the line of intersection. One must, of course, consider the intersections of each of the cutting planes with the two bases. In some cases, placing both bases on the same plane, if they are not already so arranged, may simplify the procedure. This can be done by extending or cutting down one of the cylinders if both bases lie in parallel planes.

In the problem being considered, the line of intersection of the cutting plane through *A* with the plane of the two bases has been denoted *HS*, which is the usual notation for the trace of plane *S* upon the *H* (or horizontal) plane. The broken trace indicates that the plane *S* is inclined to the horizontal plane. Once this trace and its direction have been established, it is necessary only to pass other cutting planes (such as planes *R* and *T*) by placing their traces parallel to *HS*. The elements cut by plane *S* are *V*, *W*, *X*, and *Y*. Their intersections provide points *1*, *2*, *3*, and *4* on the lines of intersection.

Observation of the position of planes *R* and *T* discloses that cutting planes farther out than these two will not cut elements from the smaller cylinder. Therefore, they are referred to as *limiting planes*. This condition also indicates that every element of the smaller cyl-

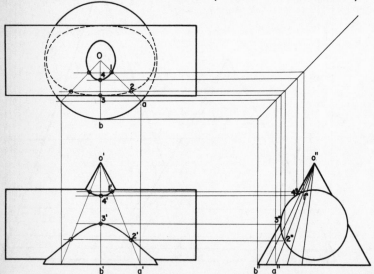

Fig. 334. Right Circular Cone and Right Circular Cylinder.

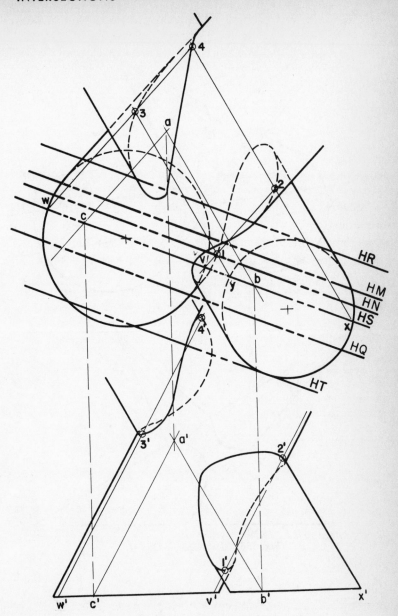

Fig. 335. Two Oblique Cylinders.

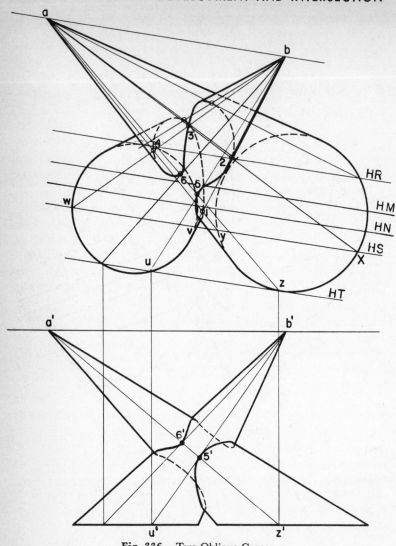

Fig. 336. Two Oblique Cones.

inder penetrates the larger cylinder. This type of intersection is referred to as *penetration*. In addition to the limiting planes, other planes which must be passed to give the contour points are M, N, and Q. Sufficient additional planes should be employed to give us a fair number of points so that a good line of intersection may be obtained.

Intersection of Two Oblique Cones. A cutting plane passed through the apex of a cone will cut elements if it cuts through the surface. This effect can readily be established by noting whether or not the plane cuts the base. In other words, the intersection of the cutting plane with the plane of the base of the cone is required. When two cones are involved, as in Fig. 336, the cutting planes must pass through the two apices. Since the apices are points, the cutting planes must contain the straight line joining these two points. The lines of intersections of the cutting planes with the planes of the two bases are required. The bases in this problem lie in the same plane, so that the lines of intersection will be common to both bases. To make sure that the cutting planes pass through the line joining the two apices (called the *control line*), the traces of the cutting planes are passed through the piercing points of the control line with the bases.

The problem under consideration shows the control line to be parallel in plan; therefore, the traces of the cutting planes will be parallel to the plan projection of the line AB. The limiting cutting planes R and T reveal that there is no penetration. This type of intersection is called *secancy*, and there is only one line of intersection. In addition to the limiting cutting planes, the planes M and N are required to give the contour points. The points obtained by the two cutting planes S and T are indicated in plan. Sufficient additional points on the line of intersection should be found in a similar way, and, with due regard to the visibility, a smooth curve should be passed through these points.

Fig. 337 again shows two intersecting oblique cones, with the pierce point 0 of the control line available. All the traces on the plane of the bases must pass through point 0. It should be noted that in this problem the limiting cutting planes again indicate a secancy intersection. Planes M, N, and S will give the necessary contour points. One can obtain additional points by passing other cutting planes.

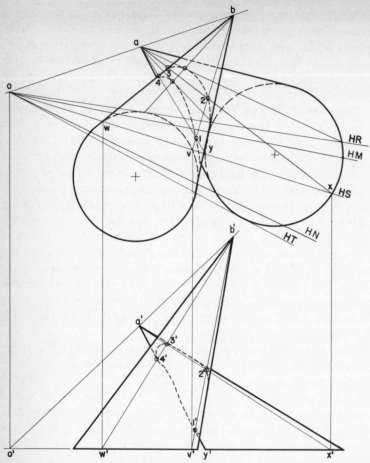

Fig. 337.   Oblique Cones.

Intersection of an Oblique Cone and an Oblique Cylinder.
As already stated, to cut elements from a cylinder the cutting plane
must be parallel to the axis, and to cut elements from a cone the
cutting plane must pass through the apex.   In the problem for
Fig. 338, comprising a cylinder and a cone, one can meet these two
requirements by passing a line through the apex of the cone which
is parallel to the axis of the cylinder.   If all of the cutting planes are
then passed through this line, elements will be cut from both surfaces.

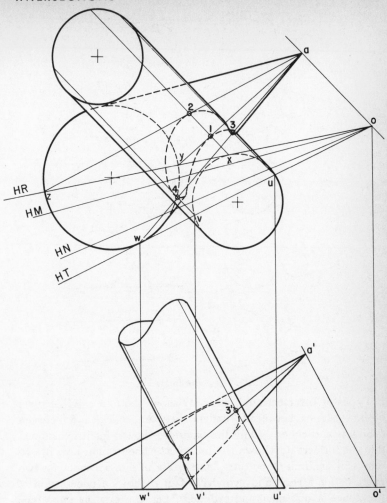

Fig. 338. Oblique Cone and Oblique Cylinder.

The base of the cone and the base of the cylinder lie in the same plane; therefore, one need only locate the pierce point of the control line on this plane and then pass all the traces of the cutting planes through this pierce point.

The two limiting planes indicate a secancy intersection; in addition to these planes, the planes M and N are needed to obtain the contour points.

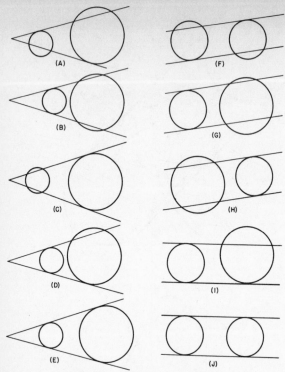

Fig. 339.   Types of Intersections.

Types of Intersections.   Fig. 339 shows the four possible types of intersections between cylinders, between cones, and between cylinders and cones. Only the bases are shown, for it is assumed that the surfaces not shown will intersect. The straight lines drawn represent the limiting cutting planes. Fig. *A* shows secancy for two cones or for a cone and cylinder. Fig. *B* shows a penetration of two cones or of a cone and cylinder. Fig. *C* shows the same type of intersection as Fig. *B* but here the penetration is reversed. Fig. *D* shows two cones, or a cone and a cylinder, which are tangent on one side. The line of intersection crosses itself at the point of tangency. Fig. *E* shows two cones, or a cone and a cylinder, which are tangent at two points. There are two lines of intersection crossing each other at the two points of tangency. Figs. *F* to *J* show the same types of intersections as Figs. *A* to *E*, in the same progressive order, but for two cylinders.

289

PROBLEMS

SUGGESTED EQUIPMENT

1. Set of drawing instruments
2. Architect's scale
3. Masking tape or scotch tape
4. Drawing pencils (F, H, 2H, 4H)
5. Sand pad (pencil pointer)
6. Ruby red pencil eraser
7. Artgum eraser
8. Black India drawing ink
9. Several French curves
10. Drawing paper
11. Dust cloth
12. Penholder
13. Lettering pen points (Henry tank pens, Nos. 4, 5, 12)
14. Drawing board
15. T-Square
16. 30°–60° triangle, 10 inches
17. 45° Braddock lettering triangle, 7 inches
18. Penknife, single-edge razor blade, and erasing shield
19. Six-inch straight edge or triangle, a pair of inexpensive pencil compasses, and cross-section paper

Introduction to Problems

The mastery of engineering drawing, which is a basic preparation for advanced work in engineering, requires diligent study and consistent, careful practice under the instructor's close supervision. The student should note that all engineering courses have a direct relationship to what he learns in engineering drawing (including both theory and practice), but that no other engineering course devotes time to teaching students how to draw. Consequently, the course in engineering drawing represents, for most students, their only opportunity to master this essential subject.

A set of instruction sheets, setting up the requirements and specifications for an engineering drawing course, is generally issued to all students at the beginning of the course, and all work must conform to the instructions issued. Instruction sheets cover grading, due dates, study assignments, plate assignments and requirements, workmanship (in which the control of appearance is stressed), drawing and tracing paper, plate arrangement, borders, prescribed title blocks, and other instructions pertaining to equipment. Procedures may vary slightly from one college to another, but drawing practice always remains the same. Therefore, the instruction sheets are important guides, and they should be read carefully.

Problems fall into two groups: (1) the study group and (2) the laboratory group.

The study group requires approximate scale drawings executed on cross-section paper, with the use of a six-inch straight edge, a pencil, and pencil compasses. Freehand drawing should be encouraged to develop the student's ability to sketch and to help him acquire a good understanding of three-dimensional visualization. Practice in lettering should also be included in this phase of the work. Workbooks containing completion problems are ideal for the study group.

The laboratory group requires complete layout drawings, including arrangement of views, border, and title blocks. These drawings should meet all the requirements specified in the instruction sheets.

Students' work should be carefully supervised throughout its many phases during the entire course of the semester. As much individual instruction as time will permit should be provided.

Sheet sizes, prescribed in Section 8 (see Appendix, p. 393) of the American Standard Drawings and Drafting Room Practice, are suggested for the problems.   Larger standard-size sheets may also be used if necessary.

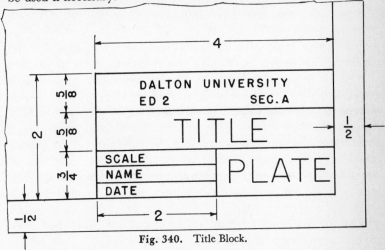

Fig. 340.   Title Block.

A title block is suggested in Fig. 340.   Title blocks vary from one college to another; consequently, the student must follow the form specified by his college and usually described in the instruction sheets distributed to him at the beginning of the semester.   At colleges where it is customary to bind the drawings, with or without a cover plate, a $1\frac{1}{2}$ inch border on the left side of the drawings should be provided to assure a border of uniform width.   Except for the sections dealing with (1) linework and the use of instruments, (2) geometric constructions, and (3) lettering, it is recommended that a title block be used in all problems.   A suggested sheet layout is shown in Fig. 341.

The student should note carefully the sheet size, border, and title block he is required to use; these data will be either stated by the instructor or listed in the instruction sheets.

The student should execute title blocks in writing, as shown in Fig. 342, until he has acquired sufficient skill in lettering.   He should not begin to letter his plates or drawings before he demonstrates the ability to letter legibly and according to acceptable standards of appearance.

Linework and the Use of Instruments

1. Reread Chapter 1 on linework and the use of instruments.

(a) Place a size A sheet ($8\frac{1}{2}'' \times 11''$) on the drawing board with the long dimension held horizontally.

(b) Sharpen pencils and point the leads.

(c) Try out your instruments and equipment by performing the operations explained in Chapter 1 of this text. Start by holding the pencil properly as indicated. Before drawing a line, make a short dash with the pencil at the start of the line and then draw it completely from the beginning. In drawing a line, the motion of the arm should be stopped approximately $\frac{1}{4}$ inch from the end of the line; the final segment is drawn with the movement of the fingers, and the pencil or pen is lifted vertically off the paper. The student should not proceed to the next problem until he has acquired efficiency in the use of all necessary instruments and adequate knowledge of their proper use.

2. Line characteristics and conventional ink lines (see Figs. 5, 6, 7 and Page 358—Fig. 18).

Sheet size A, border and title block as specified. (See Fig. 341 or other sources specified by the instructor.) Names, titles, date, and so forth should be written, unless the student's ability to letter proficiently has been approved by the instructor. The conventional line symbols should then be reproduced in pencil on one half and in ink on the other half of the paper. The pencil and ink lines should be placed on the paper in a balanced and pleasing arrangement. (The student may refer to pp. 5–6 for the relative weight of each line and for their distinguishing characteristics.) Dimension numerals and arrowheads should not be drawn at this stage. These conventional line symbols will be used in all subsequent work in engineering drawing; it is imperative that the student master them thoroughly.

3. (a) Sheet size, border, title block, and other instructions as in Problem 2. Reproduce the symbol for cast iron (see Appendix Fig. 25) in a rectangle $3'' \times 4''$. This problem makes use of two conventional lines: (1) outline of parts and (2) section lines.

(b) Ink in the same problem.

4. (a) Same instructions as in Problem 3. Reproduce the symbol for steel (see Appendix Fig. 25).

(b) Reproduce the same problem in ink by going over the pencil lines.

5. (a) Same instructions as in Problem 3. Reproduce the symbol for brick and stone masonry (see Appendix Fig. 25).

(b) Ink in the same problem.

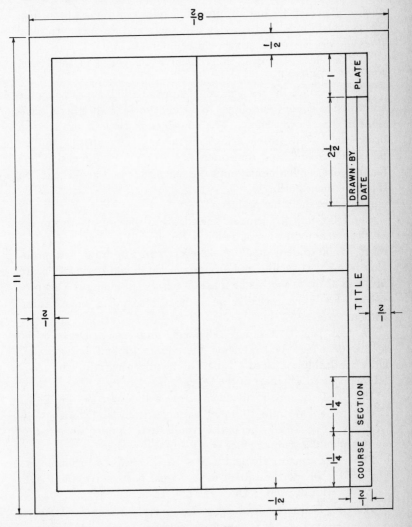

Fig. 341. Sheet Layout.

6. (a) Same instructions as in Problem 3. Reproduce the symbol for water and other liquids (see Appendix Fig. 25).

(b) Ink in the same problem.

7. Same instructions as in Problem 2, in regard to sheet size, border, and title block.

Reproduce the bottom half of Appendix Fig. 27, making the outside diameter 4″ and all other dimensions in direct proportion. This problem involves the use of compasses and three conventional line symbols. Arrowheads should be omitted.

8. Same instructions as in Problem 2, in regard to sheet size, border, and title block.

(a) Reproduce the bottom half of Appendix Fig. 68, drawing the construction circle (bolt circle) to a radius of $1\frac{1}{2}″$; all other dimensions in direct proportion. The construction circle is drawn as a center line. This problem involves the use of compasses, outline parts, center line, and dimension line. Omit the dimension line for the construction circle; omit the magnitude and arrowheads on the dimensions given.

(b) Ink in the same problem.

The following problems in linework and the use of instruments illustrate that a drawing or design in pencil must be exact before it is inked. The student should make every effort to draw these problems in ink with facility and accuracy. He should begin the entire problem again as soon as he makes a mistake in inking. This procedure should be repeated until the problem can be executed without error.

9. Use pencil, T-square, dividers, and scale. Draw a 5″ square (see Fig. 343). Divide the square in half horizontally. Draw vertical lines spaced $\frac{1}{2}″$ apart in the upper half; draw horizontal lines spaced $\frac{1}{2}″$ apart in the lower half.

10. Use T-square and dividers. Draw a 4″ square (see Fig. 344). Divide the square into 10 equal parts vertically and horizontally with dividers. Draw the pattern indicated. Under no circumstances should a scale or ruler be used in this problem.

11. Use T-square, dividers, and scale. Draw a 4″ square (see Fig. 345). Divide the square into 7 equal parts horizontally and vertically with dividers. Draw the pattern indicated.

12. Use T-square, dividers, scale, and 45° triangle. Draw a 5″ square (see Fig. 346). Draw 45° parallel lines spaced $\frac{1}{4}″$ apart as indicated, and complete the design.

Fig. 342. Title Block.

13. Use T-square, triangles, dividers, and scale. Draw a 4″ square (see Fig. 347). Draw the two diagonals of the square. These diagonals form 45° lines. Draw a series of parallel lines at 45°, spaced $\frac{1}{8}$″ apart, on both sides of the two diagonals. When the pattern indicated in Fig. 347 has been made, the spaces between the intersecting lines will form a $\frac{1}{2}$″ square.

14. Use bow compasses and scale. Draw a circle with a 4″ diameter (see Fig. 348). Starting from the center of the circle, draw concentric circles at $\frac{1}{2}$″ intervals as indicated in the illustration. Two conventional lines are used.

15. Use bow pencil compasses, T-square, triangles, and scale. Draw a 2″ square and divide it into four equal parts (see Fig. 349). Using the four inside corners, draw multiple radii $\frac{1}{4}$″ apart to complete the pattern illustrated.

16. Use T-square, triangles, bow compasses, and scale. Draw a 4″ square (see Fig. 350). Draw concentric arcs, with the four corners as centers, using radii varying by $\frac{1}{4}$″ with the smallest radius $1\frac{1}{4}$″. Complete the design.

17. Use T-square, bow pencil compasses, dividers, triangles, and scale. Draw a 3″ square (see Fig. 351). Divide the square into four equal parts. From the outside corners of each square draw intersecting arcs to form the design shown.

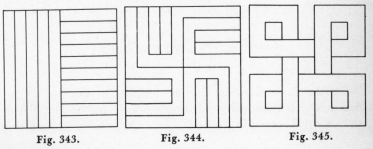

Fig. 343.   **Fig. 344.**   **Fig. 345.**

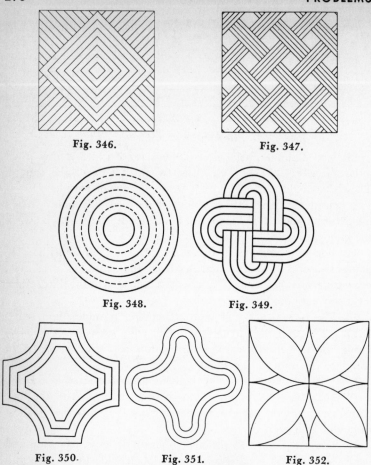

Fig. 346.

Fig. 347.

Fig. 348.

Fig. 349.

Fig. 350.

Fig. 351.

Fig. 352.

18. Use bow pencil compasses and scale. Draw a 4″ square (see Fig. 352). Divide the square into four equal parts. Using the corners of the squares as centers, complete the design as indicated.

Geometric Constructions

Sheet size A, border, and title as specified in your instruction sheets or by your instructor. Divide the available working space into four equal areas.

No specific dimensions are given for these problems. To start work on any problem, draw the lines and arcs with magnitudes, positions, and directions comparable to those shown in the illustrated problems. Draw these lines initially as construction lines and designate all points as indicated.

Construction lines must be shown in all problems. For construction lines use the pencil, properly pointed, recommended in the discussion, "Choice of Pencil," page 2. Construction lines are very light lines, yet legible and clear-cut. Construction lines should be drawn just long enough to indicate centers, tangents, or intersections.

All points of tangency must be indicated by a short dash and marked with the capital letter T. Centers should be shown by the intersection of construction lines.

All lines in the following geometric constructions must conform to the alphabet of lines shown in Fig. 7.

The problems in this group are shown in the same sheet layout illustrated in Fig. 341.

1. Fig. 353.   Bisect line *AB*, using dividers.   Bisect line *CD*, using compasses.   Bisect line *EF*, using a 45° triangle.

2. Fig. 354.   Divide line *GH* into five equal parts, using dividers. Divide line *JK* into five equal parts, using the method shown in Fig. 41.

3. Fig. 355.   Divide line *LM* into parts proportional to 1, 3, 4, 6, 9.

4. Fig. 356.   Trisect line *RS*.

5. Fig. 357.   Bisect angle *AOB*, using compasses.

6. Fig. 358.   Bisect arc *AB*, using compasses.

7. Fig. 359.   Draw a perpendicular from point *C* to line *AB*, using compasses.   Draw a perpendicular from point *F* to line *DE*, using a combination of triangles.

8. Fig. 360.   Draw a line parallel to *GH* and $\frac{3}{4}''$ from it, using compasses.   Draw a line parallel to line *JK* and 1″ from it, using a combination of triangles.

9. Fig. 361.   Draw a right triangle on *AB* with *AB* as the hypotenuse and *CD* as one leg.

10. Fig. 362.   Draw an equilateral triangle on side *EF*, using compasses.   Draw an equilateral triangle on side *GH*, using a triangle only.

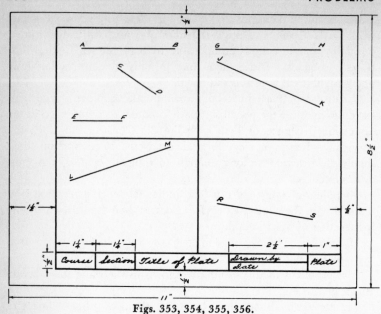

Figs. 353, 354, 355, 356.

11. Fig. 363. Draw a triangle on side *KL* with sides of length *MN* and *OP*.

12. Fig. 364. Draw a curve, using the proper French curve, parallel to *AB* and $1\frac{1}{4}''$ from it.

13. Fig. 365. Draw a square 2″ "across flats" (a dimension in the drawing of bolt heads) on center *O*, using a T-square, a 45° triangle, and compasses.

14. Fig. 366. Draw a regular hexagon with a distance "across flats" of $1\frac{7}{8}''$ on center *O*, using a T-square, compasses, and a 30°–60° triangle.

15. Fig. 367. Draw regular octagons, one circumscribed and another inscribed, in the given circle.

16. Fig. 368. Inscribe a regular pentagon in the circle given.

17. Fig. 369. Draw a regular hexagon with a distance across corners of 3″ on center *O*, using compasses.

18. Fig. 370. Draw a regular nonagon on side *AB*.

19. Fig. 371. Construct a square with a distance *CD* as the distance across corners and inscribe an octagon.

20. Fig. 372. Transfer the given figure so that line *EF* is enlarged to *GH*.

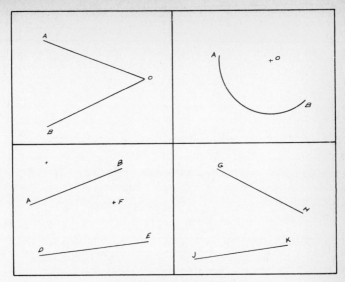

Figs. 357, 358, 359, 360.

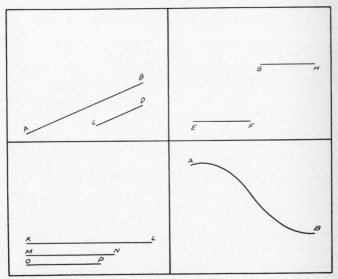

Figs. 361, 362, 363, 364.

21. Fig. 373. Draw an arc of $1\frac{1}{2}''$ radius tangent to the right angle *ABC*.

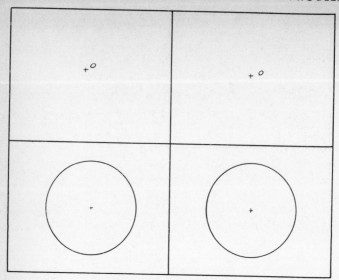

Figs. 365, 366, 367, 368.

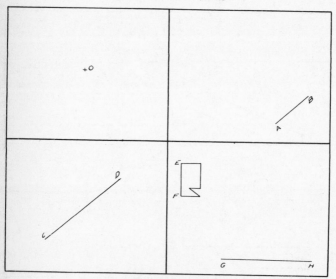

Figs. 369, 370, 371, 372.

22. Fig. 374. Draw an arc of 2″ radius tangent to the two non-parallel lines *EF* and *GH*.

23. Fig. 375.   Draw an arc of $1\frac{1}{2}''$ radius tangent to the two non-parallel lines JK and LM.

24. Fig. 376.   Draw arcs of $\frac{3}{8}''$ radius tangent to the sides of the given figure and to the sides at point O.

25. Fig. 377.   Draw an arc of $1\frac{1}{4}''$ radius tangent to arc AB and line CD.

26. Fig. 378.   Draw an arc of $\frac{7}{8}''$ radius tangent to the inside of arc EF and line GH.

27. Fig. 379.   Draw a line through G tangent to circle O. Draw a line through H tangent to circle O.

28. Fig. 380.   Draw an arc that will be the arc of a circle through C, D, and E, and then draw a smooth curve through points shown, using tangent GH and arcs.   Do not, however, use a French curve.

29. Fig. 381.   Draw an arc of $\frac{7}{8}''$ radius tangent to the "outside" of arcs KL and MN.

30. Fig. 382.   Draw an arc of $\frac{3}{4}''$ radius tangent to the "inside" of arc ST and tangent to the "outside" of arc PR.

31. Fig. 383.   Draw a circle $4''$ in diameter tangent to arcs UV and WX, but enclosing arc UV only.

32. Fig. 384.   Draw a circle $5''$ in diameter tangent to arcs AB and CD and enclosing both arcs.

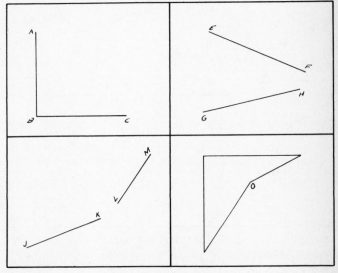

Figs. 373, 374, 375, 376.

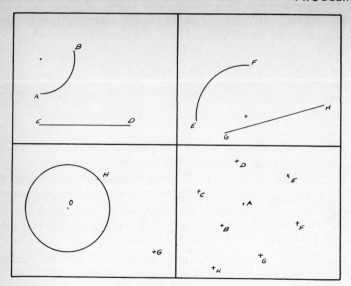

Figs. 377, 378, 379, 380.

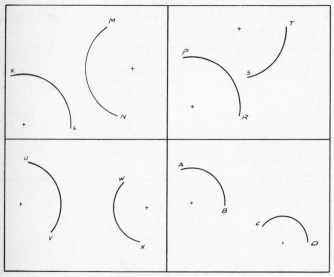

Figs. 381, 382, 383, 384.

33. Fig. 385. Draw a semi-ellipse, using the foci method, with *LM* as the minor axis and *NO* as half the major axis.

34. Fig. 386. Draw an ellipse by the concentric circle method on minor axis *AB* and major axis *CD*.

35. Fig. 387. Draw a semi-ellipse by the trammel method on minor axis *KL* and half the major axis *OM*.

36. Fig. 388. Draw an approximate ellipse by the four-center method on minor axis *AB* and major axis *CD*.

Lettering

During his work on the problems and exercises in this section, the student should refer to Chapter 3 (on lettering) and to the Appendix, page 395.

Lettering for technical drawings is fully standardized. Letters, words, sentences, and titles are designed according to specific standards. The size of a letter may vary but never its form. The letterer must know the correct form of every letter in the alphabet.

Letters are made with finger motions. The pencil or pen is held with the fingers (not too tightly) and the hand and forearm rest on the drawing board. The position of the hand in lettering is similar to its position in ruling a line. In fact, the motion to complete the

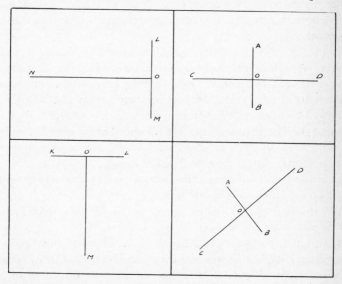

Figs. 385, 386, 387, 388.

ruling of a line involves precisely the same finger movement used in lettering.

A good letterer always uses guide lines. In drawings to be lettered in pencil, guide lines may be erased until they are barely visible. This technique obviates the need of making erasures around individual letters and words.

The student should learn the sequence of strokes in drawing letters (see Figs. 95, 100). Adherence to the recommended sequence of strokes not only helps the draftsman to form the proper shape of each letter but also aids him in acquiring facility in this work. Further, the use of the suggested sequence of strokes prevents the nibs of the pen from scratching or catching in the paper and spattering ink over the drawing, or the point of the pencil from catching in the paper and damaging its surface.

The function of lettering, like that of writing, is to convey information to the reader. Legibility, which is of primary importance, depends upon the proper spacing of letters within a word and of words within a sentence. Even poorly constructed letters can be read if the spacing is proper. A thorough understanding of spacing is essential to good lettering. Therefore, the student is urged to study the material on spacing (pp. 60–62) carefully. In addition, he is urged to carry out the following practical suggestions and instructions.

Learn the form of each letter and each numeral, noting its width in relation to its height; learn how to make the letters and numerals appear straight and steady. Compare the heights of fractions with the heights of whole numbers, noting the extent of the differences. Learn to form letters into words and words into sentences, bearing in mind the fact that good spacing is important for ease in reading. Be careful not to dot a capital I, and do not use lower case letters in a word that should consist of capital letters.

Center letters about a center line in making up a title or in completing a line of lettering or a title box.

Where lettering must first be done in pencil, preparatory to inking, ink directly over the penciled letters.

1. Cut a strip of paper to a length of one inch and to a height of the vertical capital letters illustrated in Fig. 85. Draw a line parallel to the 1″ side that bisects the narrow dimension of the strip. Prepare a table as follows.

Letter Shown with Correct Shape and Sequence of Strokes	Width in Respect to Height			Stability			
	Narrower	Same	Wider	Smaller above Center Line	Crosses above Center Line	Crosses at Center Line	Crosses below Center Line
M			√ s				

Measure the letters with the strip of paper and complete the table by placing a √ and your estimated value of variation under the proper headings.   Use an *S* if the variation is slight; otherwise, use multiples of $\frac{1}{6}$.   Compare with the corresponding alphabet in the Appendix (Section 9 of American Standard Drawings and Drafting Room Practice).   Use the completed problem as a guide until memorized.

2. Use the same procedure as in the preceding problem, but for the vertical numerals.

3. Without preparing a table as above, note and memorize the differences between the vertical capitals and the inclined capitals.

4. The same as the preceding problem, but for the inclined numerals.

5. The same as Problem 1, but for the inclined lower case letters. Use the completed problem as a guide until memorized.   (Consider the height to be from the base line to the waist line (see Fig. 98), even though the stem extends above and below these lines.)

On the lettering problems above, work about twenty minutes at a time, less if the hand becomes tired and cramped.   Do not squeeze the pencil so tightly that your hand will be cramped and shaking at the very start.   Learn the shape of the letter and the sequence of strokes, be relaxed, and work diligently.   Learning to letter like a professional will be a source of immense satisfaction to you, and careful lettering will please everyone who has occasion to view your work.

6. Sheet size A, border as specified in Fig. 341, strip title.   Divide the available working space into two equal areas, using a vertical line, and prepare the sheet as in the preceding lettering problems. Draw a series of 18 sets of guide lines, using the Braddock-Rowe

Lettering Triangle (Fig. 89), for letters $\frac{1}{4}''$ high, starting $\frac{1}{8}''$ from the top border and leaving a uniform space of $\frac{1}{8}''$ between each set of guide rules and the next set.

6(a). On the left side reproduce the Type 1 ASA vertical capitals and numerals (see Appendix Fig. 98), reproducing each 4 or 5 times in pencil, in the following order: I H T L E F N K Z Y V A M W X O Q C G D U J B B P R S & 1 2 3 8 6 9 5 7 0 4 $\frac{1}{2}$ $\frac{3}{4}$ $\frac{5}{8}$. Draw additional guide lines for the fractions.

6(b). On the right side, using Type 1 ASA vertical capitals and numerals, letter the following, one to a line: ATLANTA, WINTER, AMERICAN, XAVIER, BOISMENUE, ALTITUDE, ZENITH, TITLE, DATE, 71785, 2B643, 9A100.

7(a). Letter the alphabet two or more times in ink, as in Problem 6(a), using the pen point to make the bold strokes indicated. Do not have too much ink on the pen point. (Note that an undesirable contrast in inked lettering is caused by allowing the pen to run out of ink. In such instances, a very faint letter, resulting from the dry pen, and a bold letter, resulting from use of a freshly filled pen, will appear side by side. Do not let the pen run dry.)

7(b). As in Problem 6(b), letter entire right side in ink.

8(a). As in Problem 6(a), using the Type 1 ASA inclined capitals and numerals. (See Appendix Fig. 99.)

8(b). As in Problem 6(b), using the Type 1 ASA inclined capitals and numerals.

9(a) (b). As in Problem 7(a) (b).

10(a). Sheet layout as in Problem 6. On the left side, using lettering guide-line device (Braddock-Rowe Lettering Triangle), draw a series of guide lines using the #8 holes (capital height $\frac{8}{32}''$). The top hole is not for drawing a guide line; it is used for matching on the last base line drawn so that additional guide lines may be continued down the sheet. Reproduce the Type 6 ASA inclined lower case letters, reproducing each letter 4 or 5 times in the order given in Section 9, ASA.

10(b). On the right-hand side, using the same height guide lines as in Problem 10(a), letter the note included under Type 6 ASA that starts "Type 6 may be used, etc." (See Appendix, p. 396.)

11(a) (b). As in Problem 7(a) (b). Note the difference in boldness between the Type 1 and Type 6 letters. Use the pen point to give the boldness indicated.

12(a). Title Blocks. Sheet size A, border as specified, strip title. Letter the strip title, using Type 2 vertical capitals for "TITLE BLOCKS" and Plate No., making these letters $\frac{7}{32}''$ high. Course and section to be Type 3, vertical capitals $\frac{3}{16}''$ high. Name and date to be Type 4, vertical capitals $\frac{1}{8}''$ high. Each part of the strip title to be centered in its respective space both vertically and horizontally. (See Figs. 340, 341, 342, for a suggested title block.)

Centering your work in the left-side working area, reproduce the standard title box used at Dalton University (Fig. 340). The numbers are of the same height as the letters, measured in thirty-seconds of an inch. For top portion of title use Type 3 letters. For the title and plate number use Type 1 or 2. For scale, name, and date use Type 3 or 4. Outline of title box is the same weight as the border. Each part of the title is to be centered in its respective space both vertically and horizontally.

Centering your work in the right-side working area, reproduce the standard title box required by your college.

12(b). After your instructor's approval of the sheet executed in pencil, ink the titles.

To develop adequate speed, accuracy, and proper appearance, both for vertical capitals and inclined capitals and for lower case composition work, you should practice lettering throughout the course.

Orthographic Projection

It is recommended that the student review Chapter 4, on orthographic projection, before attempting to work the problems in this section. Although he is not required to dimension the problems at this point, he should provide ample space between and around views for dimensioning.

The vertical space above the title block (see Appendix Fig. 96) is sometimes used for notes and other pertinent data. In such instances the drawing should not extend into this area.

Sheet size A or B as noted in the Appendix (Section 8, ASA Drawings and Drafting Room Practice). Sheet size, border, and title as specified in Fig. 341.

Single-view problems are a direct application of the subject matter in the first three chapters of this text.

1. Draw the gasket shown in Fig. 389.

2. Draw the gasket shown in Fig. 390.

3. Draw the T-square Head shown in Fig. 391.

4. Draw the gasket shown in Fig. 393.

5. Draw the rail cross section shown in Fig. 392. Dimensions shown are to intersections of tangents.

6. Draw the wrench shown in Fig. 394.

7. Draw the sprocket shown in Fig. 395. Keep drawing clear of title box. The $\frac{1}{2}$ inch radius reverses on the $5\frac{5}{8}$ inch construction circle.

8. Draw the hook shown in Fig. 396. Keep drawing clear of title box.

9–25. Problems 9 to 25 on orthographic projection require you to draw three complete views (front, top, and right-side view) of the pieces illustrated in Figs. 397 to 413. Review the discussion on pages 67–83 before beginning these problems, and note carefully the

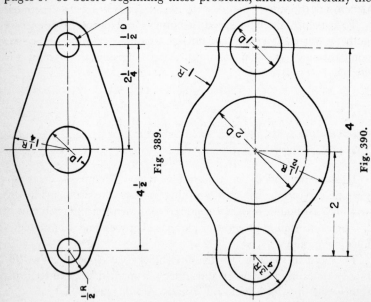

Fig. 389.

Fig. 390.

arrangement of views. Sheet size B (11 × 17), border and title, as specified in Appendix Fig. 96, should be used.

26. Compute the volume of the object assigned from Figs. 397 to 413 in cubic inches. Tabulate on computation sheet in a form similar to the following.

Part No.	Geometrical Shape	Computed Volume (Cu. In.)	
		Plus	Minus
1	Negative Cylinder		10.3
2	Rectangular Prism	50.1	
Etc.			
	Totals		
	Net		

Show all computations below tabulation. Original computation sheets must be submitted. A computation sheet should also contain such information as title, date, computer's name, and a ruled sketch or sketches. This information is lettered and engineer's numerals are used. Computations are to decimals and not to fractions. A 3H pencil should be used and a dull or soft pencil avoided. If more than one sheet is required, the sheets should be numbered consecutively, briefly titled and dated. Only one side of a computation sheet should be used.

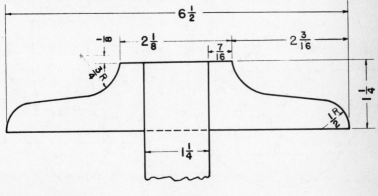

Fig. 391.

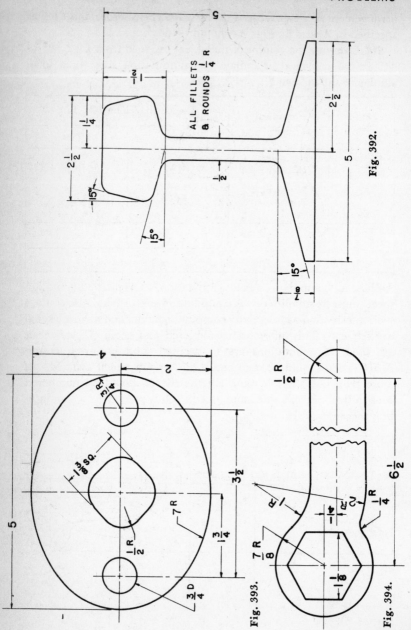

ALL FILLETS & ROUNDS $\frac{1}{4}$ R

Fig. 392.

Fig. 393.

Fig. 394.

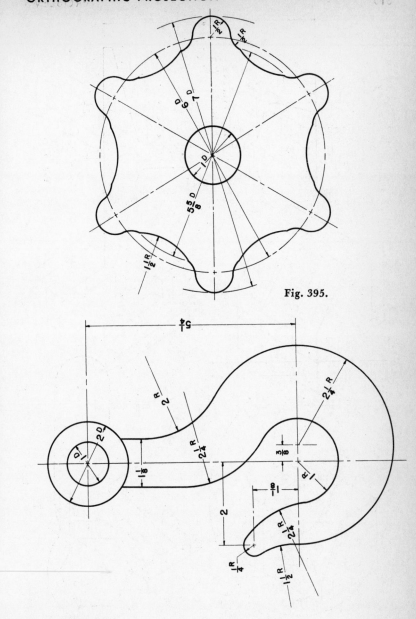

Fig. 395.

Fig. 396.

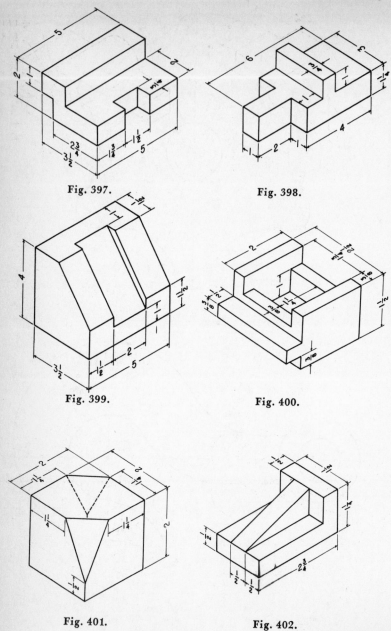

Fig. 397.

Fig. 398.

Fig. 399.

Fig. 400.

Fig. 401.

Fig. 402.

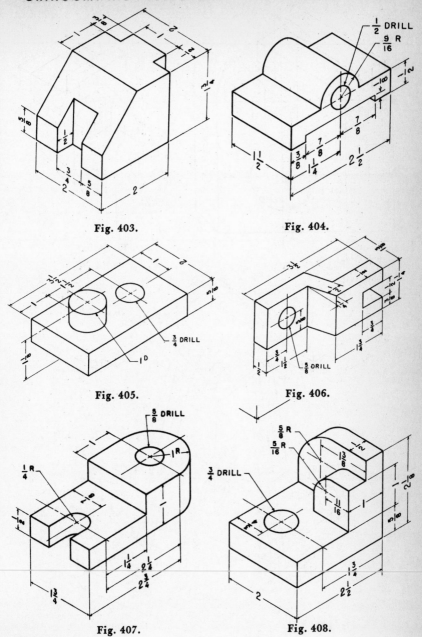

Fig. 403.

Fig. 404.

Fig. 405.

Fig. 406.

Fig. 407.

Fig. 408.

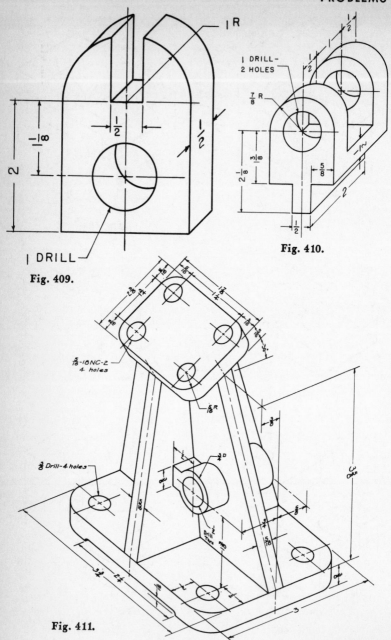

1 R

1/2

2

1/2

1 1/8

1/2

1 DRILL

Fig. 409.

1 DRILL— 2 HOLES

7/8 R

1/2

1

1/2

1/2

3/8

2 1/8

5/8

1/2

2

Fig. 410.

5/16-18NC-2 4 holes

5/8 R

3/8 D

3/8 Drill—4 holes

1/2 Drill Thru FND

3/4

3 1/4

2 1/4

1/8

3

Fig. 411.

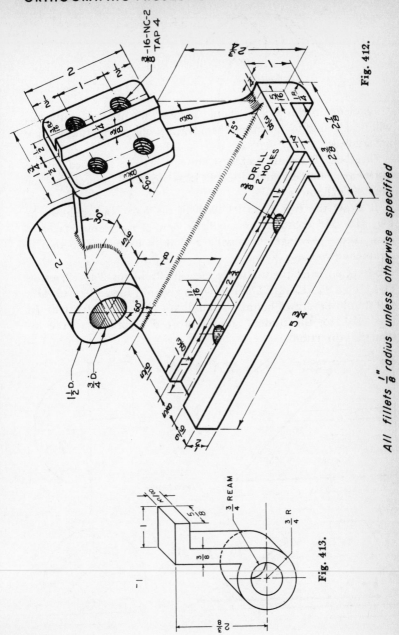

Fig. 412.

Fig. 413.

All fillets $\frac{1}{8}$ radius unless otherwise specified

Auxiliary Views

Problems in this section should not be dimensioned. Students will be required to dimension them when problems in dimensioning are studied.

Sheet size B for all problems unless otherwise specified by the instructor. Borders and title block as specified in problems for preceding chapters.

1. Draw the two views for each of the four objects shown in Fig. 416, and construct an auxiliary view of the sloping faces of each piece. Arrange the auxiliary view in each case so that it clears the two views given.

2-10. Construct the auxiliary view in Problems 2 to 10, using Figs. 414, 415, 417-421. The two views given in Figs. 414, 415, 417-419 should be drawn before the auxiliary view is constructed. In Figs. 420-423, the student should proceed according to the instructor's directions.

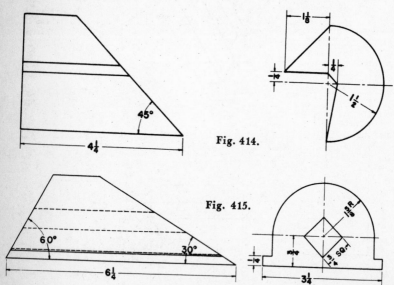

Fig. 414.

Fig. 415.

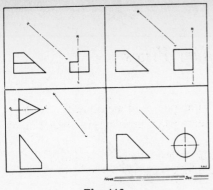

Fig. 416.

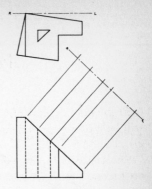

Fig. 417.

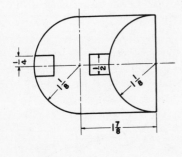

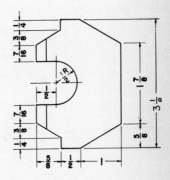

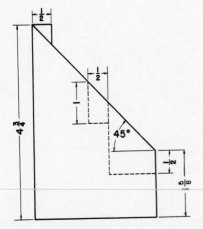

Fig. 418.

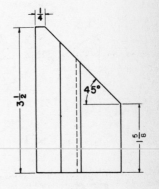

Fig. 419.

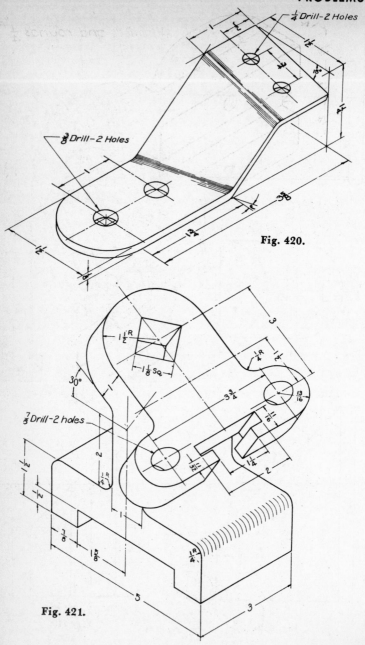

Fig. 420.

Fig. 421.

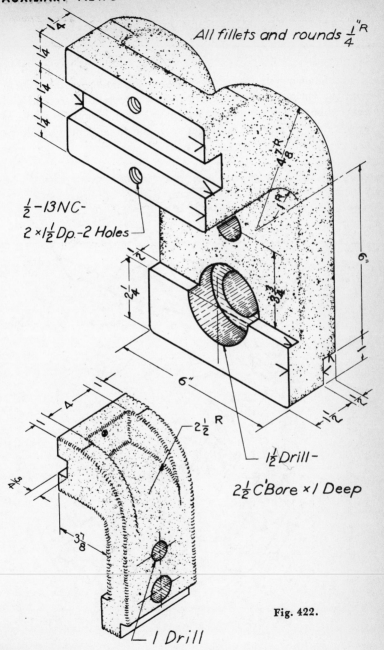

All fillets and rounds $\frac{1}{4}$"R

$\frac{1}{4}$

$\frac{1}{4}$

$\frac{1}{4}$

$\frac{1}{4}$

$4\frac{7}{8}$R

1R

$\frac{1}{2}-13NC-$
$2 \times 1\frac{1}{2}$Dp.-2 Holes

$\frac{1}{2}$

$2\frac{1}{4}$

$3\frac{3}{4}$

$6''$

$6''$

1

$\frac{1}{2}$

$\frac{1}{2}$

$1\frac{1}{2}$Drill$-$

$2\frac{1}{2}$C'Bore $\times 1$ Deep

4

$2\frac{1}{2}$R

$\frac{3}{4}$

$3\frac{7}{8}$

1 Drill

Fig. 422.

Sections and Conventions

The following problems are designed to familiarize the student with the various methods of drawing or representing sections and conventions. The student is not required to dimension the problems at this time. However, sufficient space for dimensioning should be

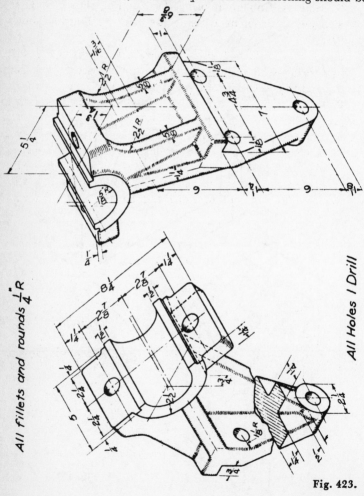

Fig. 423.

provided around all drawings. The drawings should be put away neatly to be completed later by the addition of the necessary dimensions.

Sheet size B, scale to be indicated by the instructor. Border and title as in previous plates.

1. Copy the front elevation of the valve bonnet shown in Fig. 424 and construct an end view in section.

2. Same as Problem 1, using the flanged sleeve shown in Fig. 425.

3. Same as Problem 1, using the coupling shown in Fig. 426.

4. Same as Problem 1, using the packing housing shown in Fig. 427.

5. Same as Problem 1, using the level seal shown in Fig. 433.

Hold sheet size B vertically, scale to be indicated by instructor. Border and title as specified in other problems.

6. Construct a plan view and a front elevation in section of the engine leg shown in Fig. 428.

7. Same as Problem 6, using the column base shown in Fig. 429.

8. Same as Problem 6, using the clamp lever shown in Fig. 430.

9. Same as Problem 6, using the jig base shown in Fig. 431.

10. Same as Problem 6, using the gear box shown in Fig. 432.

11. Same as Problem 6, using the flanged pulley shown in Fig. 434.

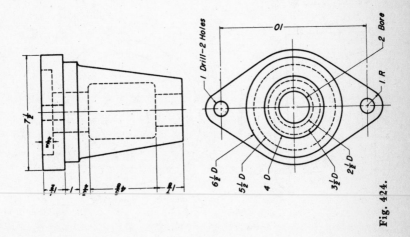

Fig. 424.

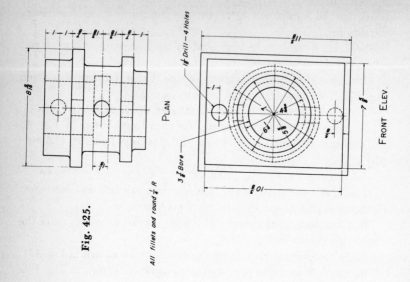

Fig. 425.

All fillets and round ¼ R

PLAN

FRONT ELEV.

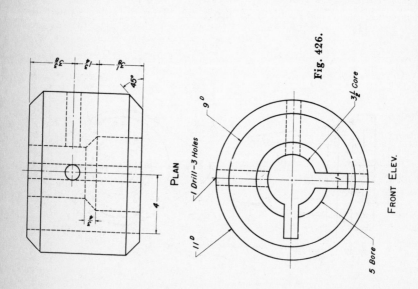

Fig. 426.

PLAN

FRONT ELEV.

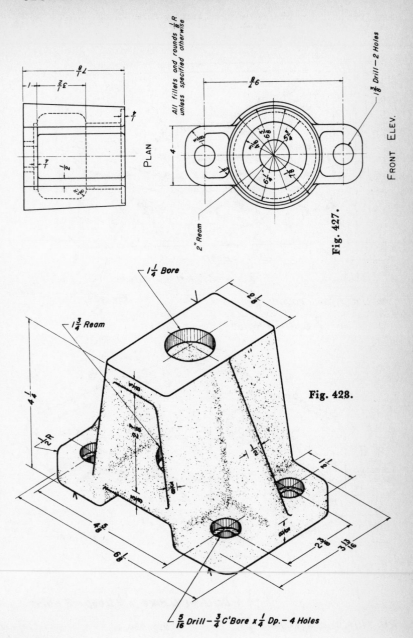

PLAN

All fillets and rounds $\frac{1}{8}$ R unless specified otherwise

$1\frac{3}{8}$ Drill — 2 Holes

2" Ream

FRONT ELEV.

Fig. 427.

$1\frac{1}{4}$ Bore

$1\frac{3}{4}$ Ream

Fig. 428.

$\frac{5}{16}$ Drill — $\frac{3}{4}$ C'Bore x $\frac{1}{4}$ Dp. — 4 Holes

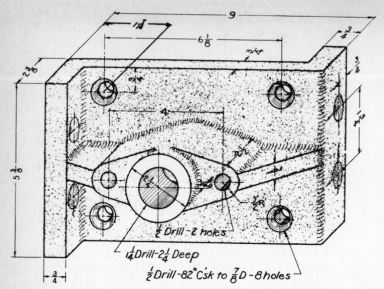

All fillets and rounds $\frac{1}{8}$"R

Fig. 429.

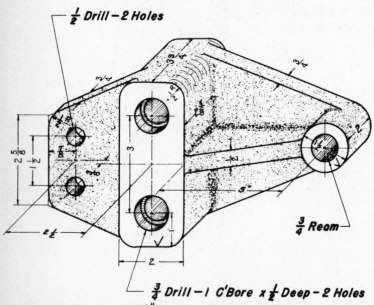

Fig. 430.

All fillets and rounds $\frac{1}{8}$"R

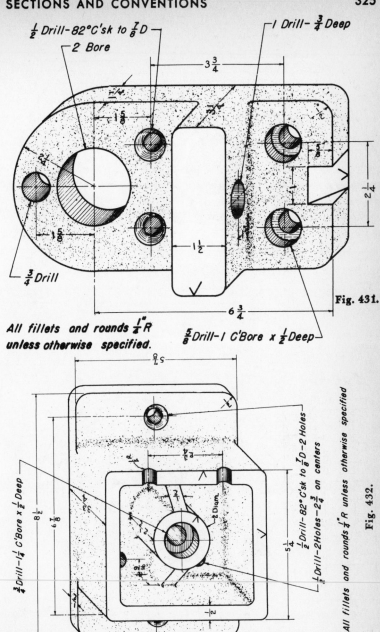

Fig. 431.

Fig. 432.

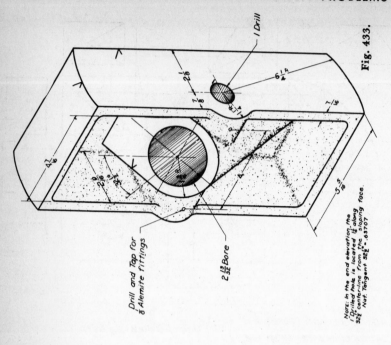

Drill and Tap for $\frac{1}{8}$ Alemite Fittings

1 Drill

$2\frac{5}{8}$

$\frac{7}{8}$

$6\frac{1}{4}R$

$4\frac{1}{1}$

$2\frac{13}{32}$ Bore

$4\frac{1}{16}$

$\frac{7}{16}$

$5\frac{5}{16}$

Note: In the end elevation the 1 Drilled hole is located $1\frac{1}{8}$ along the centre-line from the sloping face. Nat. Tangent $32\frac{1}{2} = .63707$

Fig. 433.

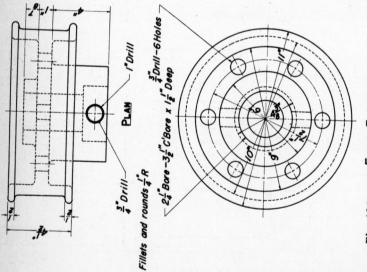

$\frac{3}{4}$ Drill

Fillets and rounds $\frac{1}{4}$ R

PLAN

1" Drill

$\frac{3}{4}$ Drill–6 Holes

$2\frac{1}{4}$ Bore–$3\frac{1}{2}$ C'Bore x $1\frac{1}{2}$ Deep

1"

6"

10"

9"

FRONT ELEVATION

Fig. 434.

Figs. 435–440.

Figs. 441–446.

Pictorial Views

Sheet size B, scale as indicated by instructor. Border and title as specified in previous problems.

1. Draw the missing lines and make a freehand isometric drawing on cross-section paper of the objects in Figs. 435-446.

Dimensioning of the following drawings may be required after study of problems in next section, p. 331.

For each of the following problems construct an isometric drawing with the use of instruments. Scale to be indicated by instructor.

2. Stand shown in Fig. 447.
3. Rocker arm shown in Fig. 448.
4. Brace shown in Fig. 449.
5. Hanger shown in Fig. 450.
6. Pedestal shown in Fig. 451.
7. Shifter fork shown in Fig. 452.
8. Hinge shown in Fig. 453.
9. Sawhorse shown in Fig. 454.
10. Bracket shown in Fig. 455.
11. Figs. 483-486 (pp. 340-343).

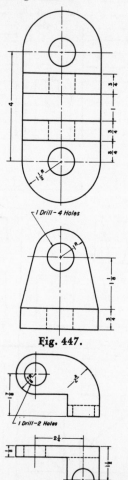

Fig. 447.

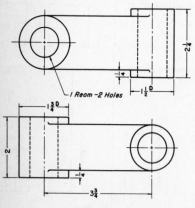

Fig. 448.

Fig. 449.

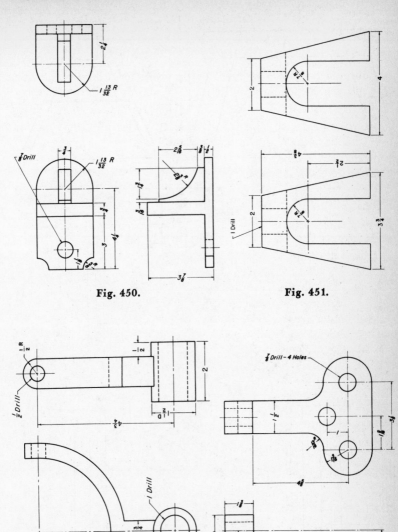

Fig. 450.

Fig. 451.

Fig. 452.

Fig. 453.

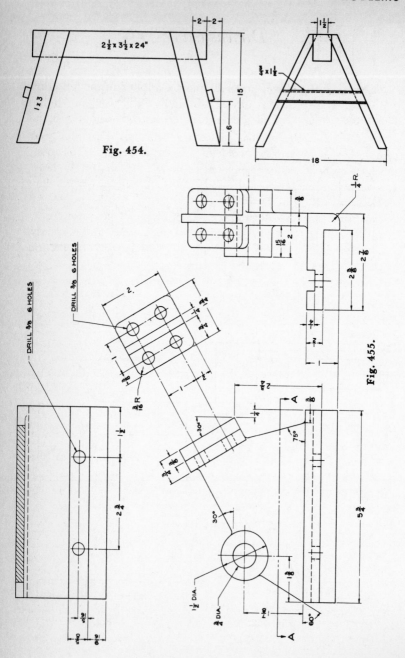

Fig. 454.

Fig. 455.

Dimensioning

The basic principles of dimensioning are applied in the following problems. The problems may be used in the study group and in the laboratory group. (The student should reread Chapter 8.)

At this point, the student may be assigned to dimension and complete the preceding problems on orthographic projection, auxiliary views, sections and conventions, and pictorial views. He may also dimension selected problems on fasteners which follow this section.

Sheet size, border, title, and scale as specified by the instructor.

1. Reproduce the drawings in Fig. 460 and dimension correctly.

2. Copy the drawings in Figs. 456-459, 461-474 and dimension properly.

In all work requiring dimensions, correct execution of the views is necessary. Drawings with incorrect views or incorrectly dimensioned must be re-drawn. Special attention should be given to linework, arrowheads, fraction heights, finish marks, arrangement of views, and the correct placing of size and location dimensions.

In the following problems, the student should not copy all the dimensions indicated. Some of these dimensions have been placed deliberately in undesirable locations, and it is the responsibility of the student to dimension the problems correctly according to the instructions on dimensioning (Chapter 8) and ASA standards (see Appendix C, Sections 5 and 6).

3. Copy the drawings in Figs. 475 to 479. Examine the dimensions of the given drawings and omit those on your copies which do not represent accepted practice. No additional dimensions are necessary.

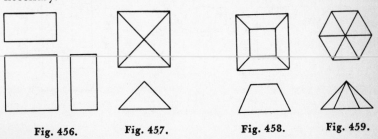

Fig. 456.   Fig. 457.   Fig. 458.   Fig. 459.

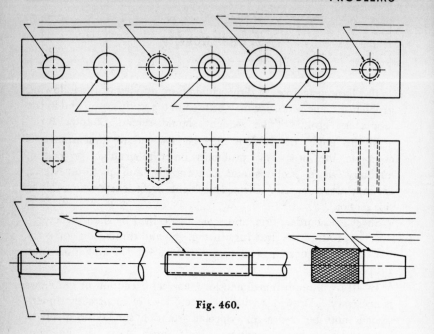

Fig. 460.

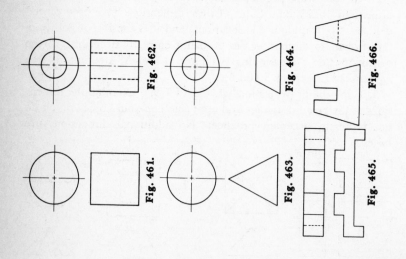

Fig. 462.

Fig. 464.

Fig. 466.

Fig. 461.

Fig. 463.

Fig. 465.

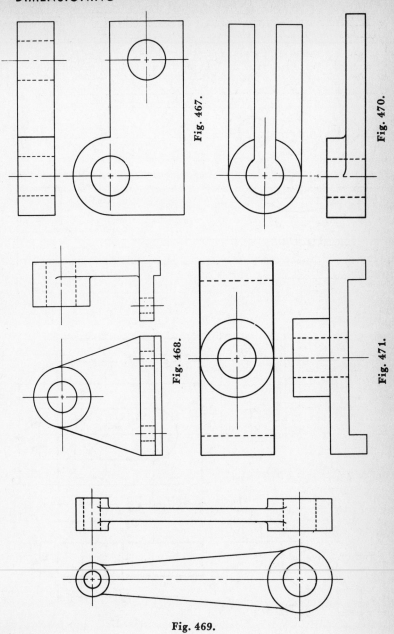

Fig. 467.

Fig. 470.

Fig. 468.

Fig. 471.

Fig. 469.

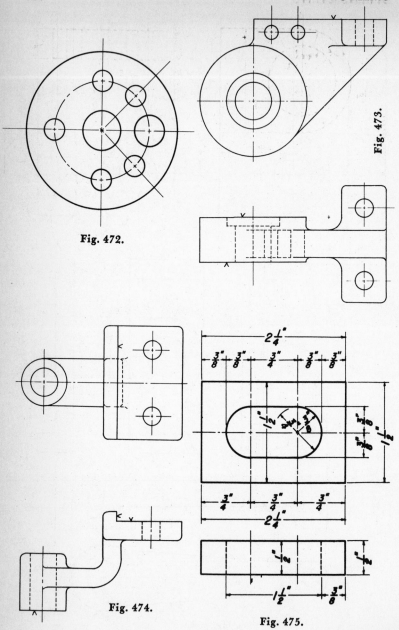

Fig. 472.

Fig. 473.

Fig. 474.

Fig. 475.

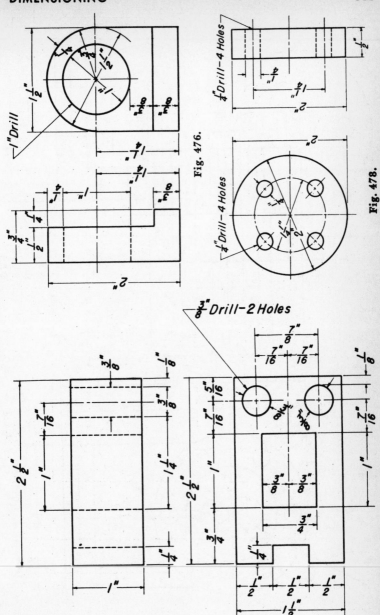

Fig. 476.

Fig. 478.

Fig. 477

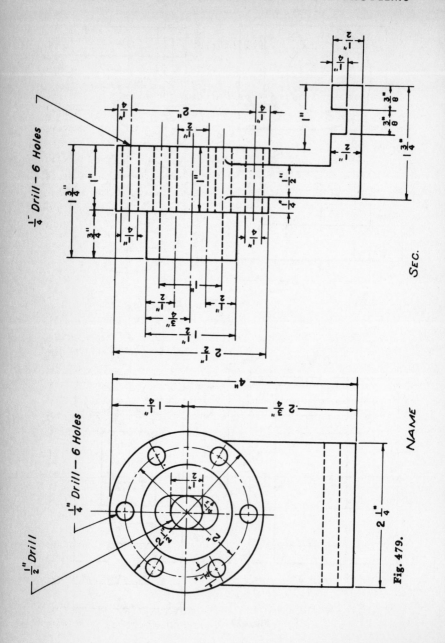

$\frac{1}{4}$" Drill – 6 Holes

$\frac{1}{4}$" Drill – 6 Holes

$\frac{1}{2}$" Drill

SEC.

NAME

Fig. 479.

Fasteners

Simplified sketches may be used in study assignments.

1. You are required by your employer, a manufacturer of steel products, to design an illustration for a new catalog showing primarily:

(a) The most common American Standard semifinished hexagonal head bolt and nut. Under the drawing and referring to the drawing, list the information you wish the customer to have about this type of bolt and nut and also the information to furnish when ordering. For example, order 100 each of the bolt and nut drawn for your illustration.

(b) Using parts of (a) applicable to studs.

(c) Using parts of (a) applicable to one particular cap screw.

(d) Using parts of (a) applicable to one particular machine screw.

(e) Using parts of (a) applicable to one particular setscrew.

(f) Using parts of (a) applicable to one particular key.

The student is not expected to reproduce tables or to include a price list. Sheet size A or B, border and title as specified. In evaluation of the illustration, the appearance of the layout, the extent of information utilized in the drawing or drawings, and the organization of materials included in the text will be considered.

2. Show the following threaded holes in elevation and section views in $1'' \times 2''$ rectangles, using ASA regular thread symbols. List the tap drill size for each hole.

(a) $\frac{1}{2}$–13Nc–2 threads for a hole tapped through the piece.

(b) $\frac{3}{4}$–16NF–3LH threads with the threads tapped the conventional depth.

(c) $\frac{5}{8}$–11NC–2 threads with the threads tapped to the bottom of the hole.

For parts (b) and (c) refer to Fig. 246 for the proper depth proportions and assume the metal to be cast iron.

3. Repeat Problem 2, using the ASA simplified thread symbols and assume the metal to be steel.

4. Fig. 480 shows a section of a flange coupling to connect two shafts. It is intended that regular hexagonal semifinished $1''$ bolts

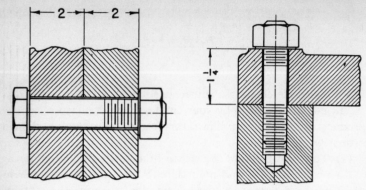

Fig. 480.   Fig. 481.

with fine threads be used.   Specify the bolt (and nut) that you think
should be used. Be sure to specify a standard length of bolt. (See
Appendix Table 2.)

5. What bolt would you specify in Problem 4 if it were intended
to put an SAE standard plain washer and an SAE standard lock
washer on the nut end of the bolt?

6. What bolt would you specify in Problem 4 if it were intended
to put two SAE standard plain washers and an SAE standard lock
washer on the nut end of the bolt?

7. Fig. 481 shows a stud that is to be used to fasten an engine
head to the block.   The block is cast iron.   A $\frac{9}{16}''$ stud with a
heavy semifinished hexagonal nut is to be used.   The end in the
block is to have coarse threads and the nut end is to have fine
threads.   Specify the stud and nut you would use.   Also specify
the tap drill size and depth and the tap size and depth.

8. Cap screws are to be used to attach a shaft bearing housing
to a cast iron speed reducer.   A partial section of the lubricating
end is shown in Fig. 482.   The cap screw is to be a $\frac{1}{2}''$ American
Standard hexagonal cap screw with coarse threads.   Specify the
standard length cap screw that you would use.   Also specify the tap
drill and tap sizes and depths for the drill in the body of the speed
reducer.   What size hole do you think should be drilled in the housing?

9. Two identical collars $3\frac{1}{2}''$ in diameter (O.D.) are to hold a
belt pulley in position on a $2''$ (diameter) shaft.   The collars are to
be held in position with $\frac{3}{8}''$ cone-pointed setscrews jammed against
the shaft.   Safety regulations require that the setscrew on the outside
(side exposed to workmen) be a socket-head setscrew at least $\frac{3}{16}''$

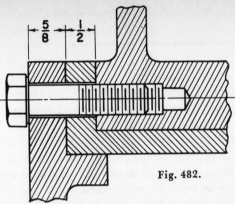

$\frac{5}{8}$ $\frac{1}{2}$

Fig. 482.

below the surface of the collar. On the other hand, it is desired to use a square-headed setscrew on the inside. In order that there will be no mistake in assembling, the outside screw is to have fine threads and the inside screw is to have coarse threads. Specify the setscrews that should be used with a Class 3 fit.

10. An electric motor with foot pads $\frac{3}{4}''$ thick is mounted on a steel plate $2''$ thick. It is proposed to use regular hexagonal semifinished $\frac{1}{2}''$ bolts as fasteners.

(a) Determine the specifications for the bolt (and nut) that will be required, using coarse threads.

(b) Determine the specifications for the cap screw that will be required, using fine threads.

(c) Determine the specifications for the stud (and nut) that will be required, using coarse threads. In order to prevent the workman from putting the stud in the wrong way, make the threaded length on both ends of the stud the same.

Specify standard lengths of bolts. For parts (b) and (c) refer to Fig. 246 for the proper depth proportions and give the specifications for drilling and tapping the hole.

(d) What type of fastener will be needed if the mounting plate is tapped rather than drilled through?

11. Two steel plates whose combined thickness is $2''$ are to be held together by square unfinished bolts with coarse threads.

(a) Specify the bolt (and nut) in the regular series.

(b) Specify the bolt (and nut) in the heavy series.

12. What is the basic difference between screw threads and pipe threads?

13. On a detail drawing of a mating part that is to have limit dimensions, why is the larger dimension given above the line for a shaft, whereas the smaller dimension is given above the line for a hole?

14. If you were the draftsman for the designer of a grain combine who told you to make a certain hole $2\frac{1}{2}''$ in diameter, what limit dimension would you put on the hole and what limit dimensions would you put on the shaft?

15. For a certain automobile, it was decided to make the piston pin holes $1''$ in diameter, using a Class 3 fit. What limit dimensions should be placed on the piston pin hole and what range of sizes of piston pins would meet this requirement?

16. After choosing a bearing from a manufacturer's catalog, a draftsman notes that the manufacturer lists the outside diameter of the bearing race as being $\dfrac{3.5000}{3.4993}$. What dimensions should be placed on the bearing housing for a medium force fit?

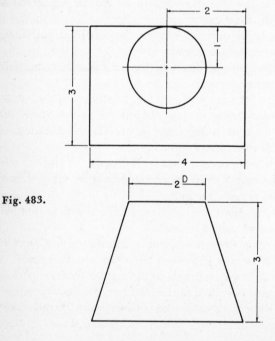

Fig. 483.

Working Drawings

Sheet sizes as specified, scale to suit.

The recommended working drawing, when facilities (listed below) and time (approximately 15 hours) are available, requires the following conditions.

The student to be assigned an object based on his proven ability. The object to be readily available in a laboratory, possibly a laboratory in the student's branch of engineering.

From the object assigned, the student makes all the field sketches and measurements necessary to lay out completely dimensioned detail drawings and assembly drawing.

The student submits his field sketches, detail drawings and assembly drawing, and a commercial type of print of the drawing. Bill of material to be part of title; all sheets to be a part of the same drawing and to be so designated.

In making the field sketches, the student may use cross-section paper on a clip board or a sketch book. In making the field measurements, he may use steel scales, inside and outside calipers, thread gauges, radius gauges, depth gauges, and other necessary equipment. The tools necessary to disassemble and reassemble the objects assigned should be available.

Parts or all of one of the following, or other suitable equipment in the laboratories, may be assigned: gate valves, globe valves, pillow blocks, prony brakes, milling attachments, bench vises, pipe vises, steady rests, lathe chucks, filter presses, couplings, pipe wrenches, testing machine grip assemblies, sheet metal ducts.

1–3. Construct a detail working drawing of the objects in Figs. 495-497.

4. Fig. 487. Following the general instructions given at the beginning of this section, make detail drawings of the Vicat Apparatus. This apparatus is used for the Standard Test of Normal Consistency of Hydraulic Cement, A.S.T.M. Designation: C–187–49, and the Standard Test of Time of Setting of Hydraulic Cement A.S.T.M. Designation: C–191–49. In the Time of Set test the movable rod is in the position shown with needle acting. In the Normal Consistency test the rod is reversed and the plunger or larger end is acting. For its protection the needle is inverted and screwed into an opening in the rod that must be designed by the student, as it is not shown in the drawing. Sizes may be taken off the drawing, where necessary, by using the ring or the length of the movable rod for making a scale.

5. Fig. 488. "Packing Gland for a Low Pressure Hydrogenative Unit." With pattern similar to that for Problem 1, make a complete detail drawing with a bill of materials for the packing gland shown in Fig. 488.

The instructor will indicate dimensions and scale to be used.

6. Fig. 489. Bear in mind the general instructions at the beginning of this section and make detail drawings of the miniature compaction device designed at Harvard University and manufactured by Soil Testing Services, Inc., 4520 W. North Avenue, Chicago 39, Illinois. The compaction mold and extension shown are made from a bronze bearing. The extension collar, base, and clamps hold the mold while the soil is being compacted.

The student is required to design the clamps, two fixed and one with a swing handle rounding the slot end of the swing handle for swing in one direction only. The student will also design the means of attaching the brass posts to the brass base.

The bottom of the extension has the same dimensions as the top of the mold with a continuous $1\frac{5}{16}''$ inside diameter throughout mold and extension.

The student is required to determine the dimensions needed for the device to lock the extension to the mold.

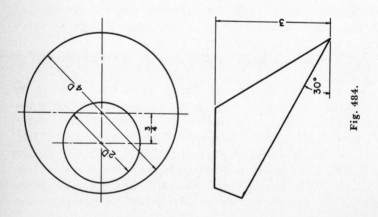

Fig. 484.

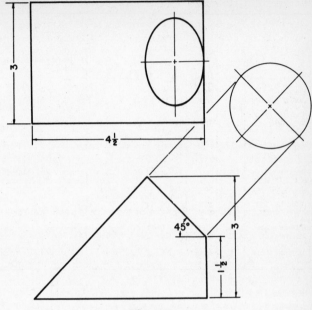

Fig. 485.

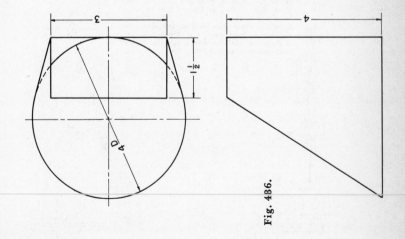

Fig. 486.

BILL OF MATERIALS

Pc. No.	Name	Quan.	Mat.	Size and Stock	Notes
1	Frame	1	C.I.		Casting purchased — surfaces to be finished and holes drilled
2	Base	1	C.I.		Casting purchased — surfaces to be finished and holes drilled
3	Plate	1	Hard rubber	$4\frac{3}{4}'' \times 4\frac{3}{4}'' \times \frac{5}{16}''$	
4	Plate	1	Glass	$4'' \times 4'' \times \frac{1}{4}''$	
5	Conical ring	1	Hard rubber	$\frac{1}{4}''$ thickness	See A.S.T.M. (American society for testing materials) specifications
6	Movable rod	1	Steel	$\frac{1}{2}''$ dia. $\times 12\frac{3}{8}''$ length	See A.S.T.M. specs. for plunger end
7	Needle	1	Steel	Threads at each end $\frac{1}{4}''$ NF–28 $\times \frac{7}{16}''$	See A.S.T.M. specs. for needle
8	Graduated plate	1	Steel	$1\frac{3}{4}'' \times 4\frac{1}{2}'' \times \frac{1}{16}''$	See A.S.T.M. specs. for graduations
9	Indicator hex nut	1	Steel	$\frac{5}{8}''$ across flats	Holes drilled—stem-interference fit, plunger clearance fit
10	Indicator stem	1	Steel	$\frac{3}{16}''$ dia. $\times \frac{7}{16}''$ length tapped thru #4 NC–40	See above for fit
11	Indicator	1	Steel	$\frac{5}{8}'' \times \frac{3}{16}'' \times \frac{1}{32}''$	Solder to stem
12	Indicator set screw	1	Steel	#4 NC–40 $\times \frac{9}{16}''$ length	Knurled circular head — dia.
13	Rod set screw	1	Steel	#4 NC–32 $\times \frac{3}{4}''$ length	Knurled circular head — dia.
14	Machine screw	2	Steel	#6 NC–32 $\times \frac{1}{4}''$ round hd.	Fasten graduated plate to frame
15	Machine screw	7	Brass	#6 NC–32 $\times \frac{3}{8}''$ round hd.	Spaced to fasten frame and rubber plate to base

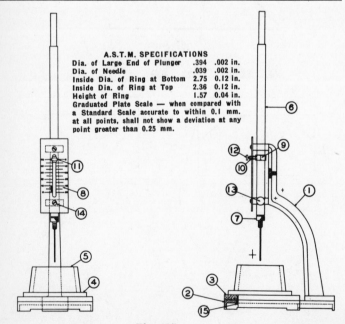

A.S.T.M. SPECIFICATIONS
Dia. of Large End of Plunger   .394   .002 in.
Dia. of Needle   .039   .002 in.
Inside Dia. of Ring at Bottom   2.75 0.12 in.
Inside Dia. of Ring at Top   2.36 0.12 in.
Height of Ring   1.57 0.04 in.
Graduated Plate Scale — when compared with
a Standard Scale accurate to within 0.1 mm.
at all points, shall not show a deviation at any
point greater than 0.25 mm.

Fig. 487.

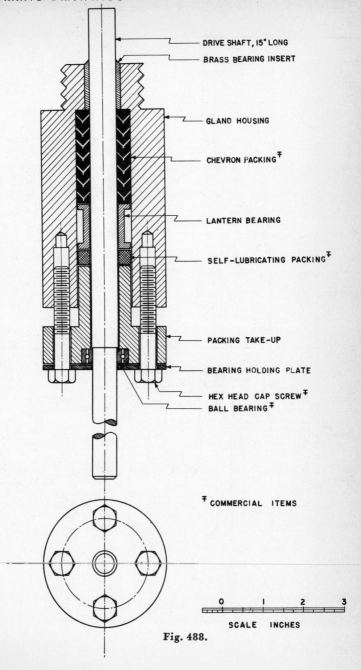

DRIVE SHAFT, 15" LONG

BRASS BEARING INSERT

GLAND HOUSING

CHEVRON PACKING[‡]

LANTERN BEARING

SELF-LUBRICATING PACKING[‡]

PACKING TAKE-UP

BEARING HOLDING PLATE

HEX HEAD CAP SCREW[‡]

BALL BEARING[‡]

‡ COMMERCIAL ITEMS

0 1 2 3
SCALE INCHES

Fig. 488.

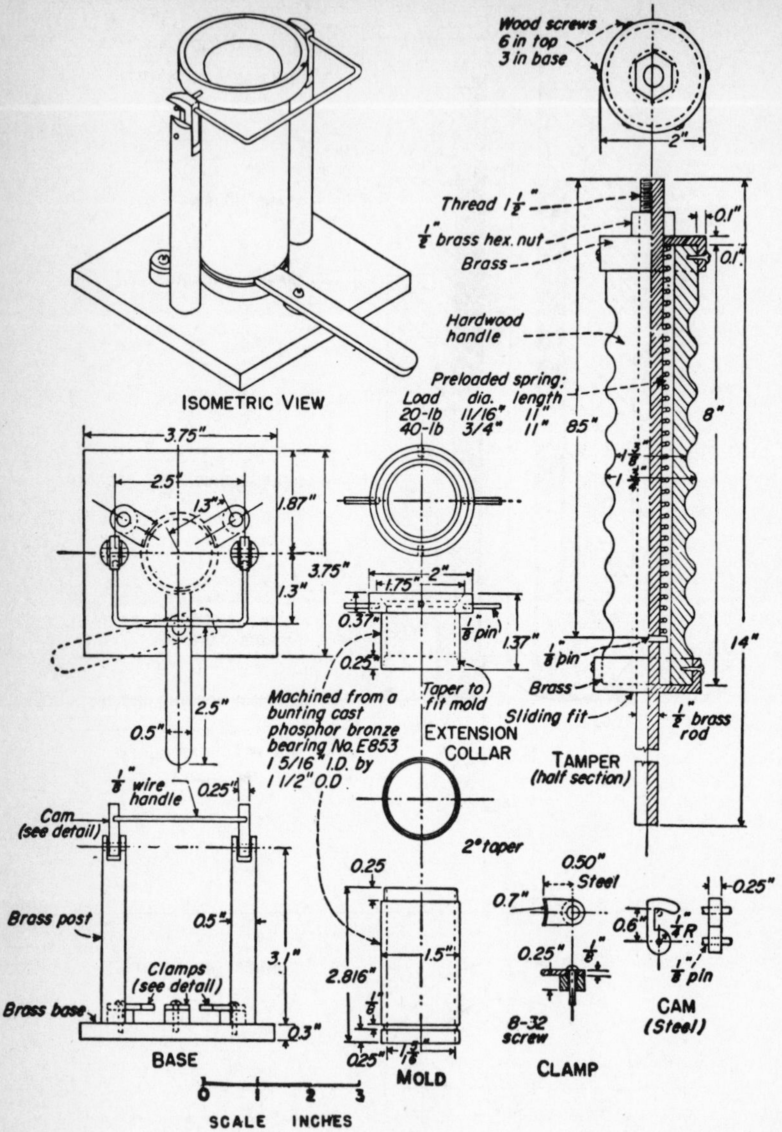
Wood screws
6 in top
3 in base
2"
Thread 1 1/2"
1/2" brass hex. nut
Brass
0.1"
0.1"
Hardwood handle
Preloaded spring:
Load dia. length
20-lb 11/16" 11"
40-lb 3/4" 11" 85"
8"
1 3/8"
1 3/4"
1/8" pin
Brass
Sliding fit
1/2" brass rod
14"
TAMPER
(half section)
ISOMETRIC VIEW
3.75"
2.5"
1.3"
1.87"
3.75"
1.3"
2.5"
0.5"
1.75"
2"
0.37"
1/8" pin
1.37"
0.25"
Taper to fit mold
Machined from a bunting cast phosphor bronze bearing No. E853 1 5/16" I.D. by 1 1/2" O.D.
EXTENSION COLLAR
1/8" wire handle
0.25"
Cam (see detail)
Brass post
0.5"
3.1"
Clamps (see detail)
Brass base
0.3"
BASE
2° taper
0.25
2.816"
1.5"
1/8"
0.25"
1 3/16"
MOLD
0.50" Steel
0.7"
0.25"
1/8"
8-32 screw
CLAMP
0.25"
0.6"
1/4" R
1/8" pin
CAM (Steel)
0 1 2 3
SCALE INCHES

Fig. 489.

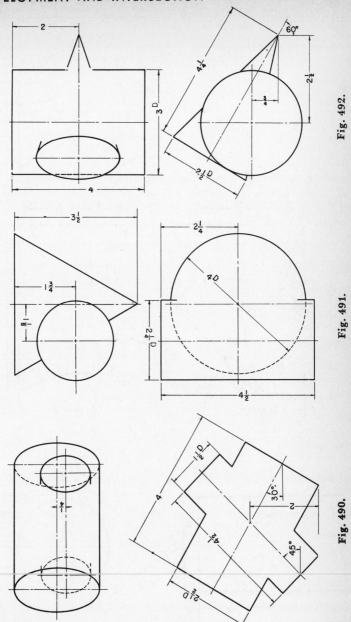

Fig. 492.

Fig. 491.

Fig. 490.

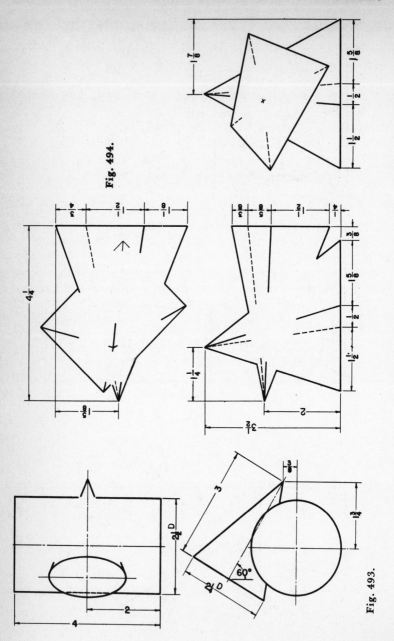

Fig. 494.

Fig. 493.

The Development and Intersection of Surfaces

The object of this section is to widen the student's experience in development and intersection problems that are commonly confronted in engineering.

1–4. Make working drawings by completing the sketches in Figs. 483 to 486. Develop the lateral surface of the object assigned and include the top and bottom surfaces. (See Fig. 324.)

5–9. Draw in orthographic projection one of the objects in Figs. 490 to 494. Find the lines of intersection and complete the views.

The instructor may also require, as an additional assignment, the development of lateral surfaces in Figs. 483 to 486 and Figs. 490 to 494; to develop the lateral surfaces, the student should add tabs to these projections, then cut out and roll or fold and construct paper models of the objects illustrated.

In laying out these problems, the student should allow sufficient space around the sketches to permit proper folding that will form the models.

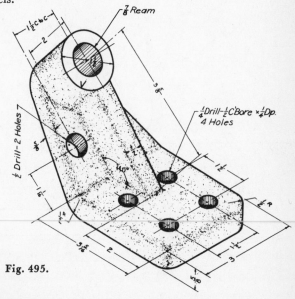

Fig. 495.

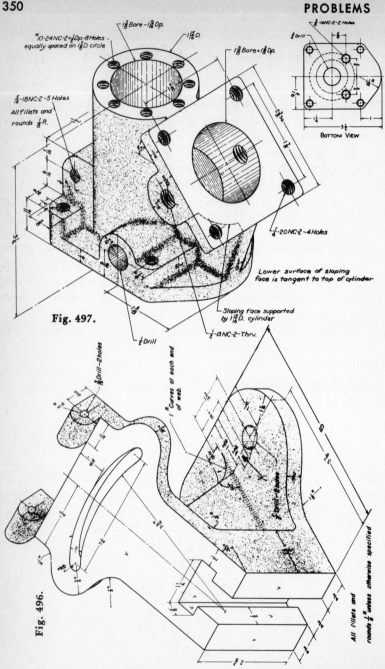

Fig. 497.

Bottom View

Fig. 496.

American Standard

Drawings and Drafting Room Practice

SECTION 1—ARRANGEMENT OF VIEWS

1 Based on Third Angle Orthographic Projection

For drawings in orthographic projection the third angle system (known in Europe

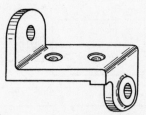

FIG. 1   PICTORIAL VIEW OF OBJECT
SHOWN IN FIG. 2

2 The Six Possible Principal Views

In third angle projections the six views, top, front, bottom, right side, left side and rear, will be arranged as shown in Fig. 2. The plane of projection is between the observer and the object, and in all cases except for the rear view will be hinged to the vertical plane and be revolved into coincidence with it, in a direction away from the object. The rear view may appear at the extreme right in reverse position to that shown in Fig. 2.

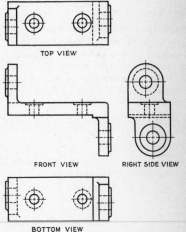

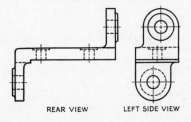

as "American Projection") has been in practically universal use in the United States for many years and is continued as the American Standard. A brief discussion of this practice based on sketches of the object shown in Fig. 1 follows.

April, 1946

FIG. 2   THE SIX POSSIBLE PRINCIPAL VIEWS
OF AN OBJECT

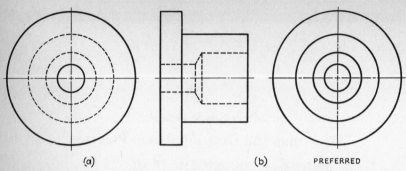

(a)   (b)   PREFERRED

FIG. 3   CHOICE OF VIEWS TO AVOID HIDDEN LINES. HIDDEN LINE TECHNIQUE

3 Choice of Views

As a general rule a view should be made in each direction in which the contour of a characteristic shape necessary to the construction would be shown.

(a)   Views should be selected to give as few hidden lines as possible. Compare side views (a) and (b) in Fig. 3.

(b)   Only those views should be drawn that are necessary to portray clearly the shape of the part.

4 One-View Drawings

In general, two views are necessary as a minimum for the description of the shape of a simple object, but many cylindrical parts may be portrayed adequately by one view, if the necessary dimensions are indicated as diameters. See Fig. 4.* Thin pieces

of uniform thickness such as shims, gaskets and plates may also be shown by one view with a note giving the thickness.

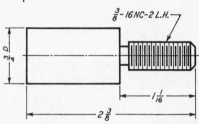

FIG. 4   ONE VIEW DRAWING *

---

* In examining the illustrations it should be kept in mind that these drawings are not necessarily complete in themselves but have been designed to illustrate principles stated in the text matter. In so far as they are complete they conform to standards recommended herein; frequently in the interest of simplicity they are fragmentary.

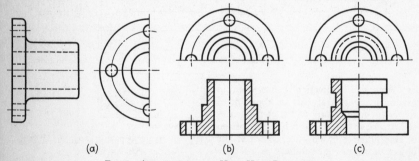

(a)   (b)   (c)

FIG. 5   ARRANGEMENT OF HALF VIEW DRAWINGS

5   Two-View Drawings

Two-view drawings may be arranged as any two adjacent views in the relation shown in Fig. 2.

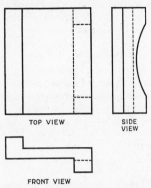

FIG. 6   ALTERNATE ARRANGEMENT OF THREE VIEWS

6   Two-View Drawings—One View a Half View

When space is limited, it is permissible to represent symmetrical objects by half views. If the adjacent view is an exterior view, the near half of the symmetrical view should be drawn, see Fig. 5(a). If the adjacent view is a full or half section, the far half of the symmetrical view should be drawn, see Fig. 5(b) and 5(c).

7   Three-View Drawings

Any three adjacent views in the relation

to each other as illustrated in Fig. 2 may be used.

8   Three-View Drawings—Alternate Positions

When space limitations require, the side view may be placed across from the top view as in Fig. 6.

9   Three-View Drawings

FRONT AND TWO SIDE VIEWS. For objects where two side views can be used to better advantage than one, these need not be complete views of the entire object, if together they describe the shape of the object, Fig. 7. In this case only the hidden lines immediately behind the face need be shown.

10   Bottom Views

A bottom view, or "view looking up," can be used to advantage instead of a top view when the shapes or operations to be shown are on the under side of the part. For example: In a punch and die drawing, the theoretical arrangement of views would be as in Fig. 8 with the view of the bottom of the punch placed in the position of the bottom view, and the top of the die in the position of the top view, each facing the front view.

(a) To conserve space this arrangement is modified by placing the drawing of the bottom of the punch to the right of and in line with the top view of the die, as if it

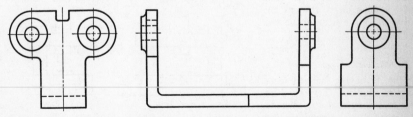

FIG. 7   ARRANGEMENT OF FRONT AND TWO SIDE VIEWS
Top view omitted to save space; two end views illustrate the principle

were turned over from the top view, Fig. 9. In drawings where any such arrangement of views is employed the views should

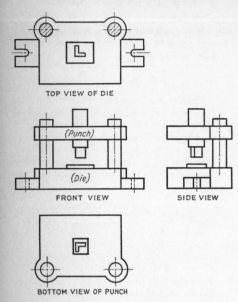

TOP VIEW OF DIE

(Punch)

(Die)

FRONT VIEW

SIDE VIEW

BOTTOM VIEW OF PUNCH

FIG. 8 THEORETICAL ARRANGEMENT OF VIEWS

always be carefully titled to aid in the reading.

(b) Bottom views (views looking up) should not be used in steel plate and structural drawings. Instead, the view should be shown as a sectional view looking down, the cutting plane passing a little above the bottom, Fig. 10.

11 Auxiliary Views

Objects having inclined faces require auxiliary views to show the true shapes of the inclined surfaces. Partial auxiliary views which show only the inclined

faces may be used to advantage in order to simplify the drawing, to eliminate difficult projections, and to show true relationships for dimensioning. The auxiliary plane is revolved into the plane of the paper by considering it to be hinged to the plane to which it is perpendicular. See Figs. 11, 12, and 13.

12 Identification of Views

When any of the standard arrangements described above are used on a drawing, it is unnecessary to identify or name the views. In unusual or special combinations of views, however, the views should be clearly identified as in Fig. 9.

13 Space Between Views

Ample space should be provided between views to permit of placing dimensions without crowding and to preclude the possibility of notes pertaining to one view overlapping or crowding the other views.

14 Hidden Lines

Hidden lines should be indicated by standard type line No. 3, Fig. 18. This

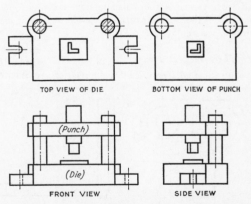

TOP VIEW OF DIE

BOTTOM VIEW OF PUNCH

(Punch)

(Die)

FRONT VIEW

SIDE VIEW

FIG. 9 APPROVED ARRANGEMENT OF VIEWS FOR PUNCH AND DIE DRAWING

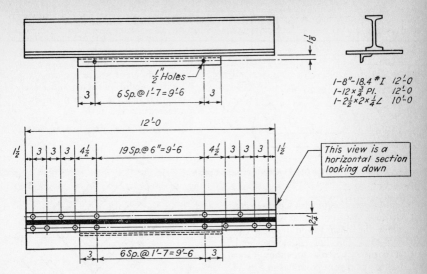

FIG. 10   ARRANGEMENT OF VIEWS IN STRUCTURAL DRAWING

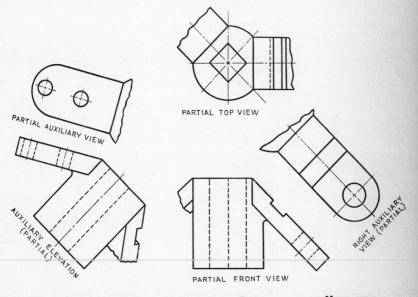

FIG. 11   PARTIAL AUXILIARY VIEW ON PLANE PERPENDICULAR TO HORIZONTAL

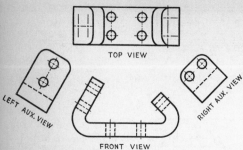

FIG. 12   AUXILIARY VIEWS ON PLANES PERPENDICULAR
TO VERTICAL

line should always begin with a dash in contact with the line from which it starts, except when the dash would form a continuation of a full line. Dashes should touch at corners. Circular arcs should start with dashes at tangent points as in Fig. 14.

15   Runouts and Filleted Intersections

The intersection of two unfinished surfaces always should be shown rounded or filleted. Intersections of two unfinished surfaces, theoretically showing no line, may be indicated by a conventional line. The location of the line should be at the theoretical intersection and the contour must be shown or specified as in Figs. 15 and 16.

16   Indication of Scale

The scale of the drawing should be indicated on the sheet. If more than one detail occurs on a sheet and different scales are used, the scale should be shown under each detail. See Fig. 17 for methods of indicating the scale.

When the drawing is much

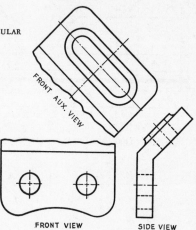

FIG. 13   AUXILIARY VIEW ON PLANE
PERPENDICULAR TO PROFILE

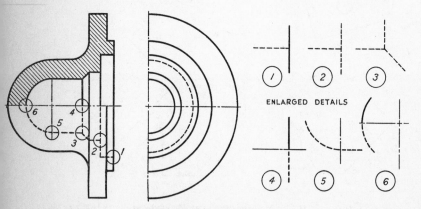

FIG. 14   HIDDEN LINE TECHNIQUE

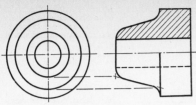

FIG. 15   REPRESENTING ROUNDED CORNERS
AND FILLETS

larger than the object, one view, in general outline, actual size, may be shown in one corner of the sheet, for identification purposes.

Drawings which are to be reduced or enlarged photographically should have the scale indicated graphically as well as numerically.

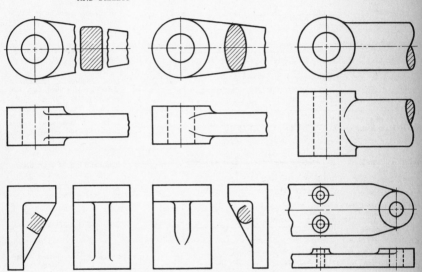

FIG. 16   RUNOUTS AND FILLETED INTERSECTIONS

DRAWING SMALLER THAN OBJECT

Scale $1\frac{1}{2}''=1'-0''$ Scale $\frac{3}{4}''=1''$

Scale $3''=1'-0''$ Full Scale

Quarter Scale   Scale $\frac{1}{2}''=1'-0''$

Scale $\frac{3}{8}''=1''$ Scale $1''=1'-0''$

Half Scale   Scale $1''=100'-0''$

DRAWING LARGER THAN OBJECT

Scale $\frac{1.5}{1}$ Scale $\frac{2}{1}$

MAP SCALES

Scale $\frac{1}{62500}$ (Representative fraction)

400   0   400   800 Ft (Graphic scale)

FIG. 17   DESIGNATION OF SCALES

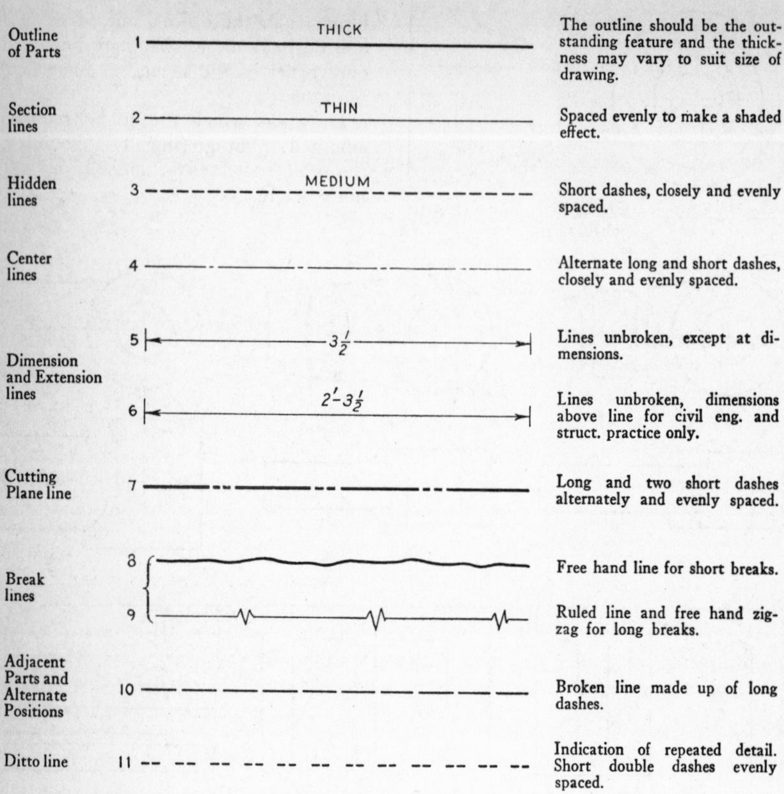

Outline of Parts
1
THICK
The outline should be the outstanding feature and the thickness may vary to suit size of drawing.
Section lines
2
THIN
Spaced evenly to make a shaded effect.
Hidden lines
3
MEDIUM
Short dashes, closely and evenly spaced.
Center lines
4
Alternate long and short dashes, closely and evenly spaced.
Dimension and Extension lines
5
3 1/2
Lines unbroken, except at dimensions.
6
2'-3 1/2
Lines unbroken, dimensions above line for civil eng. and struct. practice only.
Cutting Plane line
7
Long and two short dashes alternately and evenly spaced.
Break lines
8
Free hand line for short breaks.
9
Ruled line and free hand zigzag for long breaks.
Adjacent Parts and Alternate Positions
10
Broken line made up of long dashes.
Ditto line
11
Indication of repeated detail. Short double dashes evenly spaced.

FIG. 18 WIDTH AND CHARACTER OF LINES

ROUND, SOLID
ROUND, (TUBULAR)
RECTANGULAR
RECTANGULAR, (WOOD)

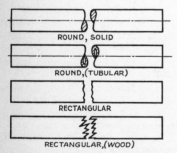

FIG. 19 CONVENTIONAL BREAKS

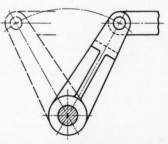

FIG. 20 INDICATION OF ALTERNATE POSITIONS

SECTION 2—LINES AND LINE WORK

17   Line Characteristics

It is recommended that the types shown in Fig. 18 be used for the purposes indicated. All lines should be clean and black. The actual width of each type of line should be governed by the size and style of the drawing, the relative widths of the lines should approximate those shown in Fig. 18.

18   Widths of Lines

Three widths of line, thick, medium and thin, are shown and are considered desirable on finished drawings in ink, both for legibility and appearance, although in rapid practice and in particular on penciled tracings from which prints are to be made this may be simplified to two widths, medium and thin, both of which must be dense black in order to print.

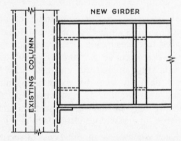

FIG. 21   INDICATION OF ADJACENT PARTS

For pencil tracings the lines should be in proportion to the ink lines, medium for outlines, hidden, cutting plane, short breaks, adjacent part and alternate position lines; and thin for section, center, extension, dimension, long break, and ditto lines.

19   Dimension and Extension Lines

Dimension and extension lines should be thin lines. Extension lines should not touch the outlines of the object, Fig. 48.

20   Break Lines Used to Shorten the View of Long Uniform Sections

Break lines may be used on both detail and assembly drawings. On small parts freehand lines are best, (Fig. 18, line 8), while on large parts the second form, made with thin ruled lines with freehand "zigzags," (Fig. 18, line 9) is preferred. When a portion of the lengths of shafts, rods, etc., are broken out to shorten the view, the breaks will be indicated as shown in Fig. 19.

In structural drawing, many parts are not drawn to detail scale in length but no break is shown unless it is necessary to show a revolved section. Symmetrical parts discontinued beyond the center line may have the break made as in Fig. 21 or Fig. 51.

21   Alternate   Positions   and   Adjacent Parts

An alternate position, or indication of the limiting positions of a moving part should be shown by a line made up of long dashes of medium width, Fig. 20.

Adjacent parts added on a drawing to indicate the position or use of the piece represented, are drawn with the same long-dash lines, Fig. 21. This line is also used in showing bosses and lugs cast on for holding purposes, which are to be removed later. On drawings of an illustrative nature adjacent parts may be shown as solid red- or diluted black-ink lines instead of black long-dash lines.

359

SECTION 3—SECTIONAL VIEWS

22 General Principles

Sectional views, commonly called "sections" should be used when the interior construction cannot be shown clearly by outside views. (In assembly drawings they also serve to indicate a difference in materials.)

A sectional view should be made as if on that view the nearest part of the object were cut or broken away. The exposed or cut surface of the material is indicated by "section lining" or "cross-hatching."

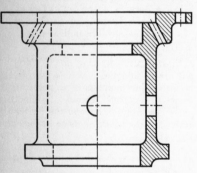

FIG. 22 HIDDEN LINES IN DETAIL HALF SECTION

Hidden lines behind the cutting plane should be omitted unless required for the necessary description of the object. In half-sectioned detail drawings hidden lines may be shown on the unsectioned side only if needed for dimensioning or clarity, Fig. 22.

23 Symbolic Section Lining

For the graphic indication of various materials of construction symbolic section lining may be used when it is desired to call special attention to them or to identify certain parts, Fig. 25. Symbols used for outside views of certain materials are shown in Fig. 26.

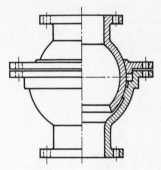

FIG. 23 HIDDEN LINES OMITTED IN HALF SECTIONED ASSEMBLY

24 Sectioning in Detail Drawings

If preferred, the section-lining of any metallic piece may be made by equally spaced full lines in one direction as for cast iron. See Figs. 22, 23, and 27. Since the specification of material must usually be more detailed than by name or symbol alone, this practice is recommended. An opening may be left in the sectioning to provide for a reference letter or dimension.

Even when the symbolic types of section lining are used it will be found frequently desirable to use reference letters to indicate the material.

25 Sectioning in Assembly Drawing

In assemblies, when it is desirable to distinguish between different classes of materials without specifying their exact composition, assemblies may be appropriately cross-sectioned to indicate specified materials, Fig. 24.

Where a large area of a piece is shown in section, it is not necessary to section line the entire area; section lining around the outline of the sectioned area should be sufficient.

26   Full Sections

When the cutting plane extends entirely through the object a "full section" is obtained as in Fig. 27. When the section is on an axis of symmetry it is not necessary to indicate its location.

27   Half Sections

A symmetrical object may be drawn as a "half-section" showing one-half up to the center line,* in section, and the other half in full view. See Figs. 22, 23, and 24. In assemblies it is customary not to show hidden lines on the unsectioned side.

28   Location of Cutting Plane

The cutting plane on which the section is taken should be indicated by type 7 line, Fig. 18, and lettered at the ends as A-A, Fig. 30. Arrows are used to indicate the direction in which the section is viewed. The letters identifying the section may be placed in a circle as the numerator of a fraction whose denominator is the sheet number on which the section will be found, Figs. 28 and 29. When the section is on the same sheet, the sheet number and circle should be omitted. The letters should be large enough to be easily found, Figs. 28 and 30.

On simple symmetrical objects the cutting plane line, letters, and arrows may be omitted when on an axis of symmetry. It is not necessary that the cutting plane be a single continuous plane; it may be bent or offset if by so doing, the construction can be shown to better advantage as, for example A-A or B-B, Fig. 30 and Fig. 29.

* The dividing line between the half-section and full view may be type 1 line, Fig. 18.

The cutting planes line may be shown only at the ends and at changes of direction as in Fig. 28.

29   Revolved Sections

These sections show the shape of the cross-section of a part, such as the arm of a wheel, the cutting plane being rotated in place, Figs. 16 and 31.

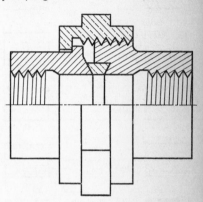

Fig. 24   Representation of Materials in Assembly

30   Removed Sections

Removed or "detail sections" should be drawn like revolved sections except that they are placed to one side and often are made to a larger scale than the view on which they are indicated, Section B-B, Fig. 30. Removed sections of symmetrical parts may be placed on an extension of the cutting plane as a center line, Fig. 32.

31   Offset Sections

When the object is not cut by one continuous plane, the section is called an offset section. Its location is shown in the usual way as in Figs. 29 and 30.

32   Broken-Out Sections

Where a sectional view of only a portion of the object is needed, broken-out sections may be used as in Figs. 33 and 36.

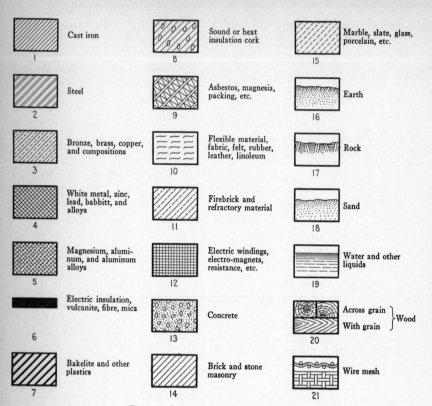

FIG. 25 SYMBOLS FOR SECTION LINING

FIG. 26 SYMBOLS FOR OUTSIDE VIEWS

33   *Direction of Section Lining*

Section lining should be made with thin parallel lines at an angle of 45 deg and spaces from 1/32 in. to ⅛ in. or more depending on the size of the drawing of the part. Two adjacent parts should be sectioned by lines at right angles to each other.

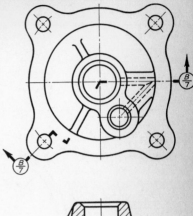

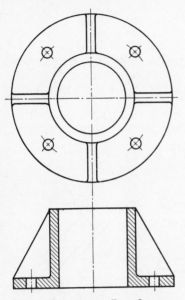

FIG. 27   SYMMETRICAL FULL SECTION

A third, adjacent to both, should be sectioned at 30 deg or 60 deg as shown in Figs. 24 and 34. If the shape or position of the part would bring 45 deg sectioning parallel or nearly parallel to one of the sides, another angle should be chosen. In all views showing sections of a part the sectioning of that part should be the same in direction and spacing.

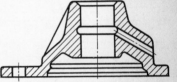

SECTION B-B
FIG. 28   INDICATION OF CUTTING PLANE
IN SECTIONED VIEWS

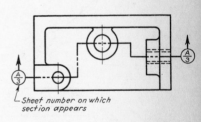

*Sheet number on which
section appears*

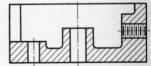

FIG. 29   CROSS-HATCHING AN OFFSET SECTION

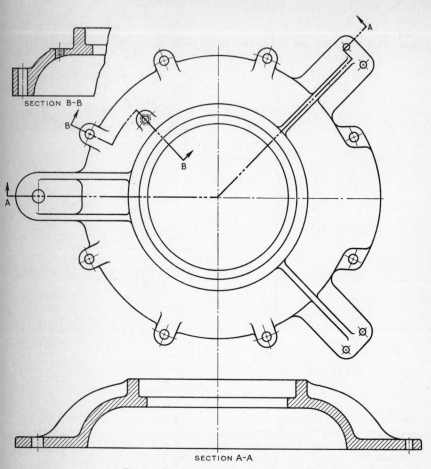

SECTION B-B

SECTION A-A

Fig. 30 Indication of Cutting Planes

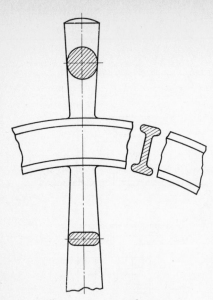

FIG. 31   REVOLVED SECTIONS

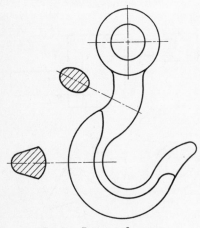

FIG. 32   REMOVED SECTIONS

34   Thin Sections

Sections which are too thin for line sectioning may be shown solid, such as structural shapes, sheet metal, packing, gaskets, etc. Where two or more adjacent parts are shown solid a space should be left between them, Fig. 35.

35   Sections Through Thin Webs, Shafts, Bolts, Pins, Keys, etc.

There is one important violation of the conventional theory which is made in the interest of clearness. When the section or cutting plane passes through a rib, web or similar parallel element, section lines should be omitted from those parts, Figs. 27 and 30.

Shafts, bolts, nuts, rods, rivets, keys, pins and similar solid parts whose axes lie in the cutting plane should not be sectioned, Fig. 37.

36   Treatment of Foreshortened Projections

When the true projection of a piece would result in confusing foreshortening, parts such as ribs or arms, should be rotated until parallel to the plane of the section or projection as shown in Figs. 38 and 40.

Drilled flanges in elevation or section should show the holes at their true distance from the center rather than the true projection, Figs. 27 and 36.

37   Representing Cylindrical Intersections

The intersection of rectangular and circular parts with other circular parts, occurs frequently. Unless very large, these intersections are conventionalized as shown in Fig. 39. The curve of intersection may be drawn as a circular arc.

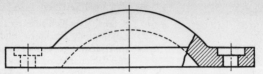

FIG. 33 BROKEN-OUT SECTION

FIG. 34 ARRANGEMENT OF SECTION LINING
FOR THREE ADJACENT PARTS

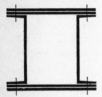

FIG. 35 SECTIONAL VIEW OF THIN PLATES

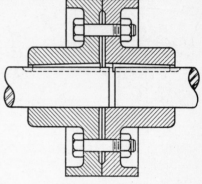

FIG. 37 SHAFTS, KEYS, BOLTS AND NUTS
IN SECTIONAL VIEW

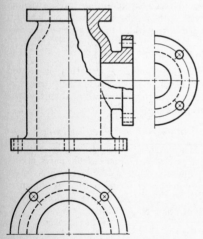

FIG. 36 HOLES REVOLVED TO SHOW TRUE
DISTANCE FROM CENTER

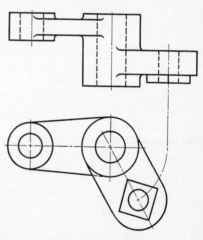

FIG. 38 REVOLUTION OF PARTS TO SHOW
TRUE RELATIONSHIPS

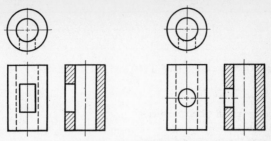

(a) CYLINDRICAL INTERSECTION IN SECTION

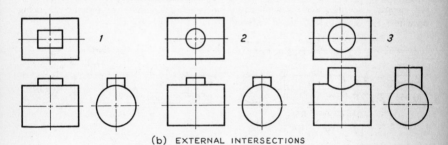

(b) EXTERNAL INTERSECTIONS

FIG. 39   REPRESENTING CYLINDRICAL INTERSECTIONS

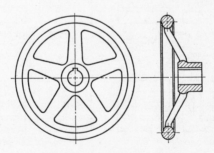

FIG. 40   SECTION THROUGH SPOKES
OF WHEELS

SECTION 4—SCREW THREAD REPRESENTATION

38 Regular Thread Symbols

Fig. 41 shows threads in section and elevation, with end view.

Fig. 41(a) shows the regular method of representing screw threads recommended for general use on assembly and detail drawings. Except in sections of external threads and hidden internal threads, the threads are indicated by alternate long and short lines at right angles to the axis representing the crests and roots of the thread, the short lines thicker than the long lines, or of equal width if preferred. They need only to approximate the actual pitch, being spaced by eye to look well.

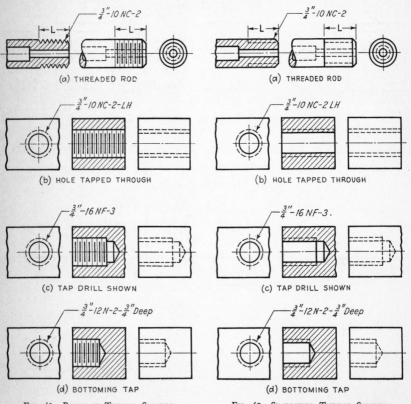

FIG. 41 REGULAR THREAD SYMBOL   FIG. 42 SIMPLIFIED THREAD SYMBOL

368

Fig. 41(b) shows internal threads tapped through. Fig. 41(c) shows internal threads where the tap drill point does not go through. The drill point should be drawn at 60 deg with the center line.

The method shown in Fig. 41(d) should be used to indicate a bottoming tap, when depth of thread is the same as depth of

at the approximate depth of the thread.

The size and length of thread and depth of tap should be given on the drawing. Threads are always considered to be "right hand" unless specified as "left hand" or "LH." The letters LH should be added after the class of fit number as shown in Figs. 41(b) or 42(b). Bolt ends should

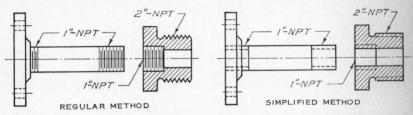

REGULAR METHOD   SIMPLIFIED METHOD

FIG. 43   PIPE THREADS

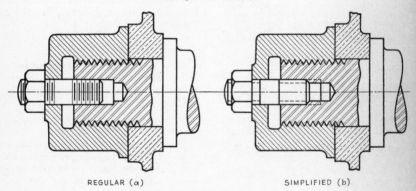

REGULAR (a)   SIMPLIFIED (b)

FIG. 44   SCREW THREADS IN ASSEMBLY

drill, or when it is not necessary to specify both depth of drill and depth of thread. Fig. 44 shows an assembly of threaded parts. The simplified method illustrated should be used with discretion to avoid possible mistakes.

39 Simplified Thread Symbols

Fig. 42 shows the simplified symbol method of screw thread representation. This method may be adopted where it is desirable to simplify drafting work. The threaded portion is indicated by lines made of short dashes drawn parallel to the axis

be shown as flat and chamfered to the thread depth at 45 deg with the flat surface.

Dimensions of screw threads for bolts, nuts, screws and threaded parts may be found in the American Standard for Screw Threads. Identification symbols and methods of designation for drawings may be found in Par. 14 of this bulletin, (ASA B1.1—1935).

40 Pipe Thread Symbols

Pipe threads should be represented in the same manner as bolt threads, Fig. 43.

It is not necessary to indicate taper on standard pipe threads but this may be done if desired. Therefore, when straight pipe threads are specified such threads must be indicated by the symbol NPS. Identification symbols and dimensions of national standard pipe threads, including diameters, form, taper, and length of thread, may be found in the American Standard for Pipe Threads (ASA B2.1—1945).

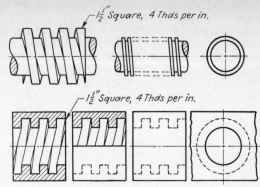

Fig. 46   Modified Square Thread

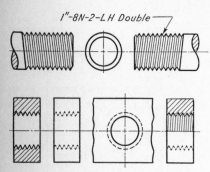

Fig. 45   Semi-Conventional Thread

41   Semi-Conventional Threads or Thread Pictures

When it is desirable to use "thread pictures" it should be done as in Fig. 45. The helices are conventionalized into slanting straight lines and the contour shown as a sharp V at 60 deg although the standard threads are truncated at the top and filled in at the root. Details of standard threads will be found in the American Standard for Screw Threads (ASA B1.1—1935).

42   Square Thread Symbols

Square threads should be shown as in Fig. 46 with a note specifying the type of

thread and the pitch. For details of modified square and acme threads see American Standard Acme and Other Translating Threads (ASA B1.3—1941).

43   Acme Thread Symbols

Acme threads should be represented as in Fig. 47 with a note specifying the type of thread and the pitch (ASA B1.3—1941).

44   Bolt Heads and Nuts

Exact dimensions of American Standard unfinished, semi-finished, and finished bolt heads and nuts, regular series and heavy series, will be found in the American Standard for Wrench Head Bolts and Nuts and Wrench Openings (ASA B18.2—1941).

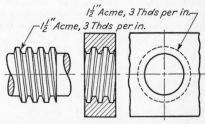

Fig. 47   Acme Thread

SECTION 5—DIMENSIONING—GENERAL RULES

45 General Principles of Dimensioning

(a) Economical production and the proper functioning of a part in service are directly dependent upon the method of dimensioning used and the manner in which dimensions are specified on the drawings.

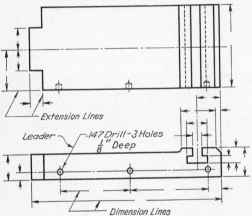

FIG. 48 LEADERS, DIMENSION AND EXTENSION LINES IN MACHINE DRAWING

(b) The dimensions should be so arranged that it never will be necessary to calculate, scale, or assume any dimensions in order to fabricate the specified part.

(c) The dimensions should include those sizes and distances which are worked

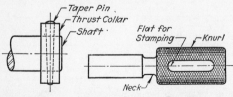

FIG. 49 APPROVED FORM OF LEADERS

to in actual shop or constructional operation and should be so placed as to minimize the cumulative error.

(d) It is essential that dimensions should be given between those points or surfaces which have a specified relation to each other or which control the location of other component or mating parts.

(e) Dimensions should not be duplicated and none should be given except those required to produce or inspect the part.

46 Technique of Dimensioning

Dimension lines should be thin full lines (broken where dimension is inserted) so as to contrast with the thicker outline of the drawing, Fig. 48. In structural drawings the dimension line is not broken and the figures are placed above the line, Figs. 50, 51, and 52.

Dimension lines should be terminated by carefully made arrowheads whose lengths are approximately three times the spread. The distance from tip to tip of the arrowheads indicates the extent of the dimension as shown in Fig. 48.

Extension lines indicate the distance measured when the dimension is placed outside the view. They are made as thin full lines, should be extended a short distance beyond the arrowhead, and should not touch the view.

In structural drawing the lines along which rivet holes are punched

371

are called gage lines. They are drawn as thin solid lines as in Figs. 51 and 52.

Leaders should be thin straight lines terminated by arrowheads. They should not be curved or made freehand, Fig. 49. The leader may terminate in a short horizontal bar at the mid-height of the lettering of the first or last line of the note.

The symbol (″) may be used to indicate inches and common and decimal fractions of an inch.

The symbol (′) may be used to indicate feet as in Figs. 50, 51, and 52.

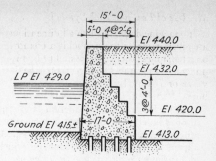

FIG. 50 DIMENSIONING IN CIVIL ENGINEERING PROJECTS

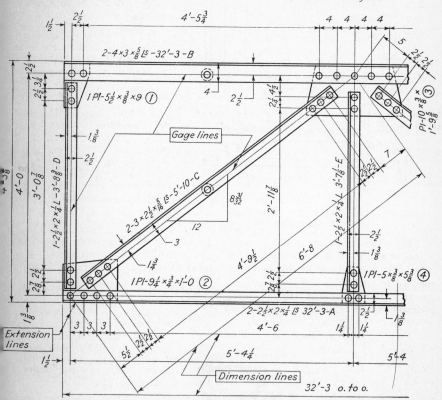

FIG. 51 DIMENSIONING ASSEMBLED STRUCTURAL WORK

47   Use of Feet and Inch Symbols

In machine drawing when all dimensions are given in inches the symbol is preferably omitted, unless there is a possibility of misunderstanding, thus 1 valve should be 1″ valve or 1 in. valve; 1 bore should be 1″ bore.

In structural drawing all length dimensions should be expressed in feet and inches. Plate widths are given in inches. Dimensions should be hyphenated thus, 4′-3; 4′-0½; 4′-0 as shown in Fig. 51. When the dimension contains only inches the inch mark may be omitted. In structural draw-

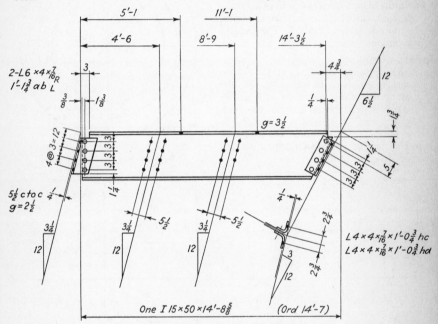

FIG. 52   DIMENSIONING STRUCTURAL STEEL BEAMS

In some industries all dimensions are specified in inches. In others dimensions up to and including 72 in. should be preferably expressed in inches and those greater than that length, in feet and inches.

ing the inch symbol is omitted even though the dimension is in feet and inches, Figs. 51 and 52.

48   Placing Dimensions

Two systems of dimensioning are approved. The older, called the aligned system, and the new, called the unidirectional system, will be found convenient under conditions described in the following:

(a) ALIGNED SYSTEM. All dimension lines and their corresponding numbers are placed so that they may be read from the bottom or right-hand edges of

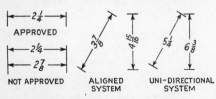

FIG. 53   POSITION OF FRACTION BAR

the drawing. Figs. 53 and 55(a). All dimensions are placed so as to read in the direction of the dimension lines as shown in Fig. 55(a). Dimension lines should not run in directions included in the shaded area as shown in Fig. 54, forty-five deg from the vertical, unless unavoidable.

In the aligned system fractions are written with the division bar in line with the dimension line, Fig. 53. The inclined bar or the omission of the bar is not approved.

(b) UNIDIRECTIONAL SYSTEM. All dimensions are made to read from the bottom of the sheet as shown in Figs. 53 and 55(b). Fractions are written with the division bar horizontal or parallel to the bottom of the sheet. Diameters of circles may be placed in any position, except along center lines.

is making its use more widespread, and therefore, acceptable as a method.

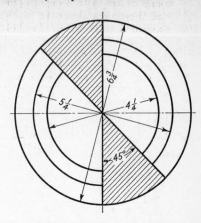

FIG. 54   AREA TO BE AVOIDED

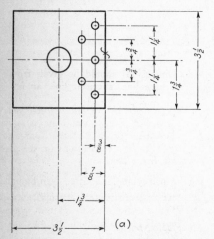

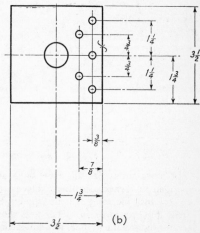

FIG. 55   ALIGNED (a) AND UNIDIRECTIONAL (b) DIMENSIONING FROM CENTER LINE AND FINISHED SURFACE

The unidirectional system of dimensioning originated in automobile and aircraft drafting rooms where long drawings made it advantageous. From the standpoint of both making and using a drawing, this system of dimensioning has advantages which

(c) GENERAL RULES. The following rules apply to both systems.

(1) The dimension line must not pass through a dimension figure, nor should a dimension figure be placed on the outline of the object.

(2) Dimensions should not be placed upon a view unless the drawing becomes clearer by so doing. In general, dimensions should be placed between views as in Figs. 57 and 61.

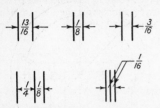

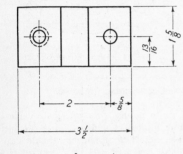

FIG. 56 DIMENSIONING NARROW SPACES

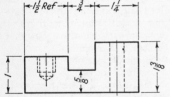

FIG. 57 PLACING OF DIMENSIONS

(3) A center line should never be used as a dimension line. A line of the piece or part illustrated, or an extension of such a line, should never be used as a dimension line.

(4) When there are several parallel dimension lines the figures should be staggered to avoid confusion as shown in Fig. 59.

(5) In general, dimension lines should

be one-half inch away from outlines and spaced uniformly at least three-eighths of an inch from each other.

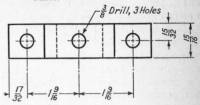

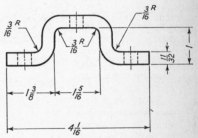

FIG. 58 DIMENSIONS FOR DIFFERENT OPERATIONS SHOULD BE SEPARATED

(6) Dimensions should be given from a base line, a center line, an important hole or a finished surface that can be readily established (based on design requirements and the relationship of other parts). See Fig. 55. Dimensions for different operations on a piece, as for example, drilling and bending should be kept separate as shown in Fig. 58 if permissible by its design.

(7) For dimensioning in limited space the arrowheads should be reversed and the methods shown in Fig. 56 may be used.

(8) In dimensioning angles an arc should be drawn and the dimension so placed as to read from the bottom of the sheet, Fig. 60. An exception is sometimes made in the dimensioning of large arcs when the dimensions are placed along the arc.

(9) Over-all dimensions should be placed outside the intermediate dimensions, Figs. 55, 58 and 77. When an over-all dimension is used, one intermediate distance * should not be dimensioned, unless for reference and so noted as shown in Figs. 57 and 61.

(10) In an object with circular ends an over-all dimension generally need not be given, Figs. 61 and 74.

(11) When the number of dimensions is large and when limited space requires that successive dimensions be given from a common reference point or surface, they may be placed in a single line as shown in Fig. 67. This practice is followed also in structural work as shown in Fig. 52.

49 Fractional and Decimal Dimensioning

GENERAL RULES. Dimensions in structural work should be expressed in units and common fractions and in machine drawing, dimensions of parts that can be produced with sufficient accuracy when measured with an ordinary scale, should be dimensioned in the same manner.

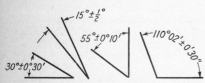

FIG. 60 DIMENSIONING ANGLES WITH LIMIT DIMENSIONS

For parts requiring greater accuracy a complete decimal system of dimensioning will be found advantageous.

* Does not apply to structural dimensioning.

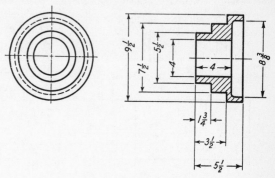

FIG. 59 DIMENSIONING CYLINDERS

Decimal dimensions should be used between finished surfaces and points which it is essential to hold in a specific relation to each other. The fundamental basis of the complete decimal system is the use of a two-place decimal, i.e., a decimal consisting of two figures after the decimal point. In all dimensions where a fraction would ordinarily be used, the two-place decimal can be applied. The figures after the decimal point, where applicable, should be in fiftieths (e.g., .02, .04, .08, .84) so that when halved (e.g., diameters to radii) two-place decimals will result. Exceptions, of course, will have to be made, but they should be kept to a minimum.

When a decimal value obtained by converting a common fraction to decimals is to be rounded off to a lesser number of places than the total number available, the procedure should be as indicated in ASA Z25.1—1940.

50 Limit Dimensioning

Accurate dimensions which are to be checked with a limit gage or micrometer should be expressed in decimals.

Limits representing the maximum and minimum dimensions allowed shall be specified for all dimensions where the tolerance is other than .01. This (.01) tolerance, or any other predominant tolerance, should be indicated on the drawing in note form. The method of writing these limits on the drawing should be as shown in Figs. 61 to 64.

For external dimensions the maximum limit is placed above the line and for internal dimensions the minimum limit is placed above the line. This method of writing should be used for smaller parts and where gages are extensively employed.

A second method is to give the calculated or basic size to the required number of decimal places, followed by the tolerance plus and minus with the plus above the minus, as $8.625^{+.002}_{-.002}$

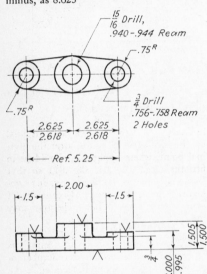

Fig. 61 Dimensioning Part With
Circular Ends

A third method, sometimes used, gives the preferred dimension with an unilateral tolerance, either plus or minus (not both) as shown in Fig. 83.

51 Dimensioning Fits

The dimensions and tolerances given in

the detail drawings of the two parts of a cylindrical fit will determine the clearance (or interference) between these parts.

52 Tolerance of Concentricity

Mating pairs of two (or more) closely fitting machined cylindrical surfaces must be concentric in order to permit assembly of parts; thus a method of giving the permissible deviation from concentricity is

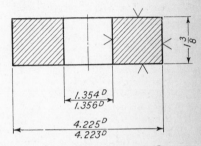

Fig. 62   Limit Dimensions for Circular
Holes and Shafts

sometimes necessary. As the center lines of adjoined cylinders coincide on the drawing, the tolerance for concentricity cannot be shown in dimensional form, and must therefore be given by note. One method is to mark the dimensions with reference letter and give the tolerance in a foot-note as in Fig. 63(a). Another method applies the note directly to the surfaces as in Fig. 63(b).

53 Dimensioning a Half Section

By a proper use of hidden lines on the external portion of a half section view and the careful observance of the usual rules, dimensioning a half-sectioned drawing becomes a fairly simple matter as shown in Fig. 64. Generous use of notes and careful placement of the dimension lines, leaders and figures will in most cases suffice to make the dimensioning clear.

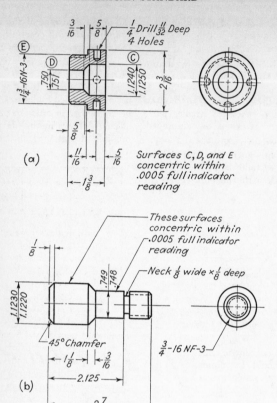

Surfaces C, D, and E
concentric within
.0005 full indicator
reading

(a)

These surfaces
concentric within
.0005 full indicator
reading

Neck ⅛ wide × ⅛ deep

45° Chamfer

¾–16 NF–3

(b)

FIG. 63   LIMIT DIMENSIONS FOR CONCENTRICITY

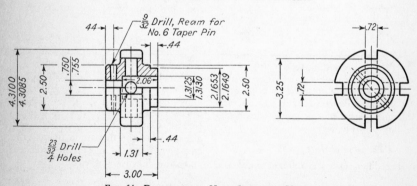

FIG. 64   DIMENSIONING HALF SECTIONED VIEWS

SECTION 6—DIMENSIONING STANDARD DETAILS

54 Circles

A dimension indicating the diameter of a circle should be followed by the letter "D" except when it is obvious from the drawing that the dimension is a diameter, Fig. 62. The dimension of a radius should

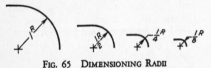

FIG. 65   DIMENSIONING RADII

always be followed by the letter "R," and the radial dimension line should have only one arrowhead, Fig. 65.

A series of concentric circular parts should be dimensioned from the side or sectioned view as in Fig. 59, rather than from the circular view. A large number of dia-

metric dimensions in the circular view is to be avoided.

55 Curves

A curved line may be dimensioned either by radii whose centers are properly located or by offsets, Figs. 66 and 67.

56 Angles

When angular dimensions are necessary a horizontal (or vertical) center line should be used as a base line, but not both, and points located from it, Fig. 68. Angular

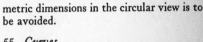

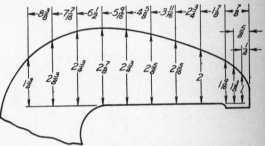

FIG. 67   PROGRESSIVE DIMENSIONING

dimensions should be written as 50°45′; the dash between degrees and minutes should not be used.

When it is necessary to give the accuracy required in an angular dimension, the tolerance is generally bilateral. When the tolerance is given in degrees it is written, for example, $\pm\frac{1}{2}°$, when given in minutes, $\pm0°10′$; and when given in seconds, $\pm0′30″$, as shown in Fig. 60.

In structural drawings angular measurements are shown by giving the ratio of run to rise with the larger side 12 in., Figs.

FIG. 66   DIMENSIONING IRREGULAR CURVE
WITH RADII

379

51 and 52. For steep angles as on retaining walls, the ratio has one factor equal to 1 as shown in Fig. 69.

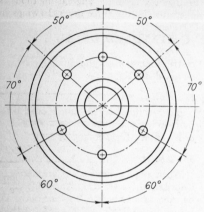

FIG. 68 DIMENSIONING ANGLES

57 Holes—Drilled, Reamed, Punched, Swaged, Cored or Bored

Holes which are to be made by any of these operations should have the diameter given, preferably on a leader, followed by the word indicating the operation, and the number of holes to be made, Fig. 70.

Notes for holes made with drills one-half inch in diameter and smaller should be written as decimal fractions, Figs. 72a, 73, and 75. The drills selected in this range should be the standard diameters given in the American Standard for Straight Shank Twist Drills (ASA B5.12—1940). The indication of the diameters of drills larger than one-half inch should be expressed in units and decimals. If common fractions are employed, the decimal equivalent should be given.

Holes which are to be bored after coring

or casting should have finish marks and finished dimensions specified, Fig. 71.

58 For counterbored holes the diameters and depths should be given as shown in Fig. 72.

59 For countersunk and counterdrilled holes the angles and diameters should be given by dimensions or notes as shown in Fig. 73. The value of the countersink angle should be given as the included angle.

60 Tapped Holes

The size and depth of tapped holes should be given by note as shown in Fig. 75 with reference to the American Standard Coarse (NC), American Standard Fine (NF) or American Standard Special (N) Screw Thread Series and the Class of Fit desired. If the American Standard form is desired with a non-standard pitch the symbol is (NS).

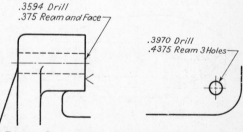

FIG. 69 INDICATING SLOPES ON CIVIL ENGINEERING PROJECTS

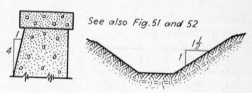

FIG. 70 DIMENSIONING DRILLED AND REAMED HOLES

61 Location of Holes

Figs. 74, 76, and 77 illustrate the coordinate method of dimensioning holes. The actual numerical values shown for location of holes in these figures have been included for illustrative purposes only. The alignment of two or more parts requires similar dimensioning from a common datum, line, or plane.

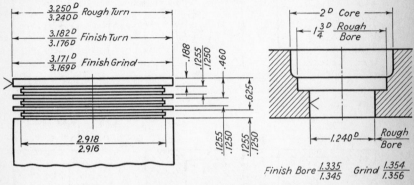

FIG. 71   DIMENSIONING MACHINED HOLES AND CYLINDERS

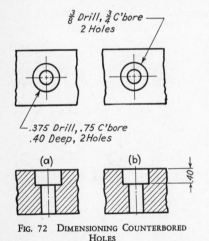

FIG. 72   DIMENSIONING COUNTERBORED HOLES

The use of angular measurements, such as degrees, minutes and seconds to locate holes and parts requiring accurate placement should be avoided as much as possible, Fig. 76.

The ordinate method of dimensioning, as illustrated in the lower right-hand drawing, Fig. 76, is preferred in precision work to the less accurate angular method as illustrated by the three other drawings in Fig. 76.

62 Tapers

The difference in diameter or width in one foot of length is known as the "taper per foot." At least three methods of dimensioning tapers are in general use.

(a) STANDARD TAPERS. Give one diameter or width, the length, and insert note on drawing designating the taper by number taken from ASA B5.10—1943, as shown in Fig. 78.

(b) SPECIAL TAPERS. In dimensioning a taper when the slope is specified, the length and only one diameter should be given or the diameters at both ends of the taper should be given and the length omitted, Fig. 78.

(c) Fig. 79 illustrates the proper method of dimensioning tapered surfaces where accuracy is required so as to obtain a close fit between internal and external tapers. The tolerance on the diameter at the gage line is ±0 and the tolerance on the angle is as shown in the figure. The

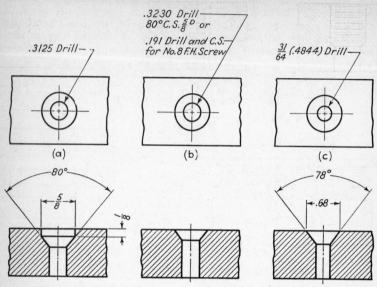

FIG. 73 DIMENSIONING COUNTERDRILLED AND COUNTERSUNK HOLES

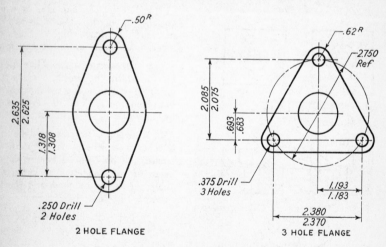

FIG. 74 LOCATION DIMENSIONING OF HOLES

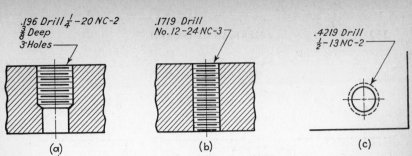

FIG. 75 DIMENSIONING TAPPED HOLES

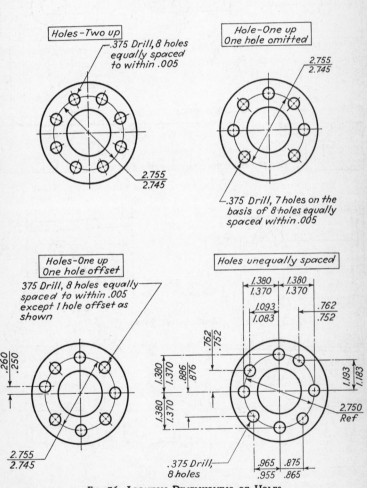

FIG. 76 LOCATION DIMENSIONING OF HOLES

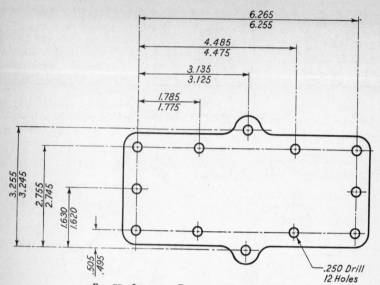

FIG. 77 LOCATION DIMENSIONING OF HOLES

.250 Drill
12 Holes

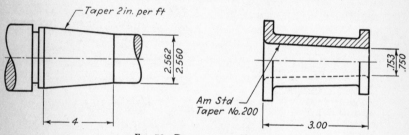

Taper 2 in. per ft

2.562
2.560

4

Am Std
Taper No.200

.753
.750

3.00

FIG. 78 DIMENSIONING TAPERS

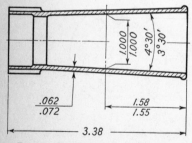

1.000
1.000

4°30'
3°30'

.062
.072

1.58
1.55

3.38

FIG. 79 DIMENSIONING TAPERS FOR
A CLOSE FIT

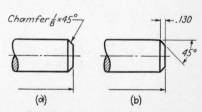

Chamfer ⅛ × 45°

.130

45°

(a)   (b)

FIG. 80 DIMENSIONING CHAMFERS

384

tolerance for location of the gage line may be varied to suit the conditions.

63 Chamfers

Ordinary chamfers may be dimensioned as shown in Fig. 80a. More accurate chamfers should be dimensioned as in Fig. 80(b).

64 Knurls

When knurls are used to roughen a surface for the purpose of giving a better grip it is only necessary to specify the pitch of the knurl and show the kind of knurl and the dimensions of the areas as shown in Fig. 81.

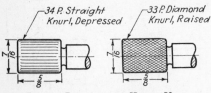

Fig. 81 Dimensioning Knurl Used to Provide Grip

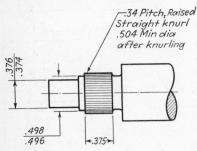

Before knurling

Fig. 82 Dimensioning Knurl for Press Fit

When knurls are used to make a press fit between two parts the original finished surface should be dimensioned with limits and then the minimum acceptable diameter of the knurl should be given in a note together with the pitch and type of knurl, straight or diamond, depressed or raised, as shown in Fig. 82.

65 Dovetail Tongues and Slots

For large quantity production, snug fitting dovetailed parts should be dimensioned as shown in Fig. 83 which provides complete information for the tool and gage maker. The so-called "plug method" is also in common use.

The important contact surfaces should be controlled by dimensions delineated to the same intersection points of mating angular flanks on each component part.

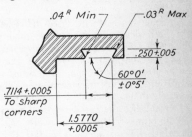

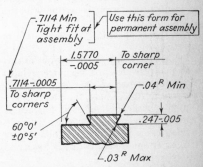

Fig. 83 Dimensioning a Dovetail Tongue and Slot for Snug Fit

Tolerances should be given on all dimensions including angular dimensions. The radii at corners should be governed by the best requirements of good tool practice and flats may be substituted if desired.

66 Finish Marks

A surface to be machined or "finished" from unfinished material such as a casting or a forging should be marked with a 60 deg "V," the bottom of the "V" touching the line representing the surface to be machined or finished. Fig. 94.

The old symbol "f" is still in use and is also acceptable for this purpose, Fig. 95. The notes, "Finish All Over," or "F.A.O.," are acceptable for parts which are to have an ordinary machine finish on the entire surface.

67 Symbols for Designating Surface Quality *

An American Standard (ASA B46) has now been developed for surface quality which (1) defines roughness, waviness, and lay, (2) establishes the specification rating and measurement of roughness in terms of height and width of irregularities and the direction of the dominant surface pattern, (3) establishes the specification of waviness in terms of height and width, with the width line in all cases greater than the width of roughness, (4) gives recommended values for roughness and waviness height, and (5) describes the meaning and use of the symbols for the designation of surface quality.

Among the many characteristics of surface quality which are intimately related to the functioning of a surface is the surface finish. Accordingly, the proper specification of the finish of such surfaces as bearings, seals, etc., is extremely important. In other cases where the finish of a surface is unimportant it may not be necessary to specify it.

A surface whose finish is to be specified should be marked with the finish mark having the general form of a check mark ($\sqrt{}$) so that the point of the symbol is

(a) On the line indicating the surface,

(b) On a leader pointing to the surface.

Where it is desired to specify only the surface roughness height, and the width of

* As recommended by the Sectional Committee on the Standardization of Classification and Designation of Surface Qualities (ASA B46).

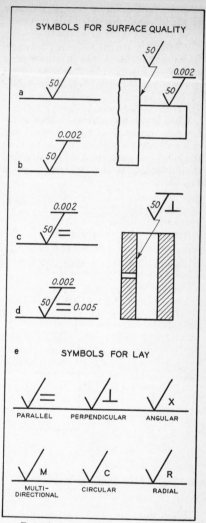

SYMBOLS FOR SURFACE QUALITY

FIG. 84   SURFACE QUALITY SYMBOLS

roughness or direction of tool marks is not important, the simplest form of the symbol should be used. See Fig. 84(a). This height may be either maximum peak to valley height, average peak to valley height, or average deviation from the mean (RMS or arithmetical). The numerical value is placed in the $\vee$ as shown.

Where it is desired to specify waviness height in addition to roughness height a straight horizontal line should be added to the top of the simple symbol. See Fig. 84(b). The numerical value of height of waviness would be shown above this line.

Then, if the nature of the preferred lay is to be shown in addition to these two characteristics, it will be indicated by the addition of a combination of lines as shown in Fig. 84(c and e). The parallel and perpendicular part of the symbol indicates that the dominant lines on the surface are parallel or perpendicular to the boundary line of the surface in contact with the symbol.

The complete symbol including the roughness width placed to the right of the lay symbol, is shown in Fig. 84(d).

The use of only one number to specify the height or width of roughness or waviness shall indicate the maximum value. Any lesser degree of roughness will be satisfactory. When two numbers are used separated by a dash, they indicate the maximum and minimum permissible values.

$$Bend\ allowance\ (B.A.) = (.01745\ R + .0078\ T)\ \theta$$

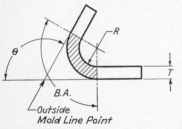

FIG. 85   BEND ALLOWANCE

68   Bend Allowance

The allowance to be made for bends in sheet metal work or thin steel is shown in Fig. 85. The intersection of the plane sur-

faces adjoining the bend is called a mold or construction line and this line is used in dimensioning rather than the center of the arc.

69 · Profile Dimensioning

Parts that are formed by bending are dimensioned as in Fig. 86. The dimensions are given to mold lines. Angles and radii must be shown.

70   Springs

Methods of representing and dimensioning springs are shown in Figs. 90, 91, and

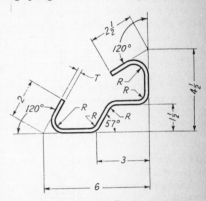

FIG. 86   PROFILE DIMENSIONING

92. Beside the length and controlling diameter (inside or outside) the size and number of turns of wire must be indicated by note. The type of end should be indicated even though standard. If the ends of the spring must be formed to fit some special condition the end must then be dimensioned in detail to secure the desired result. Single line symbols are shown in Fig. 93.

71   Gears

A gear may be shown satisfactorily by a section through the axis, except when additional views may be required to show the construction of a large blank or other details. In principle the dimensions placed on the drawing should be sufficient for machining the gear blank. The gear-cutting data which include the tooth-form standard and method of cutting, and information for measurement and inspection, should be given in a table. Notes for material and heat treatment are also required, Figs. 87 and 88.

72 Keys

Plain square, flat, taper and Gib-head taper stock keys are dimensioned by note giving the width, height and length. Whenever possible, sizes should conform to standards established in the American Standard for Shafting and Stock Keys (ASA B17.1—1943). The keys need not be drawn except for special keys or when limits other than those of the standard are necessary. American Standard Woodruff Keys, Keyslots and Cutter (ASA B17f—1930) may be specified by key number.

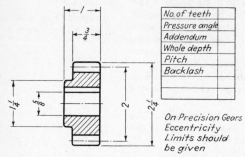

No. of teeth	
Pressure angle	
Addendum	
Whole depth	
Pitch	
Backlash	

On Precision Gears
Eccentricity
Limits should
be given

FIG. 87 DIMENSIONING SPUR PINION

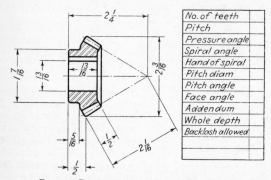

No. of teeth	
Pitch	
Pressure angle	
Spiral angle	
Hand of spiral	
Pitch diam	
Pitch angle	
Face angle	
Addendum	
Whole depth	
Backlash allowed	

FIG. 88 DIMENSIONING SPIRAL BEVEL PINION

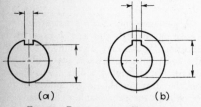

(a)   (b)

FIG. 89 DIMENSIONING KEYWAYS

73 Keyways

Keyways on shafts or internal members may be dimensioned as shown in Fig. 89(a). On the hub or external member the keyway may be dimensioned as shown in Fig. 89(b). The key seat for patented varieties may be specified by the key number.

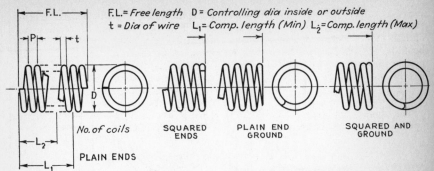

FIG. 90   REPRESENTING AND DIMENSIONING COMPRESSION SPRINGS

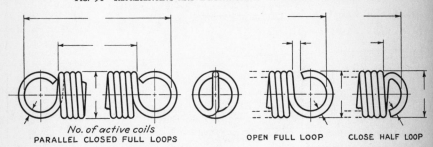

FIG. 91   REPRESENTING AND DIMENSIONING TENSION SPRINGS

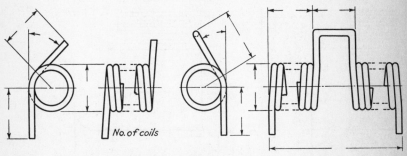

FIG. 92   REPRESENTING AND DIMENSIONING TORSION SPRINGS

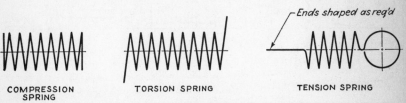

FIG. 93   SINGLE LINE REPRESENTATION OF SPRINGS

389

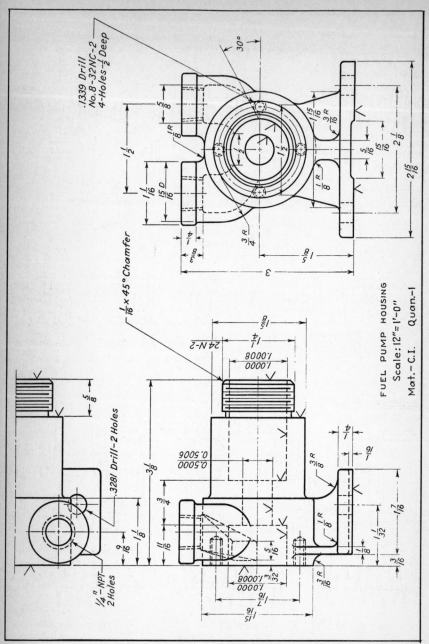

FIG. 94 APPLICATION OF SURFACE FINISH SYMBOLS

390

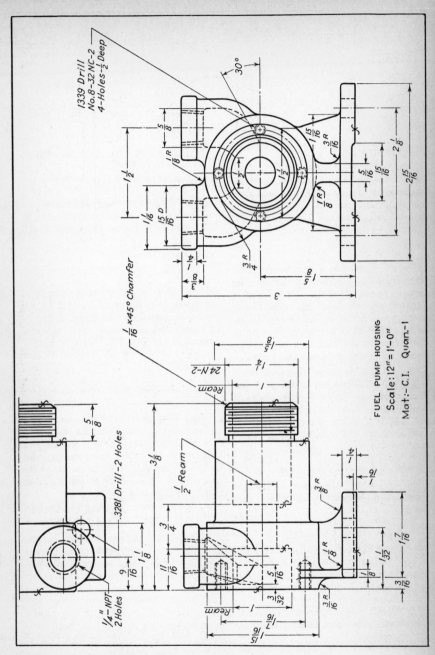

FIG. 95 APPLICATION OF SURFACE FINISH SYMBOLS

391

SECTION 7—NOTES

74 Definition

Notes are supplementary to dimensioning and are used to indicate necessary information on the drawing in a condensed and systematic manner. Notes may be classified as General and Local or Specific, according to their character.

75 General Notes

General notes should be placed in the lower right hand corner of the drawing above or to the left of the title block or in a central position below the view of the object to which they apply. General notes, as the name implies, means those notes which refer to the part as a whole, e.g.: "Finish All Over" or "Paint One Coat."

Also classified as general notes, are notes that apply to dimensions of the part and which might be repeated many times if general notes were not used, e.g.: "All draft angles 3° unless otherwise specified" or "Tolerance ±.001 unless shown otherwise."

76 Miscellaneous General Notes

The following miscellaneous General Notes are suggested for use where necessary.

(1) Finish All Over.
(2) Finish All Over Except—
(3) Break Sharp Edges .01-, .03 Approx. R Unless Otherwise Specified.
(4) Break Sharp Edges On All (Drilled Holes) (Chamfers) (Countersinks) Unless Otherwise Specified.
(5) All (Casting) (Forging) (Finished) Radii .xxx- .xxx Unless Otherwise Specified.

(6) All Draft Angles X° Unless Otherwise Specified.
(7) All Dimensions To Be Met After Plating.
(8) Must Be Flat and Free From Burrs.
(9) All Small Unfinished Radii and Fillets .XX Unless Otherwise Specified.
(10) Remove Burrs.

77 Local Notes

Local notes are those that apply to local operations only and should be placed adjacent, connected by a leader, to the point at which such operations are to be performed, e.g.: ".248-.255," "Drill, 4 holes." See Figs. 64 and 70 to 75 inclusive, for examples.

78 Specification of Materials and Heat Treatments

Many companies have their own method and standards. A method commonly available is to indicate ferrous materials and heat treatments by specifying the steels by the SAE Numbers, and the hardness required by a Rockwell, or Brinell hardness number, as for example:

SAE—1095—Rockwell C 60-64
SAE—3345—Brinell 340-380

For steel in buildings, bridges, boilers, railroads, and reinforced concrete the A.S.T.M. specifications or special specifications prepared by the firm or department making the drawing are used. Treatments such as case-hardening, carburizing (by any method), cyaniding, nitriding, should be indicated by a specific local note completely covering the requirements.

392

SECTION 8—TRIMMED SIZES OF DRAWING PAPER AND CLOTH. TITLES

79 Sizes of Paper

The recommended standard trimmed sheet sizes of drawing paper and cloth are as follows:

A	8½×11	D	22×34
B	11×17	E	34×44
C	17×22		

The use of the basic sheet size 8½×11 in. and its multiple permits filing of small tracings and folded prints in commercial standard files with or without correspondence. These sheet sizes also cut without waste from the present 36 in. rolls of paper and cloth. These standard sizes are based on the dimensions of the commercial letter head, 8½×11 in., in general use in the United States.

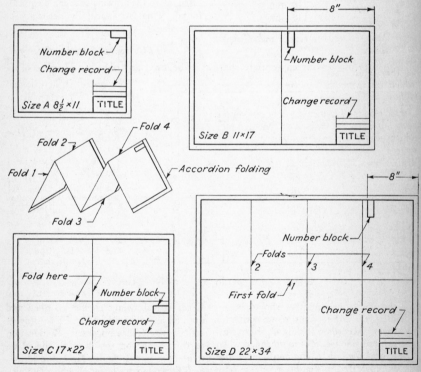

FIG. 96 TITLE BLOCK, CHANGE RECORD, AND FOLDING

Drawings larger than standard sheet sizes may be made as "rolled" drawings. Widths are controlled by standard paper sizes, and lengths are in multiples of 11 in.

80 Sizes of Paper in the Metric System

For drawings made in the metric system of units or for foreign correspondence it is recommended that the metric standard trimmed sheet sizes be used. These sizes are based on the width to length ratio of 1 to $\sqrt{2}$ and are as follows:

A0 841×1189 mm
A1 594×841 mm
A2 420×594 mm
A3 297×420 mm
A4 210×297 mm
A5 148×210 mm
A6 105×148 mm

81 Title, Change Record and Number Blocks

The title block with appropriate space

accordion folded so that the closed fold will be up and the number still be visible, it is necessary to add a supplementary number block (approximately 1.75 in. by .5 in.) to each size sheet as shown in Fig. 96. This supplementary number block may be either parallel or normal to the border line of the drawing. If change notes or general notes reach this supplementary number block a minimum clearance of .25 in. should be left above and below the block.

82 Location of Change Record

The change record should be placed immediately above the title space as shown in Fig. 96. The change record must be "tied in" to the drawing so it can be quickly found. This is particularly necessary on large sheets.

83 Zoning System of Locating Changes

The lower and right hand borders of the

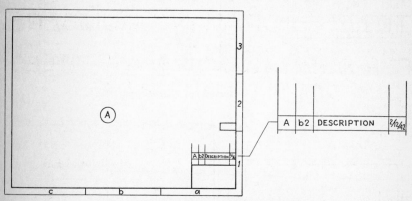

FIG. 97 ZONE METHOD OF LOCATING CHANGES

for the identifying number should be located at the lower right hand corner of the sheet. Accordion folding of prints with the printed side out is recommended when prints are filed in a standard letter size file as illustrated in Fig. 96.

In order to file prints which have been

larger size drawings should be ruled and marked as indicated in Fig. 97 to provide zones for reference purposes. The location of the change on the drawing should be referenced in the change block and identified by a reference letter which should also appear on the drawing near the change and in a position where it can be readily seen. For example a change referenced (b2) would be found upward from b and over from 2. For purposes of clarity a circle of approximately 5/16 in. in diameter should be drawn around the change letter as illustrated in Fig. 97. Letters I, O and Q should not be used to avoid misinterpretation and resultant errors. Other methods not illustrated here are also in common use.

SECTION 9—LETTERING

84 The most important requirement for lettering as used on working drawings is legibility. The second is ease and rapidity of execution. These two requirements are met in the single stroke commercial gothic letter, now in almost universal use throughout the technical world. Preference seems to be divided between the vertical and the inclined styles.

The following standard practice is recommended:

(a) That single stroke commercial gothic lettering either vertical or inclined at a slope of 2 in 5 be used on all working drawings for titles, notes, etc.

85 It is not desirable to grade the size of lettering with the size of the drawing

TYPE 1

ABCDEFGHIJKLMNOP
QRSTUVWXYZ&
1234567890 $\frac{1}{2}$ $\frac{3}{4}$ $\frac{5}{8}$
TITLES & DRAWING NUMBERS

TYPE 2

FOR SUB-TITLES OR MAIN TITLES
ON SMALL DRAWINGS

TYPE 3

ABCDEFGHIJKLMNOPQRSTUVWXYZ&
1234567890 $\frac{1}{2}$ $\frac{3}{4}$ $\frac{5}{8}$ $\frac{9}{32}$
FOR HEADINGS AND PROMINENT NOTES

TYPE 4

ABCDEFGHIJKLMNOPQRSTUVWXYZ&
1234567890 $\frac{1}{2}$ $\frac{3}{4}$ $\frac{5}{8}$ $\frac{23}{64}$
FOR BILLS OF MATERIAL, DIMENSIONS & GENERAL NOTES

TYPE 5

OPTIONAL TYPE SAME AS TYPE 4 BUT USING TYPE 3 FOR FIRST
LETTER OF PRINCIPAL WORDS. MAY BE USED FOR SUB-TITLES
AND NOTES ON THE BODY OF DRAWINGS.

TYPE 6

abcdefghijklmnopqrstuvwxyz

FIG. 98
52

except when a reduced photographic reproduction of the drawing is to be made. In
other words the size and weight of the
lettering should be such as will produce
legible prints from tracings either in pencil
or in ink.

Lettering should not be underlined except for particular emphasis.

Approved specimens of vertical and inclined letters are shown in Figs. 98 and 99.

TYPE 1
ABCDEFGHIJKLMNOP
QRSTUVWXYZ&
1234567890 $\frac{1}{2} \frac{3}{4} \frac{5}{8} \frac{7}{16}$
TO BE USED FOR MAIN TITLES
& DRAWING NUMBERS

TYPE 2
ABCDEFGHIJKLMNOPQR
STUVWXYZ&
1234567890 $\frac{13}{64} \frac{5}{8} \frac{1}{2}$
TO BE USED FOR SUB-TITLES

TYPE 3
ABCDEFGHIJKLMNOPQRSTUVWXYZ&
1234567890 $\frac{1}{2} \frac{3}{4} \frac{5}{8} \frac{7}{16}$
FOR HEADINGS AND PROMINENT NOTES

TYPE 4
ABCDEFGHIJKLMNOPQRSTUVWXYZ&
1234567890 $\frac{1}{2} \frac{1}{4} \frac{3}{8} \frac{5}{16} \frac{7}{32} \frac{1}{8}$
FOR BILLS OF MATERIAL, DIMENSIONS & GENERAL NOTES

TYPE 5
OPTIONAL TYPE SAME AS TYPE 4 BUT USING TYPE 3 FOR FIRST
LETTER OF PRINCIPAL WORDS. MAY BE USED FOR SUB-TITLES &
NOTES ON THE BODY OF DRAWINGS.

TYPE 6
abcdefghijklmnopqrstuvwxyz
Type 6 may be used in place of
Type 4 with capitals of Type 3,
for Bills of Material and Notes
on Body of Drawing.

FIG. 99

Appendix Tables

TABLE 1. THREAD DIMENSIONS AND TAP DRILL SIZES

Size	Threads per Inch			Outside Diameter	Root Diameter	Tap Drill 75% Full Thread	Decimal Equiv. of Tap Drill
	NC	NF	SAE				
0		80		.0600	.0438	$\frac{3}{64}$	.0469
1	64			.0730	.0527	53	.0595
1		72		.0730	.0550	53	.0595
2	56			.0860	.0628	50	.0700
2		64		.0860	.0657	49	.0730
3	48			.0990	.0719	47	.0785
3		56		.0990	.0758	45	.0820
4	40			.1120	.0795	43	.0890
4		48		.1120	.0849	42	.0935
5	40			.1250	.0925	38	.1015
5		44		.1250	.0955	37	.1040
6	32			.1380	.0974	35	.1065
6		40		.1380	.1055	33	.1130
8	32			.1640	.1234	29	.1360
8		36		.1640	.1279	29	.1360
10	24			.1900	.1359	25	.1495
10		32		.1900	.1494	21	.1590
12	24			.2160	.1619	16	.1770
12		28		.2160	.1696	14	.1820
$\frac{1}{4}$	20			.2500	.1850	7	.2010
$\frac{1}{4}$		28		.2500	.2036	3	.2130
$\frac{1}{4}$			36	.2500	.2136	D	.2460
$\frac{5}{16}$	18			.3125	.2403	F	.2570
$\frac{5}{16}$		24		.3125	.2585	I	.2720
$\frac{5}{16}$			32	.3125	.2742	I	.2720
$\frac{3}{8}$	16			.3750	.2938	$\frac{5}{16}$	.3125
$\frac{3}{8}$		24		.3750	.3209	Q	.3320
$\frac{3}{8}$			32	.3750	.3367	R	.3390
$\frac{7}{16}$	14			.4375	.3447	U	.3680
$\frac{7}{16}$		20		.4375	.3726	$\frac{25}{64}$	.3906
$\frac{7}{16}$			28	.4375	.3937	Y	.4040
$\frac{1}{2}$	13			.5000	.4001	$\frac{27}{64}$	.4219
$\frac{1}{2}$		20		.5000	.4351	$\frac{29}{64}$	.4531
$\frac{1}{2}$			28	.5000	.4562	$\frac{15}{32}$	.4687
$\frac{9}{16}$	12			.5625	.4542	$\frac{31}{64}$	.4844
$\frac{9}{16}$		18		.5625	.4903	$\frac{33}{64}$	.5156
$\frac{9}{16}$			24	.5625	.5114	$\frac{33}{64}$	.5156
$\frac{5}{8}$	11			.6250	.5069	$\frac{17}{32}$	.5312
$\frac{5}{8}$		18		.6250	.5528	$\frac{37}{64}$	.5781
$\frac{5}{8}$			24	.6250	.5739	$\frac{37}{64}$	.5781
$\frac{3}{4}$	10			.7500	.6201	$\frac{21}{32}$	.6562
$\frac{3}{4}$		16		.7500	.6688	$\frac{11}{16}$	.6875
$\frac{3}{4}$			20	.7500	.6887	$\frac{11}{16}$	.6875
$\frac{7}{8}$	9			.8750	.7307	$\frac{49}{64}$	.7656

TABLE 1.   THREAD DIMENSIONS AND TAP DRILL SIZES
(*Continued*)

Size	Threads per Inch			Outside Diameter	Root Diameter	Tap Drill 75% Full Thread	Decimal Equiv. of Tap Drill
	NC	NF	SAE				
7/8		14		.8750	.7822	13/16	.8125
7/8			20	.8750	.8137	53/64	.8281
1	8			1.0000	.8376	7/8	.8750
1		14		1.0000	.9072	15/16	.9375
1			20	1.0000	.9387	15/16	.9375
1 1/8	7			1.1250	.9394	63/64	.9844
1 1/8		12		1.1250	1.0168	1 3/64	1.0469
1 1/8			18	1.1250	1.0568	1 1/16	1.0625
1 1/4	7			1.2500	1.0644	1 7/64	1.1094
1 1/4		12		1.2500	1.1418	1 11/64	1.1719
1 1/4			18	1.2500	1.1418	1 3/16	1.1875
1 3/8	6			1.3750	1.1585	1 7/32	1.2187
1 3/8		12		1.3750	1.2668	1 19/64	1.2969
1 1/2	6			1.5000	1.2835	1 11/32	1.3437
1 1/2		12		1.5000	1.3918	1 27/64	1.4219
1 1/2			18	1.5000	1.4318	1 7/16	1.4375
1 3/4	5			1.7500	1.4902	1 9/16	1.5625
2	4 1/2			2.0000	1.7113	1 25/32	1.7812
2 1/4	4 1/2			2.2500	1.9613	2 1/32	2.0313
2 1/2	4			2.5000	2.1752	2 1/4	2.2500
2 3/4	4			2.7500	2.4252	2 1/2	2.5000
3	4			3.0000	2.6752	2 3/4	2.7500
3 1/4	4			3.2500	2.9252	3	3.0000
3 1/2	4			3.5000	3.1752	3 1/4	3.2500
3 3/4	4			3.7500	3.4252	3 1/2	3.5000
4	4			4.0000	3.6752	3 3/4	3.7500

TABLE 2. STANDARD BOLTS

Type	Description	Application
Machine Bolts Rough	Unfinished Square Heads only. Always come with Unfinished Hexagon Nuts.	Used only as THROUGH BOLTS in cast, drilled or punched clearance holes where bottom of bolthead does not rest on a finished surface and where a square head is not objectionable. For general use on structural assemblies such as car frames, counterweights, rail brackets, etc.
Set-over Head Bolts 10° Rough	Unfinished, Square, Set-over (Askew) Heads. Always come with Unfinished Hexagon Nuts.	Same As Above Heads are made to fit over tapered flanges of angles, beams, and channels. Angle of head is 10°.
Tap Bolts Machined	Semifinished, Hexagon Heads only. (Machined only under head.)	Used to hold together two or more parts, one or more having cast, drilled or punched clearance holes and only one part having a tapped hole. Bottom of bolt head may or may not rest on a finished surface.
Finished Body Bolts, Commercial ±.003" Ground Machined	Semifinished, Hexagon Heads only. (Machined only under head.) Bodies ground to diameter ±.003". *Semifinished Hexagon Nuts are used with all Finished Body Bolts.*	Used where accuracy of bolt body, head, and threads is essential to good fits. Used as THROUGH BOLTS with drilled clearance holes to fasten sheave rims to sheave centers, bearing caps to gear cases and outboard stands, etc. Used as TAP BOLTS with drilled clearance holes to fasten motor feet, brake frames, lower gear cases and outboard stands to bedplates.
Finished Body Bolts, Oversize +.002" −.000" Ground Machined	Semifinished Hexagon Heads only. (Machined only under head.) Bodies ground to diameter $^{+.002''}_{-.000}$.	Used where accuracy of bolt body, head, and threads is essential to good fits. Used as THROUGH BOLTS with standard reamed clearance holes where a tight or drive fit is required so that bolts may act as dowels.
Finished Body Bolts, Undersize +.000" −.003" Ground Machined	Semifinished Hexagon Heads only. (Machined only under head.) Bodies ground to diameter $^{+.000}_{-.003''}$. *SAE Finished Body Bolts come* $-.001''$ $-.003''$.	Used where accuracy of bolt body, head, and threads is essential to good fits. Used as THROUGH BOLTS with standard reamed clearance holes where a tight or drive fit is not required and where clearances of several bolts should be uniform. For Brake Coupling, hub and web bolts. Bearing Caps, where location of cap is dependent on the bolts instead of on mating flanges, lips, or recesses.
Lag Bolts Rough	Unfinished Square Heads and Gimlet Points are standard. May be obtained with Special Washer Heads.	Used as wood screws, primarily to fasten structural shapes to wood.
Carriage Bolts Rough	Unfinished Round Heads with Square Necks only. Always come with Unfinished Square Nuts.	Used only as THROUGH BOLTS, primarily to fasten wood to structural shapes.
Stove Bolts Rough	Unfinished Round or Flat Heads (Round preferred). Always come with Unfinished Square Nuts. Sizes 1/8″, 5/32″, 3/16″, 1/4″, 5/16″, 3/8″, or 1/2″ (Diameters).	Used only as THROUGH BOLTS, primarily to fasten together various parts of steel enclosures of freight elevators. Similar to machine screws but are of inferior quality, less expensive, and come in standard lengths up to 6″.

TABLE 3. DIMENSIONS OF AMERICAN STANDARD REGULAR BOLTHEADS AND NUTS *

Bolt Diam.	Regular Boltheads					Nuts						
	Across Flats [1]	Width – Across Corners		Height		Across Flats [1]	Width – Across Corners		Thickness – Regular Nuts		Thickness – Regular Jam Nuts [2]	
		Sq.	Hex.	Unfin.	Semifin.		Sq.	Hex.	Unfin.	Semifin.	Unfin.	Semifin.
1/4	3/8	0.498	0.413	11/64	5/32	3/8	0.584	0.484	7/32	13/64	5/32	9/64
5/16	1/2	0.665	0.552	13/64	3/16	1/2	0.751	0.624	17/64	1/4	3/16	11/64
3/8	9/16	0.747	0.620	1/4	13/64	5/8	0.832	0.691	21/64	5/16	7/32	13/64
7/16	5/8	0.828	0.687	19/64	9/32	3/4	1.000	0.830	3/8	27/64	1/4	15/64
1/2	3/4	0.995	0.826	21/64	11/32	13/16	1.082	0.898	7/16	31/64	5/16	19/64
9/16	7/8	1.163	0.966	3/8	11/32	7/8	1.163	0.966	1/2	35/64	11/32	21/64
5/8	15/16	1.244	1.033	27/64	23/64	1	1.330	1.104	35/64	17/32	3/8	23/64
3/4	1 1/8	1.494	1.240	1/2	15/32	1 1/8	1.494	1.240	21/32	41/64	7/16	27/64
7/8	1 5/16	1.742	1.447	19/32	9/16	1 5/16	1.742	1.447	49/64	3/4	1/2	31/64
1	1 1/2	1.991	1.653	21/32	19/32	1 1/2	1.991	1.653	7/8	55/64	9/16	35/64
1 1/8	1 11/16	2.239	1.859	3/4	11/16	1 11/16	2.239	1.859	1	31/32	5/8	39/64
1 1/4	1 7/8	2.489	2.066	27/32	25/32	1 7/8	2.489	2.066	1 3/32	1 1/16	3/4	23/32
1 3/8	2 1/16	2.738	2.273	29/32	27/32	2 1/16	2.738	2.273	1 13/64	1 9/32	13/16	25/32
1 1/2	2 1/4	2.986	2.480	1	15/16	2 1/4	2.986	2.480	1 5/16	1 9/32	7/8	27/32
1 5/8	2 7/16	3.235	2.686	1 3/32	1 1/32	2 7/16	3.235	2.686	1 27/64	1 25/64	15/16	29/32
1 3/4	2 5/8	3.485	2.893	1 5/32	1 3/32	2 5/8	3.485	2.893	1 17/32	1 1/2	1	31/32
1 7/8	2 13/16	3.733	3.100	1 1/4	1 3/16	2 13/16	3.733	3.100	1 9/16	1 39/64	1 1/16	1 1/32
2	3	3.982	3.306	1 11/32	1 7/32	3	3.982	3.306	1 3/4	1 23/32	1 1/8	1 3/32
2 1/4	3 3/8	4.479	3.719	1 1/2	1 3/8	3 3/8	4.479	3.719	1 31/32	1 59/64	1 1/4	1 13/64
2 1/2	3 3/4	4.977	4.133	1 21/32	1 17/32	3 3/4	4.977	4.133	2 3/16	2 9/64	1 3/8	1 29/64
2 3/4	4 1/8	5.476	4.546	1 13/16	1 11/16	4 1/8	5.476	4.546	2 13/32	2 23/64	1 5/8	1 37/64
3	4 1/2	5.973	4.959	2	1 7/8	4 1/2	5.973	4.959	2 5/8	2 37/64	1 3/4	1 45/64

* Compiled from ASA B18.2 — 1941.

[1] Unfinished Square and Hexagonal Semi-finished (Hexagonal Head only).

[2] Jam Nuts (Hexagonal only).

TABLE 4. DIMENSIONS OF AMERICAN STANDARD HEXAGONAL SOCKET AND FLUTED SOCKET CAP SCREWS *

Nominal Size D	Head Diam. A	Head Height H	Head Side Height		J	M	N
			S	K			
8	9/32	0.164	0.1503	1/8	0.127	0.147	0.035
10	5/16	0.190	0.1741	5/32	0.127	0.147	0.035
12	11/32	0.216	0.1980	5/32	0.160	0.185	0.042
1/4	3/8	1/4	0.2291	3/16	0.190	0.219	0.052
5/16	7/16	5/16	0.2864	7/32	0.221	0.256	0.062
3/8	9/16	3/8	0.3437	5/16	0.312	0.380	0.092
7/16	5/8	7/16	0.4010	5/16	0.312	0.380	0.092
1/2	3/4	1/2	0.4583	3/8	0.386	0.463	0.112
9/16	13/16	9/16	0.5156	3/8	0.386	0.463	0.112
5/8	7/8	5/8	0.5729	1/2	0.506	0.600	0.142
3/4	1	3/4	0.6875	9/16	0.568	0.654	0.157
7/8	1 1/8	7/8	0.8020	9/16	0.568	0.654	0.157
1	1 5/16	1	0.9166	5/8	0.631	0.790	0.184
1 1/8	1 1/2	1 1/8	1.0312	3/4	0.756	0.957	0.221
1 1/4	1 3/4	1 1/4	1.1457	3/4	0.756	0.957	0.221
1 3/8	1 7/8	1 3/8	1.2604	3/4	0.756	0.957	0.221
1 1/2	2	1 1/2	1.3750	1	1.007	1.275	0.298

* Compiled from ASA B18.3 — 1936.

Length under Head (L). The length of the screw shall be measured on a line parallel to the axis, from the plane of the bearing surface under the head to the plane of the flat of the point. The difference between consecutive lengths shall be as follows: (a) for screw lengths 1/4 to 1 in. shall be 1/8 in.; (b) for screw lengths 1 to 4 in. shall be 1/4 in.; (c) for screw lengths 4 to 6 in. shall be 1/2 in.

Thread Length (l). The length of the screw thread is measured from the extreme point to the last useable thread and shall be as follows:

For National Coarse —

1 2D 1/2 in. (where this length of thread is greater than 1/2 L).
1 1/2L (where this length of thread is greater than 2D 1/2 in.).

For National Fine —

1 1 1/2D 1/2 in. (where this length of thread would be greater than three-eighths the screw length).
1 3/8L (where this length of thread would be greater than 1 1/2D 1/2 in.).

Screws too short to allow application of these formulas shall be threaded as close to the head as practicable.

TABLE 5. DIMENSIONS OF AMERICAN STANDARD SLOTTED–HEAD CAP SCREWS *

Size D	Head Diameter			Height of Head			
	A	B	C	E	F	G	H
1/4	1/2	7/16	3/8	.146	.188	11/64	.044
5/16	5/8	9/16	7/16	.183	.236	13/64	.050
3/8	3/4	5/8	9/16	.220	.262	1/4	.064
7/16	13/16	3/4	5/8	.220	.315	19/64	.071
1/2	7/8	13/16	3/4	.220	.342	21/64	.084
9/16	1	15/16	13/16	.256	.394	3/8	.091
5/8	1 1/8	1	7/8	.293	.421	27/64	.099
3/4	1 3/8	1 1/4	1	.366	.526	1/2	.112
7/8	....	....	1 1/8	....	....	19/32	.126
1	....	....	1 5/16	....	....	21/32	.146

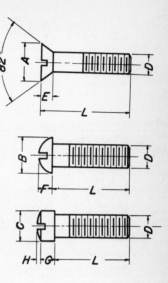

* Compiled from ASA B18c — 1930.

Cap Screw Lengths. The difference between consecutive lengths of screws: for screw lengths 1/4 in. to 1 in. shall be 1/8 in.; for screw lengths 1 in. to 4 in. shall be 1/4 in.; for screw lengths 4 in. to 6 in. shall be 1/2 in.

Thread Lengths. Slotted-head cap screws shall be regularly threaded coarse pitch and when so threaded shall have a length of thread equal to 2D 1/4 in. Screws too short to allow the formula length of thread may be threaded as close to the head as practicable.

Screw Points. The points of all cap screws shall be flat, the flat being normal to the axis of the screw, and shall be chamfered at an angle of 35° with the surface of the flat.

TABLE 6. DIMENSIONS OF AMERICAN STANDARD HEXAGONAL CAP SCREWS *

Size	Width Across Flats	Height of Head
1/4	7/16	3/16
5/16	1/2	15/64
3/8	9/16	9/32
7/16	5/8	21/64
1/2	3/4	3/8
9/16	13/16	27/64
5/8	7/8	15/32
3/4	1	9/16
7/8	1 1/8	21/32
1	1 9/16	3/4
1 1/8	1 1/2	27/32
1 1/4	1 11/16	15/16

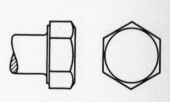

* Compiled from ASA B18.2 — 1941.

Full finished cap screws have all surfaces, including body and all surfaces of the head, machined or otherwise treated to provide a surface equivalent in appearance.

Cap screws are threaded with either the coarse or fine threads and shall have a length of thread equal to twice the diameter plus 1/4 in. Screws too short to allow this length of thread shall be threaded as close to the head as practicable.

The top of the head shall be chamfered at an angle of 30° with the top of the head.

Bearing surfaces shall be washer faced. The thickness of these shall be 1/64 in., including the height of the head The diameter of the washer face shall be the same as the distance across flats of the head.

TABLE 7. DIMENSIONS OF AMERICAN STANDARD MACHINE SCREWS *

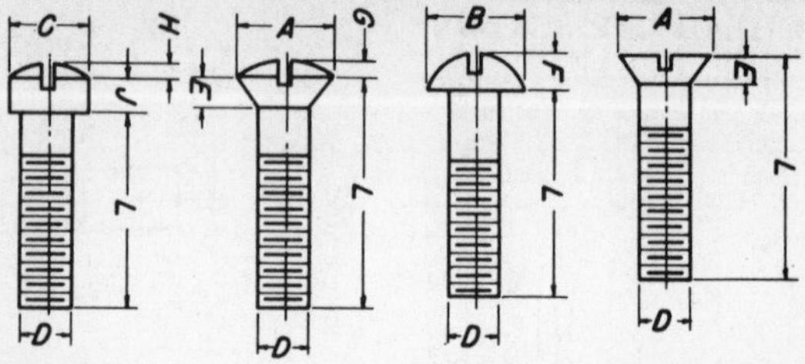

Size	Diam. D	A	B	C	E	F	G	H	J
2	.086	.172	.162	.140	.051	.070	.029	.028	.055
3	.099	.199	.187	.161	.059	.078	.033	.032	.063
4	.112	.225	.211	.183	.067	.086	.037	.035	.072
5	.125	.252	.236	.205	.075	.095	.041	.039	.081
6	.138	.279	.260	.226	.083	.103	.045	.043	.089
8	.164	.332	.309	.270	.100	.119	.053	.050	.106
10	.190	.385	.359	.313	.116	.136	.061	.057	.123
12	.216	.438	.408	.357	.132	.152	.069	.064	.141
1/4	.250	.507	.472	.414	.153	.174	.079	.074	.163
5/16	.3125	.636	.591	.519	.192	.214	.098	.092	.205
3/8	.375	.762	.708	.622	.230	.254	.117	.109	.246

* Compiled from ASA B18c — 1930.
Where the length of screw (*L*) is 1¼ in. or less, the length of thread will extend to as near the head as is practicable. Where the length of screw is over 1¼ in., the thread length will not be less than 1¼ in.

TABLE 8. DIMENSIONS OF AMERICAN STANDARD SET SCREW HEADS *

Nominal Size or Basic Diameter of Thread	Width Across Flats	Width Across Corners	Height
1/4	1/4	0.331	3/16
5/16	5/16	0.415	15/64
3/8	3/8	0.497	9/32
7/16	7/16	0.581	21/64
1/2	1/2	0.665	3/8
9/16	9/16	0.748	27/64
5/8	5/8	0.833	15/32
3/4	3/4	1.001	9/16
7/8	7/8	1.170	21/32
1	1	1.337	3/4
1 1/8	1 1/8	1.505	27/32
1 1/4	1 1/4	1.674	15/16
1 3/8	1 3/8	1.843	1 1/32
1 1/2	1 1/2	2.010	1 1/8

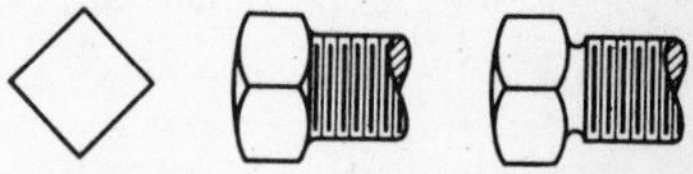

* Compiled from ASA B18.2 — 1941.
All dimensions given in inches.
The under surface of the head should be beveled not more than 40 deg.
Top or crown of head shall be rounded to a radius of two and a half times the major diameter of the thread.

TABLE 9. DIMENSIONS OF AMERICAN STANDARD HEXAGONAL SOCKET SET SCREWS *

D	C	R	Y		P	Q	q	J
			Cone Point Angle [3]		Full Dog Point and Half Dog Point,[1, 2, 3]			
Nominal Diameter	Cup and Flat [3] Point Dia.	Oval Point Radius	118° ± 2° for These Lengths and Under	90° ± 2° for These Lengths and Over	Diameter	Full	Half	Socket Width [4] Across Flats
5	1/16	3/32	1/8	3/16	0.083	0.06	0.03	1/16
6	.069	7/64	1/8	3/16	0.092	0.07	0.03	1/16
8	5/64	1/8	3/16	1/4	0.109	0.08	0.04	5/64
10	3/32	9/64	3/16	1/4	0.127	0.09	0.04	3/32
12	7/64	5/32	3/16	1/4	0.144	0.11	0.06	3/32
1/4	1/8	3/16	1/4	5/16	5/32	1/8	1/16	1/8
5/16	11/64	15/64	5/16	3/8	13/64	5/32	5/64	5/32
3/8	13/64	9/32	3/8	7/16	1/4	3/16	3/32	3/16
7/16	15/64	21/64	7/16	1/2	19/64	7/32	7/64	7/32
1/2	9/32	3/8	1/2	9/16	11/32	1/4	1/8	1/4
9/16	5/16	27/64	9/16	5/8	25/64	9/32	9/64	1/4
5/8	23/64	15/32	5/8	3/4	15/32	5/16	5/32	5/16
3/4	7/16	9/16	3/4	7/8	9/16	3/8	3/16	3/8
7/8	33/64	21/32	7/8	1	21/32	7/16	7/32	1/2
1	19/32	3/4	1	1 1/8	3/4	1/2	1/4	9/16
1 1/8	43/64	27/32	1 1/8	1 1/4	27/32	9/16	9/32	9/16
1 1/4	3/4	15/16	1 1/4	1 1/2	15/16	5/8	5/16	5/8
1 3/8	53/64	1 1/32	1 3/8	1 5/8	1 1/32	11/16	11/32	5/8
1 1/2	29/32	1 1/8	1 1/2	1 3/4	1 1/8	3/4	3/8	3/4
1 3/4	1 1/16	1 5/16	1 3/4	2	1 5/16	7/8	7/16	1
2	1 7/32	1 1/2	2	2 1/4	1 1/2	1	1/2	1

* Compiled from ASA B18.3 — 1936.

All dimensions in inches.

[1] Where usable length of thread is less than nominal diameter, half dog point shall be used.

[2] Allowable eccentricity of dog point axis with respect to axis of screw shall not exceed 3 per cent of nominal diameter of screw with a minimum of 0.005 in.

[3] CHAMFERS AND POINT ANGLES. $W = 45° + 5°, -0°$; $X = 118° ± 5°$; $Y = $ (see Table 1); $Z = 35° + 5°, -0°$.

[4] SOCKET DEPTH (T). The depth of the socket shall be as great as practicable but varying conditions render it inadvisable to specify definite values.

5 SOCKET END CHAMFER (V). Socket end of screw shall be flat and chamfered. The flat shall be normal to the axis of the screw and the chamfer (V) shall be at an angle of $35° + 5°, -0°$ with the surface of the flat. The chamfer shall extend to the bottom of the thread and the edge between flat and chamfer shall be slightly rounded.

6 LENGTH (L). The length of the screw shall be measured overall on a line parallel to the axis. The difference between consecutive lengths shall be as follows:

(a) for screw lengths 1/4 to 5/8 in. difference = 1/16 in.
(b) for screw lengths 5/8 to 1 in. difference = 1/8 in.
(c) for screw lengths 1 to 4 in. difference = 1/4 in.
(d) for screw lengths 4 to 6 in. difference = 1/2 in.

7 LENGTH TOLERANCE. Allowable tolerance on length (L) shall be 3 per cent on lengths 2 in. and under with a minimum of 0.020 in., one-half to be applied plus and one-half minus; on lengths over 2 in. to 6 in. plus or minus 1/32 in.; on lengths over 6 in. plus or minus 1/16 in.

8 SCREW THREADS shall conform to the American Standard for Screw Threads. (B1.1 — 1935).

TABLE 10.   AMERICAN STANDARD WOODRUFF KEY
DIMENSIONS

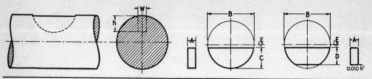

Key [1] Number	Nominal Key Size A × B	Height of Key		Distance Below Center	Keyslot	
		C	D		Width W	Depth h
204	$\frac{1}{16} \times \frac{1}{2}$	0.203	0.194	$\frac{3}{64}$	0.0630	0.1718
304	$\frac{3}{32} \times \frac{1}{2}$	.203	.194	$\frac{3}{64}$	0.0943	0.1561
305	$\frac{3}{32} \times \frac{5}{8}$	.250	.240	$\frac{1}{16}$	0.0943	0.2031
404	$\frac{1}{8} \times \frac{1}{2}$	.203	.194	$\frac{3}{64}$	0.1255	0.1405
405	$\frac{1}{8} \times \frac{5}{8}$	.250	.240	$\frac{1}{16}$	0.1255	0.1875
406	$\frac{1}{8} \times \frac{3}{4}$	.313	.303	$\frac{1}{16}$	0.1255	0.2505
505	$\frac{5}{32} \times \frac{5}{8}$	.250	.240	$\frac{1}{16}$	0.1568	0.1719
506	$\frac{5}{32} \times \frac{3}{4}$	.313	.303	$\frac{1}{16}$	0.1568	0.2349
507	$\frac{5}{32} \times \frac{7}{8}$	.375	.365	$\frac{1}{16}$	0.1568	0.2969
606	$\frac{3}{16} \times \frac{3}{4}$	.313	.303	$\frac{1}{16}$	0.1880	0.2193
607	$\frac{3}{16} \times \frac{7}{8}$	.375	.365	$\frac{1}{16}$	0.1880	0.2813
608	$\frac{3}{16} \times 1$	.438	.428	$\frac{1}{16}$	0.1880	0.3443
609	$\frac{3}{16} \times 1\frac{1}{8}$	.484	.475	$\frac{5}{64}$	0.1880	0.3903
807	$\frac{1}{4} \times \frac{7}{8}$	.375	.365	$\frac{1}{16}$	0.2505	0.2500
808	$\frac{1}{4} \times 1$	.438	.428	$\frac{1}{16}$	0.2505	0.3130
809	$\frac{1}{4} \times 1\frac{1}{8}$	.484	.475	$\frac{5}{64}$	0.2505	0.3590
810	$\frac{1}{4} \times 1\frac{1}{4}$	.547	.537	$\frac{5}{64}$	0.2505	0.4220
811	$\frac{1}{4} \times 1\frac{3}{8}$	.594	.584	$\frac{3}{32}$	0.2505	0.4690
812	$\frac{1}{4} \times 1\frac{1}{2}$	.641	.631	$\frac{7}{64}$	0.2505	0.5160
1008	$\frac{5}{16} \times 1$	.438	.428	$\frac{1}{16}$	0.3130	0.2818
1009	$\frac{5}{16} \times 1\frac{1}{8}$	.484	.475	$\frac{5}{64}$	0.3130	0.3278
1010	$\frac{5}{16} \times 1\frac{1}{4}$	.547	.537	$\frac{5}{64}$	0.3130	0.3908
1011	$\frac{5}{16} \times 1\frac{3}{8}$	.594	.584	$\frac{3}{32}$	0.3130	0.4378
1012	$\frac{5}{16} \times 1\frac{1}{2}$	.641	.631	$\frac{7}{64}$	0.3130	0.4848
1210	$\frac{3}{8} \times 1\frac{1}{4}$	.547	.537	$\frac{5}{64}$	0.3755	0.3595
1211	$\frac{3}{8} \times 1\frac{3}{8}$	.594	.584	$\frac{3}{32}$	0.3755	0.4065
1212	$\frac{3}{8} \times 1\frac{1}{2}$	.641	.631	$\frac{7}{64}$	0.3755	0.4535

All dimensions given in inches.

[1] Note: Key numbers indicate the nominal key dimensions. The last two digits give the nominal diameter (B) in eighths of an inch and the digits preceding the last two give the nominal width (A) in thirty-seconds of an inch. Thus, 204 indicates a key $\frac{2}{32} \times \frac{4}{8}$ or $\frac{1}{16} \times \frac{1}{2}$ inches; 1210 indicates a key $\frac{12}{32} \times \frac{10}{8}$ or $\frac{3}{8} \times 1\frac{1}{4}$ inches.

TABLE 11. DIMENSIONS OF PRATT AND WHITNEY KEYS

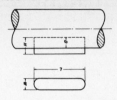

Key No.	L	W or D	H	Key No.	L	W or D	H
1	$\frac{1}{2}$	$\frac{1}{16}$	$\frac{3}{32}$	22	$1\frac{3}{8}$	$\frac{1}{4}$	$\frac{3}{8}$
2	$\frac{1}{2}$	$\frac{3}{32}$	$\frac{9}{64}$	23	$1\frac{3}{8}$	$\frac{5}{16}$	$\frac{15}{32}$
3	$\frac{1}{2}$	$\frac{1}{8}$	$\frac{3}{16}$	F	$1\frac{3}{8}$	$\frac{3}{8}$	$\frac{9}{16}$
4	$\frac{5}{8}$	$\frac{3}{32}$	$\frac{9}{64}$	24	$1\frac{1}{2}$	$\frac{1}{4}$	$\frac{3}{8}$
5	$\frac{5}{8}$	$\frac{1}{8}$	$\frac{3}{16}$	25	$1\frac{1}{2}$	$\frac{5}{16}$	$\frac{15}{32}$
6	$\frac{5}{8}$	$\frac{5}{32}$	$\frac{15}{64}$	G	$1\frac{1}{2}$	$\frac{3}{8}$	$\frac{9}{16}$
7	$\frac{3}{4}$	$\frac{1}{8}$	$\frac{3}{16}$	51	$1\frac{3}{4}$	$\frac{1}{4}$	$\frac{3}{8}$
8	$\frac{3}{4}$	$\frac{5}{32}$	$\frac{15}{64}$	52	$1\frac{3}{4}$	$\frac{5}{16}$	$\frac{15}{32}$
9	$\frac{3}{4}$	$\frac{3}{16}$	$\frac{9}{32}$	53	$1\frac{3}{4}$	$\frac{3}{8}$	$\frac{9}{16}$
10	$\frac{7}{8}$	$\frac{5}{32}$	$\frac{15}{64}$	26	2	$\frac{3}{16}$	$\frac{9}{32}$
11	$\frac{7}{8}$	$\frac{3}{16}$	$\frac{9}{32}$	27	2	$\frac{1}{4}$	$\frac{3}{8}$
12	$\frac{7}{8}$	$\frac{7}{32}$	$\frac{21}{64}$	28	2	$\frac{5}{16}$	$\frac{15}{32}$
A	$\frac{7}{8}$	$\frac{1}{4}$	$\frac{3}{8}$	29	2	$\frac{3}{8}$	$\frac{9}{16}$
13	1	$\frac{3}{16}$	$\frac{9}{32}$	54	$2\frac{1}{4}$	$\frac{1}{4}$	$\frac{3}{8}$
14	1	$\frac{7}{32}$	$\frac{21}{64}$	55	$2\frac{1}{4}$	$\frac{5}{16}$	$\frac{15}{32}$
15	1	$\frac{1}{4}$	$\frac{3}{8}$	56	$2\frac{1}{4}$	$\frac{3}{8}$	$\frac{9}{16}$
B	1	$\frac{5}{16}$	$\frac{15}{32}$	57	$2\frac{1}{4}$	$\frac{7}{16}$	$\frac{21}{32}$
16	$1\frac{1}{8}$	$\frac{3}{16}$	$\frac{9}{32}$	58	$2\frac{1}{2}$	$\frac{5}{16}$	$\frac{15}{32}$
17	$1\frac{1}{8}$	$\frac{7}{32}$	$\frac{21}{64}$	59	$2\frac{1}{2}$	$\frac{3}{8}$	$\frac{9}{16}$
18	$1\frac{1}{8}$	$\frac{1}{4}$	$\frac{3}{8}$	60	$2\frac{1}{2}$	$\frac{7}{16}$	$\frac{21}{32}$
C	$1\frac{1}{8}$	$\frac{5}{16}$	$\frac{15}{32}$	61	$2\frac{1}{2}$	$\frac{1}{2}$	$\frac{3}{4}$
19	$1\frac{1}{4}$	$\frac{3}{16}$	$\frac{9}{32}$	30	3	$\frac{3}{8}$	$\frac{9}{16}$
20	$1\frac{1}{4}$	$\frac{7}{32}$	$\frac{21}{64}$	31	3	$\frac{7}{16}$	$\frac{21}{32}$
21	$1\frac{1}{4}$	$\frac{1}{4}$	$\frac{3}{8}$	32	3	$\frac{1}{2}$	$\frac{3}{4}$
D	$1\frac{1}{4}$	$\frac{5}{16}$	$\frac{15}{32}$	33	3	$\frac{9}{16}$	$\frac{27}{32}$
E	$1\frac{1}{4}$	$\frac{3}{8}$	$\frac{9}{16}$	34	3	$\frac{5}{8}$	$\frac{15}{16}$

The length L may vary from the table, but must at least equal $2 \times W$.

TABLE 12. DIMENSIONS OF AMERICAN STANDARD SQUARE AND FLAT PLAIN PARALLEL STOCK KEYS *

Shaft Diameter	Square Key W × H	Flat Key W × H	Bottom of Key-seat to Opposite Side of Shaft — Square Key S	Bottom of Key-seat to Opposite Side of Shaft — Flat Key T
1/2	1/8 × 1/8	1/8 × 3/32	0.430	0.445
9/16	1/8 × 1/8	1/8 × 3/32	0.493	0.509
5/8	3/16 × 3/16	3/16 × 1/8	0.517	0.548
11/16	3/16 × 3/16	3/16 × 1/8	0.581	0.612
3/4	3/16 × 3/16	3/16 × 1/8	0.644	0.676
13/16	3/16 × 3/16	3/16 × 1/8	0.708	0.739
7/8	3/16 × 3/16	3/16 × 1/8	0.771	0.802
15/16	3/16 × 3/16	3/16 × 1/8	0.796	0.827
1	1/4 × 1/4	1/4 × 3/16	0.859	0.890
1 1/16	1/4 × 1/4	1/4 × 3/16	0.923	0.954
1 1/8	1/4 × 1/4	1/4 × 3/16	0.986	1.017
1 3/16	1/4 × 1/4	1/4 × 3/16	1.049	1.081
1 1/4	1/4 × 1/4	1/4 × 3/16	1.112	1.144
1 5/16	5/16 × 5/16	5/16 × 1/4	1.137	1.169
1 3/8	5/16 × 5/16	5/16 × 1/4	1.201	1.232
1 7/16	3/8 × 3/8	3/8 × 1/4	1.225	1.288
1 1/2	3/8 × 3/8	3/8 × 1/4	1.289	1.351
1 9/16	3/8 × 3/8	3/8 × 1/4	1.352	1.415
1 5/8	3/8 × 3/8	3/8 × 1/4	1.416	1.478
1 11/16	3/8 × 3/8	3/8 × 1/4	1.479	1.542
1 3/4	1/2 × 1/2	1/2 × 3/8	1.542	1.605
1 13/16	1/2 × 1/2	1/2 × 3/8	1.527	1.590
1 7/8	1/2 × 1/2	1/2 × 3/8	1.591	1.654
1 15/16	1/2 × 1/2	1/2 × 3/8	1.655	1.717
2	1/2 × 1/2	1/2 × 3/8	1.718	1.781
2 1/16	1/2 × 1/2	1/2 × 3/8	1.782	1.843
2 3/16	1/2 × 1/2	1/2 × 3/8	1.845	1.908
2 1/4	1/2 × 1/2	1/2 × 3/8	1.909	1.971
2 5/16	1/2 × 1/2	1/2 × 3/8	1.972	2.034
	5/8 × 5/8	5/8 × 7/16	1.957	2.051

Square Key W × H	Flat Key W × H	Shaft Diameter	Bottom of Key-seat to Opposite Side of Shaft — Square Key S	Bottom of Key-seat to Opposite Side of Shaft — Flat Key T
5/8 × 5/8	5/8 × 7/16	2 3/8	2.021	2.114
5/8 × 5/8	5/8 × 7/16	2 7/16	2.084	2.178
5/8 × 5/8	5/8 × 7/16	2 1/2	2.148	2.242
5/8 × 5/8	5/8 × 7/16	2 9/16	2.275	2.368
5/8 × 5/8	5/8 × 7/16	2 5/8	2.402	2.495
3/4 × 3/4	3/4 × 1/2	2 3/4	2.450	2.575
3/4 × 3/4	3/4 × 1/2	2 7/8	2.514	2.639
3/4 × 3/4	3/4 × 1/2	2 15/16	2.577	2.702
3/4 × 3/4	3/4 × 1/2	3	2.704	2.829
3/4 × 3/4	3/4 × 1/2	3 1/16	2.831	2.956
7/8 × 7/8	7/8 × 5/8	3 1/8	2.880	3.005
7/8 × 7/8	7/8 × 5/8	3 3/16	2.944	3.069
7/8 × 7/8	7/8 × 5/8	3 1/4	3.007	3.132
7/8 × 7/8	7/8 × 5/8	3 3/8	3.140	3.259
7/8 × 7/8	7/8 × 5/8	3 1/2	3.261	3.386
1 × 1	1 × 3/4	3 5/8	3.309	3.434
1 × 1	1 × 3/4	3 3/4	3.373	3.498
1 × 1	1 × 3/4	3 7/8	3.437	3.562
1 × 1	1 × 3/4	4	3.690	3.815
1 × 1	1 × 3/4	4 1/4	3.881	4.006
1 × 1	1 × 3/4	4 3/8	3.944	4.069
1 1/4 × 1 1/4	1 1/4 × 7/8	4 1/2	4.042	4.229
1 1/4 × 1 1/4	1 1/4 × 7/8	4 11/16	4.232	4.420
1 1/4 × 1 1/4	1 1/4 × 7/8	5	4.296	4.483
1 1/4 × 1 1/4	1 1/4 × 7/8	5 1/4	4.550	4.733
1 1/4 × 1 1/4	1 1/4 × 7/8	5 7/16	4.740	4.927
1 1/4 × 1 1/4	1 1/4 × 7/8	5 3/4	4.803	4.991
1 1/4 × 1 1/4	1 1/4 × 7/8	5 15/16	4.900	5.150
1 1/2 × 1 1/2	1 1/2 × 1	6	5.091	5.341
1 1/2 × 1 1/2	1 1/2 × 1		5.155	5.405

* Compiled from ASA B17.1 — 1934.

TABLE 13.　DIMENSIONS OF AMERICAN STANDARD SQUARE AND FLAT PLAIN TAPER STOCK KEYS *

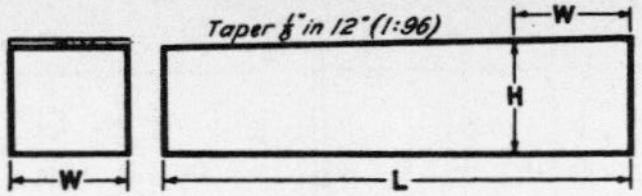

Taper ⅛ in 12" (1:96)

Shaft Diameter (Incl.)	Square Type		Flat Type		Length of Key [1] L						
	Maximum Width W	Height at Large End [1] H	Maximum Width W	Height at Large End [1] H							
½ – 9/16	⅛	⅛	⅛	3/32	½	¾	1	1¼	1½	1¾	2
⅝ – ⅞	3/16	3/16	3/16	⅛	¾	1⅛	1½	1⅞	2¼	2⅝	3
15/16 –1¼	¼	¼	¼	3/16	1	1½	2	2½	3	3½	4
1 5/16 –1⅜	5/16	5/16	5/16	¼	1¼	1⅞	2½	3⅛	3¾	4½	5¼
1 7/16 –1¾	⅜	⅜	⅜	¼	1½	2¼	3	3¾	4½	5¼	6
1 13/16 –2¼	½	½	½	⅜	2	3	4	5	6	7	8
2 5/16 –2¾	⅝	⅝	⅝	7/16	2½	3¾	5	6¼	7½	8¾	10
2⅞ –3¼	¾	¾	¾	½	3	4½	6	7½	9	10½	12
3⅜ –3⅜	⅞	⅞	⅞	⅝	3½	5¼	7	8¾	10½	12¼	14
3⅞ –4½	1	1	1	¾	4	6	8	10	12	14	16
4¾ –5½	1¼	1¼	1¼	⅞	5	7½	10	12½	15	17½	20
4¾ –6	1½	1½	1½	1	6	9	12	15	18	21	24

* Compiled from ASA B17.1 — 1934.

[1] Note: The minimum stock length of keys is equal to four times the key width, and the maximum stock length is equal to sixteen times the key width. The increments of increase in length are equal to twice the width.

TABLE 14. DIMENSIONS OF AMERICAN STANDARD SQUARE AND FLAT GIB-HEAD TAPER STOCK KEYS *

Shaft Diameter (Incl.)	Square Type					Flat Type					Length of Key[1] L						
	Key		Gib Head			Key		Gib Head									
	Maximum Width W	Height at Large End[1] H	Height C	Length D	Height Edge of Chamfer E	Maximum Width W	Height at Large End[1] H	Height C	Length D	Height Edge of Chamfer E							
1/2 – 9/16	1/8	1/8	1/4	7/32	5/32	1/8	3/32	3/16	1/8	1/8	1/2	3/4	1	1 1/4	1 1/2	1 3/4	2
5/8 – 7/8	3/16	3/16	5/16	9/32	7/32	3/16	1/8	1/4	3/16	5/32	3/4	1 1/8	1 1/2	1 7/8	2 1/4	2 5/8	3
15/16 – 1 1/4	1/4	1/4	7/16	11/32	11/32	1/4	3/16	5/16	1/4	3/16	1	1 1/8	2	2 1/2	3	3 1/2	4
1 5/16 – 1 3/8	5/16	5/16	9/16	13/32	13/32	5/16	1/4	3/8	5/16	1/4	1 1/4	1 7/8	2 1/2	3 1/8	3 3/4	4 3/8	5 1/2
1 7/16 – 1 3/4	3/8	3/8	11/16	15/32	15/32	3/8	1/4	7/16	3/8	5/16	1 1/2	2 1/4	3	3 3/4	4 1/2	5 1/4	6
1 13/16 – 2 1/4	1/2	1/2	7/8	19/32	5/8	1/2	3/8	5/8	1/2	7/16	2	3	4	5	6	7	8
2 5/16 – 2 3/4	5/8	5/8	1 1/16	23/32	3/4	5/8	7/16	3/4	5/8	1/2	2 1/2	3 3/4	5	6 1/4	7 1/2	8 3/4	10
2 7/8 – 3 1/4	3/4	3/4	1 1/4	7/8	7/8	3/4	1/2	7/8	3/4	5/8	3	4 1/2	6	7 1/2	9	10 1/2	12
3 3/8 – 3 3/4	7/8	7/8	1 1/2	1	1	7/8	5/8	1 1/16	7/8	3/4	3 1/2	5 1/4	7	8 3/4	10 1/2	12 1/4	14
3 7/8 – 4 1/2	1	1	1 3/4	1 3/16	13/16	1	3/4	1 1/4	1	13/16	4	6	8	10	12	14	16
4 3/4 – 5 1/2	1 1/4	1 1/4	2	1 7/16	1 7/16	1 1/4	7/8	1 1/2	1 1/4	1	5	7 1/2	10	12 1/2	15	17 1/2	20
5 3/4 – 6	1 1/2	1 1/2	2 1/2	1 3/4	1 3/4	1 1/2	1	1 3/4	1 1/2	1 1/4	6	9	12	15	18	21	24

* Compiled from ASA B17.1 — 1934.

[1] Note: This height of the key is measured at the distance W, equal to the width of the key, from the gib head.

TABLE 15. STRUCTURAL RIVETS

Note: These lengths are for rivets that are hot riveted in the field.

A.I.S.C. Standard

Lengths of Undriven Rivets for Various Grips

Dimensions in Inches

Grip, a	Diameter of Rivet 1/2	5/8	3/4	7/8	1	1 1/8	1 1/4
1/2	1 5/8	1 7/8	1 7/8	2	2 1/8		
5/8	1 3/4	2	2	2 1/8	2 1/4		
3/4	1 7/8	2 1/8	2 1/8	2 1/4	2 3/8		
7/8	2	2 1/4	2 1/4	2 3/8	2 1/2		
1	2 1/4	2 3/8	2 3/8	2 1/2	2 5/8	2 3/4	2 7/8
1/8	2 3/8	2 1/2	2 1/2	2 5/8	2 3/4	2 7/8	3
1/4	2 1/2	2 5/8	2 5/8	2 3/4	2 7/8	3	3 1/8
3/8	2 5/8	2 3/4	2 3/4	2 7/8	3	3 1/8	3 1/4
1/2	2 7/8	3	3	3 1/8	3 1/4	3 3/8	3 1/2
5/8	3	3 1/8	3 1/8	3 1/4	3 3/8	3 1/2	3 5/8
3/4	3 1/8	3 1/4	3 1/4	3 1/2	3 5/8	3 3/4	3 7/8
7/8	3 1/4	3 3/8	3 3/8	3 5/8	3 3/4	3 7/8	4
2	3 1/2	3 1/2	3 5/8	3 3/4	3 7/8	4	4 1/8
1/8	3 5/8	3 5/8	3 3/4	3 7/8	4	4 1/8	4 1/4
1/4	3 3/4	3 7/8	3 7/8	4	4 1/8	4 1/4	4 3/8
3/8	4	4	4	4 1/8	4 1/4	4 3/8	4 1/2
1/2	4 1/8	4 1/8	4 1/8	4 1/4	4 3/8	4 1/2	4 5/8
5/8	4 1/4	4 1/4	4 1/4	4 3/8	4 1/2	4 5/8	4 3/4
3/4	4 3/8	4 3/8	4 3/8	4 1/2	4 5/8	4 3/4	4 7/8
7/8	4 5/8	4 5/8	4 5/8	4 5/8	4 3/4	4 7/8	5
3	...	4 3/4	4 3/4	4 7/8	5	5 1/8	5 1/4
1/8	...	4 7/8	4 7/8	5	5 1/8	5 1/4	5 3/8
1/4	...	5	5	5 1/8	5 1/4	5 3/8	5 1/2
3/8	...	5 1/8	5 1/8	5 1/4	5 3/8	5 1/2	5 5/8
1/2	...	5 3/8	5 3/8	5 3/8	5 1/2	5 5/8	5 3/4
5/8	...	5 1/2	5 1/2	5 1/2	5 5/8	5 3/4	5 7/8
3/4	...	5 5/8	5 5/8	5 5/8	5 3/4	5 7/8	6
7/8	...	5 3/4	5 3/4	5 3/4	5 7/8	6	6 1/8
4	...	...	5 7/8	6	6	6 1/8	6 1/4
1/8	...	...	6	6 1/8	6 1/4	6 3/8	6 1/2
1/4	...	...	6 1/8	6 1/4	6 3/8	6 1/2	6 5/8
3/8	...	...	6 3/8	6 1/2	6 1/2	6 5/8	6 3/4
1/2	...	...	6 1/2	6 5/8	6 5/8	6 3/4	6 7/8
5/8	...	...	6 5/8	6 3/4	6 3/4	6 7/8	7
3/4	...	...	6 3/4	6 7/8	6 7/8	7	7 1/8
7/8	...	...	6 7/8	7	7	7 1/8	7 1/4

Grip, a	Diameter of Rivet 7/8	1	1 1/8	1 1/4
5	7 1/8	7 1/8	7 1/4	7 3/8
1/8	7 1/4	7 1/4	7 3/8	7 1/2
1/4	7 3/8	7 3/8	7 1/2	7 5/8
3/8	7 5/8	7 5/8	7 3/4	7 3/4
1/2	7 3/4	7 3/4	7 7/8	7 7/8
5/8	7 7/8	7 7/8	8	8
3/4	8	8	8 1/8	8 1/8
7/8	8 1/8	8 1/8	8 1/4	8 1/4
6	8 3/8	8 3/8	8 3/8	8 3/8
1/8	8 1/2	8 1/2	8 1/2	8 1/2
1/4	8 5/8	8 5/8	8 5/8	8 5/8
3/8	8 3/4	8 3/4	8 3/4	8 3/4
1/2	8 7/8	8 7/8	8 7/8	8 7/8
5/8	9	9	9 1/8	9 1/8
3/4	9 1/8	9 1/8	9 1/4	9 1/4
7/8	9 1/4	9 1/4	9 3/8	9 3/8

Grip, b	Diameter of Rivet 1/2	5/8	3/4	7/8	1	1 1/8	1 1/4
1/2	1	1	1 1/8	1 1/4	1 1/4		
5/8	1 1/8	1 1/4	1 1/4	1 3/8	1 3/8		
3/4	1 3/8	1 3/8	1 3/8	1 1/2	1 1/2		
7/8	1 1/2	1 1/2	1 1/2	1 5/8	1 5/8		
1	1 5/8	1 5/8	1 5/8	1 3/4	1 3/4	1 7/8	1 7/8
1/8	1 3/4	1 3/4	1 7/8	1 7/8	1 7/8	2	2
1/4	2	2	2	2	2	2 1/8	2 1/8
3/8	2 1/8	2 1/8	2 1/8	2 1/4	2 1/4	2 3/8	2 3/8
1/2	2 1/4	2 1/4	2 1/4	2 3/8	2 3/8	2 1/2	2 1/2
5/8	2 3/8	2 3/8	2 3/8	2 1/2	2 1/2	2 5/8	2 5/8
3/4	2 5/8	2 5/8	2 5/8	2 5/8	2 5/8	2 3/4	2 3/4
7/8	2 3/4	2 3/4	2 3/4	2 3/4	2 3/4	2 7/8	2 7/8
2	2 7/8	2 7/8	2 7/8	2 7/8	2 7/8	3	3
1/8	3 1/8	3	3	3	3	3 1/8	3 1/8
1/4	3 1/4	3 1/8	3 1/8	3 1/8	3 1/4	3 1/4	3 1/4
3/8	3 3/8	3 3/8	3 3/8	3 3/8	3 3/8	3 3/8	3 3/8
1/2	3 1/2	3 1/2	3 1/2	3 1/2	3 1/2	3 5/8	3 5/8
5/8	3 3/4	3 5/8	3 5/8	3 5/8	3 5/8	3 3/4	3 3/4
3/4	3 7/8	3 3/4	3 3/4	3 3/4	3 3/4	3 7/8	3 7/8
7/8	4	3 7/8	3 7/8	3 7/8	3 7/8	4	4
3	...	4 1/8	4 1/8	4 1/8	4 1/8	4 1/8	4 1/8
1/8	...	4 1/4	4 1/4	4 1/4	4 1/4	4 1/4	4 1/4
1/4	...	4 3/8	4 3/8	4 3/8	4 3/8	4 3/8	4 3/8
3/8	...	4 1/2	4 1/2	4 1/2	4 1/2	4 1/2	4 1/2
1/2	...	4 5/8	4 5/8	4 5/8	4 5/8	4 5/8	4 5/8
5/8	...	4 3/4	4 3/4	4 3/4	4 3/4	4 7/8	4 7/8
3/4	...	5	5	5	5	5	5
7/8	...	5 1/8	5 1/8	5 1/8	5 1/8	5 1/8	5 1/8
4	...	...	5 1/4	5 1/4	5 1/4	5 1/4	5 1/4
1/8	...	...	5 3/8	5 3/8	5 3/8	5 3/8	5 3/8
1/4	...	...	5 1/2	5 1/2	5 1/2	5 1/2	5 1/2
3/8	...	...	5 5/8	5 5/8	5 5/8	5 5/8	5 5/8
1/2	...	...	5 3/4	5 3/4	5 3/4	5 3/4	5 3/4
5/8	...	...	6	6	6	6	6
3/4	...	...	6 1/8	6 1/8	6 1/8	6 1/8	6 1/8
7/8	...	...	6 1/4	6 1/4	6 1/4	6 1/4	6 1/4

Grip, b	Diameter of Rivet 7/8	1	1 1/8	1 1/4
5	6 3/8	6 3/8	6 3/8	6 3/8
1/8	6 1/2	6 1/2	6 1/2	6 1/2
1/4	6 5/8	6 5/8	6 5/8	6 5/8
3/8	6 3/4	6 3/4	6 3/4	6 3/4
1/2	6 7/8	6 7/8	6 7/8	6 7/8
5/8	7	7	7	7
3/4	7 1/4	7 1/4	7 1/4	7 1/4
7/8	7 3/8	7 3/8	7 3/8	7 3/8
6	7 1/2	7 1/2	7 1/2	7 1/2
1/8	7 5/8	7 5/8	7 5/8	7 5/8
1/4	7 3/4	7 3/4	7 3/4	7 3/4
3/8	7 7/8	7 7/8	7 7/8	7 7/8
1/2	8	8	8	8
5/8	8 1/4	8 1/4	8 1/4	8 1/4
3/4	8 3/8	8 3/8	8 3/8	8 3/8
7/8	8 1/2	8 1/2	8 1/2	8 1/2

Lengths given may vary from standards of fabricators and should be checked against any such standard.

TABLE 16. LIMITS FOR METAL FITS *

Loose Fit (Class 1) — Large Allowance Interchangeable

This fit provides for considerable freedom and embraces certain fits where accuracy is not essential.

| Size | Limits | | | | Tightest Fit | Loosest Fit |
	Hole or External Member +		Shaft or Internal Member −	−	Allowance + +	Allowance + Tolerances + +
0 − 3⁄16	0.001	0.000	0.001	0.002	0.001	0.003
3⁄16 − 5⁄16	0.002	0.000	0.001	0.003	0.001	0.005
5⁄16 − 7⁄16	0.002	0.000	0.001	0.003	0.002	0.005
7⁄16 − 9⁄16	0.002	0.000	0.002	0.004	0.002	0.006
9⁄16 − 11⁄16	0.002	0.000	0.002	0.004	0.002	0.006
11⁄16 − 13⁄16	0.002	0.000	0.002	0.004	0.002	0.006
13⁄16 − 15⁄16	0.002	0.000	0.002	0.004	0.003	0.006
15⁄16 − 1 3⁄16	0.003	0.000	0.003	0.006	0.003	0.009
1 3⁄16 − 1 5⁄16	0.003	0.000	0.003	0.006	0.003	0.009
1 5⁄16 − 1 3⁄8	0.003	0.000	0.003	0.006	0.003	0.009
1 3⁄8 − 1 5⁄8	0.003	0.000	0.003	0.006	0.004	0.009
1 5⁄8 − 1 7⁄8	0.003	0.000	0.004	0.007	0.004	0.010
1 7⁄8 − 2 1⁄8	0.003	0.000	0.004	0.007	0.004	0.010
2 1⁄8 − 2 3⁄8	0.003	0.000	0.004	0.007	0.005	0.010
2 3⁄8 − 2 5⁄8	0.003	0.000	0.005	0.008	0.005	0.011
2 5⁄8 − 2 7⁄8	0.004	0.000	0.005	0.009	0.006	0.013
2 7⁄8 − 3 1⁄4	0.004	0.000	0.006	0.010	0.006	0.014
3 1⁄4 − 3 3⁄4	0.004	0.000	0.006	0.010	0.007	0.014
3 3⁄4 − 4 1⁄4	0.004	0.000	0.007	0.011	0.007	0.015
4 1⁄4 − 4 3⁄4	0.004	0.000	0.007	0.011	0.008	0.015
4 3⁄4 − 5 1⁄2	0.005	0.000	0.008	0.013	0.009	0.018
5 1⁄2 − 6 1⁄2	0.005	0.000	0.009	0.014	0.009	0.019
6 1⁄2 − 7 1⁄2	0.005	0.000	0.010	0.015	0.010	0.020

* Compiled from ASA B4a — 1925.
† Note: (+) denotes clearance or amount of looseness.   All dimensions in inches.

TABLE 17. LIMITS FOR METAL FITS *

Free Fit (Class 2) — Liberal Allowance Interchangeable

For running fits with speeds of 600 r.p.m. or over, and journal pressures of 600 lb. per sq. in. or over.

| Size | Limits | | | | Tightest Fit | Loosest Fit |
	Hole or External Member +		Shaft or Internal Member −	−	Allowance + +	Allowance + Tolerances + +
0 − 3⁄16	0.0007	0.0000	0.0004	0.0011	0.0004	0.0018
3⁄16 − 5⁄16	0.0008	0.0000	0.0006	0.0014	0.0006	0.0022
5⁄16 − 7⁄16	0.0009	0.0000	0.0007	0.0016	0.0007	0.0025
7⁄16 − 9⁄16	0.0010	0.0000	0.0009	0.0019	0.0009	0.0029
9⁄16 − 11⁄16	0.0011	0.0000	0.0010	0.0021	0.0010	0.0032
11⁄16 − 13⁄16	0.0012	0.0000	0.0012	0.0024	0.0012	0.0036
13⁄16 − 15⁄16	0.0013	0.0000	0.0013	0.0025	0.0013	0.0037
15⁄16 − 1 3⁄16	0.0013	0.0000	0.0014	0.0027	0.0014	0.0040
1 3⁄16 − 1 5⁄16	0.0014	0.0000	0.0015	0.0029	0.0015	0.0043
1 5⁄16 − 1 3⁄8	0.0014	0.0000	0.0016	0.0030	0.0016	0.0044
1 3⁄8 − 1 5⁄8	0.0015	0.0000	0.0018	0.0033	0.0018	0.0048
1 5⁄8 − 1 7⁄8	0.0016	0.0000	0.0020	0.0036	0.0020	0.0052
1 7⁄8 − 2 1⁄8	0.0016	0.0000	0.0022	0.0038	0.0022	0.0054
2 1⁄8 − 2 3⁄8	0.0017	0.0000	0.0024	0.0041	0.0024	0.0058
2 3⁄8 − 2 5⁄8	0.0018	0.0000	0.0026	0.0044	0.0026	0.0062
2 5⁄8 − 2 7⁄8	0.0019	0.0000	0.0029	0.0048	0.0029	0.0067
2 7⁄8 − 3 1⁄4	0.0020	0.0000	0.0032	0.0052	0.0032	0.0072
3 1⁄4 − 3 3⁄4	0.0021	0.0000	0.0035	0.0056	0.0035	0.0077
3 3⁄4 − 4 1⁄4	0.0021	0.0000	0.0038	0.0059	0.0038	0.0080
4 1⁄4 − 4 3⁄4	0.0022	0.0000	0.0041	0.0063	0.0041	0.0085
4 3⁄4 − 5 1⁄2	0.0024	0.0000	0.0046	0.0070	0.0046	0.0094
5 1⁄2 − 6 1⁄2	0.0025	0.0000	0.0051	0.0076	0.0051	0.0101
6 1⁄2 − 7 1⁄2	0.0026	0.0000	0.0056	0.0082	0.0056	0.0108

* Compiled from ASA B4a — 1925.
† Note: (+) denotes clearance or amount of looseness.   All dimensions in inches.

TABLE 18. LIMITS FOR METAL FITS *

Medium Fit (Class 3) — Medium Allowance Interchangeable

For running fits under 600 r.p.m. and with journal pressures less than 600 lb. per sq. in.; also for sliding fits, and the more accurate machine-tool and automotive parts.

Size	Limits — Hole or External Member +	Limits — (0.0000)	Limits — Shaft or Internal Member −	Tightest Fit Allowance +†	Loosest Fit Allowance + Tolerances +†
0 – 3/16	0.0004	0.0000	0.0006	0.0002	0.0010
3/16 – 5/16	0.0005	0.0000	0.0009	0.0004	0.0014
5/16 – 7/16	0.0006	0.0000	0.0011	0.0005	0.0017
7/16 – 9/16	0.0006	0.0000	0.0012	0.0006	0.0018
9/16 – 11/16	0.0007	0.0000	0.0014	0.0007	0.0021
11/16 – 13/16	0.0007	0.0000	0.0014	0.0007	0.0021
13/16 – 15/16	0.0008	0.0000	0.0016	0.0008	0.0024
15/16 – 1 3/16	0.0008	0.0000	0.0017	0.0009	0.0025
1 3/16 – 1 5/16	0.0009	0.0000	0.0017	0.0010	0.0026
1 5/16 – 1 3/8	0.0009	0.0000	0.0019	0.0010	0.0028
1 3/8 – 1 5/8	0.0010	0.0000	0.0020	0.0012	0.0030
1 5/8 – 1 7/8	0.0010	0.0000	0.0023	0.0013	0.0033
1 7/8 – 2 1/8	0.0010	0.0000	0.0024	0.0014	0.0034
2 1/8 – 2 3/8	0.0011	0.0000	0.0024	0.0015	0.0035
2 3/8 – 2 5/8	0.0011	0.0000	0.0028	0.0017	0.0039
2 5/8 – 3 1/8	0.0012	0.0000	0.0031	0.0019	0.0043
3 1/8 – 3 3/4	0.0012	0.0000	0.0033	0.0021	0.0045
3 3/4 – 4 1/4	0.0013	0.0000	0.0036	0.0023	0.0049
4 1/4 – 4 3/4	0.0013	0.0000	0.0038	0.0025	0.0051
4 3/4 – 5 1/2	0.0014	0.0000	0.0040	0.0026	0.0054
5 1/2 – 6 1/2	0.0015	0.0000	0.0045	0.0030	0.0060
6 1/2 – 7 1/2	0.0015	0.0000	0.0048	0.0033	0.0063
7 1/2 – 8 1/2	0.0016	0.0000	0.0052	0.0036	0.0068

* Compiled from ASA B4a — 1925.
† Note: (+) denotes clearance or amount of looseness.
All dimensions in inches.

TABLE 19. LIMITS FOR METAL FITS *

Snug Fit (Class 4) — Zero Allowance Interchangeable

This is the closest fit which can be assembled by hand and necessitates work of considerable precision. It should be used where no perceptible shake is permissible and where moving parts are not intended to move freely under load.

Size	Limits — Hole or External Member +	Limits — (0.0000)	Limits — (0.0000)	Limits — Shaft or Internal Member −	Tightest Fit Allowance	Loosest Fit Allowance + Tolerances +†
0 – 3/16	0.0003	0.0000	0.0000	0.0002	0.0000	0.0005
3/16 – 5/16	0.0004	0.0000	0.0000	0.0003	0.0000	0.0007
5/16 – 7/16	0.0004	0.0000	0.0000	0.0003	0.0000	0.0007
7/16 – 9/16	0.0005	0.0000	0.0000	0.0003	0.0000	0.0008
9/16 – 11/16	0.0005	0.0000	0.0000	0.0004	0.0000	0.0009
11/16 – 13/16	0.0005	0.0000	0.0000	0.0004	0.0000	0.0009
13/16 – 15/16	0.0006	0.0000	0.0000	0.0004	0.0000	0.0010
15/16 – 1 3/16	0.0006	0.0000	0.0000	0.0004	0.0000	0.0010
1 3/16 – 1 5/16	0.0006	0.0000	0.0000	0.0004	0.0000	0.0010
1 5/16 – 1 3/8	0.0006	0.0000	0.0000	0.0004	0.0000	0.0010
1 3/8 – 1 5/8	0.0007	0.0000	0.0000	0.0005	0.0000	0.0012
1 5/8 – 1 7/8	0.0007	0.0000	0.0000	0.0005	0.0000	0.0012
1 7/8 – 2 1/8	0.0008	0.0000	0.0000	0.0005	0.0000	0.0013
2 1/8 – 2 3/8	0.0008	0.0000	0.0000	0.0005	0.0000	0.0013
2 3/8 – 2 5/8	0.0008	0.0000	0.0000	0.0005	0.0000	0.0013
2 5/8 – 3 1/8	0.0009	0.0000	0.0000	0.0006	0.0000	0.0015
3 1/8 – 3 3/4	0.0009	0.0000	0.0000	0.0006	0.0000	0.0015
3 3/4 – 4 1/4	0.0010	0.0000	0.0000	0.0006	0.0000	0.0016
4 1/4 – 4 3/4	0.0010	0.0000	0.0000	0.0007	0.0000	0.0017
4 3/4 – 5 1/2	0.0010	0.0000	0.0000	0.0007	0.0000	0.0017
5 1/2 – 6 1/2	0.0011	0.0000	0.0000	0.0007	0.0000	0.0018
6 1/2 – 7 1/2	0.0011	0.0000	0.0000	0.0008	0.0000	0.0019
7 1/2 – 8 1/2	0.0012	0.0000	0.0000	0.0008	0.0000	0.0020

* Compiled from ASA B4a — 1925.
† Note: (+) denotes clearance or amount of looseness.
All dimensions in inches.

TABLE 20. LIMITS FOR METAL FITS *
Wringing Fit (Class 5) — Zero to Negative Allowance Selective Assembly

This is also known as a "tunking fit" and it is practically metal-to-metal. Assembly is usually selective and not interchangeable.

Size	Limits — Hole or External Member (+)	Limits — Shaft or Internal Member (+)	Tightest Fit — Allowance (−†)	Loosest Fit — Allowance + Tolerances (+†)	Selected Fit — Average Interference of Metal
0 – 3/16	0.0003	0.0002	0.0002	0.0003	0.0000
3/16 – 5/16	0.0004	0.0003	0.0003	0.0004	0.0000
5/16 – 7/16	0.0004	0.0003	0.0003	0.0004	0.0000
7/16 – 9/16	0.0005	0.0003	0.0003	0.0005	0.0000
9/16 – 11/16	0.0005	0.0003	0.0004	0.0005	0.0000
11/16 – 13/16	0.0005	0.0004	0.0004	0.0005	0.0000
13/16 – 15/16	0.0006	0.0004	0.0004	0.0006	0.0000
15/16 – 1 1/16	0.0006	0.0004	0.0004	0.0006	0.0000
1 1/16 – 1 3/16	0.0006	0.0004	0.0005	0.0006	0.0000
1 3/16 – 1 3/8	0.0007	0.0005	0.0005	0.0007	0.0000
1 3/8 – 1 5/8	0.0007	0.0005	0.0005	0.0007	0.0000
1 5/8 – 1 7/8	0.0007	0.0005	0.0005	0.0008	0.0000
1 7/8 – 2 1/8	0.0008	0.0005	0.0005	0.0008	0.0000
2 1/8 – 2 3/8	0.0008	0.0006	0.0006	0.0008	0.0000
2 3/8 – 2 5/8	0.0008	0.0006	0.0006	0.0009	0.0000
2 5/8 – 3 1/8	0.0009	0.0006	0.0006	0.0009	0.0000
3 1/8 – 3 5/8	0.0009	0.0006	0.0006	0.0010	0.0000
3 5/8 – 4 1/8	0.0010	0.0007	0.0007	0.0010	0.0000
4 1/8 – 4 5/8	0.0010	0.0007	0.0007	0.0010	0.0000
4 5/8 – 5 1/8	0.0010	0.0007	0.0007	0.0011	0.0000
5 1/8 – 6 1/8	0.0011	0.0007	0.0008	0.0011	0.0000
6 1/8 – 7 1/8	0.0011	0.0008	0.0008	0.0012	0.0000
7 1/8 – 8 1/2	0.0012	0.0008	0.0008	0.0012	0.0000

* Compiled from ASA B4a — 1925.
† Note: (−) denotes interference of metal or negative allowance. (+) denotes clearance or amount of looseness.
All dimensions in inches.

TABLE 21. LIMITS FOR METAL FITS *
Tight Fit (Class 6) — Slight Negative Allowance Selective Assembly

Light pressure is required to assemble these fits and the parts are more or less permanently assembled, such as the fixed ends of studs for gears, pulleys, rocker arms, etc. These fits are used for drive fits in thin sections or extremely long fits in other sections, and also for shrink fits on very light sections. Used in automotive, ordnance, and general machine manufacturing.

Size	Limits — Hole or External Member (+)	Limits — Shaft or Internal Member (+)	Limits — Shaft or Internal Member (+)	Tightest Fit — Allowance (−†)	Loosest Fit — Allowance + Tolerances (+†)	Selected Fit — Average Interference of Metal (−†)
0 – 3/16	0.0003	0.0003	0.0000	0.0003	+0.0003	0.0000
3/16 – 5/16	0.0004	0.0005	0.0001	0.0005	+0.0003	0.0001
5/16 – 7/16	0.0004	0.0005	0.0001	0.0005	+0.0003	0.0001
7/16 – 9/16	0.0005	0.0006	0.0001	0.0006	+0.0004	0.0001
9/16 – 11/16	0.0005	0.0007	0.0002	0.0007	+0.0003	0.0002
11/16 – 13/16	0.0005	0.0007	0.0002	0.0007	+0.0003	0.0002
13/16 – 15/16	0.0006	0.0008	0.0002	0.0008	+0.0004	0.0002
15/16 – 1 1/16	0.0006	0.0009	0.0003	0.0009	+0.0003	0.0003
1 1/16 – 1 3/16	0.0006	0.0009	0.0003	0.0009	+0.0003	0.0003
1 3/16 – 1 3/8	0.0006	0.0011	0.0003	0.0011	+0.0003	0.0003
1 3/8 – 1 5/8	0.0007	0.0011	0.0004	0.0011	+0.0003	0.0004
1 5/8 – 1 7/8	0.0007	0.0013	0.0004	0.0013	+0.0003	0.0004
1 7/8 – 2 1/8	0.0007	0.0014	0.0005	0.0014	+0.0002	0.0005
2 1/8 – 2 3/8	0.0008	0.0014	0.0006	0.0014	+0.0001	0.0006
2 3/8 – 2 5/8	0.0008	0.0017	0.0006	0.0017	+0.0000	0.0006
2 5/8 – 3 1/8	0.0008	0.0018	0.0008	0.0018	0.0000	0.0008
3 1/8 – 3 5/8	0.0009	0.0020	0.0009	0.0020	−0.0001	0.0009
3 5/8 – 4 1/8	0.0010	0.0021	0.0010	0.0021	−0.0001	0.0010
4 1/8 – 4 5/8	0.0010	0.0023	0.0011	0.0023	−0.0003	0.0011
4 5/8 – 5 1/8	0.0010	0.0026	0.0013	0.0026	−0.0004	0.0013
5 1/8 – 6 1/8	0.0011	0.0029	0.0015	0.0029	−0.0007	0.0015
6 1/8 – 7 1/8	0.0011	0.0029	0.0018	0.0029	−0.0007	0.0018
7 1/8 – 8 1/2	0.0012	0.0032	0.0020	0.0032	−0.0008	0.0020

* Compiled from ASA B4a — 1925.
† Note: (−) denotes interference of metal or negative allowance. (+) denotes clearance or amount of looseness.
All dimensions in inches.

TABLE 22. LIMITS FOR METAL FITS *
Medium Force Fit (Class 7) — Negative Allowance Selective Assembly

Considerable pressure is required to assemble these fits and the parts are considered permanently assembled. These fits are used in fastening locomotive wheels, car wheels, armatures of dynamos and motors, and crank disks to their axles or shafts. They are also used for shrink fits on medium sections or long fits. These fits are the tightest which are recommended for cast-iron holes or external members as they stress cast iron to its elastic limit.

| Size | Limits | | | Tightest Fit | Loosest Fit | Selected Fit |
| | Hole or External Member | | Shaft or Internal Member | Allowance | Allowance + Tolerances | Average Interference of Metal |
	+	0.0000	+	+	−†	+†	−†
0 − 3/16	0.0003	0.0000	0.0004	0.0001	0.0004	+0.0002	0.0001
3/16 − 5/16	0.0004	0.0000	0.0005	0.0001	0.0005	+0.0003	0.0001
5/16 − 7/16	0.0004	0.0000	0.0006	0.0002	0.0006	+0.0002	0.0002
7/16 − 9/16	0.0005	0.0000	0.0008	0.0003	0.0008	+0.0002	0.0003
9/16 − 11/16	0.0005	0.0000	0.0009	0.0003	0.0008	+0.0002	0.0003
11/16 − 13/16	0.0005	0.0000	0.0010	0.0004	0.0009	+0.0001	0.0004
13/16 − 15/16	0.0006	0.0000	0.0011	0.0004	0.0010	+0.0002	0.0004
15/16 − 1 1/16	0.0006	0.0000	0.0011	0.0005	0.0011	+0.0001	0.0005
1 1/16 − 1 3/16	0.0006	0.0000	0.0012	0.0006	0.0012	0.0000	0.0006
1 3/16 − 1 3/8	0.0006	0.0000	0.0012	0.0006	0.0012	0.0000	0.0006
1 3/8 − 1 5/8	0.0007	0.0000	0.0015	0.0008	0.0015	−0.0001	0.0008
1 5/8 − 1 7/8	0.0007	0.0000	0.0016	0.0009	0.0016	−0.0002	0.0009
1 7/8 − 2 1/8	0.0007	0.0000	0.0018	0.0010	0.0018	−0.0002	0.0010
2 1/8 − 2 3/8	0.0008	0.0000	0.0019	0.0011	0.0019	−0.0003	0.0011
2 3/8 − 2 5/8	0.0008	0.0000	0.0021	0.0013	0.0021	−0.0005	0.0013
2 5/8 − 3 1/8	0.0008	0.0000	0.0024	0.0015	0.0024	−0.0006	0.0015
3 1/8 − 3 5/8	0.0009	0.0000	0.0027	0.0018	0.0027	−0.0009	0.0018
3 5/8 − 4 1/8	0.0009	0.0000	0.0030	0.0020	0.0030	−0.0010	0.0020
4 1/8 − 4 5/8	0.0010	0.0000	0.0033	0.0023	0.0033	−0.0013	0.0023
4 5/8 − 5 1/2	0.0010	0.0000	0.0035	0.0025	0.0035	−0.0015	0.0025
5 1/2 − 6 1/2	0.0011	0.0000	0.0041	0.0030	0.0041	−0.0019	0.0030
6 1/2 − 7 1/2	0.0011	0.0000	0.0046	0.0035	0.0046	−0.0024	0.0035
7 1/2 − 8 1/2	0.0012	0.0000	0.0052	0.0040	0.0052	−0.0028	0.0040

* Compiled from ASA B4a — 1925.
† Note: (—) denotes interference of metal or negative allowance. (+) denotes clearance or amount of looseness.
All dimensions in inches.

TABLE 23. LIMITS FOR METAL FITS *
Heavy Force and Shrink Fit (Class 8) — Considerable Negative Allowance, Selective Assembly

These fits are used for steel holes where the metal can be stressed to its elastic limit. These fits cause excessive stress for cast-iron holes. Shrink fits are used where heavy force fits are impractical, as on locomotive wheel tires, heavy crank disks of large engines, etc.

| Size | Limits | | | Tightest Fit | Loosest Fit | Selected Fit |
| | Hole or External Member | | Shaft or Internal Member | Allowance | Allowance + Tolerances | Average Interference of Metal |
	+	0.0000	+	+	−†	+†	−†
0 − 3/16	0.0003	0.0000	0.0004	0.0001	0.0004	+0.0002	0.0001
3/16 − 5/16	0.0004	0.0000	0.0007	0.0003	0.0007	+0.0001	0.0003
5/16 − 7/16	0.0004	0.0000	0.0008	0.0004	0.0008	0.0000	0.0004
7/16 − 9/16	0.0005	0.0000	0.0010	0.0005	0.0010	0.0000	0.0005
9/16 − 11/16	0.0005	0.0000	0.0011	0.0006	0.0011	−0.0001	0.0006
11/16 − 13/16	0.0006	0.0000	0.0013	0.0008	0.0013	−0.0003	0.0008
13/16 − 15/16	0.0006	0.0000	0.0015	0.0009	0.0015	−0.0003	0.0009
15/16 − 1 1/16	0.0006	0.0000	0.0016	0.0010	0.0016	−0.0004	0.0010
1 1/16 − 1 3/16	0.0006	0.0000	0.0017	0.0011	0.0017	−0.0005	0.0011
1 3/16 − 1 3/8	0.0007	0.0000	0.0019	0.0013	0.0019	−0.0007	0.0013
1 3/8 − 1 5/8	0.0007	0.0000	0.0022	0.0015	0.0022	−0.0008	0.0015
1 5/8 − 1 7/8	0.0007	0.0000	0.0025	0.0018	0.0025	−0.0011	0.0018
1 7/8 − 2 1/8	0.0008	0.0000	0.0028	0.0020	0.0028	−0.0012	0.0020
2 1/8 − 2 3/8	0.0008	0.0000	0.0031	0.0023	0.0031	−0.0015	0.0023
2 3/8 − 2 5/8	0.0008	0.0000	0.0033	0.0025	0.0033	−0.0017	0.0025
2 5/8 − 3 1/8	0.0009	0.0000	0.0039	0.0030	0.0039	−0.0021	0.0030
3 1/8 − 3 5/8	0.0009	0.0000	0.0044	0.0035	0.0044	−0.0026	0.0035
3 5/8 − 4 1/8	0.0010	0.0000	0.0050	0.0040	0.0050	−0.0030	0.0040
4 1/8 − 4 5/8	0.0010	0.0000	0.0055	0.0045	0.0055	−0.0035	0.0045
4 5/8 − 5 1/2	0.0010	0.0000	0.0060	0.0050	0.0060	−0.0040	0.0050
5 1/2 − 6 1/2	0.0011	0.0000	0.0071	0.0060	0.0071	−0.0049	0.0060
6 1/2 − 7 1/2	0.0011	0.0000	0.0081	0.0070	0.0081	−0.0059	0.0070
7 1/2 − 8 1/2	0.0012	0.0000	0.0092	0.0080	0.0092	−0.0068	0.0080

* Compiled from ASA B4a — 1925.
† Note: (—) denotes interference of metal or negative allowance. (+) denotes clearance or amount of looseness.
All dimensions in inches.

TABLE 24.   HOLES MADE BY STANDARD AND OVERSIZE REAMERS

Nominal Diameter	Standard	Oversize	
	Actual Diameter	Actual Diameter	Average Amount of Oversize
¼	.249 .251	.251 .253	.002
⁵⁄₁₆	.3115 .3135	.3135 .3155	.002
⅜	.374 .376	.377 .379	.003
⁷⁄₁₆	.4365 .4385	.4395 .4415	.003
½	.499 .501	.502 .504	.003
⁹⁄₁₆	.5615 .5635	.5645 .5665	.003
⅝	.624 .626	.628 .630	.004
¾	.749 .751	.753 .755	.004
⅞	.874 .876	.878 .880	.004
1	.999 1.001	1.003 1.005	.004
1⅛	1.124 1.126	1.128 1.130	.004
1¼	1.249 1.251	1.253 1.255	.004
1⅜	1.374 1.376	1.379 1.381	.005
1½	1.499 1.501	1.504 1.506	.005
1⅝	1.624 1.626	1.629 1.631	.005
1¾	1.749 1.751	1.754 1.756	.005
2	1.999 2.001	2.004 2.006	.005
2¼	2.249 2.251	2.254 2.256	.005
2½	2.499 2.501	2.504 2.506	.005

All dimensions in inches.

STANDARD REAMERS should be used for making holes for turned shafts; the shafts should be fitted to the reamed holes.

OVERSIZE REAMERS should be used for making clearance holes for Cold Drawn Steel and Brass Rods which are not turned.

For closer fits the rods may be ground to suit clearance holes made by Standard Reamers.

Where more clearances are desired, use next size standard drill and omit reaming.

Note: For sizes smaller than ¼", use standard numbered or lettered drills.

TABLE 25. CLEARANCE HOLES FOR COUNTERSINKING FLATHEAD SCREWS IN THIN STOCK

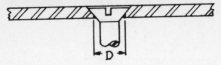

Sizes given decrease amount of work for countersinking operation and avoid objectionable burrs.

Thickness of Metal * (U.S.S. Gauge)		Machine Screw Size									
		#2	#3	#4	#5	#6	#8	#10	#12	¼"
		Outside Diameter of Screw								
		.086	.099	.112	.125	.138	.164	.190	.216	.250
		Height of Head								
		.051	.059	.067	.075	.083	.100	.116	.132	.153
No.	Decimal	Diameter (D) of Clearance Hole								
26	.0188	.152	.177	.201						
25	.0219	.144	.173	.199	.221					
24	.025	.144	.166	.191	.221	¼				
23	.0281	.140	.166	.191	.221	¼				
22	.0313–¹⁄₃₂	.136	.154	.182	.209	¹⁵⁄₆₄	.290			
21	.0344	⅛	.154	.180	.209	¹⁵⁄₆₄	.290	.339		
20	.0375	.120	.144	.173	.199	.228	⁹⁄₃₂	.339		
19	.0438	.110	.136	.166	.191	.221	.272	²¹⁄₆₄		
18	.0500		⅛	.154	.180	.209	.261	⁵⁄₁₆	.368	
17	.0563			.144	.169	.199	¼	.302	²³⁄₆₄	⁷⁄₁₆
16	.0625–¹⁄₁₆				.157	.185	¼	¹⁹⁄₆₄	¹¹⁄₃₂	⁷⁄₁₆
15	.070					.169	.228	⁹⁄₃₂	.339	.413
14	.0781					.161	.221	.272	²¹⁄₆₄	.397
13	.0938–³⁄₃₂						.196	¼	.302	⅜
12	.1094							.221	⁹⁄₃₂	¹¹⁄₃₂
11	.125–⅛								¼	²¹⁄₆₄
10	.1406								¹⁵⁄₆₄	.302

All dimensions in inches.

Clearance Holes, except for fractional sizes, conform to numbered and lettered sizes of drills, and are applicable also for Flathead Wood Screws up to #14 (¼" Approx.).

* For other gauges, use Diameter of Hole (D) for the U.S.S. Gauge which is nearest to thickness of metal used.

TABLE 26.   CLEARANCE HOLES FOR COLD ROLLED STEEL PINS

Pin Diameter		Drill or Hole for Free Fit (Rotating Parts)	Drill or Hole When Pin Is Riveted Over (Pin Stationary)
Nominal	Decimal		
1/32	.03125	#66(.033)	#68(.0310)
1/16	.0625	52(.0635)	52(.0635)
3/32	.09375	41(.0960)	42(.0935)
1/8	.125	30(.1285)	30(.1285)
5/32	.15625	22(.157)	22(.1570)
3/16	.1875	12(.189)	12(.189)
1/4	.250	F.R. .251 / .253	F.R. .249 / .251
5/16	.3125	F.R. .3135 / .3155	F.R. .3115 / .3135
3/8	.375	F.R. .377 / .379	F.R. .374 / .376
7/16	.4375	F.R. .4395 / .4415	F.R. .4365 / .4385
1/2	.500	F.R. .502 / .504	F.R. .499 / .501
9/16	.5625	F.R. .5645 / .5665	F.R. .5615 / .5635
5/8	.625	F.R. .628 / .630	F.R. .624 / .626
3/4	.750	F.R. .753 / .755	F.R. .749 / .751
7/8	.875	F.R. .878 / .880	F.R. .874 / .876
1	1.000	F.R. 1.003 / 1.005	F.R. .999 / 1.001
1 1/8	1.125	F.R. 1.128 / 1.130	F.R. 1.124 / 1.126
1 1/4	1.250	F.R. 1.253 / 1.255	F.R. 1.249 / 1.251
1 3/8	1.375	F.R. 1.379 / 1.381	F.R. 1.374 / 1.376
1 1/2	1.500	F.R. 1.504 / 1.506	F.R. 1.499 / 1.501
1 5/8	1.625	F.R. 1.629 / 1.631	F.R. 1.624 / 1.626
1 3/4	1.750	F.R. 1.754 / 1.756	F.R. 1.749 / 1.751
2	2.000	F.R. 2.004 / 2.006	F.R. 1.999 / 2.001
2 1/4	2.250	F.R. 2.254 / 2.256	F.R. 2.249 / 2.251
2 1/2	2.500	F.R. 2.504 / 2.506	F.R. 2.499 / 2.501
All dimensions in inches		Approximately .001 to .005 clearance	Approximately size to size

(These Are Standard Oversize Reamers)

(These Are Standard Reamer Sizes)

These sizes are intended only as a general guide.   Where less clearance is desirable on a FREE FIT use standard reamer sizes.   Where more clearance is desirable on a FREE FIT use standard drill sizes slightly larger than the Pin diameter.

TABLE 27. PLUG ENDS FOR RIVETING AND WELDING PINS TO PLATES

A	d	C	D
1/8	.063 / .061	1/64	1/16
3/16	.128 / .126	1/64	1/16
1/4	.189 / .187	1/64	1/16
* 5/16	.221 / .219	1/64	3/32
3/8	.251 / .249	1/64	1/8

A	d	C	D
1/2	.313 / .311	1/64	7/32
5/8	.376 / .374	1/32	9/32
3/4	.501 / .499	1/32	13/32
7/8	.626 / .624	1/32	17/32

A	d	C
1	.751 / .749	1/32
1 1/8	.876 / .874	1/32
1 1/4	1.001 / .999	1/32
1 3/8	1.126 / 1.124	1/32
† 1 1/2	1.188 / 1.186	1/16
1 5/8	1.251 / 1.249	1/16
1 3/4	1.376 / 1.374	1/16
1 7/8	1.501 / 1.499	1/16
2	1.626 / 1.624	1/16
‡ 2 1/4	1.876 / 1.874	3/32
2 1/2	2.001 / 1.999	3/32

d = diameter of Pin.

Note: For size of hole in plate see with following exceptions:

PINS
CLEARANCE HOLES

* Hole in plate should be No. 2 (.2210″) drill.

† Hole in plate should be F.R. 1.1865″ / 1.1885″

‡ Hole in plate should be F.R. 1.874″ / 1.876″

All dimensions in inches.

TABLE 28. DRILLED HOLES FOR COTTER PINS

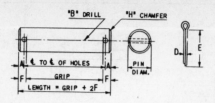

$\mathcal{C}$ to $\mathcal{C}$ of holes = Grip plus drill diameter "B" specified to next largest even fractional dimension.

Pin Diam.	A	Drill Size "B"	Cotter Pin		F	Chamfer H
			Diam. D	Length E		
$3/16$	$3/32$	47(.0785)	$1/16$	$1/2$	$9/64$	$1/32$
$1/4$	$3/32$	47(.0785)	$1/16$	$1/2$	$9/64$	$1/32$
$5/16$	$3/32$	47(.0785)	$1/16$	$1/2$	$9/64$	$1/32$
$3/8$	$1/8$	35(.1100)	$3/32$	$3/4$	$3/16$	$1/32$
$7/16$	$1/8$	35(.1100)	$3/32$	$3/4$	$3/16$	$1/32$
$1/2$	$1/8$	35(.1100)	$3/32$	$3/4$	$3/16$	$1/32$
$9/16$	$5/32$	28(.1405)	$1/8$	1	$15/64$	$1/16$
$5/8$	$5/32$	28(.1405)	$1/8$	1	$15/64$	$1/16$
$3/4$	$5/32$	28(.1405)	$1/8$	$1 1/4$	$15/64$	$1/16$
$7/8$	$5/32$	28(.1405)	$1/8$	$1 1/4$	$15/64$	$1/16$
1	$5/32$	28(.1405)	$1/8$	$1 1/2$	$15/64$	$1/16$
$1 1/8$	$7/32$	$3/16$	$5/32$	$1 1/2$	$5/16$	$3/32$
$1 1/4$	$7/32$	$3/16$	$5/32$	$1 3/4$	$5/16$	$3/32$
$1 3/8$	$9/32$	$7/32$	$3/16$	$1 3/4$	$25/64$	$1/8$
$1 1/2$	$9/32$	$7/32$	$3/16$	2	$25/64$	$1/8$
$1 5/8$	$5/16$	$9/32$	$1/4$	$2 1/4$	$29/64$	$1/8$
$1 3/4$	$5/16$	$9/32$	$1/4$	$2 1/4$	$29/64$	$1/8$
2	$13/32$	$11/32$	$5/16$	$2 3/4$	$37/64$	$3/16$
$2 1/4$	$13/32$	$11/32$	$5/16$	3	$37/64$	$3/16$
$2 1/2$	$7/16$	$13/32$	$3/8$	$3 1/2$	$47/64$	$3/16$

All dimensions in inches.

Note: Distance from end of pin to drilled hole should, where possible, be the same on both ends of pin.   Chamfer is at 45°.

Do not indicate dimensions for "Grip," "F" and "$\mathcal{C}$ to $\mathcal{C}$ of Holes" on drawings unless it is necessary to clarify machining requirements.

TABLE 29. GAUGES FOR STRUCTURAL ANGLES, CHANNELS, AND BEAMS

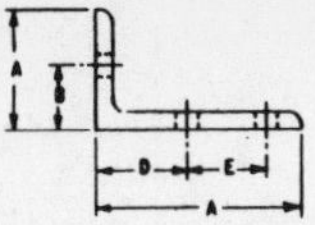

Usual Gauges for Angles

A	8	7	6	5	4	3½	3	2½	2	1¾	1½	1⅜	1¼	1	¾
B	4½	4	3½	3	2½	2	1¾	1⅜	1⅛	1	⅞	⅞	¾	⅝	½
D	3	2½	2¼	2											
E	3	3	2½	1¾											
Max. Rivet	1⅛	1	⅞	⅞	⅞	⅞	⅞	¾	⅝	½	⅜	⅜	⅜	¼	¼

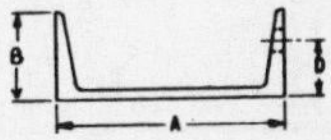

Usual Gauges for Channels

A	18	15	12	10	9	8	7	6	5	4	3
B	4	3⅜	3	2⅝	2½	2¼	2⅛	2	1¾	1⅝	1⅜
D	2½	2	1¾	1½	1⅜	1⅜	1¼	1⅛	1⅛	1	⅞
Max. Rivet	1	1	⅞	¾	¾	¾	⅝	⅝	½	½	½

Dimensions shown are for American Standard Light Sections.

Usual Gauges for Beams

A	24	20	18	15	12	10	8	7	6	5	4	3
B	7	6¼	6	5½	5	4⅝	4	3⅝	3⅜	3	2⅝	2⅜
D	4	3½	3½	3½	3	2¾	2¼	2¼	2	1¾	1½	1½
Max. Rivet	1	⅞	⅞	¾	¾	¾	¾	⅝	⅝	½	½	⅜

Dimensions shown are for American Standard Light Sections.
All dimensions in inches.
Note: Dimensions may be varied to suit applications.

TABLE 30. MINIMUM GAUGES IN ANGLES FOR BOLTS AND NUTS

(Note: Dimensions given allow for lock washers.)

BOLT SIZE	1/8" R	3/16" R			1/4" R					5/16" R				3/8" R				7/16" R		1/2" R		
ANGLE THICKNESS	1/8"	1/8"	3/16"	1/4"	1/8"	3/16"	1/4"	5/16"	3/8"	1/4"	5/16"	3/8"	1/2"	1/4"	5/16"	3/8"	1/2"	7/16"	1/2"	3/8"	7/16"	1/2"
1/4"	9/16"	5/8"	11/16"	3/4"	11/16"	3/4"	13/16"	7/8"	15/16"	7/8"	15/16"	1"	1 1/8"	15/16"	1"	1"	1 3/16"	1 3/16"	1 3/16"	1 3/16"	1 1/4"	1 5/16"
5/16"		11/16"	3/4"	13/16"	3/4"	13/16"	7/8"	15/16"	1"	15/16"	1"	1 1/16"	1 3/16"	1"	1 1/16"	1 1/16"	1 1/4"	1 1/4"	1 1/4"	1 1/4"	1 5/16"	1 3/8"
3/8"		3/4"	13/16"	7/8"	13/16"	7/8"	15/16"	1"	1 1/16"	1"	1 1/16"	1 1/8"	1 1/4"	1 1/16"	1 1/8"	1 1/8"	1 5/16"	1 5/16"	1 5/16"	1 5/16"	1 3/8"	1 7/16"
1/2"					15/16"	1"	1 1/16"	1 1/8"	1 3/16"	1 1/8"	1 3/16"	1 1/4"	1 3/8"	1 3/16"	1 1/4"	1 1/4"	1 7/16"	1 7/16"	1 7/16"	1 7/16"	1 1/2"	1 9/16"
5/8"					1"	1 1/16"	1 1/8"	1 3/16"	1 1/4"	1 3/16"	1 1/4"	1 5/16"	1 7/16"	1 1/4"	1 5/16"	1 5/16"	1 1/2"	1 1/2"	1 1/2"	1 1/2"	1 9/16"	1 5/8"
3/4"					1 1/8"	1 3/16"	1 1/4"	1 5/16"	1 3/8"	1 5/16"	1 3/8"	1 7/16"	1 9/16"	1 3/8"	1 7/16"	1 7/16"	1 5/8"	1 5/8"	1 5/8"	1 5/8"	1 11/16"	1 3/4"
7/8"										1 7/16"	1 1/2"	1 9/16"	1 11/16"	1 1/2"	1 9/16"	1 9/16"	1 3/4"	1 3/4"	1 3/4"	1 3/4"	1 13/16"	1 7/8"
1"										1 9/16"	1 5/8"	1 11/16"	1 13/16"	1 5/8"	1 11/16"	1 3/4"	1 7/8"	1 7/8"	1 7/8"	1 7/8"	1 15/16"	2"

TABLE 31. FRACTION AND DECIMAL EQUIVALENTS

Fraction	Decimal	Fraction	Decimal
1/64	.015625	33/64	.515625
1/32	.03125	17/32	.53125
3/64	.046875	35/64	.546875
1/16	.0625	9/16	.5625
5/64	.078125	37/64	.578125
3/32	.09375	19/32	.59375
7/64	.109375	39/64	.609375
1-8	.125	5-8	.625
9/64	.140625	41/64	.640625
5/32	.15625	21/32	.65625
11/64	.171875	43/64	.671875
3/16	.1875	11/16	.6875
13/64	.203125	45/64	.703125
7/32	.21875	23/32	.71875
15/64	.234375	47/64	.734375
1-4	.25	3-4	.75
17/64	.265625	49/64	.765625
9/32	.28125	25/32	.78125
19/64	.296875	51/64	.796875
5/16	.3125	13/16	.8125
21/64	.328125	53/64	.828125
11/32	.34375	27/32	.84375
23/64	.359375	55/64	.859375
3-8	.375	7-8	.875
25/64	.390625	57/64	.890625
13/32	.40625	29/32	.90625
27/64	.421875	59/64	.921875
7/16	.4375	15/16	.9375
29/64	.453125	61/64	.953125
15/32	.46875	31/32	.96875
31/64	.484375	63/64	.984375
1-2	.5	1	1.

TABLE 32. ISOMETRIC CONVERSION

Isometric Ellipse	Size of Hole or Round
1/8	5/32
3/16	7/32
1/4	1 1/32
5/16	3/8
7/16	9/16
1/2	1 1/16
9/16	3/4
5/8	13/16
11/16	7/8
3/4	15/16
13/16	1 1/8
7/8	1 1/4
15/16	1 1/4
1	1 3/8
1 1/8	1 3/8
1 3/16	1 1/2
1 1/4	1 5/8
1 3/8	1 3/4
1 1/2	1 7/8
1 5/8	2

Index

(Figures in italics refer to problems.)

Left-side view, 72
Lengthening bar, 14
LeRoy Lettering Set, 55
Lettering, 52–62, *306–310*
  American Standard, 52
  ampersand, 60
  angle, 56
  guide lines, 54, 55–60
  inclined letters, 53, 56, 58
  inking, 55
  LeRoy Set, 55
  lower- and upper-case, 59, *308–310*
  numerals and fractions, 59–60, *308–309*
  pencils, 55
  problems, *306–310*
  single-stroke Gothic, 52, 55
  spacing, 60–61
  triangle, 55–56, 60
  vertical letters, 53, *309–310*
Limit dimensions, 190–192, *339*
  computation of, 192–193, *339*
Line gauge, 21
Lines
  alphabet of, 21
  conventional, 5–6
  dimension, 148–149
  extension, 147–148
  hidden, 84, 87, 96, 130
  horizontal, 6
  inclined, 8
  invisible, 84, 87, 96, 130
  nonisometric, 130
  parallel, 9, 29
  perpendicular, 11, 30–33, *300*
  reference, 91–92, 95
  section, 107–110
  to bisect straight, 26, *300*
  to divide into equal parts, 30, *300*
  to divide into proportional parts, 30, *300*
  to trisect straight, 27–28, *300*
  true length, 99–102
  vertical, 7–8
Linework, 1–25, *295–299*
Location dimensions, 154, 155

Machine, drawing of, 120, 121
Machine screws, 186, *336*
Mann's line gauge, 1, 7, 21
Multiple threads, 169–170
Multiple views, 63

Necking, 204, 206, 207
Nonisometric lines, 130
Nonisometric planes, 133–135
Notes, 161–163, 179–181
Numerals, 59–60
Nuts, 181–186

Oblique
  axes in, 139
  cabinet, 140–145
  cabinet vs. isometric, 145
  cavalier, 139–140
  cone, 266–267
  cylinder, 258
  invisible lines, 144
  prism, 255–256
  projection, 139–144
  pyramid, 261–262
  types of, 139–140
Octagon, to construct, 38–41, *303*
Offset method, 42
Offset sections, 117–118
Orthographic projection, 67–71, *310–313*
  pictorial vs., 145
Over-all dimensions, 155

Paper, 2
Parallel lines, 9, 29
Partial auxiliary views, 98
Partial sections, 113
Patent drawings, 200
Patternmaking, 238–246
Pen
  bow, 16
  ruling, 16–21
  selection and care, 17
  use, 17–21
Pencils
  artist, 4
  bow, 16